Change and Continuity among Tribes

Change and Continuity among Tribes

The Idu Mishmis of Arunachal Pradesh

Edited by

TARUN MENE
SARIT K. CHAUDHURI

Indira Gandhi Rashtriya Manav Sangrahalaya, Bhopal
(National Museum of Mankind)

RAWAT PUBLICATIONS
Jaipur • New Delhi • Bangalore • Guwahati • Kolkata

ISBN 978-81-316-0984-2

Published by
Indira Gandhi Rashtriya Manav Sangrahalaya
Shamla Hills, Bhopal 462 013 (Madhya Pradesh)
E-mail: directorigrms@gmail.com

and

Prem Rawat for **Rawat Publications**
Satyam Apts., Sector 3, Jawahar Nagar, Jaipur 302 004 (India)
Phone: 0141 265 1748 / 7006 Fax: 0141 265 1748
E-mail: info@rawatbooks.com
Website: www.rawatbooks.com

New Delhi Office
4858/24, Ansari Road, Daryaganj, New Delhi 110 002
Phone: 011-23263290

Also at Bangalore, Guwahati and Kolkata

Typeset by Rawat Computers, Jaipur
Printed at Nice Printing Press, New Delhi

Dedicated to the Idu Mishmi community of Arunachal Pradesh

Contents

Foreword

I am delighted to pen a few lines to this joint endeavour by Professor Sarit K Chaudhuri and Dr Tarun Mene which is an outcome of combined efforts of a numbers of scholars on various aspects of socioculture life of the Idu Mishmis of Arunachal Pradesh. They have contributed original and scholarly papers through which one can see the society and culture of the people.

It is my humble appreciation that this work of significant domain in a contemporary tribal society of the state explores a wide range of problems and issues in specific area and locates them within wider debates on society, economy, public policies, health, language, history, religion, culture and tradition. The variety of perspectives and approaches deployed by scholars of different disciplines in each paper is an attempt in understanding the dynamic of social forces and processes that bring forth to the readers the interface and relationships between number of issues pertaining to a tribal society that is passing through the phase of rapid social transformation.

We are aware of the fact that there are a series of studies made on different tribes of Arunachal Pradesh but negligibly few on the Idu Mishmi, leaving all ethnographic works. This book which contains important papers based on empirical research is timely and fills the existing knowledge gap in a sense that it reflects a holistic attempt to understand the dynamics of historicity, change and continuity concerning a tribal society.

The effort of the editors is praiseworthy and I congratulate them for bringing out this book for the benefit of the academic community and the society at large. It will be of immense interest to researchers, students of anthropology, sociology, history, NGO activists and policy makers.

Professor Tamo Mibang
Vice Chancellor
Rajiv Gandhi University
Rono Hills, Doimukh, Arunachal Pradesh

Acknowledgements

In the context of India's North-East and more specifically, former NEFA as well as present Arunachal Pradesh, the Idu Mishmis remained one of the important tribes which had attracted attention of both colonial as well as post-colonial writers, such as administrators, anthropologists and others, cutting across the disciplinary frames. Obviously, this focus is gaining much more ground within last few decades though unfortunately, after T.K. Barua (1960) and T.K. Bhattacharjee (1983) we did not have any book which could have explored the new areas of research focussing on the Idu Mishmis from multidisciplinary perspectives, so that one can locate the comparative epistemological praxis and holistic understanding of the frontier tribes who are passing through a phase of transition like many other tribes of this region. As both of us are involved with the Idu Mishmi tribes for our sustained research commitment, we thought of bringing together major works on this tribe in a single volume which can lead or reshape future research on this tribe and may be other tribes located in similar eco-cultural context.

We are highly indebted to all the chapter contributors for their valuable work on the Idu Mishmi tribe, most of whom represent the young academicians of our time affiliated to various institutions both in India and abroad. As an academic discourse, it is also pertinent to mention here that this book is a special one of its own kind as many of the chapter contributors represent the tribe itself.

We also take this opportunity to acknowledge the editorial boards of the various international and national journals for giving necessary permission to reprint some of the chapters in this volume which have appeared previously and their complete citations are provided in the respective chapters. We also express our heartfelt thanks to the members of Academic Advisory Board of the IGRMS, Bhopal and the entire institution for their constant encouragement and support in the publication of this present book.

We are also very much thankful to our colleagues and friends working in different Colleges and Universities for their valuable support for giving the final shape of this book. We are particularly thankful to Professor S. Simon John, Dr Jumyir Basar, Dr Wanglit Mongchang and Miss Lisa Lomdak from Arunachal Institute of Tribal Studies (AITS), and Dr Lijum Nochi, Department of Economics of Rajiv Gandhi University, Arunachal Pradesh.

Editors

1

Introduction

The State of Arunachal Pradesh, on India's North-East frontier, forms a part of the eastern Himalayas which is characterized by breathtaking natural beauty with plenty of natural resources and rich cultural heritage. Being a tribal state, people of Arunachal Pradesh are highly dependent on forest and forest resources and have strong cultural linkage with their immediate natural surroundings. It is home to more than 25 indigenous groups based on ethno-linguistic characteristics and number of subgroups who primarily practise shifting cultivation along with various other strategies of livelihood.[1] All of them have their own distinct language, belief system and cultural practices, thus representing a cultural mosaic of its own kind. Though many of them lack written history, these groups through their rich oral tradition trace their origin from neighbouring regions of China, Myanmar and Bhutan.

In the modern-day context, the state of Arunachal Pradesh is often in the headlines for various reasons. On the one hand, the state is known to the outside world for its natural resources and tourism potentials, cultural heritage and ethnic heterogeneity, agriculture and horticulture products but, on the other, there are issues related to border dispute, insurgency, opium menace, ethnic conflicts, political instability, underdevelopment, etc. Amidst these possibilities of potentials and existing sociocultural, economic and political dynamics, this piece of work is a contribution for the students, researchers and academicians alike, in understanding the potentials and the contemporary issues faced by the Idu Mishmis, a tribe which is at the centre of discussion in this book, who have inhabited the easternmost part of India for centuries but very little has been known and written on them except for two old ethnographic books which are referred in various chapters of this book.

In fact, this book aims to provide a comprehensive understanding about the post-colonial research trends on this community which was considered as important tribe since the precolonial to colonial days because of multiple reasons. It takes stock of some ground realities pertaining to issues of daily life, sociocultural aspects and the issues of resource mobilization. It also takes into account the historicity of the tribe and brings into light the change and continuity in various aspects of the community in the context of emerging modernity as well as involvement of the state. To explore these issues and concerns confronting the Idu Mishmis, the challenge has been taken up by the current generation scholars having different academic backgrounds, cutting across the disciplinary boundaries. The effort has been largely to get the scholars who are deeply rooted in their respective fields of research, especially those who had their experience of doing research among the Idu Mishmis. To add further, there are as many contributors who represent the community itself and some are obviously representing the 'others'. So, in the course of this exercise, there emerged more importantly the views and observations on the tribe from two different perspectives, i.e. both 'emic' and 'ethic' perspectives, an approach which has its own significance in understanding any community.

Before we proceed to the main chapters of this book, a brief ethnographic understanding of the Idu Mishmi tribe we have given, especially for those readers and researchers who are interested to know about the tribe. This has been done after a careful review of literatures which are available in the form of ethnographic accounts and also published articles on the tribe. Thus, in fulfilling this information the opening chapter by Tarun Mene and Sarit K. Chaudhuri (editors) titled, 'The Idu Mishmi Tribe of Frontier State of Arunachal Pradesh', introduces the Idu Mishmi tribe basically dealing with the historicity of the tribe, their daily life, religious life, social institutions, etc. keeping in mind the changing perspectives in the context of contemporary Arunachal Pradesh.

The next two chapters provide a historical and cultural account of the Mishmi tribe written in both pre- and post-colonial context. The chapter titled, 'Narrating the Tribe: Colonial Constructs and Voicing the Savage: A Post-colonial Study of the Colonial Writings on the Mishmis of Arunachal Pradesh', by Razzeko Delley, noted that these writings are highly prejudiced, deeply misinterpreted and misrepresented, and these underwritings are being deemed as authentic academic sources of the Mishmi culture and history today. The study looks at the colonial discourse as a form of Cultural Imperialism. Similarly, the chapter, 'Examining the Narratives of Mishmi's Status and its Peregrination of Baptism into Contemporary India' by Tilu Linggi, engages in the critical analysis on the political, social, economic and cultural changes that had undergone during the British control. In doing so, the author has attempted to assess the arguments surrounding the Mishmi's origin and migration, and examines their resemblance or divergence with the ethnic tribes of neighbouring countries.

Similarly, the chapter by Rajiv Miso on 'Border Trade in Mishmi Hills: A Historical Perspective', provide various aspects of border trade relation of the

Mishmi tribe with their neighbours and argues that the policy of loose political control in the twentieth century was to bring the Mishmi hills closer to British administration and to increase their trade with the Assam plains. To the author, this has resulted in the closure of all the passes connecting the Idu Mishmi country with Tibet and China and thus, the trade and cultural contacts of the two sides came to an end.

Following the above historical accounts of the tribe, Ambika Aiyadurai in her chapter, 'Idu Mishmis' Social Worlds: Animals, Humans and Spirits', explores the Idu Mishmi's relations with animals and spirits and throws perspectives as how Mishmi's social world is part of a complex human-animal-spirit cosmology accompanied by hunting rituals, taboos and the practices that are in conflict with the modern laws. She stresses that the local sociocultural concerns and indigenous knowledge of the wildlife and forests need to be incorporated in both research and conservation programmes, so that wildlife conservation works for both wildlife and local people.

The chapter, 'Aspects of Marriage System of the Idu Mishmi Tribe of Arunachal Pradesh', by Justina Umbrey and Razzeko Delley deals with different aspects of traditional institution of marriage that govern the community since ages and also provides aspects of change and continuity of the institution.

Rumo Meto and Tarun Mene in their chapter, 'The Great Fire and the Creation Myth: The Oral Tradition of the Idu Mishmis of Arunachal Pradesh', traces the oral tradition of the Idu Mishmis and provides an understanding of the creation myths of the tribe. The chapter informs that there are different oral versions of the creation myths available with the society with variations in name of the place, legends, etc.

The next two chapters are dealing with the language question as it comes under endangered domain. Mite Lingi in his chapter, 'The Writing System of the Idu Mishmi Language: An Introduction', traces the history of community's effort in preserving the Idu Mishmi language. Precisely, it provides chronological information on the formation of various Committees who are engaged for the creation of writing system and documentation of the Idu Mishmi language. However, the chapter, 'Attempts to Write the Idu Mishmi Language and a Proposal for a Modern Orthography' by Roger Blench, attempts to write the Idu Mishmi language and presents the phonology and explores options to write the language in a practical way. To the author, the writing system of the tribe has scope of further improvement and could be used as a basis for written publications in the Idu Mishmi language.

The chapter, 'Festival and Emerging Social Reality: A Study of the Idu Mishmis of Arunachal Pradesh' by Tarun Mene and Sarit K. Chaudhuri, offers a detailed organizational and functional aspect of the *Reh* festival of the Idu Mishmis. In particular, it highlights both the traditional and the modern forms of *Reh* festival which, to the authors, is the demand of time and is inevitable as the society is passing through the phase of transitions due to multiple factors.

Eva Umpo in her chapter titled, 'Cultural Epidemiology of Malaria among the Idu Mishmis of Arunachal Pradesh', explores the local perceptions of malaria disease. The study provides the linkages and the processes through which social and cultural factors affect the biomedical burden of malaria, better known as Cultural Epidemiology, using anthropologic approach and methods among the Idu Mishmi tribe.

There are four chapters dealing with various aspects of death and related issues among the Idu Mishmi tribe. The chapter on, 'Funeral Traditions of the Idu Mishmi Tribe of Arunachal Pradesh' by S. Simon John and Maya Pulu, deals with various aspects of the funeral traditions of the Idu Mishmi tribe and discusses the funeral rites and customs, beliefs associated with death and funeral, mourning period, preparation and disposal of the body, taboos, rituals, narratives, etc. and highlights the changing aspects in the present-day context. Another chapter by Tarun Mene titled, 'Underestimation of Suicide: A Study of the Idu Mishmi Tribe of Arunachal Pradesh', compares and examines the existing official data of suicide with field data on suicide and thereby validates the reliability of official data and addresses the issue of underestimation of completed suicides in the study area. He suggests that reliable suicide statistics are a prerequisite to understand the vulnerability of suicide, its monitoring and prevention.

Similarly, the chapter, 'Sineru Monomyth: The Idu Mishmi Funeral Mythography' by Razzeko Delley, explores the mythological aspect of the Idu Mishmi funeral oration, i.e. Sineru myth and tries to unravel the cultural and psychological dimension associated with it. The author interprets the death ritual among the Idu Mishmis called *Ya* which is centred around a mythical shaman called Sineru. The chapter, 'Euthanasia among the Idu Mishmis of Arunachal Pradesh: Understanding Issues and Concerns of a Frontier Tribe' by Tarun Mene and Sarit K. Chaudhuri, presents an account of the historical and cultural aspects of euthanasia as existed among the Idu Mishmi tribe. It addresses the practical issue of management in which the family members of the victim had to make difficult decisions when faced with a person expressing a wish to die. Focussing on case studies, the authors have tried to explore how, when and why an Idu Mishmi desires for such distinct form of dying. An attempt has also been made to extract how the attitudes toward such practice have varied over time and space.

Much in the contemporary discourses of discussion, the issues pertaining to women have been well placed in the chapter titled, 'Women in the Face of Globalization: Observations on the Idu Mishmi Society of Arunachal Pradesh' by Justina Umbrey and Tarun Mene. The authors have highlighted the gender-specific responses to the processes of globalization, especially that of women who are often found excluded in the discussions on globalization. Similarly, Sarit K. Chaudhuri in his chapter, 'Plight of the *Igu*s: Notes on Shamanism among the Idu Mishmis of Arunachal Pradesh', brings into light various intricate aspects of shamanism and reveal how pervasive the role of the *Igus* is in the life of the Idu Mishmis. The author discusses the concerning issues of change and continuity of the institution of the shamanism and concludes that as long as village life exists, shamanism will continue to survive, though it is bound to introduce some modifications in keeping in tune with emerging socio-political transformations in Arunachal Pradesh.

The remaining chapters basically address the issues of resource and resource mobilization available with the tribe. The chapter titled, 'Traditional Use of Indigenous Medicinal Plants: A Case Study on Idu Mishmis of Arunachal Pradesh' by Athuko Tayu, deals with the indigenous healing practices and treatments with traditionally known medicinal plants and herbs available with the tribe. In doing so, the author also suggests measures for the protection and conservation of these indigenous resources and knowledge for future biomedical research.

There are two chapters dealing with the Mehao Lake located in the Mishmi Hills. The chapter titled, 'Mehao Lake of Arunachal Pradesh: A Biological Treasure' by Boni Amin Laskar et al. reveals that the introduced fish in the Mehao Lake are thriving well and suggests for a thorough survey and collection of fish species available in the river and the outlet of the lake for biological, ecological and particularly *ichthyological* interest. Another chapter titled, 'Mehao Wetland: A Treasure of Mishmi Hills' by Fames Linggi, emphasizes that wetland is an important component of biodiversity in terms of generating goods and services, as well as supporting livelihood of the locality living adjacent to the lake. However, as noted by the author, due to absence of property rights and open access nature and also due to information gap, its importance has never been realized in the market context.

The chapter by Rajen Miwu titled, 'Managing Tourism Assets: A Case Study of Lower Dibang Valley District of Arunachal Pradesh', explores the tourism potentials of the study area and identifies various factors affecting the mobilization of these resources. And finally, the last chapter by Riko Mihu titled, 'Probable Economic Impact of Hydropower Project: A Case Study on 3,000 MW Dibang Multipurpose Project', determines the possible economic impact of such huge mega dam project on the community living in the periphery of the proposed dam site. In particular, it is an assessment of the Corporate Social Responsibility (CSR) Schemes in realizing the socio-economic status of the indigenous population of the study area.

With the above brief note, we hope that the chapters included in this book serves the purpose of understanding the tribe and its dynamic aspects in the changing phase of globalized era. We further hope that, this much needed book also serves the academic purposes as well as benefits students, researchers and policy makers as it has covered a wide range of topics and research areas. Some of the chapters raise very pertinent issues and explore the plight of the peripheral tribe within a tribal state of India's North-East region. We are sure that this academic exercise, on a lesser known tribe, provides plenty of scope for future enquiry and in-depth probing with immense policy implications.

Note

1. Regarding the number of tribes in Arunachal Pradesh, there is always a contested debate surrounding what the terms 'Major', 'Minor' or 'Subgroup' exactly imply, and also regarding the number of tribe scholars claim from time to time are challenged. In many of the writings it is said that there are 26 major tribes and more than 110 subgroups. But the fact remains that no cultural group is static as also seen among some of the tribes in Arunachal Pradesh. In fact, there is visibly an ongoing process of new social formations or new ethnic assertions among many tribes across the globe. In the context of Arunachal Pradesh, formerly the Gallong tribe was known with an identity as a subgroup of larger Adi tribe but in the present day they identify themselves as Galo tribe, an independent identity separated from the former and is one of the best examples of this process. Similarly, erstwhile 'Hills Miri' as an identity of a tribe is no more in use as this tribe assumed and imbibed a new social identity as Nyishi tribe. This 'in and out process' of tribes makes it difficult to figure out the exact number of ethnic groups in Arunachal Pradesh. Thus, at least for now, we may safely say that based on ethno-linguistic characteristics there are as many as 25 tribal groups and many more with dialectic variations inhabiting the state of Arunachal Pradesh.

2

The Idu Mishmi Tribe of Frontier State of Arunachal Pradesh

TARUN MENE AND SARIT K. CHAUDHURI

The Idu Mishmis, a scheduled tribe of India, primarily inhabit two districts, i.e. the Lower Dibang Valley and the Dibang Valley districts along with a few population in Lohit, East Siang and Upper Siang districts of Arunachal Pradesh. They are one of the three subgroups of the Mishmi tribe and the other two subgroups are Taraon (Digaru) and Kaman (Miju).[1] Culturally, the Idu Mishmis are a distinct group from the other two which are very much reflected in various aspects of their day-to-day life and social structure as well as value systems. In terms of population, they are approximately 12,000 in total which are spread in as many as 250 villages.[2]

Though the terms 'Idu' and 'Mishmi' have precolonial origin; they call themselves *Keraa-a*, meaning children of *Keraa*, a remote ancestor of the Idu Mishmis as they assume. They were also popularly known to outsiders as the Chulikata Mishmis during colonial and post-colonial periods because of their distinct hairstyle which is said to be a nomenclature given by the people of the plains with whom they had trade relations (Bhattacharjee, 1983). Dalton (1872: 18) also reported them as *Midhi* people and mentioned that they are greatly detested and mistrusted by their neighbours, the Abors and Tains, and they are much dreaded by the Saudiya population in consequence of the prowling expeditions to kidnap women and children.

From the time they came in contact with the outside world, various scholars have shed light on their origin, but to this date, no general consensus could be attained. In this regard, Baruah (1960: 11–13) claimed that they have come from the north and their migration took them from Tibet. Similarly, Bhattacharjee (1983: 13) had the notion that they have come from the triangle of Burma between Salween Mekong and Yangten where similar tribe lives. Very recently, Lingi (2011), breaking the code of shaman's chants provided some information on the numbers of migratory routes which was followed by the Idu Mishmis in the past along the river *Etho* (Siang), *Taloh* (Dibang) and *Illu* (Lohit). Along the river *Etho* (Siang) and *Taloh* (Dibang) he provided the following major places: *Mudu (inika-ellaka), Iniyo (iniyo Chengo Pu), Iniyo Selo Pu, Iniyo Maselo Pu, Inika Kandi Phiti, Iniyo Azumboli, Iniyo Akhrika, Aduya, Inigomo, Locho lasa* (present-day Tibet), *Layi Lagu, Suli Pra Po*, to the present habitation *Chokonati.* Another route was along the river *Illu* (Lohit) which includes places like *Tsinji Gema, Dili, Axi Aka, Sili Leya* and *Chokonati.*

Thus, it is an undeniable fact that whatever information one collects on the origin of the tribe, it tell us about their memoirs of migration and their migratory routes which often indicate places located in the upper ridge of the present-day habitation. Even today, one may note that the Idu Mishmis identify themselves by their place of settlement which lies in the river valleys called *Chithus* and are said to be twelve in number. They are: (a) *Ihil* (b) *Siku* (c) *Illu* (d) *Emma* (e) *Emmra* (f) *Ahi* (g) *Mathu* (h) *Dri* (i) *Taloh* (j) *Ithu* (k) *Chiyu* and (l) *Chifu*. The present-day landmass between the rivers *Etho* (Siang) and *Taloh* (Dibang) is called *Shoko Payu-Bo* and the region between rivers *Taloh* (Dibang) and *Illu* (Lohit) is called *Shoko Awa-No* (Lingi, 2011).

The Idu Mishmis are Mongoloid and speak Tibeto-Burman family language (Simon, 1976). Their habitation is mostly located in the river valleys and few in the mountain plains. Their village may be categorized into two, viz. uniclan and multi-clan villages. But most distinctively, there exists another type of village which may be called a single homestead village. Such a village consists of single or nuclear or extended type of family living in a single household. For example, villages like Ingulin, Induli, Ebali, Grinli, etc. located at Mipi and Aneli administrative circle of Dibang Valley district have only single household.

While bypassing through an Idu Mishmi village, one may find another unique feature of an Idu Mishmi village which basically lies in the length of their dwelling houses. This is, however, not an exclusive feature of the entire village but true to some only. Interestingly, looking at this unique structure of house, Baruah (1960: 22) once remarked it as 'Corridor train' which still exists in some villages. Such a traditional house may be of 40 to 50 metres in length with 6 to 7 metres in widths and may consist of as many as 10 to 15 apartments, each room having its own hearth.[3] The front room is called *Alonga* for the male members and the northern side of this *Alonga* is considered a sacred place for men called *Amenido* where they hung the skulls of wild and domestic animals which they hunt. The rooms for females follow through the *Alonga* called *Apinuku*. Each room has hearth and above it there are three layers of shelves called *Ato, Andu* and *Apo*. The house is built upon raised platform and the floor and the walls are made of spilt bamboo.

Having such a unique feature and among others, it is observed that there exists both nuclear and joint or extended types of families among the Idu Mishmis. Sometimes two or more lineally related kinsman, their wives and children also occupy a single homestead similar to a joint family structure.

Generally, the authoritative power goes to father or married male of the family and women in the family are traditionally responsible for all the domestic activities such as collection of firewood and fodder, food preparation, etc. All the immovable properties are inherited by the sons; daughters get their mother's possessions. The succession of power is maintained through the male line and generally the eldest son is expected to inherit the position of father in family. However, these traditional norms are changing due to various factors. Nowadays, nuclear type of family is mostly visible, especially in the villages near to urban township area. Women are no more subjected to domestic affairs.

The institution of marriage is an important aspect of sociocultural set-up in every society. This institution plays an important role in reflecting the culture of the people and assuring the continuity of the society. Among the Idu Mishmis, a person is considered incomplete without marriage. The one who fails to marry is seen as socially inferior and a failure in life. The basic rule of marriage is clan exogamy and for establishing a matrimonial relationship, persons involved should not have any blood relationship either from the patrilineal or matrilineal line of descendants. However, this traditional norm experienced challenges with changing time. There is seen relaxation in matrilineal line of descendants in establishing a marital tie only after getting the consent of the respective clan members. Polygamy was once considered a matter of pride but as of now it is becoming a rare practice. Widow remarriage is allowed provided the customary rules of marriage are followed.

The religious world of the Idu Mishmi is largely animism and they believe in number of spirits called *khinu* whom they appease from time to time involving scores of animal and bird sacrifices. These man-spirit relationships are well communicated by the community shaman called *Igu* through various rites and rituals. However, changes in various aspects are quite visible. Conversion to greater religion such as Christianity and Hinduism is a reality and in an attempt to counterbalance this process, people have already started revivalist movement to institutionalize their own traditional religious belief and practices. This movement is termed as Nani Intayaism[4] where an effort has been made to create images of Goddess Intaya or Maselo Zeno. This movement was initiated by the Idu Cultural and Literary Society (ICLS) during 1997–98.

The material culture life of the Idu Mishmis is deeply rooted with their immediate natural surroundings. They are known to others for their expert handloom and handicraft works. From there everyday use of domestic articles to dwelling place all are mainly made up of forest materials. Their domestic articles as well as art and craft, like baskets, mats, headgear, mug, strainer, spoon, tray, winnow, rain shield, haversack, mortar, etc. are the reflection of bamboo and cane works.

Idu Mishmi men and women are experts in weaving and knitting. Their handlooms are generally designed with mix colour of black, red, white, yellow and dark green. An Idu man wears a sleeveless black coat called *Etoma, Etopu, Etowe Yambu, Etomaju, Etoambu, Etoko,* with embroidered borders. Men also wear thick war coat called *Atondren* made of nettle fibre and human hair. Ear rings and bead necklaces are used irrespective of gender and these include *Arulo, Lekepo, Andisu, Akokhre,* etc. An Idu woman wears blouse in upper level called *Atopolo*. The lower garment consists of *Thuwe, Thuwe Pupra, Thuwe Juputu, Thuma*, etc. Also there a special variety of upper garment called *Anatubi* which is worn by both the gender. Other male attire includes variety of hats like *Apotolo Juhi, Apotolo Gerandu, Apotolo Kulutu,* etc. Their swords include *Era-ah, Sissa, Ambre. Aache*. The community shaman (*Igu*) has its own special variety of costumes which include *Ethomabra, Atoti, Amraala,* and *Auoto.*

Society is never static so are its components. With the options wide open for substitutions in the present-day context, many elements are losing its utility and significance and are on the verge of extinction. For example, present-day house structure of an Idu Mishmi is built of concrete materials and roof with metal sheet which is opted over the traditional bamboo house due to its durability. Similarly, traditional domestic articles are gradually substituted with the metallic fibre, plastic articles. With the acceptance of latest in vogue, be it dress or ornaments, people are fast changing in their outlook. In this process of replacement, the traditional art and crafts as well as skills and techniques are disappearing.

In terms of economic life, their day-to-day activities mainly revolve around agriculture, hunting and gathering, fishing, cane and bamboo work, weaving, etc. Since the habitation of the tribe is mostly in hilly terrains, people practise jhuming form of agriculture. Those living in the foot plains practise settled form of wet rice cultivation. Generally, agricultural land, area of hunting and trapping are deemed as individual, family or clan or community land. Thus, ownership of land varies from community, clan to individual level.

During the precolonial periods, the Idu Mishmis had their trade relation with the people of Tibet (*Puwu*) in the form of barter system. Items like deer musk (*Alapea*), coptis tita (*Aroh*), bear bile (*Ahumuh*), tiger skin (*Amrako*), deer skin (*Manjoko*), etc., were used as commodity for exchange and in return they used to get beads, swords, utensils, cloths, salt, etc. With the expansion of British colony to the land of this frontier tribe, Sadiya, located at Upper Assam, became the centre of trade for the people. Here also goods were exchanged. They had also good trade relation with their neighbouring tribe. References are there where it is said that the Padams supplied the Mishmis with Mithuns in exchange for Mishmi coats, helmets and hand bags (Singh, 1995: 27).[5] Srivastava (1988: 29) also observed that through traditional trade weaved Idu Mishmi clothes reached the land of the Adi and Galo tribe.

However, with the advent of developmental activities and education, occupational mobility is observable. People have now started allied activities like contract works, business, commercial farming, horticulture, fisheries, etc. Many are now engaged in various government jobs also. Many are shifting towards commercial farming of crops like ginger, mustard, potato, tea plantation, cardamom, etc. One more important feature of lower plain agriculturist is the system of sharecropping which exist between the land owner and the tenant. Most of the tenants are Nepali's who seasonally share their agriculture production with the landowner.

Among the Idu Mishmis, traditional system of administration of justice exists and functions as per the age-old traditions and customs. This traditional village political organization is called '*Abbelah*'. The term *Abbelah* is composed of two words; i.e. '*Abbe*' meaning 'in between' and '*lah*' meaning 'to speak or talk'. Thus, a group of person who talks in between the two parties as mediators constitute the village political organization called '*Abbelah*'. To solve any sort of disputes, arbitration is done through negotiation and therefore, their political organization may be termed as 'Arbiter System.' This village political organization is composed of few elderly villagers (i.e. two to four in most cases) who are renowned for their traditional wisdom, persuasive capacity, wisdom and experience in settling disputes, good oratory and soundness in their judgement. Disputes related to theft, quarrel, marriage, murder, property, etc. are resolved through this institution. Sometimes, shamans are also called upon for help in resolving issues through different types of oaths and ordeals such as *Ata, Aseya, Ikuta*, etc.

However, in the present-day context, having the modern judiciary and administration system, the traditional institution of *Abbelah* is losing its role it had played in the past. Earlier, for example, in case of murder and adultery, it was *Abbelah* who were held responsible in sorting out the issue between the two disputant parties and their verdict was supposed to be final. But at present days such issues are settled mostly in modern judiciary system.

There are some recent developments in terms of identity consciousness not only visible among the Idu Mishmis but among most of the tribal groups of the state. Identity is dominant question today and identity markers are observed in various movements that are taking place in the region. Prominent among these remained the religious and the language oriented. Of late, people started a revivalist movement in an attempt to institutionalize their age-old religion. This has generated a numbers of religious elements which were not there in the past, for example, the images of goddess Nana Intaya. Similarly, in case of language, the Idu Mishmi language has only a spoken form and that the language is listed among the endangered languages of India;[6] some eminent members of the society took up the issue for the first time in 2003 by forming Idu Ekobe Kebange (IEK), a Non-Governmental Organization. This Organization in collaboration with Central Institute of Indian Languages (CIIL), Mysore, developed a writing system which is still in the process of refinement which is looked after by Idu Language Development Committee (ILDC), a new nomenclature for IEK, in giving its best for the creation of Idu Mishmi writing system and dictionary. This movement also reflects the linkages of language and ethnic identity, concerns and consciousness of the community in preserving their language as an identity marker, vis-à-vis continuity of their culture.

Another such concern is reflected in the celebration of two important festivals, i.e. *Reh* and *Ke-meh-ha* festivals. These festivals are primarily clan and family based festival involving rituals and animal sacrifices. These festivals are observed for the prosperity and well-being of the family and clan members by seeking blessings from the supreme goddess *Inni* and from different benevolent spirits. However, these traditional forms of festivals have itself a new identity and new dimensions, basically in response and pertaining to new ideologies and larger social interactions and exposure of the people in the light of cultural identity. To them, it was first realized when some eminent member of the society took initiative to celebrate these festivals at community level by bringing all the community members into a single platform on a fixed calendar date. It was on 1st February 1968, the then Additional Deputy Commissioner, I.P. Gupta, for the first time made a history by inaugurating the central form of *Reh* festival on community basis at Roing, now the Headquarters of Lower Dibang Valley district. Similarly, the *Ke-meh-ha* festival was celebrated at community level during September 2004 and it was first held at *Simare* village in the Lower Dibang Valley district. Both the festivals are celebrated at a particular place calling it a central celebration representing as community festival. Along with the traditional elements, such as rituals and sacrifices, these centrally celebrated festivals also accommodate modern songs and dances, sports and literary competitions, fashion shows, etc. To be precise, in these centrally celebrated festivals, programmes are too often designed keeping the concerns of 'others' and defined in the eyes of the non-indigenous culture.

Like many other tribes of Arunachal Pradesh, the Idu Mishmis are also passing through the phase of transition. And these are manifested in terms of their economy, social structure, material culture and other basic elements of society as well as culture. Such changes are inevitable as they are exposed to the wider realities of life through the development of communication, monetary economy, formal education systems, modern political processes and initiation of state sponsored development programmes. However, amidst such changes, Idu Mishmis in general, are conscious of retaining some of their core identity markers, which have given them a distinct space within the varied cultural mosaic of the tribes of a frontier state. Thus, keeping in mind the process of change and continuity, this book on the Idu Mishmis will further clear all doubts.

Acknowledgement

The paper is a revised version of the original paper titled 'The Idu Mishmis of Arunachal Pradesh: A Frontier Tribe in Transition' by Tarun Mene and Sarit K. Chaudhuri, In Medhi, B.K., Athparia, et al. 2009: 154–70. *Tribes of North East India; Issues and Challenges*, Omsons Publications, New Delhi.

Notes

1. The Kamans were also known as 'Miju Mishmis' and Taraon as 'Digaru Mishmis'. Their material culture such as dresses and ornaments, housing design and pattern, etc. is so similar that it is difficult to distinguish them; however, the Idu Mishmis are quite distinct in this matter. One distinguishing feature of the Idu Mishmis is their hair style.
2. As per 2001 census report, they were numerically figured at 9,350. Available at: censusindia.gov.in/tables_published/scst/dh_st_arunachal.pdf
3. One Mr Adema Mimi of Aneya village in the Dibang Valley district had once as many as 30 rooms (*egu*) with each room having a hearth (*engoko*) in his house.

4. The concept is coined from the term *Innitaya* or *Maselo Zeno* (the sun) whom the Idus regard as supreme Goddess. The prefix *Nani* meaning Mother is added to it to create a sense of supreme authority like in the concept of *Ma Durga, Ma Kali* in Hinduism.
5. Singh (1995: 27).
6. Language endangerment in India is divided in two broad categories: (i) languages that are endangered due to certain speech communities are biologically endangered, viz. Andamanese, Jarawas, Onges, Sentenalese and Shompens in the Union Territory of Andaman and Nicobar Islands and (ii) languages that are endangered due to other reasons, viz. speech communities having considerably very small population of few hundreds to few thousands like the Idu Mishmis in Arunachal Pradesh (around eight thousand only) ... Reference from the web: http://www.ciil.org/main/announcement/abstracts/abstacts/14.htm. Accessed on 5 November 2007.

References

Aiyadurai, Ambika (2014). *Traditional Ecological Knowledge of the Idu Mishmis: What Do People Say about Wildlife?* Report submitted for the 2nd Rufford Small Grant for Nature Conservation. Available at: www.rufford.org/files/12697-2%20 detailed%20final%20report.pdf. Accessed on 12 May 2016.

Baruah, S. (2003). 'Nationalising Space: Cosmetic Federalism and the Politics of Development in the Northeast India', *Development and Change*, 34(5): 915–39.

Baruah, T.K. (1960). *The Idu Mishmis*, Directorate of Research, Government of Arunachal Pradesh, Itanagar.

Behera, M.C. and S.K. Chaudhuri (1998). *Indigenous Faiths and Practices of the Tribes of Arunachal Pradesh*, Himalayan Publications, Itanagar.

Bhattacharjee, T.K. (1983). *Idus of Mathu and Dri Valley*, Directorate of Research, Government of Arunachal Pradesh, Itanagar.

Bose, M.L. (1997). *History of Arunachal Pradesh*, Concept Publishing, New Delhi.

Chakravorty, L.N. (1989). *Glimpses of the Early History of Arunachal*, Directorate of Research, Government of Arunachal Pradesh, Itanagar.

Committee of the Royal Anthropological Institute of Great Britain and Ireland (1951). *Notes and Queries on Anthropology*, Sixth edition, Routledge and Kegan Paul Ltd., London.

Dalton, E.T. (1872). *Descriptive Ethnology of Bengal*, German edition 1875, Asiatic Society of Bengal, Calcutta, pp. 13–21.

Datta, B., N.C. Sarma and P.C. Das (1994). *A Handbook of Folklore Material of North-East India*, ABILAC, Guwahati.

Elwin, V. (1958). *Myths of the NEFA*, Directorate of Research, Government of Arunachal Pradesh, Itanagar.

—— (1959). *A Philosophy for NEFA*, Director of Research, Government of Arunachal Pradesh, Itanagar.

Gopalakrishanan, R. (1994). *Arunachal Pradesh*, Omsons Publications, New Delhi.

Lingi, Mite (2011). 'Origin of the Idu Mishmis and the Igu', in *Reh Souvenir, Roing*, Central Reh Celebration Committee, Roing Lower Dibang Valley, Arunachal Pradesh, pp. 8–14.

Mibang, T. and M.C. Behera (eds) (2004). *Dynamics of Tribal Villages in Arunachal Pradesh*, Mittal Publications, New Delhi.

—— (2007). *Marriage in Tribal Societies*, Bookwell Publications, New Delhi.

Pulu, J. (1999). 'Reh Festival of Idu Mishmi', *Resarun*, 25(1-2), Directorate of Research, Government of Arunachal Pradesh, Itanagar.

Simon, I.M. (1976). 'Note on the Languages of Arunachal Pradesh', *Resarun*, 2(3), Directorate of Research, Government of Arunachal Pradesh, Itanagar, p. 60.

Singh, K.S. (ed. 1995). *People of India, Arunachal Pradesh*, Vol. XIV, Anthropological Survey of India, Calcutta.

Srivastava, L.R.N. (1988). *The Gallongs*, Directorate of Research, Government of Arunachal Pradesh, Itanagar.

Vidyarth, L.P. and B.K. Rai (1976). *The Tribal Culture of India*, Concept Publishing Company, New Delhi.

3

Narrating the Tribe: Colonial Constructs and Voicing the Savage

A Post-colonial Study of the Colonial Writings on the Mishmis of Arunachal Pradesh

RAZZEKO DELLEY

History is one of the most significant components of a society. The individuals or society construct their identity and selfhood around it. Moreover, history is a source of pride for any society. It acts as a guiding principle in situation of chaos and confusion. The figures from historical past are a perennial source of inspiration for the whole community and therefore, society gets knowledge and insight of itself through history. The society without history is similar to man without memory or self-knowledge; cut adrift from everything. Probably, that may be the reason behind Plato's proclamation that history is the highest form of knowledge (Rowe, 2006).

Sense of history, most probably, is imbued in human consciousness. The pride people take in their family names even today in the modern world manifest the significance of the past. The past it can be said lives in the present through different human endeavours. The diverse literature since prehistoric times manifests that the past played a crucial role in the affairs of mankind. The importance of connecting with the past is revealed in earliest writings, especially in epics where the heroes are portrayed as being genealogically connected to royalty or divinity. The heroes are never rootless.

Among the Idu Mishmis, the sense of the past plays a very significant role as they are basis of the sociocultural set up. Their unique pattern of fostering kinship system, which only traces the bloodline in both matrilineal and patrilineal sides, is regarded as an exclusive factor among the tribes of Arunachal Pradesh. However, the community's history is shrouded in mystery.

The oral narratives throw very little light about their past. There is mention of places and communities but most of them are untraceable and, therefore, unverifiable today.

Moreover, there is very less documented text about the tribe's past. The earlier writings, few in Ahom chronicle and British texts mention only Mishmi and do not classify them. Therefore, this work henceforth shall take into account the available literature written by the British colonial powers before the Indian independence about the Mishmis. The available literatures also highlight very less about the tribe and moreover, the problem arises in their notion about the tribe. Most of the literatures are highly derogatory representation of the community. Verrier Elwin while writing about the Mishmis notes:

> ... nearly all the early visitors came away with lowest opinion of the Mishmis. Wilcox wrote that they were excessively 'dirty and as rude looking' as could possibly be imagined. 'Excessively filthy', echoed Robinson in 1841; their clothing were inferior, their cultivation 'very rude' 'Disgustingly dirty', adds Rowlatt, varying the adverb for a change ' a very wild roaming race of people, capable of most remorseless reprisal and massacres', declared Butler. The general view says yet another visitor is that they are 'deceitful and bloodthirsty devils' ... not one of them ever bothered to say that the Mishmis were beautiful. And I was entirely unprepared for the wealth and beauty of their weaving designs, for their sense of colour and pattern, for the bright clean faces of the children, the shining white teeth .... The friendly hospitality of everyone, and the quite wonderful coiffure of the Taraon and Kaman women which would not disgrace a Parisian lady of fashion. (1957: 21)

Underwriting and derogatory presentation of the non-European communities had been a widespread phenomenon during the colonial times. As it had been noted earlier, the history is a medium for self-identity and source of inspiration, the derogatory generalizations of the indigenous community are today deemed as history and have crept into the academic curriculum. Regarding the Mishmi community, most materials written on them were part of military expeditions, environmental and trade route surveys and moreover, significant amount of data were collected from the neighbouring tribes of Arunachal Pradesh and Assam. These resources in real sense do not amount to a real history as it is defined as:

> The word history has its origin in the Greek ηιστορια (historia), from the Proto-Indo-European wid-tor-, from the root weid 'to know, to see'. This root is also present in the English words wit; wise, wisdom, vision, and idea, in the Sanskrit word veda and in the Slavic word videti and vedati. The Ancient Greek word ηιστορια, historía, means 'inquiry, knowledge acquired by investigation'. It was in that sense that Aristotle used the word Historia Animalium. The term is derived from ηιστορ, history meaning wise man, witness, or judge. The form historeîn 'to inquire' is an Ionic derivation, which spread first in Classical Greece It was still in the Greek sense that and ultimately over all of Hellenistic civilization (Comprehensive Etymological Dictionary of the English Language, 1971)

Apart from dates of various records, most of the data are unverifiable. History ought to present facts from the perspectives of both the sides but the histories of Mishmis were written by their adversaries like the history of Mongol emperor Ghangis Khan.

These dimensions of the historical records about the Mishmis have made me to look at the colonial writings about the tribe as prejudiced which narrates only the colonial perspectives in order to serve their purposes. I have arrived to this conclusion by founding the study upon the political, sociological and anthropological theories laid down by the Poststructuralists and New Historicists.

Theoretical Background

Edward Said in his book *Orientalism* (1978) coins the phrase 'cultural imperialism' for the tendency to underwrite the communities through derogatory presentation of them by the colonial powers. Cultural imperialism according to Said is carried out through Eurocentric discourse which subjected the western 'occidental' as normal and superior by portraying eastern 'oriental' as an exotic inferior; the other. Said views cultural imperialism as a mode of non-violent imperialism, which was an effective tool to subjugate their colonies through the discourse.

The book reveals how Eurocentric discourses presented the Middle Eastern cultures as timeless societies full of savagery and exotic in a highly romanticized and distorted manner. Said argues that distorted portrayals were political as well as culturally motivated, exhibiting western European superiority and thereby vindicating military conquests and colonizations.

The work had far reaching impact on the social science. Orientalism became an interdisciplinary tool to look at the established works of the colonial masters about the colonized people. Post-colonialism today spans across diverse fields and cannot be regarded as a unified movement but they all reject the 'master-narrative' of western imperialism in which the colonized are the other who are not only marginalized and subordinated but also in effect deleted as cultural agency. The former colonial cultures today, fight their way back into the world history written by Europeans and endeavour to replace these colonial texts by 'counter-narrative' of their own. M.H. Abraham in 'A Glossary of Literary Terms' explains the meaning of post-colonialism thus:

> The rejection of the master-narrative of Western imperialism – in which the colonial other is not only subordinated and marginalized, counter-narrative in which the colonial cultures fight their way back into a world history written by Europeans. The influential collection of essays, 'The Empire Writes Back: Theory and Practice in Post-Colonial Literatures' (1989), ed. Bill Ashcroft, Gareth Griffiths, and Helen Tiffins, stresses what it terms the hybridization of colonial languages and cultures, in which imperialist importations are superimposed on indigenous traditions; it also includes a number of postcolonial counter texts to the hegemonic texts that present a Eurocentric version of colonial history. (1999: 306)

Louis Althusser, in his essay 'Ideology and Ideological State Apparatuses' (1970) lays down the theory of 'ideology' and elaborates the concept by expanding the theory beyond what Karl Marx and Fredrich Engel had defined. Althusser supplements the theory by drawing ideas from later writings of

Antonio Gramsci, Sigmund Freud and Jacques Lacan. He argues that the ideologies of the ruling class are manifested in various forms of discourses of the period. He further contends that ideology as a state apparatus operates covertly to form and position the users of language as a subject in the discourse, in a way that in fact 'subjects' them – that is, subordinates them – to the interests of the ruling classes.

Similarly, Michel Foucault in his discourse analysis observes that the discourse of an era is both products and propagators of 'power' or social force for the master class. In his book *The Archaeology of Knowledge* (1969), Foucault draws the term 'discourse' beyond the formal linguistic aspects and brands it as an institutionalized patterns of knowledge which are manifested in various branches of disciplines and are directly associated with power and knowledge. Discourse as an institutionalized knowledge of the ruling class determines the 'knowledge' and 'truth' as well as what is considered to be criminal, insane or sexually deviant of that era.

Louis Montrose in his essay, 'Professing the Renaissance: The Poetics and Politics of Culture' (1989) considers history as a text to be interpreted like literature. Therefore, as an interpretive text, history is not set of fixed objective facts. Thereby, he further contends that as a text, history is a discourse which overtly may reflect or present a reality but it also is infused with narratives which are representations of ideological products or cultural constructs of the historical environment of that era. These ideological representations in the texts according to Montrose and other new historicists; operates to reproduce, confirm and propagate the complex power structures of domination and subordination of the ruled class in a society.

New historicists like Stephen Greenblatt in his work 'Towards a Poetic of Culture in New Historicisms' (1989) and Raymond Williams in his work 'Marxism and Literature' (1977) attribute these cultural constructs as economy driven. Raymond William in his book coins the phrase cultural materialism to drive the point that the textuality of history, culture and literary product are conditioned by material forces and relation of the production.

In a similar manner, the colonial economic interest made the Britishers to venture in the Mishmi Hills. These hilly ranges since ages were the most viable trade route to Tibet used by many traders from various part of India. However, the colonial powers had to face a highly territorial tribe; the Mishmis. It seems the colonial masters first employed the tried and tested agent, the missionaries, which they had successfully used in America and Africa to subdue the tribes. But the earliest clergy to venture in the hills, Mr Krick, was killed by a Mishmi. Looked from this perspective the Mishmis were impeding the colonial economic interest and, therefore, they were probably derogatory branded. Inappropriate and derogatory branding of the tribe apart from ideological construct and cultural hegemony results from not understanding the native culture but writing about them. It is noteworthy to draw attention to the cultural anthropological theory as proposed by Glifford Geertz regarding the misinterpretation of a culture and misrepresenting it. Geertz looks at culture as being constituted with distinctive set of signifying systems which he calls 'thick description'. Culture according to this idea is governed by language and other behaviours that surround the individual. Moreover, it also encompasses other cultural artefacts like ritual, myth and art. Therefore, anthropologists and ethnographers need to look beyond the collection of cultural data and interpret cultural phenomenon as if it were stored in an archival data. Through the analogy of Moroccan Jew, Geertz demonstrate how the lack of cultural knowledge results into narrative of cultural misunderstanding. Therefore, for the right interpretation or right presentation of facts of any culture, one needs to adopt 'thick descriptions' – the close analysis, or 'reading', of a particular social production or event so as to recover the meanings it has for the people involved in it, as well as to discover, within the cultural system, the general patterns of conventions, codes, and modes of thinking that invest the item with those meanings (Cited in *Glossary of Literary Terms*, Abraham, 1999: 245).

Agreeing upon the concept of 'thick description', I also propose that for the right presentation of facts of any culture, the researcher needs to look beyond what had actually happened. It is essential to study the hidden meanings of cultural conducts in a community's action and look at what had happened before that event and significantly how the participant community gives meaning to that event. Most of the colonial accounts about Mishmis are one sided, highly misrepresentation and misinterpretation of the tribe.

Though post-colonialists and new historicists endeavour to rewrite history and literature, my attempt is just to throw light on how the Mishmi tribe had been misrepresented and misinterpreted by colonial writers. The study tries to give voice to the misinterpreted community.

The Tribe and Territory

The Mishmi people living in the Mishmi Hills and having interaction with the Chutia kingdom gets mentioned in few records (Needham, 1900). During the Ahom period, the chronicle *Buranji* records many instances of Mishmi and Ahom contacts. Few instances are setting up of rampart called 'Mishmi Garh' in 1644 and famous Sadhiya stone pillar inscription from 1687. It is important to note that the earlier recordings do not classify the Mishmi people. The classification of them starts from British records.

The European accounts divide these Mishmis into three groups; Chullikatas, Digarus and Mijus. Further, later on from the last decades of Nineteenth century one more group is included the Bebejiyas.

The branch of Mishmi tribe which is known today as Idu Mishmis called themselves *Kra-aa* which means children of *Kera*. The way of hair dressing earns them the name Chullikatta Mishmi which means cropped hair. However, it is difficult to pin the origin of the term Bebejiya which means outcasts. As per the records, in most of the occasions, they are deemed as an entirely different tribe by the British Administration. The Idu Mishmi society has no concept of an outcast; therefore the people referred here are the members of the tribe itself. However it is significant to note that, the Bebejiya people belonged from middle part of the Dibang Valley especially Ithun Valley, who speak Mithu dialect and were deemed responsible for most of the raids and, therefore, a source of colonial anxiety. Needham in his *Report of the Bebejiya Mishmi Expedition, 1899–1900* clearly divides the Idu Mishmis into two sections when he claims, 'The tribal name of the Bebejiyas is Mithun, and the Chulikattas, Midu' (1900: 13). Moreover, he also reveals how the (Midus) had been incessantly claiming that the Bebejiyas (Mithus) were different community altogether, however, interestingly Needham rightly observes when he writes:

> The Bebejiyas, they (Midus) declare, are of Digaro origin, and they insist upon impressing upon me-as they have always hitherto done-that they are in no way related to the Bebejiyas, though the two tribes appear to me to be identically the same, for they live in exactly the same manner, their customs are similar, they are clothed alike, and their language is undoubtedly the same, and although a Chulikatta never marries a Digaro girl, and a Bebejiya does, the two tribes (Chulikattas and Bebejiyas) intermarry freely. (1990: 13)*

It is difficult to ascertain the origin of Bebejiya concept as it goes against the Idu Mishmi norms. As rightly observed by Needham, the Bebejiya and Chullikatta are the same tribe having the same culture. The reason for some of the members of tribe being branded as outcasts may have resulted due to their actions in the plains. As manifested by the colonial accounts, many Chullikatta people were in good terms with the British Government. Most probably, these people to save themselves from punitive sanctions might have branded the troublemakers as outcasts and a different tribe altogether. Therefore, Keraa is the indonym of the tribe and Chulikattas, Bebejiya and Idu being the exonym. Similarly, Mijus call themselves Kaman and Digaru's Tawra.

The earliest Europeans to visit the Mishmi Hills were Burton (1825) and Wilcox (1827). They both found the Mishmis 'very averse to receive strangers' (Mackenzie, 1884: 47). Same opinions were echoed by most of the Britishers and as quoted by Elwin in earlier passage. These arguments became louder after killing of Hindu Fakir Parmananda by Jingsha in 1848 and French Missionary Krick with his physician subordinate by Kaisha Manyu in 1854.

The reason of unfriendliness to the strangers arises because of the Mishmi attitude which is extremely territorial. Within the community also the villages, clans and individuals have their own territory which is subject to the community regulations. There is no concept of barren independent land as all territories are claimed by villages and clans and, therefore, trespassers are bound to pay penalty. One has to obtain permission for different purposes and exploits. Example of the Mishmi territorial attitude can be witnessed in the Sadiya Snake pillar inscription which dates back to 1687, wherein it is clearly written that trespassing in Hills are strictly prohibited. The inscription reads as follow:

> I, the Dihingia Borgohain, do engrave on the stone pillar and the copper plate these writings (with strength of which) the Mishmis are to dwell on the hills near the Dibong River with their females, children attendants and followers. They will

* Hamilton also refers the Mithu clans as Bebejiyas (1912(a): 19).

> occupy all the hills. They will give four basket full of poison other things as tribute and keep watch on the body of the fat Gohain (Sadhiyakhowa Gohain). If anybody happens to be in procession of and wishes to remain on all sides (of the hills) he is prohibited from encroachment. If anybody would dwell by the side of the hills, he would surely become a slave (of the Mishmis). I do proclaim wide if anybody sits exalted (i.e. comes in power, i.e. become ruler) he should not break (the agreement) and break the stone. (*Assam District Gazetteers*, Vol. XI, 1928: 18–19)

The Colonialists were drawn towards the Mishmi Hills as it was the most suitable passage to Tibet and China. In his book, *North-East Frontier of India: Topographical, Political and Military Reports*, Captain F. Michell John of Intelligence Branch serving in Quarter Master Generals Department in India writes:

> More interest attaches to the Mishmis than to some of the other tribes of the Assam valley, for through their territory one of the roads to the trade of China lies, and the progress of civilization in Assam points to this route being opened up at some future period. (1883: 85)

The Mishmi Hill ranges of Lohit Valley were being used as safe and viable trade route to Tibet, China and Burma for many centuries. Not only the Mishmis and other tribes of Arunachal Pradesh but people from other places like Assam also frequented and carried out their trade (Cooper, 1873: 230). At different Passes, the traders used to be levied taxes by the Mishmis. These payments were for using the territory of a particular clan and also, the levying clan after receiving the dues ensured the safety as well as hospitality of the traders in their territories as they deemed this aspect their responsibility. T.T. Cooper in his book *The Mishmee Hills* (1873), records an episode in which some Khampti traders were plundered by Lamat clan (Romat), however as they were in Bowsong Prun's (Pul) territory, he negotiates with them and consequently all the items are restored to the traders. T.T. Cooper does not mention the cause of the altercations, but probably the episode might have occurred due to non-payment of taxes to the Romat clan or might have resulted because of non-agreement on the sum of the taxes. Lamat clan or in some instances Romat clan as Cooper himself mentions inhabited immediate territory to the Tibetan Frontiers and thereby enjoyed the taxes of the traders.

The Westerners might have assumed the hills as chaotic and devoid of any regulations but mutual exchanges of dues and cooperation have prevailed in these regions since ages. However, to the bewilderment of the native people, the colonial whites had their own codes and regulations which were dictated by their notion of 'white men's burden'. For them savage codes were irrelevant, inapplicable and, above all, unacceptable. Likewise, the fakir and missionaries breached the existing regulations by not paying dues to the clan members after passing through their territory. As they had broken the law, the people thought it appropriate to punish them. If not sternly punished, there were dangers of other people following the suit and throttling the source of their economy. These killings, it may look marred with savagery and treachery however, had resulted from the wrongdoings of the victims themselves.

Another significant aspect which the colonialist raises is the inability of bringing to justice the Mishmis who had raided their territory and killed their subjects. In most episodes, like as in the Chulikatta Mishmi raid of Sadiya in 1855, 1879, 1884, 1899 and 1911, the attempt to book the culprit failed. These episodes seem to have infuriated the colonial power. The Raj proclaims of engaging various 'chiefs' for their purpose but were futile endeavours.

The vital point which the Britishers could not grasp is that there is no concept of chieftaincy among the Mishmis. They are a highly independent tribe without any prescribed laws but are governed by their community specific ethical conducts and regulations. These people whom they have referred as chiefs were most influential people of their clan during their lifetime. The so-called Mishmi chiefs are very different from chiefs of Africa or America who have considerable influence on their people. As there is no concept of chieftaincy therefore, the inheritance of it doesn't arise. Among the Mishmis one earns reputation and status in the clan as well as in the community through their endeavours. Despite their position in the clan, these 'chiefs' might have very less or no say in the matters concerning the people from other clans.

Culture

Attire and Appearance

The early writers describe in detail the weapons possessed by the Mishmis. Dalton, Cooper and Hamilton indicate the violent nature of the Mishmis by describing in detail what they carry; the swords, spears and bows with quiver full of poisoned arrows, etc.

According to the Mishmi tradition, weapons are an essential component of an attire. All are expected to wear at least a sword or machete whenever out of the house. Only the slaves roam disarmed. Moreover, these tribal people had to cross hundreds of miles to get into Sadiya by spending nights in caves and jungles. Travelling without arms would have been highly impractical during those days. As observed rightly by Elwin, all the foreigners had very low opinion about the conduct as well as appearance of the Mishmis. The Civil Assistant Surgeon of Goalpara, J. McCosh in his paper, 'Account of the Mountain Tribes on the Extreme N.E. Frontier of Bengal' calls them 'one of tribe with lowest grade of civilization' (1836: 195). At times, the derogatory levelling seems out of context as in case of Dalton (1872), who while demeaning the hairstyle of the Idu Mishmis writes: 'The front hair is combed down on the brow, then cut straight across from ear to ear, giving them foreheads villainous low'. Moreover in the same vein, Dalton narrates an incident involving an Idu Mishmi man who had come to trade in Sadiya market thus:

> It was very interesting to watch the barter that took place there between these suspicious, excitable savages and the cool, wily traders of the plains. The former took salt chiefly in exchange for the commodities they brought down, and they would not submit to its being measured or weighed to them by any known process. Seated in front of the trader's stall, they cautiously take from a well-guarded basket one of the articles they wish to exchange. Of this they still retain a hold with their toe or their knee as they plunge two dirty paws into the bright white salt. They make an attempt to transfer all they can grasp to their own basket, but the trader,

> with a sweep of his hand, knocks off half the quantity, and then there is a fiery altercation, which is generally terminated by a concession on the part of the trader of a few additional pinches. (1872: 220)

The concept of beauty is cultural specific and varies from time to time as well as from place to place. Travelling for hundreds of miles by spending nights in caves and jungles will give tiresome and shabby countenance. The Mishmis traded their goods in the plains especially in Sadiya fairs. As noted above by Dalton, if there were no way of weighing or measuring, one can assume the kind of trade that were going on in the past. The tribal people in many occasions were duped and cheated by the Dalton's 'wily and cool' traders. The commerce without regulations could have been one of the reasons for the mistrust and misunderstanding between the tribal and plain people.

T.T. Cooper's 'The Mishmee Hills' is marred with description of Mishmis as lazy, dirty, brutish savages, in most of the chapters. In some instances, much unknown brutish practices are also attributed to the 'savages'. For instance, Cooper describes of Mishmi way of slaughtering the Mithun wherein he claims 'a chief' was first to strike the beast and thereafter:

> The chief then retires, and all the men rush in and with horrible yells hack and hew at the wretched beast until it falls with piteous groans, and long before life is extinct lumps of the quivering flesh are cut off and thrown to the women and children, who scramble for the warm bloody pieces, and, amidst frantic shouts of delight carry them to the house, where they are boiled for the feast. This ceremony is a ghastly spectacle, and sickened me .... (1880: 234)

Marriage and Morals

Dalton and Cooper have observed that the marriage system among the Mishmis exclusively consists of bargains and purchase where the women are traded as commodities. Dalton writes:

> Marriage ceremony there is, I believe, none; it is simply an affair of purchase, and the women thus obtained, if they can be called wives, are not much bound by the tie. The husbands do not expect them to be chaste; they take no cognizance of their temporary liaisons so long as they are not deprived of their services. If a man is dispossessed of one of his wives, he has a private injury to avenge, and takes the earliest opportunity of retaliating, but he cannot see that the woman is a bit the worse for a little incontinency. (1872: 19)

For the outsiders, the Mishmi marriage system may look as a simple trade but their institution of marriage is highly complex where the past of the clans are scanned and enquired upon. The whole marriage process involves most of the clan members, and both the parties have to maintain and follow strictly various customs and regulations for rest of their life.

Strangely, the colonial writers were also attracted towards the sexual morality of the 'savages'. In his fantasized version, Dalton mentions a kind of orgy indulged by the Idu Mishmi men and women when he writes:

> The Midhi, like the Mishmis previously described, are a trading people. Large parties are continually on the move trading with Tibet. On such occasions, men

> send their wives if they cannot go themselves, and to anyone who has seen how the men and women promiscuously bivouac at night, the exceeding complaisance of the husband will not appear wonderful. (1872: 19)

Similarly, Hamilton in his book, *In Abor Jungles* (1912a) writes about the Mishmi morality:

> Sexual morality is not imposed on men or women until after marriage. The inevitable result is that the great majority of women have large and happy families, though only the minority possess husbands. Where the lady boasts a lover, and honours her intercourse with him after the eternal fashion, some sort of permanent alliance is set up. Such an arrangement is optional none the less; more often than not it is disregarded. (1912: 99)

The account of Hamilton seems to be based on the misinformation probably furnished by neighbouring tribes. Dalton's assumptions seem to be cooked up fantasy of his own as he had never been to the hills and not to talk of visiting the trade routes towards Tibet. The reason for these assumptions whether were out of misinformation or whether it is fantasy of the white head about the 'savages' may not surface today. Sex is not a tabooed subject among the Mishmis, however, the society is deeply rooted in the concept of clan relations which is strengthened by taking into account both the patrilineal and matrilineal sides and continues for many generations. This structure make most of the people as relatives and leaves very less scope of finding a non-relative with whom one can establish sexual relationships. This dimension of the Idu Mishmi society has been the impeding factor in getting a choice of marital partner even today. Moreover, illicit affairs are handled with iron hand and the offending male has to pay a huge penalty. Just a couple of years ago, a man had to pay a sum of fifty lakh for eloping with another man's wife.

The Tribal Religion and Colonial Reservations

Demeaning a community and derogatory portrayal of them would have been incomplete without savaging their religion. To show the Mishmis in poorest of light they need to be portrayed as being practitioners of lowest and rudimentary religious forms. Therefore, Dalton seems to have left no stone unturned when he writes:

> I have met with no people so entirely devoid of religious feeling as are the Chalikatas. I had long conversations on the subject with several of the chiefs, and they utterly rejected all notions of a future state, or of immortality of any kind. ... Men die and worms eat them, is their creed .... (1872: 21)

Cooper also makes similar findings, 'The Mishmees being polytheists, though of the lowest order' ... (1883: 197) and therefore, he preaches them the concept of the great monotheistic single 'Great Spirit' when he says,

> I described monotheism to him, and it seemed to create a very pleasing impression. Of course I did not speak to him of the Saviour, as I feared that the Christian religion with its wonderful mystery might be too much for the half fetishist and half-polytheistic savage to understand, besides which, I saw that Poso was

> beginning to be excessively uncomfortable, and Chowsam told me not to talk about demons, as the Mishmees disliked it, and begged of me for the future to abstain from this subject. (1883: 197)

Moreover late in the night, Cooper further discusses the compassion which is brimming up in his conscience for the lesser mortal savages:

> Here I was among a people who knew nothing of a God, their lives spent amidst a slavish fear of unseen evil spirits, and yet ready in the slow progress of their thoughts to offer up allegiance to one Great Spirit, of whom they might now be said to have heard for the first time. Their poor reasons were incapable of conceiving a notion of anything great and good. Alas! It was a sorry picture, and I almost wished that I was a missionary that I might teach them to become worshippers of one God instead of many, for it was evident that as polytheists they were ripe for receiving monotheism. (1883: 199)

Religion is a very private matter among the Mishmis; therefore, unlike the Christians, they don't harp around and preach their religion to convert others. Many subjects relating to faith are tabooed by the people even today; thereby, the reluctance of the people to discuss about their belief system is quite sensible. Among the entire subject about the belief systems, the death related customs are most tabooed subject even in present times therefore; it is not hard to see the reasons behind the utter failure of Dalton to extract the information relating to the subject. For comprehending a faith, one needs to be a keen observer and have understanding sights and not contempt glances like that of Mr Dalton.

It is highly irreconcilable why the western monotheistic Christians are not able to comprehend the tribal polytheism. What is the issue in believing that there are many elements which control the nature as well as affairs of humans? What is ill in not submitting oneself to one single almighty god but revering many forces of nature which structure and shape the universe? The Mishmis as mentioned earlier are highly independent tribe and have no concept of supreme ruler or chieftaincy. However, it should not be assumed that their society is highly chaotic, as they follow strictly the traditional ethics and regulations of the community. Even the Mishmi religion is not about submitting oneself to god, there is no idea of submission at all and thereby there is no concept of 'God is great' kind of notion. Their religion is very much rooted to their life and surroundings. Viewed with reason, their religion is inseparable from their other aspects of life. It is not an abstract practice but holistic, literal and implicit in all actions. Even most of the day-to-day activities like eating, sleeping and other daily mundane chores are ingrained with religious beliefs. What outsiders view as the demons or evil spirits are actually supernatural beings who are embodiment of various ailments and elements of nature. These supernatural beings are everywhere and in everyplace, in most instances rubbing shoulders with the human affairs. They are not to be offended so that they don't disturb the human world. When a Mishmi senses the presence of supernatural beings nearby, especially when one feel at stake, then he would utter thus, 'I'm on my way minding my own business and not at all concerned with you. You go your way and let me go my way'. Therefore, the cruxes of the Mishmi religion is simply 'mind your own businesses' and live and let live. However at times, these entities get offended and inflict people with various miseries. The reason for the annoyance may be breach of regulations by humans, knowing or unknowingly. During these times, shamans are employed as they have powers to communicate with these entities. Significantly, the shamanic discourse also does not comprise of praising those beings with invocatory songs. The shaman after diagnosing the cause, reasons, debates, consoles and bargains and thereafter makes amendment with the supernatural entities. Sacrifice is the last step to appease as well as seal the bond between the aggrieved and aggressor. However, at times the powerful shamans even warn and threaten these spirits. The shaman during the communiqué mostly employ intelligent discourse as he reasons and debates and does not flatter the spiritual beings by prostrating and singing invocatory praises as in case of other religions.

Dalton and Cooper both display deep angst against the Mishmi religion. Moreover, Cooper even thinks of imposing monotheistic religion on the tribal people. The idea of only one supreme god who is also maker and saviour of the world and the attitude of regarding other gods being lesser gods or false has been one of the main source of ills in the world today. The concept of one ruler also seems to have developed from this idea. Therefore, they are so insistent on the chieftaincy among the tribal people. To refer the influential people of different clans being chiefs manifests the urge to submit to one single entity and therefore, view community being controlled by chiefs. The insistent urge to submit oneself to one god, one king seems to control their attitude while viewing the world but the same instinct, among the Mishmis is absent as they are highly independent.

It is not difficult to ascertain the thoughts of Poso when Cooper insisted and preached monotheistic religion to him. He might have felt astonished to see a man vouching for his religion, so insistent and adamant about the superiority of his faith. He would have not reconciled with the higher 'metaphysical idea' that is persistent to prove his faith as superior without knowing the faith of others and imposing one great single saviour to the world. To divert the topic and please the guest, the 'savage' gentleman seems to have uttered politely 'Ah! You English people must be very happy in having such a good and powerful demon in your country. The Mishmees are very unfortunate ... .'

The Mishmis do not establish an emotional connection with the supernatural beings unlike other religions who connect themselves emotionally to a great saviour of the world. The Mishmis believe in supernatural beings that are dynamic by nature and at times are benevolent and malevolent. This belief system seems to have evolved out of their keen observance of nature which is benevolent as well as malevolent. There prevails no concept of praying everyday and prostrating in front of a supreme being. The nature, surrounding and environment are governed by certain principles and regulations. The people only need to follow certain restrictions and regulations in order to save themselves from the wrath of these superior beings. One keeps a safe distance and at times they need to be appropriated. Unlike the European guest, the 'savage' might have viewed no point in insisting that there is only one great being of theirs who is most superior in the world. For the 'savage' there was no problem to accept the great saviour as one of the supernatural being as Mishmi culture is full of them and there is no reservations in accommodating one more. They don't have temples or churches but different places are of religious importance guarded by supernatural beings. Every place has its own spiritual significance and needs to be revered. The human establishments like agricultural plot and houses even have different entities. Even the house is guarded by many spirits. The entrance has different guarding spirit and males and females of the house have their own spiritual space.

The above-mentioned way of life and spiritual beliefs, seen today, does not make them a lesser a human being. Another European who came half a century after Dalton and Cooper, Verrier Elwin after studying the tribal religions of Arunachal, in his book, 'A Philosophy for NEFA' (1957) observes:

> But a careful study of tribal religion, both in NEFA and elsewhere, does not suggest that it is noticeably inferior to its competitors. It has its drawbacks, it is not fully thought out, there are many problems to which it has no answer. But as a working way of life it brings consolation to its adherents and gives them hope and courage. (1957: 210)

Further, Elwin draws attention towards significant qualities of tribal religions in NEFA:

> Tribal religion is associated with a social ethic that unites the tribe in its discipline and undoubtedly makes for a certain nobility of conduct. The great tribal virtues are discipline, devotion to work, generosity, and hospitality, truth, kindness. Many tribes, while permitting considerable freedom to the unmarried insist high standard of marital fidelity. (1957: 210)

Further writing on the concept of sin and punishment among the NEFA people, Elwin elaborates:

> This ethic is not related to the religion in the sense that virtue will normally be rewarded and vice punished in the after-life. But the absence of eschatology of rewards and punishments is no disadvantage: it rather links tribal religion with the most advanced ethical and religious systems.
>
> Finally, tribal religion gives the people the power to reconcile themselves to the eternal emergencies of life. It has been said that fear is the father of religion and love its late-born daughter, and it is true that there is an element of fear in all primitive religion. But this is true also of the great world religions, and a celebrated psychologist has pointed out that a merely 'healthy minded' and optimistic religion may prove inadequate when faced with the deeper tragedies of existence.
>
> In their religion, the tribesmen have created a realistic picture of life seen sub specie eternitatis; they face it, in all its dismal trappings, with courage; yet it is not fear of things as they are, but a heroic appreciation of them which has brought it into being. The tribesmen are realists; till recently they lived a life of constant anxiety and they projected this onto the wider canvas of their theology. Today, as they discover a more friendly world on earth, they may come to believe in a kinder world in heaven.

> Above all, the tribesmen have faced the problem of death; they have not solved it any more than we have solved it; but they have devised means whereby it can be made more tolerable. The lengthy course of funerary ceremonial, the elaborate tombs, the carvings, the feasts of mourning are not due only to a desire to propitiate the ghost; they give the mourners an opportunity of separating themselves psychologically from the departed object, always a protracted and painful process. Modern psychology suggests that their efforts are well adapted to this end.
>
> The tribesmen believe in a life after death and that living and dead continue to be united in one family. (1957: 213–14)

As observed by Elwin, there is no concept of redemption or dreadful punishment for the wrong doers. Among the Idu Mishmis, the wrong doers while descending to the underworld need to confess their crimes but they are not damned for eternal. For breaching ethical regulations, the soul is humiliated and may be denied water as well as may be forced to pass through dangerous paths; however there are also means and devices to overcome these impending hindrances during the arduous ultimate quest. This idea makes a radical departure from other well organized religions like Christianity where the sinner is damned and roasted in hell for eternal. This tribal approach draws our attention to the significant dimension that, despite concept of such a meagre punishment, tribal societies in the past were devoid of much wrongdoings or sinnings. Their knowledge of the belief that they would face little consequences in next world should have motivated them to commit more ills. However, scanned closely, we find that the ills which one has done in his life are punished during lifetime itself. This aspect probably raises the strong impulse of revenge among the Mishmis, one need to pay everything in lifetime itself.

Elwin, further elaborating the essence of tribal religion which needs to be preserved for the good of the people writes:

> Tribal religion, developed and reformed from within, is thus not bound to be destroyed by science.
>
> In one of his rare utterances on tribal problems, Mahatma Gandhi urged that the tribesmen should be persuaded to abolish animal sacrifice and the use of alcohol in worship. It is probably true that these are the main features which divide the tribal from other religions in India. Yet, although there is much to be done in the way of teaching the tribesmen to kill their animals before the altar more mercifully, the general practice of animal sacrifice is more innocuous than it sounds. In 'civilized' life, one's meat is provided by the butcher; in tribal life, it is provided by the clergyman. The sacrifice is a sacrament, where the people eat in the name of the gods. To give the sanction of religion to the eating of meat may offend the vegetarian, but it surely cannot be regarded as offensive to the religious spirit.
>
> I submit, therefore, that we should not be defeatist about tribal religion. It is worthy of preservation; I believe that it contains the seeds of growth. Anyone who reads Sir James Frazer's Folklore of the Old Testament may see from what humble beginnings two of the great world-religions have developed. A study, says Fraser, of the elements that underlay the civilization of ancient Israel, as they underlie the civilization of modern Europe, 'serves as a foil to enhance by contrast the glory of a

people which, from such dark depths of ignorance and cruelty, could rise to such bright heights of wisdom and virtue, as sunbeams appear to shine with a greater effulgence of beauty when they break through the murky clouds of a winter evening than when they flood the earth from the serene splendour of a summer noon. (1957: 215–16)

Colonial Punitive Expeditions and Tribal Endurance

The British India archival records mention four prominent military punitive expeditions against the Mishmis. The first being expedition against Kaisha Manyu in 1855 and other three being, Bebejiya Expeditions of 1900 against the people of Mithun valley and other two against the people of Elope in 1914 and 1920.

1855 Expedition and Aftermath

Furnishing a heroic account of 1855 expedition against Kaisha Manyu, Col. Shakespeare in his book 'History of the Assam Rifles' (1929) calls it '... one of, if not the most successful minor expedition of all our punitive outings in Assam'. And further elaborates the successful expedition thus:

> A friendly Menu chief, by name Lumling, with some of his own followers, joined Eden in time for the sharp fight which at once ensued, in which Kaisha was captured, his two sons and many of his men were killed, and the village was destroyed. The murder of the missionaries was amply avenged .... Eden brought Kaisha back, who was duly hanged at Dibrugarh, but not before the sturdy ruffian had managed to kill two warders. (1929: 46)

It is important to note that the Raj had planted a mole within the Mishmis itself in form of Lumling and Krosha for 'successful' expedition. Deception is one of the most influential tools of the British colonists.

It will be very difficult to know what led to murder of Krick and Bourri. Colonial powers had concealed most of the facts and revealed the aspects which would only demonize Kaisha Manyu. The biggest example is the secret government communication prepared by N. Williamson reports the incident thus:

> I also heard last night that the reason for Kai-ee-sha's murdering Messr. Krick and Bourri was due to some trouble about a mithun. It is said these gentlemen were camped near Samelying and one night the mithun roamed about their camp and annoyed them a good deal. One of the mithuns which belonged to Kai-ee-sha was shot by the missionaries. Kai-ee-sha considered that he had not received a present sufficient for his services. The small offer combined with his loss of mithun, angered him so much that he rose in his wrath and following the strangers slew them near the border where they had gone from Sameyling via the Du river route. (Assam Secretariat, 1886, File No. 1735, Tribal Records, p. 26)

From this report two things are certain; Kaisha Manyu was not paid adequately for his work as guide and porter.

Second aspect is more significant as well as more reasonable. Mithun is not just an animal for the Mishmis as well as most of the tribes of Arunachal Pradesh.

They have social as well as cultural significance. As a social symbol they are nearly equivalent to humans in many aspects. According to the tribal ethics of Arunachal Pradesh, slaying of someone's mithun is equal to killing the owner or killing the clan member of the owner. Today also, slaying someone's Mithun is one of the gravest offence second only to killing a human, therefore, the slayer is made to pay huge penalty amounting to three or four times the price of the killed mithun. If penalty is not paid, the blood fueds are carried on for generations. Getting away by killing someone's mithun was unthinkable in 1855.

According to the local version,[1] apart from killing Kaisha Manyu's mithun, the missionaries' were engaging themselves in hunting spree wherever they went. As mentioned earlier, Mishmis being territorial might have had reservations for this action. The missionaries should have respected the regulations of the land. The consequence of a Mishmi, or for that matter, anybody indulging according to their will freely in 1855 France is unimaginable.

Another local version also mentions of Kaisha Manyu's son dying in Sadiya by drowning while being employed as a porter. Moreover, the family was not paid any wages of the deceased man. For this episode also, Kaisha Manyu was considering himself as a wronged man.

The colonial accounts also exhibit the air of white supremacy and deep contempt for tribal culture. Being a missionary, by nature they might have also demeaned the Mishmi belief system. The disparaging of indigenous culture and branding them demonical is still a prevalent tool for the missionaries to proselytize in tribal regions of India.

Capturing of Kaisha Manyu and subsequently hanging him had a far-reaching effect on the Mishmi-British relationship. The British ambition of extending the imperial commerce to China through Tibet and plan of scuttling the Chinese tea trade monopoly was stalled forever. Moreover, the most significant aspect was the collaboration of both Mijus and Idus (Chullikata) to avenge the death of Kaisha Manyu. The archival reports attribute series of raids in Sadiya mostly in Khampti territory carried out by the Chullikatas were to avenge the death of Kaisha Manyu. Apart from T.T. Cooper (1880: 244–45), Hamilton throws light on Mishmi-British relation in the light of Kaisha Manyu episode thus:

> For many years from this date, the Kaisha affair 1856 and 1857 the same tribesmen For many years from this date, the Kaisha affair became one of the burning questions of the border; for, in his operations against Kaisha's village, Lieutenant Eden had been assisted by the supporters of a Menu chieftain by the name of Lumling. This circumstance not unnaturally roused the ire of Kaisha's people, and when the news of Kaisha's execution was received by his son, that youth enlisted the help of the Chulikattas and immediately attacked the renegade village. Lumling, who had received both money and gifts for his services, appealed for aid to the British authorities at Sadiya, but was refused, with the result that he and his people were massacred. A little later, Chulikattas contrived the seizure of three of Lieutenant Eden's servants, while in carried out some successful raids on the Kampti villages near Sadiya. During the next few years, in part by way of avenging themselves on the Kamptis for their share in the Kaisha expedition, one or other of

> the Mishmi tribes constantly harried the Kamptis in the region about the Kundil and Deopani Rivers. So serious did the resulting situation become that in 1866, the British authorities, as the only means in their power, issued firearms to the Sadiya Kamptis, when the raids at once ceased. Two years later, moreover, peace had been so far restored that a large party of Chulikattas, as a special concession, was allowed to settle in the Kundil Valley. Unfortunately for the general condition of the border, the act of grace shown to the Chulikattas had little immediate effect, for Mr T.T. Cooper was turned back by the Menu chiefs at Prun, a few miles west of the point reached by Wilcox in 1827, when he attempted in the winter of 1869–70 to travel along the southern bank of the Brahmaputra to Tibet. (1912(b): 195–96)

As mentioned by Hamilton, Cooper was sent to survey for a viable trade to Tibet and China, but the Mishmis stopped him from further advancement. The account of T.T. Cooper attribute apart from Kaisha Manyu episode to scheming Chinese Officers and intolerant Lama Priests. However, viewed from the perspective of the Mishmis, they were against the advancement of British Government.

The following reasons can be drawn after studying the various sources, why Mijus were averse to the European presence in their soil:

1. The British interferences had resulted into depravation of many Mishmis who used to levy taxes from the pilgrims in Brahamakund since ages.
2. Many slaves were accorded free status by the Raj. They had now settled in British territory as free people. Many of the slaves were even armed to fight against their masters.
3. The most significant and immediate reason was inapt handling of Kaisha Manyu episode. He had become the symbol of imperial atrocities. He and his family had to face the brunt despite they being wronged party in the first place.
4. Another reason for mistrust is due to betrayal of the Mishmi people who had collaborated with the Raj in arresting Kaisha Manyu. Despite their plea, British Government declined to offer any aid when Kaisha Manyu clan members in collaboration with the Idu Mishmis (Chulikatttas) attacked them. Subsequently they were all killed in revenge feud.
5. The Mishmis also might have sensed the danger of being deprived of their traditional taxes which they had been levying in different trade routes. The colonial trade route would have surely stripped them of this privilege.
6. Moreover the relationship between the Tibetans and Mishmis were time tested and continuing since many ages. Therefore, it is not hard to see the preferences of the Mishmis.

Bebejiya Mishmi Expedition of 1899

The 1899, Bebejiya Expedition was carried out to punish the Bebejiya Mishmis who were responsible for series of raids in British territory.

The earliest raids are reported in 1855, 1856, and 1857. The report attributes the Apelong clan (Aprollo Linggi) responsible for these raids. The reasons for first two raids are not mentioned but the last 1857 raid which were carried out in a Khampti village according to the British account was in retaliation to the hanging of Kaisha Manyu. The Khamptis were most of the time part of British expeditions to the hills as was in case of Kaisha's arrest.

Again in October and November 1857, the Bebejiyas raided a Khampti village to avenge the death of their people. According to the archival account some Bebejiyas died after returning from Khampti village in a suspicious condition. The Bebejiyas viewed it as a foul play by the Khamptis and, therefore, raided their village.

Another raid is reported in 1878. A. Mackenzie cites the reasons for the raid thus:

> The reason alleged of the murder of the Assamese was an old feud dating from 1865, when the Mishmis stated that some of their people had been killed by British subjects, and in the other case it was stated that the Khamptis had on some previous occasion killed some of their people. (1884: 51)

Similarly raid of 1884 is attributed to the death of Lako (Lako Menda) who died while on touring programme to Calcutta organized by the British Government.

Again in 1893, Aiyu Mimi and his clan members from Anaya killed three sepoys and carried away their arms.

The immediate consequence of the Bebejiya Expedition, however, was raid in Khampti village Mitaigaon by Midere clan (Dele) of Abragon village. The reason revealed by the government was a case in which Thruso Midere (Dele) of Abragon was killed by some Khamptis. Aholo Midere, the son of Thruso Midere had avenged the killing by raiding the village.

As per the above records most of the raids were carried out in form of revenge retaliations. Very strong sense of revenge prevails among the Idu Mishmis. The revenge feuds, if it is not solved amicably, are carried on for several generations. However, through discourse and negotiations everything can be resolved. The cultural ethos of Mishmis is based on meaningful discourse and mutual negotiations. Even the spiritual aspects are engrained with this syndrome, the give and take, bargain and console, etc. but this dimension needs a planned strategy wherein an appropriate agent has to be engaged for the mission. The negotiator need to possess statesmanship skills as well as good relations with both the parties. This method is employed by the Mishmis to resolve even grave conflicts. The colonial masters if they had employed right persons, then most of the matters could have been solved amicably.

Another significant aspect behind the revelation of the motives of the raid are furnished because of the cultural practices. An Idu Mishmi culture does not permit to hide the killing of a person. No murder can be hidden as the killers are bound to observe the *Ahumu* ritual and declare the reason as well as intent of slaying someone. If this ritual is not followed, the Idus believe that the killer will get insane.

The colonists had planned to undertake the expedition in 1857 itself after series of raids. However, due to revolt of 1857, the Raj could not execute their mission against the Bebejiya Mishmis. Therefore, in 1899, the Raj wanted to punish the tribe. Assistant Political Officer of Sadiya, J.F. Needham while reporting the Mitaigaon raid writes to the DC Lakhimpur 6 May 1899, urging the high offices for the urgent need of undertaking punitive expeditions against the Bebejiyas by concluding the report thus:

> Mishmis, including Bebejiyas, are bloodthirsty wretches of the first water, who take a life for the mere devilry of it, and it must not be forgotten that they have on two previous occasions, viz. at Dikrang in 1885, when they killed a Khampti volunteer, and again in 1893, when they waylaid and murdered three of our sepoys murdered our subjects with impunity, for no attempt, beyond blockading them for a time, was made in either of the cases mentioned to punish them for their atrocity. It is quite time therefore that we called them to account. (Assam Secretariat, 1899, Foreign, p. 4)

While forwarding the letter to Chief Commissioner of Assam, the Deputy Commissioner of Lakhimpur notes:

> ... I am inclined to think that the dates given for the two previous outrageous are not quite correct. It further appears that for the said murders to have been committed in Dikrang in 1885, the Mishmis were fined two thousand rupees, and they were induced to return the rifles they acquired after murdering three sepoys near Bomjur; .... (Assam Secretariat, 1899, Foreign, p. 1)

The Bebejiya expedition lasted for three months; from November 1899 to 8 February 1900. The report of the APO, Needham proclaims that the expeditions were highly successful. Similarly, A. Hamilton regards the operation as 'eminently successful'. However, the Viceroy Lord Curzon had his own reservations and not at all convinced of the expedition. The expedition had cost a heavy burden to the colonial coffers. In his reply he observes:

> ... so far from, regarding this expedition as having been satisfactory, either in its conception or in its results, I hold it to have been marked by serious miscalculation from the start, by a sacrifice of life which ought, with reasonable precaution to have been avoided, by an expenditure of money for which there has been no proportionate return and by political and scientific results that are all but worthless .... .

The expedition team reached Hunli in January 1900 after finding the village deserted, they burnt down all the houses. Thereafter, Pika and nearby villages up to Denge were all burnt down. The imperial army then turned toward Abrango, Elope, Athroma and Athoro, and destroyed the villages. The last targeted village was Anaya. The small villages and hamlets which are scattered two to three days march apart were no match against the imperial army.

The impacts of the punitive expedition were severe. For three months people of these villages, infant, child, old, sick and everyone else spent their days and nights in the jungle. The winter is very severe in these places. Frostbites are everyday affair. The beginning of the new century for these tribal people was marred with anguish and misery.

It is hard to reconcile the tall claims of the British Raj on freedom and justice. The modus operandi they adopted was more savage than their savage counterpart. Punishing the whole community for crime of few manifests the hypocrisy of the people who profess compassion and salvation in their religion. As the record shows, most of the raids carried out by the Bebejiyas were revenge strikes. The issue could have been solved in the first instance itself by engaging in negotiations. However, the cultured savages choose to adopt highest form of revenge by punishing even the children, women, sick and old.

Needham vindicating the need to punish all the tribe writes:

> I will endeavour to get the names and residence of the culprits, but this is not, in my opinion, an important matter. We know the tribe to which the offenders belong, and this is sufficient, and only question now is how to punish them. In my opinion it is useless to attempt to punish individuals. The whole tribe must be held responsible, and we must give them to thoroughly understand that whenever any outrage like the present one is committed, we shall hold the whole tribe responsible. (Assam Secretariat. 1899, Foreign, p. 5)

Further, Needham argues why all need to be punished:

> Even supposing that the whole tribe did not actually sanction the outrage, one and all would nevertheless glory in feat of the kind, for this Mishmis are innately blood thirsty devils, and no one would raise a finger to see the culprits, and hand them over to us for punishment, unless perhaps compelled to do so by arrival of force in their midst which threatened to punish all unless the murderers were delivered up within a specified time, for such a practice is against Mishmi custom. (Assam Secretariat, 1899, Foreign, p. 5)

For the Bebejiya people the expedition was a new experience. They had never faced an enemy who destroyed houses, granaries and agricultural fields.

The only positive thing that came out of the punitive expedition for the Bebejiya people it seems to be the elevation of their status, which of course they were unaware of. Needham who had earlier declared, 'Mishmis, including Bebejiyas, are bloodthirsty wretches of the first water, who take a life for the mere devilry of it', after getting into direct contact with them during the expedition writes:

> During my sojourn in the hills I became gradually agreeably aware of the fact that the Bebejiyas are, as a whole, very desirous of being on friendly terms with us, and I have almost begun to believe that they are a maligned race! There are, of course, bad characters among them, as there are amongst every nation under the sun, but I do not believe that the tribe, as a whole, is nearly as black as it has been painted. For generations past the Assamese, and plains people including Khamtis, Singphos, Dowaniyas, etc., etc., residing on the north bank of the Brahmaputra have learnt to look upon them as a bloodthirsty and dangerous race, and all works of reference on the tribes on our North-East Frontier speak of them as such, vide page 47 of Mackenzie's History of the relations of the Government with the Hill Tribes, and page 328, Volume I of W. W. Hunter's Statistical Account of Assam, ... Report on the Bebejiya Mishmi Expedition, 1899–1900 (1900: 13)

The last two punitive expeditions were undertaken against the Mishmis of Elope village in 1913 and 1920. The cause of the expedition was killing of three British subjects by Ponge Dele. The blockade was imposed on the Bebejiya Mishmis for three years but subsequently revoked in 1909. One of the suspects,

Taji Dele, was arrested and hanged in 1918. Avenging the death of Taji, Ponge and people from Elope killed a British sepoy. The British Government's ₹ 1,000 reward for capturing each culprit had no takers. Therefore, in 1920 the British forces under captain Nevill destroyed the Elope village. Ponge was killed while trying to ambush the cavalcade.

The main cause leading to the expedition, according to the British Archival record is the confinement of Ponge Dele during the previous Bebejiya Expedition of 1900. Ponge Dele as reported was arrested and confined despite his noninvolvement in the case.

Among the Idu Mishmis arresting or handcuffing of a person is grave offence. Only the slaves are tied and confined or arrested. Handcuffing in a way is viewed as enslaving the person. Therefore, the arrest and confinement were unimaginable to Ponge Dele, who held a high esteem not only among his clan brethrens but also in the community. The torture and humiliation which he would have endured in captivity will never surface.

The British Government was also furious of the general Chullikatta attitude concerning the raids in their territory. The 'savages' were very difficult to book and arrest as their tribe was always reluctant to pass information and cooperate with the Raj. In this regard Dalton notes:

> If an injury is inflicted on one of them by a member of another tribe, it is incumbent on the tribe of the injured party to avenge it; if one of his own tribe offends, it is the business of the person offended only. He has no law except that which he can take in his own hands, and between people in the same village feuds are thus perpetuated, for ages. (1872: 19)

Informing or cooperating with the British Government directly would have sowed the seed of feuds and conflicts among themselves for generations. Moreover, the community had witnessed the fate of the people who had collaborated with the British for arresting Kaisha Manyu.

The other reason for the noncooperation with the British demand may be that, as all these raids were not a bloody venture as perceived by the government but revenge of the wrongs which they had endured. Among the Mishmis revenge is just and accepted norm.

Moreover, it is significant to note that most of the time the confrontation had its roots in humiliations meted to the tribal people as in case of Kaisha Manyu, Ponge Dele and Matmur Jamoh.

The 1920 Bebejiya Mishmi Expedition once again brought miseries and sorrow for the people of Elope village.[2] The imperial army after reaching the deserted village of Elope, burnt down all the houses. Agricultural crops were destroyed. For two months the British army camped in the village. Every possible destructive method was executed over the village. People's sources of sustenance, as well as those employed for multiple purposes; bamboos were destroyed. The army had cut down every species of bamboo and burnt them down. Sago palm which is used by the tribal people as food during the non-harvesting season as well as used as swine fodder were all felled and destroyed. The forces even attempted to uproot the roots of *abrato*, a special species of bamboo by ploughing them out. However, the task was highly toiling and within this period of stay, the forces could only uproot not more than 100 metres.

This was the second time that the people of Elope were bearing the brunt of imperial expedition. Once again, all the folks had to take shelter in the jungle and caves for two months. During that time the village had not more than 40 houses. They were no match for the British forces. It is bewildering to imagine the hardship and chaos endured by these people; without house, without food and without any domestic animals. The domesticated animals among the Mishmis are not only food and pet but every ritual is incomplete without sacrifice of pig or chicken. All kinds of ritual from birth to death demand sacrifices.

The Sago palm and bamboo which were their necessity were destroyed and it would take many years for them to grow again.

Abrato is not only a bamboo for the Idu Mishmis. It is significant cultural symbol used in all religious rituals. The shamanic ritual at the time of birth, death, and Amrase cannot be conducted without physical as well as spiritual employment of *abrato.* The British massive destructive approaches shocked the tribal ethos.

Above all these aspects, the expedition also sowed the seed of discord among the different clans of the tribe. Aftermath of expedition unfolded the turmoil and bloodbath within the community. There were people from the tribe itself who had collaborated with the British army and had guided them. All three of them, Adama Linggi, Asoti Mega and Athakhro Pecha were all killed in revenge operation, masterminded by Lolyi Dele, the son of Ponge Dele. The revenge feud among these people continued for many more generations.

In 1947, the Bebejiyas directly came under the Indian Government. Despite compassionate approaches of the government, the people of Elope had still deep mistrust and discontentment for the outsiders as they opposed the road project in their village and preferred to be left alone.

Conclusion

Most of the data collected by the colonial writers probably is based on information collected from the neighbouring tribes. Especially, Dalton seems to have collected considerable amount of data from the Adis as he refers the Chullikatas as 'Midhi' an Adi term for the Idu Mishmis.

The main reasons for branding the Mishmis as bloodthirsty savages seems to be based on their way of executing the revenge feuds and kidnapping the people. Kidnapping, during those times was a lucrative source of economy. They were sold as slaves in hills. The slave trade among the Idu Mishmis was highly prevalent. The Adis bought slaves from them and, therefore, many Britishers even assumed that the Mishmis were employed as slaves by the Adis. However, in this context the colonial writers seem to have forgotten their deeds in Africa. The European imperialism had in between 1500 to 1900 enslaved half of the population of many countries in Africa.

As far as the notion of revenge is concerned, it seems not only the Mishmi savages, but the civilized European as well, seem to have been drawn towards the concept of 'an eye for an eye'. If an act of revenge were just the affairs of the 'savages' then the great bards like Shakespeare, Marlowe, Kyd and Webster would have not written the great revenge tragedies.

After going through the colonial accounts, one is also able to sense the covert motive of the earlier explorers. The reason for blackening and savaging the people in most derogatory way seems to arise from the urge of these writers to demonstrate themselves as valiant noble souls who are walking among the bloodthirsty brutes and enlightening them through the dispensation of justice and knowledge.

Notes

1. Oral history was collected from Shri Sokhep Kri (State Gazetteer, Itanagar), Shri Hakresha Kri (Extra Assistant Commissioner, Hayuliang) and Shri Ritemso Manyu (Youth Leader from Manyu Clan).
2. Oral history was collected from Shri Mengo Dele (Head Gaon Bura), Shri Rao Dele (Public Leader) and Shri Ethadu Dele (84 years, the eldest surviving man from Dele Clan) from Elope village.

References

Abraham, M.H. (1999). *A Glossary of Literary Terms*, Heinle and Heinle, USA.

Althusser, Louis (1971 [1970]). 'Ideology and Ideological State Apparatuses', in *Lenin and Philosophy and Other Essays*, Monthly Review Press, New York.

—— (1968). 'Lenin and Philosophy', in *Lenin and Philosophy and Other Essays*, English translation 1971, Monthly Review Press, New York.

Ashcroft, Bill, Gareth Griffiths and Helen Tiffins (eds) (1989). *The Empire Writes Back: Theory and Practice in Post-Colonial Literatures*, Routledge, London and New York.

Assam Secretariat (1886). File No. 1735, Tribal Records, p. 26.

Barnhart, Robert K. (ed.) (1971). *A Comprehensive Etymological Dictionary of the English Language*, Elsevier Scientific Publishing Co., Amsterdam.

Benson, Hugh H. (2006). *A Companion to Plato*, Blackwell Publishing, Australia.

Comprehensive Etymological Dictionary of the English Language (1971). Elsevier Scientific Publishing Co., Amsterdam.

Cooper, T.T. (1873). *The Mishmee Hills: An Account of a Journey Made in an Attempt to Penetrate Thibet from Assam to Open New Routes for Commerce*, H.S. King & Co., London.

Dalton, E.T. (1872). *Descriptive Ethnology of Bengal*, German edition 1875, Asiatic Society of Bengal, Calcutta, pp. 13–21.

Elwin, Verrier (1957). *A Philosophy for NEFA*, Directorate of Research, Government of Arunachal Pradesh, Itanagar.

Foucault, Michel (1972 [1969]). *The Archaeology of Knowledge*, Translated from the French by A.M. Sheridan Smith, Routledge, London.

Geertz, Clifford (1973). *The Interpretation of Cultures: Selected Essays*, Basic Books, New York.

Geertz, Clifford (ed.) (1963). *Old Societies and New States: The Quest of Modernity in Asia and Africa*, Amerind Publishing Co., New Delhi.

Greenblatt, Stephen (1989). 'Towards a Poetic of Culture in New Historicisms', in *Shakespearean Negotiations: The Circulation of Social Energy in Renaissance England (The New Historicism: Studies in Cultural Poetics)*, University of California Press, USA.

Hamilton, A. (1912a). *In Abor Jungles: An Account of the Abor Expedition and the Mishmi and Miri Missions*, E. Nash, London.

—— (1912b). 'The Mishmi Mission', *Fortnightly Review*, XCI: 552–65.

Mackenzie, Alexander (1884). *History of the Relations of the Government with the Hill Tribes of the North-East Frontier of Bengal, Calcutta*, Home Department Press, Calcutta, pp. 47–54.

McCosh, J. (1836). 'Account of the Mountain Tribes on the Extreme N.E. Frontier of Bengal', *Journal of the Royal Asiatic Society*, V: 193–207.

Michell, John F. (1883). *North-East Frontier of India: Topographical, Political and Military Reports*, Intelligence Branch, Quarter Master-General's Department, Government of India.

Montrose, Louis A. (1989). 'Professing the Renaissance: The Poetics and Politics of Culture', in H. Aram Veeser (ed.), *The New Historicism*, Routledge, New York, pp. 15–36.

Needham, J.F. (1900). *Report of the Bebejiya Mishmi Expedition, 1899–1900*, Shillong.

Rowe, Christopher (2006). Interpreting Plato. In Hugh H. Benson (ed.), *A Companion to Plato*, pp. 13–24, Blackwell Publishing Ltd., Australia.

Said, Edward W. (1978). *Orientalism*, Pantheon, New York.

—— (1993). *Culture and Imperialism*, Chatto and Windus, London.

Shakespear, L.W. (1914). *History of Upper Assam, Upper Burmah and North-Eastern Frontier*, Macmillan, London.

—— (1929). *History of the Assam Rifles*, Firma KLM, Calcutta.

Veeser, H. Aram (ed.) (1989). *The New Historicism*, Routledge, New York.

Williams, Raymond (1977). *Marxism and Literature*, Oxford University Press, Oxford.

4

Examining the Narratives of Mishmi's Status and its Peregrination of Baptism into Contemporary India

TILU LINGGI

One could not have imagined the romanticism that once prevailed in the West that the 'Roof of the World' was an ultimate place of bliss, could one day significantly shape the fate of contemporary South-East (SE) Asia. The frequent reference of *Shangri La*[1] in various literatures including James Hilton's book 'Lost Horizon' would show to offer that such illustration about Tibet[2] indeed prevailed (Kapadia, 2007). It is significant to consider how such desires backed by the Industrial Revolution had let a remote west country like Britain to come in contact with 'primitive' tribes in the far east the then SE Tibet. Various scholars and explorers were dispatched arguably with different tasks during different periods in the then SE Tibet, or North-East (NE) Frontier side of British India. However, it cannot be denied that the motive of the broad plan to assign tasks to these officers was same in one major aspect in this part of Asiatic civilization – securing a lasting political and commercial interest for the British Empire, mostly after First World War. While political interest included territorial expansion by means of mapping and surveying of unexplored region and to pre-emptively check against the growing influence of Russian, Japanese and Chinese occupation in SE Tibet, the commercial interest was to pave way for exploiting raw produce, exchange and extract all other precious species of floras and faunas to cater its growing industrialized European society by opening up the frontier through railway and other means of communication and transportation (Holdich, 1912; Marshall, 2005). Hence, a new chapter was unfolded in the British exploration and discovery of whole of Mishmis,[3] in fact the whole NE frontier tribes[4] of British India came to be known to the world as a result of such desire to explore, expand and control.

The main aim of this article is to examine who these Mishmis, were, did these tribes enjoy an independent social, economic, cultural and political status and if so, how and at what point of time the independent and scarcely inhabited Mishmi tribes gave way to coercive authority, only to be merged into the concept of new 'India'.

Brief Background of British Expansion in the Mishmi Hills

The knowledge of the existence of the Mishmis to the outsiders at large came only after the contact of British Survey of India initially with NE frontier hill tribes as a part of 'Forward Policy', a policy that advocated filling the vacuum acknowledged to be of strategic importance for the British Raj. There were certain reasons as to why Mishmi Hills was the obvious choice for British explorers to venture into. According to Marshall, firstly, *Near* States of Nepal valley having good ties with Tibet were invaded by Hindu Gurkhas under *Prithvinarayan* in 1767, an opportunity that the East India Company had lost to extend trade relation with Tibet by failing to support *Near* on their request, thus forcing them to find other alternative route (Marshall, 2003). Secondly, though there was a route that passed through *Tawang* over the *Se/Tse La* in the west, *Rima* was the preferable route as it was shortest route in the east to Tibet that connected *Sadiya* through *Lohit* river valley (Marshall, 2003; Ward and Smith, 1934). Banking on new avenue such as North-Eastern Frontier hills to trade with Tibetan was an obvious factor as Sikdar noted:

> The trade through the frontier was important for the British India as it would minimise enormous cost while opening trade with Tibetans and Burma rather than opting other practically difficult routes such as Sikkim and Nepal. For that the buffer zone of hill tribes were to be pierced through first. (Sikdar, 1982: 21)

Prior to First World War, Tibet was a mere parochial issue. However, the reasons for aggressive policy of the British with Tibet post-war as Christie attributes was owing to apprehensions of threat from Japanese expansion, Russian re-emergence post-Bolshevik Revolution and political turmoil in China as a result of 1911 Revolution, especially in the far North-Eastern Frontier hills (Christie, 1976). It was particularly due to emphasis placed by Viceroy like Lord George Nathaniel Curzon[5] seeking increased contact with the Dalai Lama because of the apprehension that Tibetan Government might appeal for Russian military assistance against China (McKay, 1997). Such international developments had wider impact on the British policy towards the Mishmi Hills as reflected from Hamilton's words:

> While cutting a road through the Lohit Valley, laying down the correct boundary-line between Tibet and the Abor marches in a northerly direction and between Tibet and the Mishmi in the east, were important tasks, the main objective of the Mission was, of course, to ascertain the precise extent of Chinese activity on Tibeto-Mishmi, Tibeto-Abor borders. (Hamilton, 1912: 228)

In particular, Mishmi Mission undertaken under Mr W.C.M. Dundas had its objective stated in Hamilton's word:

> Mr Dundas's Mission to the Mishmis was concerned almost wholly with the political issues, set afoot by the activity of Chinese on the Mishmi marches. (Hamilton, 1912: 192)

Thus, to argue that the British explorers came to the Mishmi Hills for survey on origin of Brahmaputra River would not be incorrect but would be an oversimplification of intention of the British Raj. It considered growing Chinese influence on the tribes lying between Sichuan, Yunnan and Tibet a threat to their empire that they believed lay within their jurisdiction (Hamilton, 1912). Hamilton notes that Captain Frederick 'Eric' Marshman Bailey (F.M. Bailey)[6] reportedly had seen Chinese flags and troops at *Menilkrai*,[7] *Walong* and *Khampti* belt adjacent to Mishmi belt had been annexed by Imperial Government of China few years ago. However, Dundas failed to find any Chinese soldiers or officials within the limit of frontier zones. In 1914, while *Walong Promenade* was undertaken under the T.P.M. O'Callaghan, the Chinese boundary pillars were reportedly removed from south of *Walong* (Marshall, 2005). Along these developments waiting to shape was consolidation of forces to advance into the Mishmi Hills to introduce the tribes to new forces of Europe.

The Mishmis, Origin and their Migration[8]

To arrive at the moot point of this chapter it is required to dwell briefly upon the life of Mishmi people. Most of the early explorers argued that Mishmis possessed Mongoloid features (Hamilton, 1912; Holdich, 1912; Ward, 1930). They were divided into numerous clans. Relying largely on the accounts of Forrest P. Mainprice who was the then political in charge of Lohit Valley from 1943 to 1945, Mills argued that there were around one hundred twenty Mishmi clans all of which were named after the place of river bank settlements and the clan names had been passed onto generations as 'tenacious memory for traditions' (Mills, 1952). Hence, the phrase *Chithuh Huluni* finds a reference in the vernaculars of Idu Mishmi,[9] which basically stands for twelve rivers representing Mishmi settlement namely *Ihi, Siku, Ahi, Emra* (a tributary of *Talon*, joining *Talon* at *Angulin*), *Ethon, Mathu, Dri* (inhabitants of *Dri* are known as *Mindri* or *Midri*), *Ithu* (inhabitants of *Ithu* are called *Mithu*), *Talon* (*Dibang*), *Chiyu, Chipu* and *Ilu*.

According to Hamilton (as per the divisions accepted by Mishmis themselves) they were categorized into four groups namely the *Chulikattas* (*Midus*), the *Bebejiyas* (*Mithus*), the *Digarus* (*Tains* or *Tawra* or *Taius*)[10] and *Kaman* (*Mijus* or *Mizhus* or *Mizus*) (Holdich, 1912). Miso argued that the *Bebejiya* and *Chulikatta* term were used as a matter of inference to distinguish between administered and partially administered Idu Mishmis where *Bebejiya* meant those who settled in the higher ranges of the hills (Miso, 2015). According to Markham, *Chulikattas* primarily resided on current Upper Dibang Valley district spread across in and around *Ahi* river valley (*Ahimro*) and *Dri* river valley such as *Anini, Mano, Mihundo, Mipi, Anelih, Brango, Etabe, Aleney, Gipuli, Ranli*

(Markham, 1871). Therefore, the clans from these regions included *Ekru* (inhabitants of *Wayin* valley), *Mithi* (inhabitants of *Ithi* river valley), *Rondo, Tacho, Mihu, Mipi, Mele, Mili, Miku, Umpo, Amow* (*Emohon*), *Mongon (Mow), Molo, Miuli, Mimi, Mito, Mepo, Melo, Lingi, Pulu, Mena, Miwu, Apralo, Aprawe, Pralo, Lombo, Miyee, Migri, Umbrey, Aprawe, Mitayu* (*Tayu*),[11] *Mengo, Pocha, Yaka, Yalan* and others.[12] On the other hand the *Bebejiyas* or *Mithus* were inhabitants of both sides of *Ithun* river valley (*Ithumro*) and some of the clans from these regions included *Apora, Dele, Elapra, Miso, Michichi, Mikasen or Mikeche* (*Keche*), *Mana, Mendo, Mene, Mepola, Miaton (Meto), Miso, Miaga (Mega), Mimi, Mitalo, Mitayi, Mitati, Umpo, Umpe*. Hamilton goes on to point out that the *Chulikattas* occupied both banks of *Dihang* (*Siang*) river while larger and prosperous *Midu* villages rested in close proximity to the Tibetan border and north of *Sadiya* to the *Digaru* river on the east (Holdich, 1912). He also noted that the *Bebejiyas,* frequented *Ithun* and *Ithi* river valley whose country was surrounded by *Sihi* range and *Saruba* Peak in south, *Chulikattas* in the west, bordered by ranges of southern Tibet in north and *Digarus* in the east (Holdich, 1912). While Digaru Mishmis situated to the east beyond *Digaru* River, *Mijus* dwelled further east towards the Tibetan valley, 'a subprefecture of *Lhasa*'. As per Mills, the *Chulikattas* were more war like than others (Mills, 1952).

While the *Digarus* comprised some of the clans such as *Ama, Tayang, Cheba* (*Chiba*), *Tabronyo, Marav* (*Marap*), *Darai* (*Drai*), *Kramblai, Manyo* (*Manyu*) *Mepu* (*Mepo*), *Dilang, Takalyang* (*Takaliang*), *Krong* and *Polong, Miju* clans consisted of *Chera, Menyin* (*Minin*), *Suiso, Halai, Yun, Mara, Longling, Tamblung* and *Rapa.* There were other clans classified as joint *Miju-Dagaru* clans by Mainprice in his accounts which included *Pul* (*Miju* (M))-*Mal* (*Digaru* (D)), *Tavshit* (*Tawsik*)(M)-*Tushi*(D), *Kri*(M)-*Tsai*(D), *Bilai*(M)-*Bali*(D), *Ngadong*(M)-*Ado*(D), *Mipung*(M)-*Po*(D), *Tamblav* (M)-*Taphlav* (D), *Mato*(M)-*Senya*(D), *Rangman* (*Rangmang*) (M)-*Tma*(D).[13]

What is more revealing from the Mainprice's account is that different clans under both Miju and Digaru Mishmis shared similarity with Chulikatta Mishmis with regard to the claim of their origin. For instance, *Chera, Cheba, Pul, Malo, Mato, Yam, Mipung, Karav* clans from *Mijus* and *Brapa, Dure, Dilang, Marav, Mepu, Ikai, Kramblai, Polong, Senya, Talampe, Taiy, Talyo, Tinda, Takathag, Takalyang,* and *Tayang* clans from *Digarus* claimed to have come from common ancestors in the *Chulikatta* country. In particular, people from *Cheba, Talampe, Karav* clans were believed to be descendants of *Maso* (*Miso*) clan of *Chulikattas.* Hamilton added further that while *Miaga, Miaton, Mepo, Mderen (Mindele), Minli (Milli), Mimi, Mikatson (Mitacho), Mongon* and *Michen (Miche)* were some of the clans under Bebejiya Mishmis whose descendants came from *Digarus*, some of the *Miju* clans like *Lapa, Prun, Manlo, Nai Smale, Hago, Towa, Ro, Tumblu* and *Lamat* had inter-marriage practices with *Digaru* clans (Hamilton, 1912; Wilcox, 1825). Mainprice during his survey found some *Mepu* clans both in the *Lohit* valley and *Chulikatta* country and such evidence is still available today (Mills, 1952). Describing about status of these clans Mills noted:

> There are no classes among the clans, and no slaves clans; all are equal, save the large and more powerful enjoy enhanced prestige. (Mills, 1952: 2)

Despite so many clans that had been reported some of the clans became extinct over a period of time.[14] Mills contemplated that the Mishmi population must have dwindled rapidly and some became extinct as a result of weaknesses and poverty or their inability to pay for bridge price (Mills, 1952).

As from the accounts of the explorers it may seemingly leave any room for skepticism on the question of Mishmi's origin from their common ancestors. There were also different viewpoints advanced for different Mishmi clans by Mills to indicate that while some among Mishmis migrated from Burma, rest of them did not. Mills claimed that the *Digaru* clans such as *Ngadong, Bilai, Yun, Hakung, Kamblung, Lamad, Kroto, Halai, Menyin, Mipung, Kri, Chikro, Suiso, Lab, Nye, Lepang, Kanzum, Rangman, Tamblav, Tavshit* and *Miju* clans such *Tushi, Tsai, Taphlav, Bali, Ado, Tma* had common ancestors who are believed to have come from *Hkampti Long* in Burma through *Krongjong Pass*, generations ago (Mills, 1952).

Mills argued that among Mishmis, Chulikattas were the first to represent the migrants from the east, i.e. Burma. Subsequently, came *Digarus* who entered current Lohit valley later followed by the ancestors of *Mijus,* from *Hkampti Long* through present *Singpho* (or *Kakhyen*) country. However, he observed that there had been hardly any displacement of existing 'aboriginal'[15] if any, because of such migration. Thus, speaking of *Digarus* Mills wrote:

> It would have been impossible for these small parties to have driven out the 'aboriginals'. Nor is there the slightest hint in tradition that they were assigned to the 'aboriginals' is indicated by the fact that they are to this day respected as 'masters of the soil.' If the immigrants found, as I have suggested, an established 'aboriginal' culture, what more natural than that they should adopt it, few in numbers as they were and largely dependent on the 'aboriginal' tribes for brides? Much the same considerations apply to the later Miju, though there is no evidence as to the size of the parties, which entered the hills. Why Digaru and Miju languages have remained separate we do not know, but I feel justified in suggesting that the extraordinarily uniform culture of the valley is basically the very ancient, undisrupted, one of the 'aboriginals,' though doubtless modified by the immigrants from the north, west and south. On the origin of the 'aboriginals' themselves there is no evidence at all. (Mills, 1952: 2)

Frank Kingdon Ward (F.K. Ward) observed in the NE direction, how migration was not uncommon, as he had reportedly seen Bebejiya Mishmis near a pass said to be just north of *Sole* in *Rong To Chu* (now in Tibet). Similarly, Tibetan inhabitants of *Putsang*, (the then last village in *Rong To Chu*) had come from Tibet through *Kangri Karpo La* (situated in the northern most tip of *Rong To Chu*) into *Pemako* and as far as *Mipi* valley (Ward and Smith, 1934). While some noted the geographical factor as a basis to argue how common stock of tribes might had at one point of time cut off from the given place of origin leading to their separation (Ward and Smith, 1934), other advances yearn for food by the foragers as the reason for migration or separation (Weatherbe, 1927).

Contrastingly, R. Kaulback's (1934) argument that the Mishmis who originally lived in SE Tibet and might have been driven to the Lohit-Irrawady divide, because of the influx of Tibetans and due to pressure from China, indicates sociopolitical reasons behind the cause for migration.

Social, Cultural, Religious and Economic Aspects

Some of areas that require revisiting for the purpose of this chapter are Mishmis languages, religious practices, architectural design, dress, food habits and other socio-economic aspects. Bradley (1997) considered that the primary languages of Himalayan and sub-Himalayan region including Tibet, China and South Asia and across Burma are Tibeto-Burman[16] languages. Blench (2015), a Cambridge linguist who had been studying Mishmi languages has ample to offer as he believed that this language belongs to one of the language phyla of SE Asia classified mainly into five different groups namely Austroasiatic, Austronesian, Daic, Sino-Tibetan and Hmong-Mien, where the Mishmi dialect, though not definitive (as many of its language group are still believed to be known), is nearly similar or accurate to other dialects falling within the same group. The reason that he attributed might have been as a result of borrowing of lexicons from same root, i.e. Tibeto-Burman group while they moved freely as foragers.[17] Kaulback (1934) reported that he had found Mishmis wearing same dress, following same custom and even speaking same dialect of *Zayul* province of Tibet. It may be noted that although both *Digarus* and *Mijus* shared uniform culture, their languages differed.[18] However, Blench (2015) observed that language of *Digarus* were identical to *Chulikattas*.

According to Dunbar all houses of the tribes of Brahmaputra belt[19] were raised on the pile, off the ground and their villages used to have minimal number of houses as large number of families were accommodated into one single house, about a length of almost 100 yards (Dunbar, 1915). According to Wilcox,[20] inside the house on one side, bamboos extended horizontally ladened with blackened skulls of all animals which owner had during the course of his life, feasted his friends (Wilcox, 1998). As per the size, Hamilton noted that a small house is forty feet long, whereas large one is about 200 feet but all 12 feet in width and its interior is divided into small compartments based on number of wives they had (Hamilton, 1912). Wilcox gives an account of one of his host who happened to be Digaru Mishmi having ten wives (Wilcox, 1825). These practices were seen almost alike throughout Mishmi society until recently.

While Wilcox and Ward had noted that Mishmi's dress had strong influence of Tibetan culture, richer men of *Kund* (*Brahmakund*) belt had distinctive coat of Tibetan coarse woolen marked dark red and ornamented with white spots, preserved by dyeing (Wilcox, 1825). Some women even wore jewellery especially in Delei valley (Ward and Smith, 1934). The Mishmis, especially *Bebejiyas* and *Chulikattas*, used to procure raw product such as silk and nettle plants. It was manufactured into finished product such as coat to exchange it with *Abors* in return for *Mithun* (*Bros frontalis*) (Clarke, 1874; Bentick, 1913). Millet was the staple food besides buckwheat and maize (Dunbar, 1915). Chief mode of commercial exchange was the barter system wherein *Aconitum fero* (used as poison in arrows), *Coptis Teeta* or *Mishmi Teeta* constituted chief source of wealth (Sikdar, 1982).

Despite sharing much of similarities with the Tibetans, the religious aspects of Mishmis had largely remained remote. While the western hill tribes of present-day Arunachal Pradesh have completely come under the influence of Tibetan Buddhism, Mishmis in the east have maintained 'animism and poly-demonism' (Dunbar, 1915). Landscapes such as water bodies, trees, lakes and passes were abode of spirits and gods. In times of ritualistic ceremonies almost all kinds of livestock were sacrificed. However, as per Mills, religion of Mishmis displayed some Tibetan influence but in no way resembled Buddhism or Hinduism (Mills, 1952). Neither, were there any temples nor any forms of idol worshipping followed. There were no priestly clan or an age bar to become a Shaman (priest). According to Blackburn, the belief of geographical journey of the soul after the demise of a person, especially in Idu Mishmi, was similar to that of the belief of Tibeto-Burman groups in the Himalayas, northern Burma and SW China especially where journey of the soul is linked with the historical experiences such as trading and pilgrimages (Blackburn, 2015). Similarly, Miso (2015) observed that there are references in the oral chants of shamans regarding halting places of souls, near China and Tibet such as *Ilu Pudu* (breeding place of Siberian birds), *Miko Dibro* (monastery region), or *Adu Pili* (where beads are found) that are rich in geographical and space specificity.

Status of the Mishmi Hills and the British Policy Towards Mishmis

Various accounts in the ensuing paragraphs would ostensibly suggest that there were ancient, independent and some form of social structure in the Mishmi society. One of the glaring evidence for such proposition could be assessed with the help of Snake Pillar available in Guwahati museum bearing an inscription of treaty signed between Mishmis and Ahoms in 1532. It reads as follows:

> I, Dihingiya Borgihain, do hereby declare on the strength of this stone inscription and copper table that the Mishmis with their wives and children will henceforth inhabit the entire hills near the Dibang River ... Should the other neighbouring tribes ever invade the Mishmis, they would become slaves of the Mishmis. (Luthra, 1971: 1145)

Myriad may be the interpretations given for what it signifies. However, what stands reasonably appropriate is it symbolized the mutual adherence to non-interference in each other's independent existence and assistance. Similar relationship between British authorities and Mishmis echoed centuries later as renewed in Hamilton's words:

> Moreover, although no treaties bind the Mishmis to us and no allowance are paid to secure their good behaviour, peace is assured because the good relations between the tribes and ourselves are based on mutual respect. The tribes both trust and honour the men whom we send to them as the representatives of the great Sirkar, and are content to accept their word that no ill shall befall them. (Hamilton, 1912: 204)

However, the difference that evolved over centuries later was that the British Raj saw much of the Mishmi Hills as nothing more than a buffer state in its initial days. As dealt in the previous paragraphs, Lord Curzon and Lord Minto, ex-Viceroys of India, shared their concerns on Chinese settling in and around Shan (Burmese ethnic) states and Mishmi border which, therefore, required them to shift their attention from NW to the NE frontier (Hamilton, 1912). Hamilton noted that the British Raj believed that unlike Afghanistan acting as buffer state in NW frontier, the NE frontier did not have any buffer state. They thought if given an opportunity geographical nature of the NE frontier region could be so used, as Hamilton wrote:

> Against this there can be placed the fact that the intervening country on the north is no loss to any one, for it is desolate, barren and unproductive, and only really fit for utilizing as a containing barrier against the peoples on the either side. (Hamilton, 1912: 235)

Some of the ambiguities regarding the status of Mishmi's territories are apparently clear when literatures available on the proceedings of Royal Society of Arts (RSA)[21] are equally analysed. From one of the proceedings of the Society that took place on 8 February 1912, it was obvious that the Mishmi Hills was perceived as a natural buffer zone between the British side of India and Tibet (which China had then taken control over).[22] The then British Ambassador on the Burma-China frontier Archibald Rose during the discussion stated:

> For many years the unadministered tribes have formed a definite buffer between the two great empires. (Holdich, 1912: 382)

Ward, after his second expedition (first expedition being *Seingkhu* valley in Burma in 1926) to *Delei* valley in 1928 made observation about the status of Mishmi Hills:

> Mishmi Hills are unadministered territory. (Ward, 1930: 423)

According to Hudson, even if Assam was considered to be a part of India and Tibet of China, there were some tribes who were unadministered, not belonging to either of the country including Mishmis (Hudson, 1962).

By the time proceedings of RSA was taking place in 1912 on the status of NE frontier tribes of British side of India, there existed no conclusive international boundary in the frontier to determine which portion of the frontier is of Tibet and that of British India's. It is important to note Hamilton's observation made in the same proceeding:

> In the opinion of all who know North-East India, moreover, it is believed that its recognition would achieve a fair and business – like adjustment of mutual differences on the Tibeto-Mishmi border, since the range marked as a 'snow range' on all maps, and employed here as the main border line, has always been regarded by the Mishmis as defining and running parallel with the northern border of their lands. (Hamilton, 1912: 236)

Therefore, for the sake of boundary adjustment the general idea that prevailed was that all the ranges marked as 'snow range' on all running parallel to China were regarded as borderline. Subsequently, he also shed some light on the confusions, British officers themselves were encountering in deciding the extent of this territory:

> It was difficult perhaps to state definitely the precise limits of the Mishmi country [for the British authority]. The tribes themselves, however had always considered that their lands ran as far as Sama, some little distance up the Rima valley, and they should be the best judges, particularly .... (Holdich, 1912: 391)

It would suffice to argue, the British Survey of India lacked the idea of exact extent of Mishmis territories, however, thought to demarcate on what they believed to their convenience was fairly accurate.[23] It is significant to note while much of the explorers had given an account of the Tibeto-Mishmi border, least was spoken about 'Anglo-Mishmi' border.[24] In 1884 and 1885 *Bebejiyas* had showed no sign of inclination to adapt to the changed conditions of border (Hamilton, 1912). In fact, incidents of raid and revenge were reported in the British account such as in 1857, 1861 and 1866; root cause being resistance by the natives to external authorities (Miso, 2015). The then Deputy Commissioner of Lakhimpur, Mr C.W.S. Clarke in referring Mr Goad's visit to Mishmi country in 1874, wrote to the then Secretary, Chief Commissioner of Assam:

> As far as I can learn, the Mishmis are in no way to blame further than in committing petty thefts and retaliating act for act, when their nearest and dearest have been killed. (Clarke, 1874: 12)

Ward and Kaulback had observed that Mishmis were an independent tribe. Kaulback had precisely pointed that Mishmis were so independent that not even their headmen had control over them (Ward, 1930; Kaulback, 1934). Mishmis were also reluctant to allow any outsiders to cross their territory for whatsoever reasons especially Miju Mishmis who were given clear instructions by the Tibetans not to allow any outsiders particularly white men into Tibet (Gregory, 1869–70). Instances were numerous when Mishmis tried to send back European travellers. *Mijus* sent back Wilcox and Dr W. Griffith (Walker, 1887). In 1854 a *Miju* chief, Kaisha, murdered French Missionary, Pere Krick and his companion Pere Bouryduring in their second attempt to pass through Mishmi country (Hamilton, 1912). Similarly, T.T. Cooper was sent back at *Prun* while he attempted to travel in 1869–70. Captain Gregory in one of his report mentioned the reasons for sending back outsiders as Chowsam Gohain, a *Khampti* chief from *Chungkham* (*Chowkham*) who was similarly asked to go back by a *Miju* man namely Jeengoo and his leader Naboo Jungbal when he tried to pass through Mishmi country to Tibet:

> The 'Naboo Jungbal' replied again vicariously that there were no Europeans in Tibet, and no road for foreigners, for the Tibetan Government know that if it once permitted the English to enter the country, they would 'covet and finally devour it, as they had devoured so many countries. (Gregory, 1869–70: 218)

It is evident from his own report that Gregory in the best of his mind realized the pessimistic feeling the Tibetans and Mishmis had for Europeans' entry into Tibet. According to Sikdar, Tibetans had also learnt of the English East India Company's desire for gold from Tibetan *Monpas* of *Tawang* (Sikdar, 1982). However, this did not seem to deter the British Raj even if it meant dividing the tribal land (Holdich, 1912). The British Raj unrelentingly continued to pursue their 'Forward Policy' to bring Mishmi country within the dominion of British Empire. Eventually, the British authority with the help of J.F. Needham adopted *Menilkrai,* supposedly as the Tibeto-Mishmi boundary in the winter of 1885–86 when he found an opportunity to survey Brahmaputra basin while heading to *Rima* and returning (as he was compelled to because of Tibetan resistance) (Hamilton, 1912). The 'policy of non-interference and forbearance' with frontier tribes eventually seemed to fade when it came to gobbling the frontier tribes' territories. What was foremost important in order to successfully implement 'Forward Policy' was to break off the habitual seclusion of the tribes. This included an inducement by luring to visit exhibitions such as one made to Kaladoi *and* Lako of *Chulikatta*, Nassi of *Bebejiya* with their sons and Chowsam Gohain of *Khampti* country in Calcutta in 1886 (Hamilton, 1912). Besides, they maintained a *Namghar* (*Assamese* word for rest house) for Mishmis in *Sadiya* but none for *Abors* (Needham, 1889).[25]

When such initiatives did not meet the expected result in their favour coupled with some raids that Mishmis did make, the Bebejiya Mishmi Expedition, 1899–1900 was carried out under the command of Lieutenant Colonel E.H. Molesworth against *Bebejiyas* of *Anaya* village, which symbolized a step towards ascendancy of British domination over independent native tribes in the Mishmi Hills (Miso, 2015). What is conspicuous in this expedition is an example of sheer military excessiveness and disproportionate use of force against the largely incoherent natives. It included a strength of 750 troops, made of 350 Naga Hills Military Police, 150 Dacca Military Police, 200 of the Ist King George's Own Sappers and Miners, 50 Survey with Lieutenant Morshead, Captain F.M. Bailey, APO, 1200 Naga coolies acting as porters and others along with 11 British officers (Hamilton, 1912). It ruthlessly burnt down the *Pika* village of *Miso* clan then proceeded later to burn down *Anaya* village.

Similarly, such excessiveness was exhibited when *Kaisha*, one of the headman along with his men murdered Pere Krick and Pere Boury; his entire village was attacked in February 1855 with the support of 20 sepoys (*Sipahi* or soldiers), 40 *Khamptis* after which he was hanged in Dibrugarh jail under Lieutenant Eden.[26] This did not end as on 4 May 1899 when Bebejiya Mishmis killed two men, two *Khampti* women and looted few guns, their whole village was destroyed on 23rd November 1900 under the command of Gurkha Rifles Commanding Officer, Colonel Molesworth, Staff Officer Major Anderson, Third Bengal Infantry, Lieutenant F.K. Ward and J.F. Needham, nearly lasting for three months. All these happened notwithstanding the fact that England was party to some of international conventions[27] and particularly a country that was considered to be a 'civilized' in the eye of the West. What more a prudent colonial master probably should have anticipated when these tribes were being forced down their throat, the systematic obedience and to break the chain of habitual seclusion against their wish ultimately abetting them to react?

Eventually, the persistent efforts to break through Mishmi country began to bear results. According to Ward, it was mostly during Needham and Dunda's period when Mishmis reasonably began showing the signs of friendly relationship with English administration (Ward, 1927). Hamilton reports that their course of relationship with Mishmis was consistently coherent and progressive unlike *Abors* (Hamilton, 1912). Hamilton reports:

> ... all expectations were surpassed, when led by Kaladoi, first one and then another of the chiefs of Chulikattas, who long since had displaced the Digarus from their predominant position in the Councils of the Mishmis, professed allegiance to the British Raj. (Hamilton, 1912: 199)

Subsequently, the policy of divide and rule began. For the convenience of the administration whole of India was divided into nine[28] divisions where the NE frontier tribes fell within Eastern Bengal and Assam Division. According to Kumar, Mishmi Hills was officially created and recognized only in 1948, though known for long as a result of the segregation of the then Assam Himalayan region into different administrative zones (Kumar, 2005).[29] During 1912–13 the Himalayan region was divided into three administrative units, namely Western Section with its headquarter at *Charduar*, Central and Eastern Section headquarter being at *Sadiya* (Marshall, 2005).[30] While the Central Section encompassed *Abors*, Eastern Section comprised Mishmis and both the sections were merged together in 1919 that came to be known as *Sadiya Frontier Tract*. On the other hand, Western Section came to be known as *Balipara Frontier Tract* in 1919, encompassing *Tawang* and *Subansiri*. In 1948, the remaining portion of *Sadiya Frontier Tract* was divided into what is now known as Abor Hills and Mishmi Hills (Kumar, 2005).

Though simultaneously, India was undergoing its political movements to achieve its independence, the status and fate of Mishmi country was recounted in crystal clear wordings of Reid:

> They are not Indian in any sense of the word, neither in origin, nor in language, nor in appearance nor in habit nor in outlook; and it is only by historical accident that they have been tacked on to an Indian Province. A new Constitution in which we may be sure, British control will be enormously diminished, is promised for India as a whole; it will be a question whether the Hill Tribes are to be included in it, or kept outside. Personally I have no doubt whatsoever that to allow them in any way to be involved in Indian politics, and with no safeguards such as now exist, would spell disaster for them. My own views runs in the direction of setting up some sort of Hill Tribe Territory, entirely separate from India, embracing the Assam Hill Tribes and possibly some of those of Burma too. The main point, however, is that we are responsible for the future welfare of a set of very loyal, primitive peoples, who are habituated to look to us for protection and will get it from no other source. They are not, by a hundred years, ready to take place in a democratic Constitution, or to compete with the sophisticated Indian politician for a place and power. It is up to us to see that they are given under our protection a period of respite within which they will develop on their own lines and without outside interference. (Reid, 1944: 247)

This observation of Reid feasibly requires no explanation to the question – how did with such distinct social organization, cultural and economic life, Mishmis were devoured by Europeans that Tibetans had long been skeptic of? Reid similarly wrote that Mishmis will 'no doubt develop' but what remained largely elusive is how these tribes would be left so as to develop by themselves. What transpired after Britain handed over the power to a new independent nation where rest of India rejoiced its freedom was the least concern to be reckoned both for British Raj and new Indian democracy which merely carried out same old colonial tradition.

Conclusion

While the English explorers were appreciated in England for their 'noble' and untiring effort to rip through rugged mountains in the frontier hills, what was hardly anticipated by the tribe was the true guise of Englishmen and their intentions.

No less harm was equally done by the Indian counterpart to the natives post-independence which effectively carried out same old colonial traits. Acharya noted that developments post-independence especially for the tribes was no less than assimilative in its nature (Acharya, 1988). What Reid mentioned long ago such as disaster without no safeguards, 'sophisticated Indian politicians' and 'development without interference' turned out to be an accurate prophecy. The political, economic, social and cultural engagements were dramatically altered. The inference of the term 'Raj' (rule or govern) attached to 'Bhavan' (Official Bungalow) of the governor in independent India denotes the existing link with the colonial context. Since the then North-East Frontier Agency (NEFA) era under the supervision of Ministry of External Affairs (MEA) the governor of Assam and governor's advisors, became a direct 'agent' to the President of India administering whole of the tribal belt. Those bureaucrats turned advisors not being from the hill belt and unaccustomed with the intricacies of hill affairs added woes to administrative complexities (Mukhopadhyay, 1992). Military mobilization as a result of strategic importance became another issue. The *Panchsheel Principles* of the then Prime Minister Nehru practically worked out only to contradict its theoretically advocated principles – to let tribal develop along their own lines. The rights of the natives to remain uncontacted and undisturbed were further systematically eroded largely because of the educational policies and institutional set-up in a manner that suited the psyche and perception of administrators that they had about Mishmi native tribes. The result was visible through foundational school textbooks which lacked how and what ought to be taught in formal educational institutions in accordance to tribal needs.[31] Besides English and Hindi medium schools like Vivekananda Kendra Vidyalaya (VKV), Ramakrishna Mission (RK Mission) and Jawahar Navodaya Vidyalaya (JNV)[32] were rigorously set up in the guise of 'nation building' and 'upliftment' of tribal people (Mukhopadhyay, 1992; Chaudhuri, 2013). The consequence is, almost whole of Mishmi people speak in Hindi at every part of their daily life (Blench and Post, 2011). Even while the *Arunachal Freedom of Indigenous Faith Bill,* 1978 was passed to protect the indigenous faiths by prohibiting 'forcible conversion' or conversion induced by 'fraudulent means,' such law nonetheless in no way could deter the activities that had considerable psychic impact that had already crept through such systematic institutional set-up.

The traditional, indigenous economic structure including subsistence economy of Mishmi native was completely altered. The primeval mode of economy like barter system, which entailed collectivism in the production, and consumption of goods were overpowered by the capitalist economy. The *Posa* (allowance) system was abolished and cash system practised introduced monetization (Sikdar, 1982). *Marwaris* took over the market monopoly replacing Tibetan salts with cheap Bengal salt from the market (Sikdar, 1982).

More variation came from post-independence Indian academia that had substantial role to play in shaping the outlook of Mishmi tribes, be it negative or positive.[33] It appeared as if the whole restructuring process had to be undertaken effectively and forever to undo the status that Mishmis enjoyed. Some of the writers have reflected integrationist approach by outrightly rejecting the claim that the NE frontier tribes of India could not be considered as a part of Tibet merely based on ethnic grounds, howsoever close resemblance they share within Tibetans (Choudhury, 1970).[34] One such glaring examples of skewed attempt is the whole narratives of linkages drawn with Mishmis with that of historical monuments, *Bhismaknagar* fort of ancient king *Bhismak,* an indicative of cultural amalgamation in the post-independent era. It is evident that Major Vetch's letter in 1848 while mentioning about his trip along with Mr Goad to Mishmi Hills mentions about an extensive fortress in *Bhismaknagar,* according to whom it might have dated back prior to *Ahom* regime (Johnson, 1874). However, there is no historical to substantiate anywhere to show that Mishmi's historical timeline came in close contact to *Bhismak's* regime in order to prove the relationship that they had with *Bhismak* and therefore, what Luthra mentioned that *Chulikatta* began embracing cropped hair as a symbol of defeat at the hands of Krishna who drove away *Rukmini* from *Bhismaknagar* seems no less than a myth (Luthra, 1971).[35] Led by such recent introspection some of the concerned members of the Mishmi community had argued that while some Indian writers had attempted to introduce piecemeal history of Mishmis to the world at large, their own untold historical record showed grave injustice done to the natives (Lingi, 2015). The underpinning inference that could be drawn from the whole debate of this is that while world powers continued their policies, Mishmis independence was systematically questioned, jeopardized and were obliterated for these tribes neither belonged to China, Tibet, Burma nor India from any aspects.

Acknowledgement

The author would like to thank especially Dr Mite Lingi, Vice-Chairman, Kera-aa Initiatives for Cultural and Ecological Security (KICES), Mrs Dibuli Linggi, Dr Tarun Mene, Asst. Professor, AITS, RGU, all other friends and colleagues and the anonymous sources who had helped the author in coming up with this work.

Notes

1. *La* is a Tibetan word for Pass. Hence, *Keya La, Bomdi La*. It is significant to note that most of the passes in *Mishmi* region have Tibetan names by virtue of their influence. While *Bomdi La* was route for people of *Kameng Valley* to trade with Tibet, *Se/Tse La* for *Tawang, Rima* for *Mishmis*, and *Hukong/Hukawng* for *Burma*. Pass was also known as *Duars* and officers who managed it were known as *Duaris*.
2. It was also known as *Bod-yul* or *Peu-yul* by the natives of Tibet.
3. For the purpose of this paper, the term '*Mishmis*' shall be employed to refer all the *Mishmi* subtribes, i.e. *Bebejiyas* and *Chulikattas* (*Idu Mishmis*), *Digaru* and *Mijus* and the clan under respective tribes unless otherwise the context requires it to be categorically mentioned.
4. The term 'frontier' in this context is relatively used to indicate the entire rugged Himalayan region in the South Eastern region of Tibet, once perceived as a buffer zone. Hence, tribes found in this frontier were termed as frontier tribes including the tribes in NE frontier.
5. It was under him when the creation of Eastern Bengal (present Bangladesh) and Assam (North-East India) was commenced and both the provinces were administered from Dacca or Dhaka.
6. F.M. Bailey was a notable linguist, explorer, diplomat and a secret British Indian Trade Agent at Gyantse, Tibet who was commissioned in the Indian Army and served in the 17th Bengal Lancers 1901–03 and 32nd Sikh Pioneers 1903–05. He served Francis Younghusband's mission to Lhasa in 1903–04 and surveyed south-eastern Tibet including *Mipi* village with Captain H.T. Morshead. Later he served as a Political Officer. See, Obituaries (1967). Lt. Col. Frederick Marshman Bailey, CIE, 1882–1967, pp. 615–16.
7. It is region situated south of *Walong*, north of *Hawai* and opposite to *Halla* region, along the northern banks of *Lohit* river.
8. The author believes that this paper has its limitations of the exact time and era of the origin of the *Mishmis*, owing to the lack of conclusive evidence yet not available to determine the human origin and migration that has always remained illusive, similar is the case with *Mishmis*.
9. For the purpose of this paper *Idu Mishmi* includes both the *Bebejiyas* and *Chulikattas*.
10. The inhabitants that resided near the bank of *Digaru* river were termed as *Digaru Mishmis*.
11. It is to be noted here that *Mitayu clan* of *Chulikattas* and *Mitayi clan* of *Bebejiyas* are two different clans.
12. The lists of the clans are not exhaustive here. They are elaborately mentioned in Report on Dibong Survey and Exploration – 1912–13 by G.A. Nevill, Appendix E, 'A List of Villages in the Midu Country', ASPO (A and P) No. 75-100-20-12-1918, pp. 35–45.
13. The basis for this classification is not known other than the information advanced that they all had come from *Hkampti Long* in Burma. Mills referred to the lists most of which were compiled by Forrest P. Mainprice. For the exhaustive list see, J.P. Mills (1952). 'The Mishmis of Lohit Valley, Assam'. *The Journal of the Royal Anthropological Institute of Great Britain and Ireland*, 82(1), Appendix A, pp. 9–10.
14. For instance, while *Mithi* and *Mitati* clan belongs to same village the latter has become extinct. Similarly, *Yaka* clan belonging to *Midu* is almost at the verge of extinction that perhaps needs urgent study.

15. The concept of who constitutes an aborigine or autochthon may be debated subjectively based on its technicalities and therefore many scholars and anthropologists like G.S. Ghurye and Virginius Xaxa had debated it. However, in this context, Mills refers to 'aborigines' as the clans that do not form a separate group but part of one or the other of the linguistic groups according to their locations. From the perspective of international law 'indigenous peoples' are synonymously to refer to aborigines. As a matter of political, social, cultural and economic rights international legal instruments such as *Indigenous and Tribal Peoples Convention* 169 (also known as *International Labour Organization* 169) in principle, subscribes to the broad concept of self-identification and uniqueness to consider as to who are indigenous or aborigines.
16. According to Max Muller, 'Tibeto-Burman' term is used for a large family of languages, which is more or less approximate to each other as a result of migration of Tibeto-Burman tribe. He believes it is this feature, which gives sufficient reason as to why tribe had separated into clans, why within few centuries a single clan might have scattered into as different tribes speaking as many dialects finding difficult to recognize their common descent. See C.J.F.S. Forbes (1878). 'On Tibeto-Burma Languages', *The Journal of the Royal Asiatic Society of Great Britain and Ireland*, 10(2), pp. 210–11.
17. Details of the similarity being shared by all *Mishmi* languages with that of Tibeto-Burman roots is provided in R. Blench and M. Post (2011). *(DE) Classifying Arunachal Languages: Reconsidering the Evidence*, Kay Williamson Educational Foundation, Cambridge, Appendix, pp. 16–17.
18. Blench argued that whether Miju languages should be brought within the category of *Mishmis* is debatable. Hence, it is maintained as an isolate language within Tibeto-Burman group. See, R. Blench and M. Post (2011). *(DE) Classifying Arunachal Languages: Reconsidering the Evidence*, Kay Williamson Educational Foundation, Cambridge, p. 9.
19. It included both the tributaries, i.e. current *Siang* river and *Lohit* or *Tellu* river or upper Brahmaputra.
20. Lieutenant R. Wilcox was in the British army who assisted Captain Bedford as his assistant in the survey of Assam and its neighbouring countries. He visited *Mishmi* country in 1825 and went up to the Brahmaputra valley and penetrated to the banks of river *Irrawady* in Burma. See, C.R. Markham (1871). *A Memoir on the Indian Surveys*, Forgotten Books, London.

    The original publications of Wilcox's reports are available as 'The Memoir of the Survey of Assam, 1825–28', with a detailed account of the discoveries, and a map, in the *Asiatic Researches*, vol. xviii. For the purpose of this paper the author has referred to its abridged version, i.e. *Memoir of a Survey of Assam and the Neighbouring Countries Executed in 1825–28,* published in 1998 by Calcutta based RNB due to unavailability of the original source. It was also found that some of the pages in the last portion of the abridged version of the book were incomplete.
21. The Royal Society of Arts used to carry out proceedings for peers on regular basis, wherein discussions used to take place on different themes among the distinguished members in their respective fields. On 8 February 1912, NE Frontier of British India was being discussed upon, because of its strategic importance and occupation of Tibet by China and partly because they believed that such occupation had pressure on tribes within British side of NE Frontier of India.

22. Observation of Colonel Thomas H. Holdich from the proceedings gives such impression when he remarks – 'If a Chinaman from Rima wished to explore Assam, we should not interfere with him. He might find a little difficulty with the *Mishmis*, but he would find none from us.'
23. To accomplish such objectives, separate Boundary Commissions were set up such as the Burma Boundary Commission to decide the fate of Indo-Burmese border.
24. The Inner Line Regulation of 1873 was merely an administrative demarcation not an international boundary.
25. To this *Abors* had later demanded when Needham visited *Nizamghat* in 1884.
26. Some believe this is one reason why *Mishmis* avenged *Khamptis* and therefore they were harassed and enslaved which altogether may not be a probable conclusion. On 4 May 1899 party of *Bebejiya* from *Abrago* visited *Khampti* village of *Mitaigaon* near *Sunpura* and killed two men, two women and carried away few guns and prisoners. There were also reports that *Khamptis* were harassed in and around *Kundil* area.
27. It may be argued that agreements may not have been made between the frontier tribes and British Raj and even if it did exist such were not recognizable, considering an international law under which an agreement has no validity when one party does not constitute a sovereign government, as was the case with *Mishmis*. However, the fact that England became a party to the *First Geneva Convention* in 1864, and laws such as *Manual on the Laws of War on Land* was drafted in the same country, symbolized how a 'civilized' country should naturally be expected to behave with its adversaries. Any nation irrespective of party to a given convention or not, by customary practices one may not resort to disproportionate use of force. See, http://www.bbc.co.uk/ethics/war/overview/rules.shtml
28. These divisions excluding the Eastern Bengal and Assam division were primarily Madras Presidency, Bombay Presidency, Bengal (current West Bengal), United Provinces of Agra and Oudh, the Central Provinces and Behar (Bihar), the Punjab, North-West Frontier and other small bodies at the headquarters of certain political agencies.
29. While Kumar mentions that the '*Mishmi Hills*' was officially created in 1948, the name *Mishmi Hills* existed long back as old as 1874 as per available records. It could be even ancient. See, W.C. Clarke (1874). 'Frontier Outposts in Lakhimpur and Mr Goad's Visit to the Mishmi Hills', Assam Secretariat Proceedings, Dibrugarh, File No. 189J of 1874, Serial No. 2.
30. In 1914, a frontier tract namely Lakhimpur Frontier Tract was created under which southern part of Western, Central and Eastern were brought in. Some parts of Lakhimpur Frontier Tract combined with Sadiya Frontier Tract and became Tirap Frontier Tract in 1943 with its headquarter at Margherita.
31. Bath had argued that some measures were taken up by the administration to include customs and cultures in the primary and secondary school textbooks. However, such measures remained minimal and temporary. See, Nani Bath (2006).
32. Institutions were strongly criticized by the people from South India mostly Dravidians who considered it an imposition upon their Tamil culture. In the North-East Frontier hills, JNV were set up more rigorously after Indo-China War of 1962.
33. Methodology of most of the scholarly writings was not unbiased. The writings like that of Verrier Elwin, T.K. Barua, P.N. Luthra, D.P. Choudhury and many others

reflect the colonialist approach of servant and master, the impoverishment and redemptory and stigmatizing of frontier tribes at the cost of other tribes.

34. Choudhury in his work 'North-East Frontier of India' attempts to provide an argument why people of hills who are Mongoloid in origin are not non-Indian in any sense by way of comparison with plainsmen of Assam to show why Mongoloid race also comprises to be an Indian. Such arguments are merely an apprehension based in order to deter ethnic identity conflicts or ethno-nationalism. If dwelled much deeper to critic Choudhary's argument, he fails to highlight to the readers of the historical fact that the ancestors of present Assam themselves were *Tais* and *Ahoms* who had migrated from Burma to Assam, annexed the land of *Chutiya* kingdom and settled in present *Dibrugarh* District, and some parts of *Sibsagar* only to become part of India after Anglo-Burmese War. The perspective that could be agreed upon here is that hill tribes indeed were and are closer to Tibetans and Burmese in most of the aspects although they were not Tibetans, nor Burmese, Chinese or at the least Indians. See, B.J. Terwiel (1996), also see, A. Guha (1983).
35. P.N. Luthra served in the capacity of the governor during the then NEFA period.

References

Acharya, S.K. (1988). Ethnic Processes in North-Eastern India, *Economic and Political Weekly*, Vol. 23, No. 21, pp. 1068–77.

Allan, J. (1909). 'The Coinage of Assam', *The Numismatic Chronicle and Journal of the Royal Numismatic Society* (Fourth Series), 9: 300–31.

Bailey, F.M. (1912). 'Journey through the Portion of Southeastern Tibet', *The Geographical Journal*, 39(4): 334–47.

—— (1914). 'Explorations of the Tsangpo or Upper Brahmaputra', *The Geographical Journal*, 44(4): 341–64.

—— (1934). 'The Source of Irrawady', *The Geographical Journal*, 84: 73–74.

—— (1957). *No Passport to Tibet*, Rupert Hart Davis, London.

Bailey, F.M., K. Mason and J. Ramsbottom (1934). 'The Himalaya East of Tsangpo: Discussion', *The Geographical Journal*, 84(5): 394–97.

Bath, Nani (2006). 'Understanding Religious Policy of Arunachal Pradesh', *Dialogue*, 7(3), p. 2.

Bentick, A. (1913). 'The Abor Expedition: Geographical Results', *The Geographical Journal*, 41(2): 97–109.

Blackburn, S. (2015). 'The Journey of the Souls: Notes on Funeral Rituals and Oral Texts in Arunachal Pradesh, India', *Reh Souvenir*, Central Reh Celebration Committee, Roing.

Blench, R. (2015). 'Origins of Ethnolinguistic Identity in Southeast Asia', in J. Habu, P. Lape and J. Oslen (eds), *Handbook of East and Southeast Asian Archaeology*, Springer, Washington, pp. 1–22.

Blench, R. and M. Post (2011). *(DE) Classifiying Arunachal Languages: Reconsidering the Evidence*, Kay Williamson Eudcational Foundation, Cambridge.

Bradley, D. (1997). 'Tibeto-Burman Languages and Classification', *Pacific Linguistics*, 81: 1–72.

Chaudhuri, S.K. (2013). 'The Institutionalization of Tribal Religion: Recasting the Donyi-Polo Movement in Arunachal Pradesh', *Asian Ethnology*, 72(2): 259–77.

Choudhury, D.P. (1970). 'The North-East Frontier of India', *Modern Asian Studies*, 4(4): 359–65.

Christie, C. (1976). 'Great Britain, China and the Status of Tibet, 1914–21', *Modern Asian Studies*, 10(4): 481–508.

Clarke, W.C. (1874). 'Frontier Outposts in Lakhimpur and Mr Goad's Visit to the Mishmi Hills', Assam Secretariat Proceedings, Dibrugarh, File No. 189J of 1874, Serial No. 2.

Close, C., F.M. Bailey and M. Barnard (1930). 'The Seinghku and Delei Valleys, North-East Frontier of India: Discussion', *The Geographical Journal*, 75(5): 433–35.

Cooper, T.T. (1873). *The Mishmi Hills: An Account of a Journey Made in an Attempt to Penetrate Tibet from Assam to Open New Routes for Commerce*, H.S. King and Co., London.

Copland, Ian (1998). 'Review', *The International History Review*, 20(4): 996–98.

Cottam, Henry (1876–1877). 'Overland Route to China viâ Assam, Tenga Pani River, Khamti, and Singpho Country, Across the Irrawaddi River into Yunan', *Proceedings of the Royal Geographical Society of London*, 21(6): 590–95.

Dunbar, G.D. (1915). 'Tribes of Brahmaputra Valley', *Journal of the Royal Society of Arts*, 63(3249): 289–303.

Elwin, V. (2005). 'The North-East Frontier Agency', in S.K. Sharma and U. Sharma (eds), *Discovery of North-East India: Geography, History, Culture, Religion, Politics, Sociology, Science, Education and Economy*, Vol. 2, Vikas Publishing House, New Delhi, pp. 1–314.

Forbes, C.J.F.S. (1878). 'On Tibeto-Burma Languages', *The Journal of the Royal Asiatic Society of Great Britain and Ireland*, 10(2): 210–27.

Geography and Travels (1887). *The American Naturalist*, 21(4): 360–66.

Gregory, J. (1869–70). 'An Account of an Attempt by a Native Envoy to Reach the Catholic Missionaries', *Proceedings of the Royal Geographical Society of London*, 14(3): 214–19.

Griffith, John (1779). *A Journal of the Life, Travels, and Labours in the Work of the Ministry*, The British Library, London.

Guha, A. (1983). 'The Ahom Political System: An Enquiry into the State Formation Process in Medieval Assam (1228–1714)', *Social Scientist*, 11(12): 3–34.

Hamilton, A. (1912). *In Abor Jungles*, The University of British Columbia, London.

Holdich, T.H. (1912). 'The North-Eastern Frontier of India', *Journal of the Royal Society of Arts*, 60(3092): 379–92.

Hudson, G.F. (1962). 'The Frontier of China and Assam: Background to the Fighting', *The China Quarterly*, 12: 203–06.

Johnson, H.L. (1874). 'Frontier Outposts in Lakhimpur and Mr Goad's Visit to the Mishmi Hills', Assam Secretariat Proceedings, Dibrugarh, File No. 189J of 1874, Serial No. 2.

Jules, S. (2011). 'Spies in Monks' Clothing', *Geographical*, 83(9). Retrieved from https://www.questia.com/magazine/1g1-271405196/spies-in-monks-clothing-as-the-british-empire-expanded

Kapadia, H. (2007). 'The Promised Land', *Himalayan Journal*, 63(5).

Kaulback, Ronald (1934). 'The Assam Border of Tibet', *The Geographical Journal*, 83(3): 177–89.

Konow, Sten (1902). 'Note on the Languages Spoken between the Assam Valley and Tibet', *Journal of the Royal Asiatic Society of Great Britain and Ireland*, 127–37.

Kumar, T.M. (2005). 'Land and People', in S.K. Sharma and U. Sharma (eds), *Discovery of North-East India: Geography, History, Culture, Religion, Politics, Sociology, Science, Education and Economy*, Vol. 2, Vikas Publishing House, New Delhi, pp. 1–314.

Lingi, M. (2015). 'Once Upon a Time in Ihili: A Thought to a Forgotten Killing', *Reh Souvenir*, Central Reh Celebration Committee, Roing, pp. 1–23.

Luthra, P.N. (1971). 'North-East Frontier Agency Tribes: Impact of Ahom and British Policy', *Economic and Political Weekly*, 1143–49.

Lyall, Charles James (1903). *Journal of the Society for Arts*, 51(2637): 611–36.

MacGregor, C.R. (1887). 'Journey of the Expedition under Colonel Woodthorpe, R.E., from Upper Assam to the Irawadi, and Return over the Patkoi Range', *Proceedings of the Royal Geographical Society and Monthly Record of Geography, New Monthly Series*, 9(1): 19–42.

Markham, C.R. (1871). *A Memoir on the Indian Surveys*, Forgotten Books, London.

Marshall, J.G. (2005). *Britain and Tibet 1765–1947: A Select Annotated Bibliography of British Relations with Tibet and the Himalayan States Including Nepal, Sikkim and Bhutan*, Routledge, London and New York.

McKay, A. (1997). *Tibet and the British Raj: The Frontier Cadre, 1904–1947*, Vol. 26, Curzon Press, Surrey.

Michell, J.F. (1833). *The North-East Frontier of India: A Topographical, Political and Military Report.*

Mills, J.P. (1952). 'The Mishmis of Lohit Valley, Assam', *The Journal of the Royal Anthropological Institute of Great Britain and Ireland*, 82(1): 1–12.

Miso, R. (2015). 'Mathun and Dri Valley: Memories of Trade, Tibetan Intrusion, Impasses and Retreat', Reh Souvenir, Central Reh Celebration Committee, Roing, pp. 1–23.

Mouat, F.J. (1868). 'A Few Notes on Some Skulls of the Hill Tribes of India', *Transactions of the Ethnological Society of London*, 6: 42–48.

Mukhopadhyay, Ela (1992). 'The Changing Profile of a Closed Culture', *Social Scientist*, 20(3/4): 68–74.

Needham, J.F. (1889). 'The Hydrography of South-Eastern Tibet: The Dibong River', *Proceedings of the Royal Geographical Society and Monthly Record of Geography*, 11(7): 440–41.

—— (1900). *Report of the Bebejiya Mishmi Expedition 1899–1900*, Shillong.

Orleans, P.H. (1896). 'Yun-nan to British India', *The Geographical Journal*, 7(3): 300–09.

Reid, Robert (1944a). 'Assam', *Journal of the Royal Society of Arts*, 92(4663): 241–47.

—— (1944b). 'The Excluded Areas of Assam', *The Geographical Journal*, 103(1/2): 18–29.

Royal Geographical Society (1902). 'The Monthly Record', *The Geographical Journal*, 20(2): 224–35.

Sikdar, S. (1982). 'Tribalism vs. Colonialism: British Capitalistic Intervention and Transformation of Primitive Economy of Arunachal Pradesh in the Nineteenth Century', *Social Scientist*, 10(12): 15–31.

Terwiel B.J. (1996). 'Recreating the Past: Revivalism in Northeastern India', *A Bijdragen tot de Taal-, Land-en Volkenkunde, Deel 152, 2de Afl*, pp. 275–92.

Walker, J.T. (1887). 'The Lu River of Tibet: Is It the Source of the Irawadi or the Salwin?', *Proceedings of the Royal Geographical Society and Monthly Record of Geography*, 9(6): 352–77.

Ward, F.K. (1927). 'The Mishmi Country', *The Geographical Journal*, 69(3): 287–88.

—— (1930). 'The Seinghku and Delei Valleys, North-East Frontier of India', *The Geographical Journal*, 75(5): 412–32.

Ward, F.K. and M. Smith (1934). 'The Himalaya East of Tsangpo', *The Geographical Journal*, 84(5): 369–94.

Weatherbe, D. (1927). 'From Burma to Assam by the Kronjong Pass', *The Geographical Journal*, 69(6): 602–04.

Wilcox, R. (1998). *Memoir of a Survey of Assam and The Neighbouring Countries Executed in 1825–28*, RNB, Calcutta.

Williamson, Noël (1909). 'The Lohit-Brahmaputra between Assam and South-Eastern Tibet, November 1907 to January 1908', *The Geographical Journal*, 34(4): 363–83.

5

Border Trade in Mishmi Hills

A Historical Perspective

RAJIV MISO

In tribal societies the production and distribution of material goods are organized by transactional principles, essentially different from market exchange. Also, transactional mechanisms used in external trade are sometimes distinctly different from those used internally. A great deal of exchange takes place in the ostensible form of a present and counter present. Sometimes, the present and its reciprocation form part of the same immediate transaction.[1] Karl Polanyi identifies a core feature of tribal economy being 'multi-centric', where the dominant centres are organized through non-market patterns of integration, such as reciprocity and redistribution; special-purpose monies are in use, and market-place exchange if it exists is subordinate and contained.[2] Exchange is often diffused or indirect and circulation does not follow a linear or cyclical trajectory of a formal western market system. The exchanges frequently have pedigree and personality, sacred uses, or moral and emotional connotations.

It is from this perspective that the aspects of border trade in the Mishmi Hills have been discussed in this chapter. The necessity has arrived from the present geopolitical reasons and emerging economic viabilities. The border war of 1962 has become a thing of past and both India and China have to move on through dialogue and economic developments. The past will show the way. The way is the opening up of old trading routes. The information and data included in the work will serve as a repository of knowledge for the scholars, administrators, planners, students and general readers.

The colonial construct regarding the tribal societies of Arunachal Pradesh and neighbouring areas as the 'primitive', 'barbarous', etc. a number of researches have been undertaken on the aspect of social formation especially on the trade practices of various tribes of Arunachal Pradesh in the past.[3] Though these researches are important source of information on the history of

Arunachal Pradesh, the Mishmi Hills have formed only a part of their studies and sometimes in a passing way. Hence, it is for the first time the aspects of border trade of Mishmi Hills have been exclusively and comprehensively studied in this work.

The Idu Mishmi who inhabits the Mishmi Hills in present Dibang Valley, Lower Dibang Valley, Lohit, Upper Siang and East Siang districts of Arunachal Pradesh had an economic relation centred on barter and exchange. The barter was the chief mode of exchange in all local, inter-tribal and interstate trade. Barter was largely necessitated to procure goods which were scarce in their habitations. The major media of exchanges among them were cattle (Mithun), hides, cloth, rice, *dao*, spearheads, arrows, etc. The form of exchange was simple and was oriented towards securing a value for their objects. In the colonial period, exchanges in Indian rupees, Chinese currency and Tibetan *tankas* were used. However, the major chunk of trade was done through barter. The articles of practical use such as metal, domestic animals, forest products, etc. and articles of decoration like beads were exchanged.

Since ancient times, trade existed between India and China in 'Kesava' and 'China-patta' which changed hands in this region through the routes of the Dibang pass, the Mishmi route, the Phugan pass and the Patkai pass.[4] This network of exchange is well reflected in the oral traditions of the tribe. In the journey of the soul, there are references of the places supposedly to be in China and Tibet such as the halting place of *Ilu Pudu* – where the Siberian birds nest during migration, *Miko dibro* – the place where monasteries are located, *Adu-Pili* – where beads are found and so on. These all stops are supposedly in the north of Idu Mishmi country.[5] Another tradition has it that Tibetans and the tribe lived together in antiquity. The ancient Idu or *Todu* was deceived by the cunning Tibetan or *Tonlo*. Exasperated and penniless, the Idu went to the mountains, collected honey, musk deer and bile of bear to sell them in the plains for good profit. The narrative is suggestive of the ancient contact between Idu Mishmis and their northern neighbour and that hill products were crucial to the exchange network (Emphasis mine).

The commercial intercourse of hill tribes with the region definitely had an important bearing in shaping their socio-economic life; their attitude towards such trading pursuits. The traders had to undergo rites of *Abhi-thu* presided by the shaman before the commencement of the journey. In fact, the trading rites and hunting rites had similar implications and observances. Similarly, after return journey, they had to undergo the same rituals. Simultaneously, restrictions or taboos in food had to be observed by the trader as well as the householders during the undertaking. The winter season was most preferred time for trade in the north as well as the south. During the time, the rain and flood receded with enough sunshine for outdoor activities. The agricultural tasks of the cycle were over. They planned for hunting expeditions, trade, construction or maintenance of the house. The womenfolk resorted to weaving.

The trading enterprises were planned and organized. When they were convinced that enough teeta, honey and musk had been collected, they contemplated of the trade. Another important consideration was the stock of salt at home. They moved in parties and halted in the temporary camps or in the caves. Rano Mihu (90 years) of Dri valley and Ataru Miso (85 years) of Ithun valley recollect of selling *Coptis teeta* to the British and Marwaris in the Hodeya (Sadiya) for 300 coins.[6] The money collected was used to purchase Mithun from the Adis. Rano Mihu fixed the price of Mishmi teeta *Coptis teeta* at ₹ 40 per kg in pre-independence period. He also visited Tibet, three days march from Keya pass with items of animal skins, musk, and *teeta*, which were exchanged for salt, *dao*, axe, vessels, beads and coins. For Ataru Miso it took four days to reach Sadiya from Ithun valley.

Articles of Exchanges

The Idu Mishmis also brought musk and Mishmi Teeta to Tibet and exchanged for salt and metals. They also procured half bred yaks called *Dzo* and *guns*. The Tibetan matchlocks were much sought after for its instantaneous effect as compared to the bows and arrows. These possessions, in addition, enhanced the man's standing in the society. Captain Mitchell (1883) notes that the Mishmis carried on a large trade in Mishmi teeta, poisons (*bih*) and mushrooms in exchange for which they obtained Tibetan goods from the valley of the Lamas like woolen goods, yak tails (for ritual costume of shaman), salt, swords, bowls and gongs. T.T. Cooper (1870) in his book – *The Mishmis*, also gives a vivid description of the Mishmis as keen traders. He observes while in his visit to a Mishmi village, the domestic kitchen use, viz. brass cup, plates, utensils, jugs, pots, etc. were all Chinese made. His accounts give insight into the economic and trade activities of the Mishmis in 19th century.

Needham (1899–1890) and J. Butler also reported of the cultivation of Mishmi teeta and its sale in Tibet along with animal skins. The *teeta* was a bitter root – 'a drug of great repute as a tonic and febrifuge',[7] greatly valued both in the north as well as south. In Tibet it was called *Duntsa* or *Shingtsa* which eventually found its market in China.[8] They also brought *gathewun* – an odiferous root, *manjeet* (madder), musk pod and grains. J.B. Goad lists the following articles traded between the Tibetans and the Idu Mishmis as follows:

> Musk deer pods Kasturi, Mishmi teetah, Elephant tusks procured from the Assam plains, Bees wax, Assam silks, slaves, Tibetan woolen clothes, Tibetan swords and spears, Mishmi bish or poison from aconite and brass and silver vessels called Dankey.[9]

Special woolen clothes from Tibet had stripes of different colours with cross marks on it. The Tibetans during their colonization of Dibang Valley in the dawn of 20th century had kept constant contact with their homeland and brought goods from Chimdro and exchanged them with Idu Mishmis along the Emra river.[10]

Trade Routes: North and South

North

In the north, the Idu Mishmis carried on a large trade in poisons, mushrooms, Mishmi teeta and dried fish, in exchange for which they obtained Tibetan goods from the valley of Lamas like woolen goods, beads, yak tails, salt, swords and gongs. The physical spaces in the form of natural mountain passes ('La' in Tibetan) across which these interactions took place connecting northwards to Tibet were as follows:

1. Andra pass in the North-West (12,000 ft approx.) – It was reached from Rinchenpung and Chimdro in Tibet into Mipi village in Mathun valley.
2. Yongyap pass (13,000 ft approx.) – Connected Chimdro in Tibet to Mipi village in Mathun valley.
3. Kangri Karo pass (18,494 ft approx.) – Led from Chimdro Chu in Tibet into Idu Mishmi country.
4. Aguia pass (17,000 ft) – It was located in the north of Dri valley. It led from Ruipu village in Rong Thod Chu (Tibet) in Zayul province into Dri valley.
5. Keya pass (15,600 ft approx.) – It lay in the North-East above the water source of Dibang river (*Taloh*). The pass connected Alupu in Zayul with the Idu Mishmi country.[11]

The above contentions could be corroborated by their references in oral traditions of the tribe. In the funeral chants the mythical soul is guided by the shaman through the Keya pass which is located in the North-East above the water source of Dibang river.[12] The Idu Mishmis of Mipi and Achuso have well remembered stories of trade as well as conflict with the Tibetans through Andra, Yanyap and Tsangkang passes. Rano Mihu of Anini is said to have visited the Tibetan villages number of times before independence to procure metals and beads.[13] The Mishmis maintained constant trade relation with the Tibetan merchandise directly or indirectly.

The Tibetan word for all the non-Buddhist in the Tibetan cultural zone is *Klopa or Lopa* meaning 'barbarian'. The Idu Mishmis of Mathun and Dri valley had old trade relations with the Tibetans of Rong To Chu. They were called *Trona Lopas* by Tibetans. The Tibetans were generally called *Pu* or *Lama*. The Ithun section of Idu Mishmi referred to them as *Tami*. Trade was conducted through all the mentioned passes.

The nature of trade with Tibet was quite flexible, in that great degree of mutual confidence was reflected. That the 'order for sword blades are given one year, executed the next and paid in the third year ...'[14] However, Bailey also notes that the Idu Mishmis were not allowed to enter inside the Tibetan villages. They were halted at the end and exchanges were thereby met.[15] The trading intercourse with the Tibetans was conducted by the Idu Mishmis of Mathun and Ithun valley, whilst the southern part was conducted by those in the foothills (*Chulikatta*). The eastern side of the Mishmis (Digarus and Mijus) also monopolized a bulk of trade between Upper Assam and Tibet which was transacted on barter terms. Dalton in his visit discovered that the southern tribes were keen traders and friendly with them while the northern part maintained aloofness and hostility.[16]

The Miju Mishmis lived in higher reaches and depended on Tibetan neighbours for supply of essential commodities. The accounts of Mr Wilcox (1827),

Dr Griffiths (1836), and Lt. Colonel E.A. Rowlatt (1845) attribute the Digaru with assuming 'independent airs'. This again was said to have been derived from their close proximity and dependence on Tibet. The hostility was ignited by their aversion to outsiders for fear of loss of resources. In 1872, Dalton also observed that:

> ... the Mishmis situated to the west of Du river are in close contact and trade with plains people and the British, whilst the people living in the east of it have much closer relation with the Tibetans whom they call Lamas ... .[17]

Besides, there are references of other passes such as the Tsangkang pass near Bruini and Abroka pass in the upper reaches of Upper Siang and Dibang valley.[18] The Abroka pass in the North-West of Idu country was also used by the Karko Adis. From the Idu Mishmis they bought coats (*Midi galuk*) in exchange for cattle and varieties of rice.[19]

In the first decade of 20th century this trade network was marred by Tibetan intrusion and colonization in Mathun and Dri valley in Dibang valley.[20] The Tibetan exodus into the Mathun and Dri valley started in 1902, especially through the Andra and Yongyap passes from Chimdro Chu (*Chu*-Tibetan word for river) in Tibet.[21] According to the reports they were forced to evacuate their abode owing to atrocities by the marching Chinese soldiers on the eastern Tibet. They thought of taking refuge in the south of their country prophesied as 'Land of promise-Pemako'. Bailey observes on the phenomenon:

> According to M. Bacot, the French traveler, this prophecy was to effect that, when their religion was persecuted in Tibet, the people should go to Pemako, where they would find a land where rivers flowed with milk, where crops grew without the necessity of any labour and whence their religion would spread over the whole world. In his book 'Le Thibet revolte' he states that the ravages of the Chinese soldiery on the eastern frontier caused a fresh migration in search of this land and he describes the villages deserted by the inhabitants who had fled from Chinese to seek this land of promise. This migration was probably responsible for the large number of Tibetans in the Dibang valley ... .[22]

Another cause of migration was the great flood in Yigrong valley in eastern Tibet and thereby destruction of their home. The immigrants were from Kham, Derge and Pome – all in southern Tibet.[23] Bhattacharjee cites 'famine' as the other cause of this migration.[24] Nyori quotes Bailey that, 'this Pemako was on the frontier of India and here they would find a land good to live in, their religion would revive and eventually spread throughout the whole world'.[25] It was because of this prophecy a number of Bhutanese had left Bhutan and settled in the lower Tsangpo valley in the beginning of nineteenth century.[26] Bhattacharjee calls them as 'Pobas'.[27] The intrusion continued as late as 1911–13, as attested by Major C. Bliss and F.M. Bailey.[28]

The migrating Tibetans passing through Andra and Yongyap pass started crowding in Mipido (Mipi) village in Mathun valley and Dri valley after pushing the Idu Mishmis forward.[29] Later, they started trespassing into Mihundo, Wanli, Angrimbolin, Elembro, Akobe, etc.[30] They brought cattle, women and children along with them. As a result, the Mipi village was deserted by Idu Mishmis.[31] In

1903, another 2,000 arrived from Kham, Derge and Pome in southern Tibet. Because of the resistance from the Idu Mishmis and previous Tibetan migrants, many of them bypassed the route and moving northwards to the source of Dri river, through Aguia and Keya pass, they again reached another Tibetan province in Zayul.

For the Tibetans, the inhabitants of high altitudes, it was not easy to survive in this new environment surrounded by hostile neighbours. Besides, the low altitude filled with wild animals and blood sucking flies worsened their continuation. In 1911, many of the families decided to return, leaving behind old, sick and children who were incapable of accomplishing the perilous journey back.[32] Bailey in his 1913 tour of Mathun and Dri valley found caves with bones and utensils of Tibetans who had perished on the return journey. The remaining Tibetans staying back had to pay twenty-five swords, twenty-five axe heads, two loads of salt, four rolls of woolen cloth and two Tibetan woolen coats; the total value between six hundred rupees.[33]

South

The Idu Mishmis maintained active trade with both the Tibetans of Alupu and Riupu in the north and Brahmaputra plains at Sadiya in the south owing to their strategic location. At the same time they maintained intra-tribe contacts with other Mishmi groups the Taroan and Miju, and inter-tribe with the Adis and the Khamptis. The Idu Mishmis had good relations of exchanges with the Khamptis even in the wake of Moamaria uprising against the Ahom monarchy. The main items procured through exchange from the Adi country were Mithun, fowls and pigs in return for Mishmi coats, Tibetan metal bowls, swords, helmets, handbags, etc. Ten coats were considered equal to the value of one cattle.[34]

The foothill, Idu Mishmis referred to as Chulikattas by the Ahoms also acted as intermediaries and organizers of trade between the highlanders known as Bebejiyas and the Adis of the Assam plain. The Bebejiyas (of Ithun valley) depended on their fellow Chulikattas and Adis for supply of Mithun. According to the colonial records they received 'commission' for the services they rendered.[35] However, in the traditional networks there was non-existence of so-called commission.

In order to reach Sadiya plains in the south they followed the downward course of Dibang river or descended through the Mayu pass (*Mayudia*). The Kuwei Dakhru pass at 14,365 ft connected the Ithun section (Bebejiyas) of Idu Mishmis with the Digaru Mishmis of Delei valley through Donli, Taloni Runli and Maunli villages.[36] Jeffrey noted that wool from Tibet was obtained by Bebejiyas through this route. The Tibetan goods from the north were further brought down to the Assam plains, Adi hills and Digaru Mishmi country through these southern passes. In the Assam plains, these passes were called as '*duars*'. In order to realize their basic requirements in the hills, the hill tribes would come down to the plains for trade and exchanges.

The Mishmis largely depended on the plains for import of salt, food grains, Mithun and metals (iron). Salt was not produced in the hills and hence the Idu

Mishmis had to come down through the southern passes (the salt route) to procure them. The important merchandise into Sadiya were textiles, their chief commodity of medicinal plants-Coptis teeta (*Aro),* poisonous roots, *Aconitum Ferox*, Pippali (*Awensi*), musk pods, bees wax, Tibetan goods hardware of silver and brass, Tibetan woolen clothes, ginger and chilies. They were carried in bamboo baskets and sold in Saikhowa market. The goods were chiefly exchanged for salt, cloth and *daos*.

In the Sadiya pillar inscription of 1687, Dihingia Bargohain recognizes the hills north of Sadiya as the territory of the Mishmis and as a tribute they were to offer four basketful of Mishmi teeta to the Ahom official in Sadiya – the Sadiyakhowa Gohain.[37] This testifies the Mishmi teeta as the main commodity of exchange at least from Ahom period. Salt was procured from the north as well as the south. The surrounding hill communities were brought into the complex trade network by products. A semblance of interdependence was visible in the permission to the Idu Mishmis to trade, particularly the latter's demand for salt.

The Ahoms observed that the Mishmis were keen traders and acted as liaison between Tibetans and Assamese traders. They brought into Assam plains Tibetan merchandise such as beads, metals and woolen articles which were in much demand. These goods were exchanged for salt and clothes. Therefore, Ahoms also felt it necessary to continue this trade. In order to facilitate this trade, various *hats* or markets were established in the foothills. Further, particular Idu Mishmi villages were asked to bring their goods to appointed Assamese families in Sadiya. These Assamese families were called *Soirengs*.[38] The system continued till the colonial period.

The Ahom administration was well aware of the fact that the Mishmis had trade monopoly in the Sadiya markets and had large volume of trade as investments in the plains. The Mishmis were dependent on Sadiya for supply of salt, clothes and metals. The trading facilities offered by Ahom Government were greatly appreciated by them.[39] Under the circumstances it might have well been thought unnecessary to grant *Posa* to them. The trading facilities were available for them as long as they maintained peace in the borders. In the event of violation and breach of agreement, an economic blockade or closure of markets were initiated.

Colonial Policy

In the nineteenth century the British Government inherited this complex network of trade activities in the plains. The initial conflict with colonial government had economic implications. The slaves who were crucial to their subsistence economy ran away and took refuge in the British territory. The economic imperative and demand for goods was crucial. Because the British territory provided an escape from the ties of bondage, the slaves would recurrently escape to British territory and greatly constrained their manpower resource as the British did not facilitate return of the slaves to their masters. Thence, the aggrieved masters would demand their extradition and upon refusal the conflict would take place.[40]

In order to facilitate the trade relations and more specifically to introduce their goods into the hills, the colonial government arranged for annual fairs (*Mela*) in Sadiya and Udalguri. The annual fairs usually commenced in winter with favourable weather to allow the hill tribes to participate. Thus, in 1876, the Sadiya fair recorded the visit of 3,000 tribesmen belonging to Miris, Mishmis, Khamptis and Singphos.[41]

Consequently, the British intended to allow Idu Mishmis to attend the fairs in Sadiya, who were also obstructed by Padam section of the Abors on the way.[42] Hence, the colonial administration resorted to prevent the Abors from crossing the Dibang river.[43] The administration was by supporting the Mishmis also supporting the cause of the plainsmen. The plainsmen of Sadiya dreaded the Abors and favoured the Mishmis. The plainsmen including Assamese, Khamptis and Marwaris were engaged in rubber tapping in the Mishmi hills and looked to Idu Mishmis for supply of hill products.

The major bulk of merchandise was forwarded from one point to another, i.e. from north to south and vice versa. Jeffrey in 1911–12 observed that Mishmis acted as middleman and carrier of trade between Assam and Tibet. The copper vessels, brass pipes, gongs, beads and medicinal plants were brought from north and exchanged for cattle, cloth, salt, money, etc. in the Assam plains. The silver was brought from the north and further traded to the Brahmaputra plains. Locally, it was used for ornamental purposes. J.B. Goad in 1874 observed that there was an arrangement of certain clans supplying goods to certain Assamese families in the plains.[44] He noted that the Meggah (*Mega*) clan brought their goods to Bettiah Ahom of the Sakang family in Kundil, the Mison (*Miso*) clan to Gobind Ahom at Singrigow and Lako Meddar (*Menda*) bringing their goods to Ghinborrah Ahom of Singrok family in Bajjalgow village.

In the 16th century, in order to facilitate the flow of hill products in the plains the Ahom Government had opened marts (*hat*) in the foothills, which was subsequently retained by the colonial government. Through these hill tribes in the north of Brahmaputra the Ahoms had procured copper and silver from China.[45] The Sadiya market in colonial regime was even visited by Burmese and Tibetan traders. The Mishmis had acted as middleman and porters for them. The British policy was to promote their goods into the hills and invariably to instil political slavery by manipulating the marts (Udalgiri, Sadiya, etc.) in the plains. The facilities and accommodations were arranged for different tribes in the fairs.[46] On the Sadiya fair, Ataru Miso, who visited the fairs number of times before 1947 narrates:

> In Sadiya, the shelters with compartments were constructed. Each tribe visiting Sadiya were assigned different compartments. But it could hardly be called a shelter as it housed plenty of lice. The Abors and Tibetans brought their goods. I communicated with them in my own language and through signs. The Tibetans coming from Walong used to bring musk, beads, woolen garments, etc. to the market. The Kotokis present there helped us in our transactions. In the evenings we spent watching British sepoys playing games. We used to stay there for two or three days and return back.

In 1875 the volume of trade by Idu Mishmis and Abors in Sadiya were assessed as:[47]

	Imports (In Rupees)	*Export (In Rupees)*
Abors	1,600	1,360
Mishmis	7,462–8	7,150

Similarly, the Sadiya fair in 1876 transacted ₹ 49,000 articles worth sold and ₹ 44,475 worth bought by Miris, Mishmis, Khamptis, Singphos and Adis.[48]

The flow of commodities and money currency into the hills colonial Assam plains brought a transition in tribal economy as well. The monetization of hill economy was thus a new feature in the colonial period. Through the sale of their articles, the money collected by Idu Mishmis was used for purchasing cattle from the Adis or the fellow tribe. W. Robinson also notes that, 'having sufficient sum of money procured they lay it out in purchasing buffaloes and country cattle'.[49] Some of the new articles of import in the colonial period included: (a) Scissors (b) Fishing hooks (c) Needles and thread (d) German silver bangles and beads (e) Norwegian knives (f) British woolen (g) Safety pins (h) Smoking pipes (i) Coarse tobacco (j) Burmese Cheroots (k) Rum (l) and Opium. The articles were deemed essential to be taken along in the expeditions and surveys to lure the hill tribes to cooperate.[50]

The policy of loose political control in the twentieth century was to bring the Mishmi hills closer to British administration and increase their trade with the Assam plains. The results were obvious, which changed the balance of trade between the north and south. The volume of trade with Tibet decreased and vanished completely after Indian independence in 1947. After the withdrawal of British the burden of developing the system of administration to its logical culmination was left to the free Indian Government. However, the independent India vary of Chinese intentions closed all the passes connecting the Idu Mishmi country with Tibet and China. Thus, the trade and cultural contacts of the Mishmis came to an end from the other side of the border.

The recent government initiatives of opening up old trade routes or the 'Look East Policy' should be rigorously pursued. The policy should not remain mere lip service and promise. It should be more development focussed than additional aims of political security all the time.

Acknowledgement

The paper is a reprint of the original paper published in Kumar, Amrendra Thakur, edt. (2013): *Proceedings of the North East India History Association (NEIHA) of 34th Session* held at Manipur University: 284–97.

Notes

1. George Dalton, 'Economic Theory and Primitive Society', *American Anthropologist*, Vol. 63, Issue 1, 1961, p. 47.

2. Ibid., p. 15.
3. J.B. Bhattacharjee, 'The Eastern Himalayan Trade of Assam in the Colonial Period', *Proceedings of North East History Association*, 1st session, Shillong, 1980, pp. 174–92; *idem*, *Trade and Colony*, NEIHA, Shillong, 2000; Sudatta Sikdar, 'Trade Fairs in Arunachal-Assam Border', *Proceedings of North East History Association*, 1st session, Shillong, 1980, pp. 158–73; Amrendra Kumar Thakur, 'Technology Aided Trade in Pre-Colonial Arunachal Pradesh', *Resarun*, Vol. 36, 60th Year Special Issue, Directorate of Research, Government of Arunachal Pradesh, Itanagar, 2011–12, pp. 7–14; *idem*, 'Reviving Indigenous Trade in Arunachal Pradesh: Some Aspects of Research and Action', in M. Sharma (ed.), *Economy of Arunachal Pradesh: Problems, Performance and Prospect*, DVS Publishers, Guwahati, 2008, pp. 112–23; *idem*, 'Trade and Culture: Some Reflections on Pre-Colonial Arunachal Pradesh', *Proceedings of North East History Association*, 27th session, Goalpar, 2007, pp. 198–209; *idem*, 'Polity of Pre-Colonial Arunachal Pradesh: Interactions in Trade, Culture, State and Buddhism', in S. Dutta and B. Tripathy (eds), *Buddhism in North-East India*, Indus Publishing Company, New Delhi, 2006, pp. 241–63; *idem*, 'Pre-Colonial Trade of Arunachal Pradesh: A Reconstruction of Economic History', *Resarun*, Vol. XXVII, 2001, pp. 17–27; Journal of the Directorate of Research, Government of Arunachal Pradesh, Special Issue on Golden Jubilee of the Directorate of Research, 2002; *idem*, 'Pattern of Pre-Colonial Trade and Polity Formations in Arunachal Pradesh: A Study of their Relationship', *Proceedings of North East History Association*, 21st session, Imphal, 2000, pp. 299–318; Todak Riba, 'Trade Practices and Trade Routes of the Galo of Arunachal Pradesh', *Proceedings of North East History Association*, 32nd session, Itanagar, 2012, pp. 235–44; Chhomu, 'Trade Practices of Monpas of Arunachal Pradesh: A Brief Study', *Proceedings of North East History Association*, 31st session, Tura, 2010, pp. 120–27 and S. Dutta and B.N. Jha, 'British Colonial Design Behind the Udalgiri and Doimara Fairs and its Impact Over the Monpas and Sherdukpens of Arunachal Pradesh', *Proceedings of North East History Association*, 20th session, Dibrugarh, 1999, pp. 305–16. This is a representative list of the publications on trade. These papers have provided directions and dimensions to the studies on trade in Arunachal Pradesh and its neighbouring areas.
4. Chitralekha Gupta, 'Trade and Markets of North-Eastern India: The Ancient Period', in Jai Prakash Singh and Gautam Sen Gupta (eds), *North East Archaeology*, Vikas Publishing House, New Delhi, 1991, p. 283.
5. Interview with Molla Milli, Shaman, Ashali, Lower Dibang Valley, 10 June 2003.
6. Field work, interview on 24 November 2003. Both are deceased during the time of writing.
7. Military Report on the Presidency and Assam District, Part II, 1931, p. 145.
8. F.M. Bailey, *Report on the Exploration on the North-Eastern Frontier*, 1913, p. 32.
9. Assam Secretariat Proceedings, File No. 189 J of 1874, p. 10.
10. Military Report, op. cit., p. 147.
11. Ibid., p. 134.
12. Interview with Mango Dele, village elder, 15 June 2003, New Elope, Lower Dibang Valley.
13. Narrated by Rano Mihu, Priest, Anini, Dibang Valley. He differentiates the colonial regime and Indian independence as period of *Lo-Imu* (white man) and Congress Government respectively.

14. R.F. Jeffrey, *Report on the Mishmi Mission*, 1911–12, p. 5.
15. F.M. Bailey, op. cit., p. 17.
16. E.T. Dalton, *Descriptive Ethnology of Bengal*, Asiatic Society of Bengal, Calcutta, 1872, Reprinted 1973, p. 13.
17. Ibid.
18. H.E. Richardson, *Tibetan Precis*, Government of India Press, Calcutta, 1945, p. 116.
19. Sachin Roy, *Aspects of Padam Minyong Culture*, Directorate of Research, Government of Arunachal Pradesh, 1960, Third Reprint 1997, p. 33.
20. Military Report, op. cit., p. 145.
21. Ibid., p. 147.
22. F.M. Bailey, op. cit., p. 2.
23. Tarun Kumar Bhattacharjee, *The Idus of Mathun and Dri Valley*, Directorate of Research, Government of Arunachal Pradesh, Shillong, 1983, p. 32.
24. Ibid.
25. Tai Nyori, *History and Culture of the Adis*, Omsons Publications, New Delhi, 1993, p. 76, as quoted by F.M. Bailey, *No Passport to Tibet*, The Travel Book Club, London, 1957, p. 35.
26. Ibid., p. 35.
27. T.K. Bhattacharjee, op. cit., p. 32.
28. F.M. Bailey, op. cit., p. 17.
29. T.K. Bhattacharjee, op. cit., p. 32.
30. Ibid., pp. 32–33.
31. Military Report, op. cit., p. 134.
32. Ibid., p. 147.
33. F.M. Bailey, op. cit., p. 3.
34. Sachin Roy, op. cit., p. 152.
35. Assam Secretariat Proceedings, File No. 189 J of 1874, p. 11.
36. Sachin Roy, op. cit., p. 32.
37. Lakshmi Devi, *Ahom-Tribal Relations*, Lawyer's Book Stall, Guwahati, 1968, p. 238.
38. Assam Secretariat Proceedings, File No. 189 J of 1874, p. 12.
39. S.L. Baruah, *A Comprehensive History of Assam*, Munshiram Manoharlal Publishers Pvt. Ltd., New Delhi, 2007, p. 375.
40. For details, see Amrendra Kumar Thakur, *Slavery in Arunachal Pradesh*, Mittal Publications, New Delhi, 2003 and *idem*, 'Colonial Penetration versus Indigenous Reaction: Slavery, Abolition in Northeast India', *Northeast Researches*, Vol. I, March 2010, pp. 82–91.
41. S. Dutta and B.N. Jha, op. cit.
42. Assam Secretariat Proceedings, File 189 J of 1874, Major W.C.S. Clarke in a letter to the Personal Assistant to the Commissioner of Assam, dated 17 October 1873, p. 1.
43. Assam Secretariat, File No. 123 J, Advance to Nizamghat and Bomjur in consequence of the threatened advance of the Abors across Dibang, 1881, p. 1.
44. Assam Secretariat Proceedings, File No. 189 J of 1874, p. 12.
45. S.L. Barua, op. cit., p. 230.
46. M.L. Bose, *History of Arunachal Pradesh*, Concept Publishing House, New Delhi, 1997, p. 33.

47. Assam Secretariat, File No. 123 J, Advance to Nizamghat and Bomjur in consequence of the threatened advance of the Abors across Dibang, 1881, p. 22.
48. J.B. Ganguly, Presidential Address, 7th session, NEIHA, J.N. College, Pasighat, 1986, published in *Studies in History, Economy and Culture of Arunachal Pradesh*, edited by S. Dutta, Himalayan Publishers, Itanagar, 1998, p. 259.
49. Verrier Elwin, *India's North-East Frontier*, Directorate of Research, Shillong, 1965, p. 314.
50. Military Report, op. cit., p. 146.

References

Assam Secretariat Proceedings, File No. 189 J of 1874, p. 10.

Bailey, F.M. (1913). Report on the Exploration on the North-Eastern Frontier, p. 32.

Baruah, S.L. (2007). *A Comprehensive History of Assam*, Munshiram Manoharlal Publishers Pvt. Ltd., New Delhi.

Bhattacharjee, Tarun Kumar (1983). *The Idus of Mathun and Dri Valley*, Directorate of Research, Government of Arunachal Pradesh, Shillong.

Bose, M.L. (1997). *History of Arunachal Pradesh*, Concept Publishing House, New Delhi.

Dalton, E.T. (1872). *Descriptive Ethnology of Bengal*, Asiatic Society of Bengal, Calcutta.

Dalton, George (1961). 'Economic Theory and Primitive Society', *American Anthropologist*, 63(1): 47.

Devi, Lakshmi (1968). *Ahom-Tribal Relations*, Lawyer's Book Stall, Gawahati.

Dutta, S. and B. Tripathy (eds) (2006). *Buddhism in North-East India*, Indus Publishing Company, New Delhi.

Elwin, Verrier (1965). *India's North-East Frontier*, Directorate of Research, Shillong.

Ganguly, J.B. (1986). Presidential Address, 7th session, NEIHA, J.N. College, Pasighat, published in *Studies in History, Economy and Culture of Arunachal Pradesh*, edited by S. Dutta, Himalayan Publishers, Itanagar, 1998, p. 259.

Gupta, Chitralekha (1991). 'Trade and Markets of North-Eastern India: The Ancient Period', in Jai Prakash Singh and Gautam Sen Gupta (eds), *North East Archaeology*, Vikas Publishing House, New Delhi, p. 283.

Military Report of Presidency and Assam District (1931). Part II, pp. 145–47.

Nyori, Tai (1993). *History and Culture of the Adis*, Omsons Publications, New Delhi.

Roy, Sachin (1997). *Aspects of Padam Minyong Culture*, Directorate of Research, Government of Arunachal Pradesh, Third Reprint.

Sharma, M. (ed.) (2008). *Economy of Arunachal Pradesh: Problems, Performance and Prospect*, DVS Publishers, Guwahati.

Thakur, Amrendra Kumar (2003). *Slavery in Arunachal Pradesh*, Mittal Publications, New Delhi.

—— (2011–12). 'Technology Aided Trade in Pre-Colonial Arunachal Pradesh', *Resarun*, 36, 60th Year Special Issue, Directorate of Research, Government of Arunachal Pradesh, Itanagar, pp. 7–14.

Todak, Riba (2012). 'Trade Practices and Trade Routes of the Galo of Arunachal Pradesh', *Proceedings of North East History Association*, 32nd Session, Itanagar.

6

Idu Mishmis' Social Worlds

Animals, Humans and Spirits

AMBIKA AIYADURAI

Like many indigenous people, the Idu Mishmis do not make a distinction between the human world and the natural environment and for them all nature is 'one', including the world of 'spirits'. Idu Mishmis constantly engage with animals and spirits during farming, hunting wildlife or slaughtering domesticated animals. Idu Mishmis believe that spirits take care of domesticated animals (*mitu-sipa*) and wild animals (*golon*) and this belief is so strong that spirits are often talked about as if they are people too, respecting and being fearful of them. For example, when I asked what will happen if women eat wildmeat? An old lady in Anini (Dibang Valley) told me '*golon humko maarega* (*golon* will beat us)', and that *golon* watches people from afar.

Idu Mishmi's social world is a network of their association with humans, animals and spirits. The presence of several spirits (Appendix 1) in farms, homes, forests and mountains and the significant role of these spirits is reflected during harvesting, healing rites, funerals and birth ceremonies. Vidyarthi (1963) proposed a concept of 'nature-man-spirit' complex. In his research among the Maler tribe of Bihar (India), he showed that the Maler is part of a world where three components (nature, humans and spirits) are independent and mutually complementary. This, according to him, is an interaction of necessity arising from the fact that the Maler interacting closely with nature is part of both religious and social organizations, similar to the Idu Mishmis. Shamans (*Igu*) have an important role as mediators between these worlds, and this makes them a central icon in religious practices and beliefs of the Idu Mishmi society (Chaudhuri, 2008). *Igus* are respected for their services during funerals, births, farming, hunting and slaughtering of domestic livestock. Idu Mishmis credit the spirits for all the events that happen in their lives and believe that their lives are ultimately controlled by spirits. The spirits, both benevolent and malevolent, are believed to rule their lives. Therefore, Idu Mishmis act in accordance with the obligation to give, to receive and to pay in a reciprocal way through a complex network of exchanges that exist between the animals, spirits and the Idu Mishmis (Figure 1).

In this work, I aim to highlight Idu Mishmi's relations with animals and spirits and how Mishmi's social world is part of a complex human-animal-spirit cosmology. I will start this chapter by providing a brief review of the theoretical ideas of human relations with animals, followed by a description of Idu Mishmi's relations with animals, and spirits. I will discuss the practice of wildlife hunting, especially hunting rituals and taboos and how Idu Mishmis engage with the spirits through animals, both wild and domesticated. The Idu Mishmi's participation with the spirits during wildlife hunting and slaughtering of domestic livestock is one example of how worlds of the Idu Mishmis, animals and spirits overlap with each other.

Figure 1

Thematic Representation of the Idu Mishmi's Social World

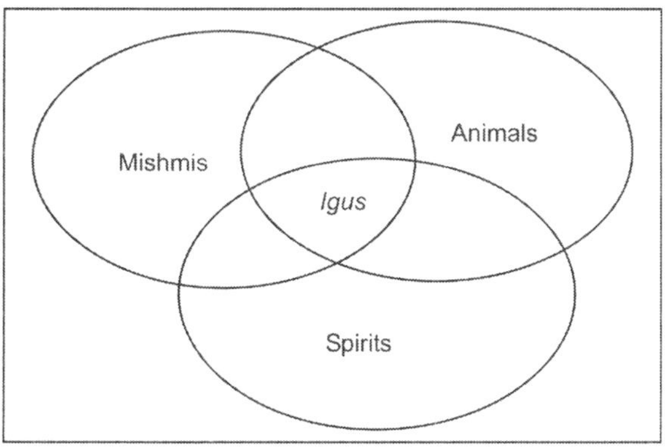

Secondly, I will discuss the role of women in hunting. Though women are prohibited from hunting wild animals or slaughtering domestic livestock, they still must follow taboos. The role of animals among the Idu Mishmis is crucial from cultural, commercial and conservation perspectives. The Idu Mishmi's relation with animals becomes particularly interesting from a conservation point of view as the Dibang Valley is witnessing conservation-related activities since the tiger cubs rescue operations that took place in 2012. Finally, I provide a brief account of the wildlife law in India that prohibits all forms of hunting and conclude with a short discussion on the impact of this law in Arunachal Pradesh.

Humans and Animals

There are various ways of perceiving human-animal relationships (Knight, 2004; Manning and Serpell, 1994; Morris, 2000). From hunter-gatherers, pastoralists, and agriculturists, up to industrial societies, the relationships between human and animal have changed tremendously. Animals can be worshipped or considered as kin; they may be loathed as evil spirits, and are slaughtered for food or offerings (Knight, 2004; Manning and Serpell, 1994). Human perception of animals in the contemporary world is also complex, where animals may be employed as entertainers in circuses, have become objects to gaze at in zoos, have become research subjects and also to considerable care and concern as pets (Bouissac, 2010; Franklin, 2006; Franklin, 2002). I focus on Ingold's work to discuss the role of animals among hunting societies and his suggestion that the relationship between humans and animals changed among the agro-pastoral cultures. I continue with a critique that Oma makes of Ingold's claims. I will show that human-animal relations are multilayered and have been changing with the transformation of human societies. It is this point that I want to consider in the case of the Idu Mishmis.

Ingold (2000) examines the changing relationship between humans and animals, specifically among the hunter-gatherers, pastoralists and agriculturalists. His claim is that hunter-gatherers' relations with animals is one of trust and reciprocity, in which hunter-gatherers feel a sense of kinship and have a trusted relation with the animals, while among the pastoralists, animals are considered as slaves. In his article, 'From trust to domination: an alternative history of human-animals relationship', Ingold explains that hunter-gatherers are basically collectors of whatever nature has to offer and they see their surroundings as 'alive' and inanimate objects as having life (2000: 50). In order to survive, they have to maintain relationship with animals, in the form of respect and due consideration. Using the example of the Cree Indians, he shows that people believe that animals intentionally present themselves to the hunters to be killed. The hunter, in return, must follow certain behaviour so that the soul of the animal is released to become another animal, which the Cree Indians see as a 'rite of regeneration' (2000: 67). Similarly, while reindeer hunting among the Yukaghirs of Siberia, it is believed that the animals offer themselves to a hunter (Willersley, 2007). When animals come to the traps, they are being 'given' or 'offered' and when they are chased and killed, for example by hunting with guns, it is equivalent to 'taking' without permission'. The Cree Indians of northern Canada, writes Ingold, believe that animals intentionally present themselves to the hunter to be killed (Ingold, 1986). He writes that failing to observe the proper, respectful procedure during hunting and during post hunting (butchering, consumption and disposal of bones) is important among indigenous societies (Ingold, 1986; Tanner, 1979).

If proper conduct is not followed, animals will not return to the hunters in their subsequent trips. This notion of reciprocity between humans and animals, Ingold believes is because hunter-gatherers depend on one another for food and these exchanges between humans and non-humans are integrated into 'cosmic economy of sharing' (2000: 44). On the contrary, the relationship of pastoralists and farming communities with animals is not of trust but of domination, says Ingold (1994). Herdsmen and farmers control their animals using whip, spur and hobble to inflict force and pain on them to make the animals behave in a certain manner. Therefore, domesticated animals are like 'slaves' under the control of humans (Ingold, 1994: 17).

This claim is challenged by Oma (2010), who sees Ingold's point of view as an oversimplified account of human-animal relationships. 'Can we see this as a universal model?', asks Oma. According to Oma, the basic assumption of Ingold is that hunter-gatherers look at animals not as individuals but as animal groups. Knight (2005) also makes this point that hunters' relations with animals are not at the individual level and they do not get familiar with the individual animals as the farming and pastoral societies do, who have connections and feelings attached to individual animals. The daily associations with individual animals give rise to mutual familiarity and trust with animals among agro-pastoral societies, whereas hunters will not get another chance to familiarize themselves with any particular animal. Therefore, although there may be an ideology of hunters having a relationship of 'trust', in fact they do not get a chance to build that trust. Trust building is possible only with domesticated animals, which results in these animals becoming docile and cooperative, for which in return humans provide food and care. Because of this reciprocity, says Oma, animals give up their autonomy for the humans to take charge of their lives. Oma, in fact turns around Ingold's argument that hunting to husbandry is not signified as a shift from 'Trust to Domination' but instead from 'Domination to Trust' (Oma, 2010: 177). Human-animal relations, therefore, cannot be simplified as either trust or domination. Instead she suggests that human-animal relations can be seen as a 'social contract'. The idea of a contract is a tool to examine human-animal relations as terms of engagement where there are a variety of roles, duties, responsibilities and obligations that people follow to maintain this relation. This point is made very well by Brian Morris (2000) who observed among the people of Malawi, that contrasting approaches to animals can coexist and people of Malawi have an ambivalent attitude to animals. On the one hand, farmers in Malawi see wild animals as destroyers of crops and as competitors. Wild animals are seen as having more power than humans. On the other hand, wild animals are a source of meat, medicine, various materials (e.g. skins used as mats) and as a subject of cosmological significance (Morris, 2000). This dual understanding of animals supports the argument made by Oma that viewing human-animal relations too simplistically is a mistake.

Among the Idu Mishmis trust and reciprocity seems to be more prevalent than domination. In the absence of herding or pastoral practices, Idu Mishmi's relations with animals are limited to wild animals in the form of hunting and trapping and with the semi-domesticated cattle, called mithun, which takes a central position in the Idu Mishmi lives. In this work, I provide a brief description of Idu Mishmi's relations with animals, both domesticated and wild. The role of animals among the Idu Mishmis is crucial from cultural, commercial and conservation perspectives.

Mishmi: A Brief Introduction

Mishmi is one of the 26 major 'tribal' groups of Arunachal. There are four subgroups recognized within the Mishmi (Idu, Digaru, Miju and Deng).

According to the Mishmi, they address the members of other Mishmi groups as their brothers and recognize each other as belonging to one major 'tribe' of Mishmi. Each subgroup has several clans that are known to disperse along the rivers and tributaries. Mishmis see themselves as a separate ethnic group from their neighbours the Adi, who belong to the Tani group. Tani group consists of Adi, Nyishi, Apatani, Tagin and Hill Miris tribes of Arunachal, who have a common ancestor, Abotani, the primal ancestor of all these tribes. Each subgroup of the Mishmi have their own primal ancestors (*Nani Initaya* for Idus, *Amik Matai* for Mijus and *Jamalo* for Digarus).

Among Mishmi scholars, there are different opinions about the status of the Mishmi. One of the senior Mishmi told me that all Idu, Miju, Digaru and Deng are different 'tribes' whereas another Mishmi scholar, who did his PhD among the Idu Mishmi, claims the groups to be 'subtribes'. In the archives, however, Mishmis are reported to be divided into 'clans' without any reasons for labelling them as clans (Mitchell, 1883). The Mishmis themselves, however, recognize separate apical ancestors, hence the term 'clan' does not seem appropriate. Idus and Digarus have language similarities but socioculturally Digarus has more affinity with the Miju and Deng Mishmis.

All the Mishmis are believed to have migrated from Burma following the course of the Lohit river (Bhattacharjee, 1983). But there are different claims about their migration routes; according to Baruah (1988), Idu Mishmis migrated from Tibet. Constant fighting and feuds separated them from each other. Miju Mishmis believe that they migrated from Burma.

Wildlife Hunting

Hunting among the Idu Mishmis is a part of an ancestral way of life and is a cultural practice. Men undertake hunting for subsistence, trade[1] and for crop protection. Shifting cultivation *(mipu mrann)* results in burning of forest patches on the mountain slopes. This opens up the land to be cultivated and facilitates regrowth of new plants that attracts animals. During shifting cultivation, villagers are in constant watch for animals that raid crops. Villagers lay different types of traps around the farm boundary to protect the crops (Appendix 2). Maize (*ambo*) and millet (*yamba*) are the major crops grown in these plots, along with a variety of vegetables (*anapra*). Bears (*ahun*), wild boars (*aamme*) and monkeys (*aame*) are reported to raid the crops during the harvest period (June–July).

Long-distance hunting trips especially ones that are undertaken for musk deer (*ala*), takin (*aakru*) and other ungulates are often carried out in the mountains. Hunters in Dibang Valley move uphill and cross mountains towards the Sino-Indian border for musk deer hunting. Animals such as barking deer and wild boars, monkeys, and bears are some of the animals commonly hunted closer to the villages or when they raid crops especially during harvesting maize (see the list of animals found in Dibang Valley in Appendix 3). Hunting is carried out both alone, in small groups or with trusted partners[2] (other village men). Hunting in groups of two or more is usually carried out during long distance trips, especially to the snow-covered areas for takin and musk deer. It is for safety reasons that they go in groups or with partners as hunting up in the mountains is a risky activity. Sometimes, hunters die due to accidents such as land or snow slides, falling off cliffs or getting injured by animal attacks. Such accidents during hunting periods are attributed to the curse of the forest spirits or because of lack of proper observations of taboos and as a curse/wrath of spirits when taboos are not observed.

According to hunters, winter (November to February) is the best season to hunt, as the high altitude animals come down in search of food when the vegetation gets covered by the snow, compelling animals to move to lower altitudes or near the foothills. Hunters prefer this season also because they need not travel very far to look for animals. Hunting in winter season is not only less tiring but there is also more time for trekking and camping as there is no farm-related work during this season.

Dibang Valley district is known for the Himalayan musk deer, *Moschus chryogaster* (*aala*). Musk pods are the scent glands of male musk deer, which are in demand in international markets because of its use as perfume. One way of searching for musk deer is to smell the rocks. The rock would smell of musk if a male animal (only males have these scent glands) had rested on it. The smell of musk is strong and remains on the rock for hours. One of the hunters said that this animal carries 'gold', by which he meant musk pods, which has a high market value, both in local and in international markets. The cost of a pod is around ₹ 20,000–30,000 (300–450 USD) per *tola.*[3] Meat is consumed and musk pods *(aalaapee)* are sold quickly. The pods are not used locally but are sold to *marwaris,*[4] which are then exported illegally to international markets and used in making perfumes. Another animal that is hunted for trade-related purposes is the black bear. It is targeted for its gall bladder from which bile is extracted and used in traditional Chinese medicine. It is sold locally for ₹ 5,000 (75 USD) per *tola*. The demand for soft and waterproof otter skins is high in the international trade and each skin is sold for ₹ 8,000–10,000 (120–150 USD) to buyers from outside the region, sometimes even from Myanmar.[5] The duration of the hunting trip varies with the species targeted. For musk deer, takin and black bears, hunters camp around 10 days or longer including travel time and search time.

Hunting Methods

Hunters use traps, guns and catapults to hunt and trap wild animals. Traps (*udru/drepa*) are made from bamboo, cane, plant fibres and small rocks (Appendix 2). In addition to that, metal wires are used which are bought from the market to make traps. Boys frequently use catapults mainly to hunt birds, squirrels and sometime bats, whereas frogs are manually captured from the ponds. Serrated leg-hold metal traps are used for capturing otters and the traps are set on the riverbanks in the evenings. These traps are left overnight and checked the following morning. There are special traps (*adapo*) for capturing rodents that are set around granaries to protect the grains. Canopy traps (*adadi*) are set for capturing small birds and small mammals in the canopy; other traps (*singrimbra, aayembya*) are designed for the ground-dwelling birds like pheasants and for large mammals.

Bows and arrows (*ilyipra-ipita*), cross-bows (*ilyipra-ticuga*) and poison-arrows (*mrala)* were commonly used in the past. Paste from a tuber of a high-altitude herb, *Aconitum ferox* (*mra*) is applied on the arrow tips which makes it powerful enough to kill a large animal. The paste is prepared away from the house for the safety of family members. Care is taken not to touch the paste with the fingers and poison arrows are placed high up near the ceiling out of the reach of children.

In gun hunting, the animals are searched and pursued. Guns are both locally made and bought in the market, usually purchased from Tezu town (capital town of Lohit district) and sometimes in Dibrugarh and Tinsukia (Assam). In Dibang Valley, the types of guns used are the double-barrel breech loading gun, (DBBL), single-barrel breech loading gun (SBBL), rifles and shotguns. The Government of Arunachal began issuing gun licenses in the 1950s for protecting crops and for personal safety against wild animals. But the arrival of guns in Arunachal goes back to the British administration. Guns were the 'political presents' or 'political gifts' given to village headmen by the British for their assistance and alliance (Bailey, 1912; Mainprice, 1945). The local Idu Mishmi gunsmiths then replicated these guns resulting in the proliferation of small arms. Guns over time have become a symbol of prestige. Furthermore, the road connectivity has increased accessibility to sophisticated weapons and ammunition.

Dogs are taken as companions on hunting trips to chase the prey. Hunters have to be alert and follow the dogs. Once the prey is spotted the dogs bark and chase the prey towards hunters, who shoot the prey.

Hunting Rituals and Taboos

The Idu Mishmis do not take hunting *(anji)* casually. Hunters (*anjiya*) equate hunting to a spiritual activity with many taboos *(aangien)* that need to be observed carefully. Taboos are observed before, during and after hunting. Hunting kits are prepared that contain essential items, such as rice, dal, salt and bedding (Appendix 4). These materials are useful for both subsistence during hunting and also for performing rituals. Women are forbidden from touching the kit (see the section on 'Women and Wildlife Hunting').

Aambo, a type of generic ritual that is performed to ask for success and safety in any endeavour, is performed by an *Igu* at a hunter's house before the trip. If the hunting is planned in a group, then one of the group members performs the ritual at his house. During this ritual, hunters pray for animals and for their own safety. An *Igu* slaughters a chicken and its blood is offered to the spirits. In exchange for this offering, the *Igu* asks for success in hunting. Hunters leave very early in the morning before the sunrise. Once they reach the hunting grounds, a symbolic gate (*la-ro*) is prepared towards the direction of their movement. A short prayer is chanted by one of the hunters before crossing this symbolic gate. Hunters camp near a large tree or a rock, close to a water source like rivers and streams. They also stay in a cave at night to protect themselves from cold weather. *Yiu* is offered to the spirits *ani anjuli zinu* and *aba abroya,* spirits associated with forests and ancestral spirits and they pray for a good hunt. Leaf cups filled with *yiu* fixed to a stick are placed either near a tree or on a rock carefully. Over this a piece of brass scratched by *dao* or a machete. A piece of brass metal is the most important item that hunters carry. In general, the base of the cartridge is used for the ritual. In the olden days, hunters said they had brass spoons from China. Hunters make a small hole in the bag to tie the metal piece to permanently attach it to this bag. Only brass *(tamba)* is preferred and no other metal such as iron, copper or aluminum. This ritual is called *yiu chi amphoo* or *yiu ampho.*

The gate is a symbolic boundary between the village and the hunting zone. Crossing the gate indicates the beginning of actually hunting which requires the hunters to follow certain rules. This is seen as the beginning of a 'spiritual' journey in which hunters engage with forest spirits and animals. This is a kind of 'rite of passage' where the transition is made to a spiritual world and where the Idu Mishmis enter into a 'social contract' with animals and spirits, as Oma (2010) suggests. This constructs the idea, in the Idu Mishmi world-view, that there are certain duties, responsibilities and rights that hunters have towards animals and the spirits, founded on terms of engagement that depend on trust, reciprocity and mutual assistance. Hunters share food and drinks with the spirits symbolically (a piece of meat or a leaf cup filled with rice beer) as one would share with other people. Both animals and spirits are seen as socially and spiritually equivalent and believe that they have feelings like people. Therefore, rituals are performed for animals like the way people perform rituals in their homes. Rites always accompany hunting trips as a mark of respect and reverence to animals. Offerings are made with the expectation that the spirits will be pleased and provide more animals in the subsequent trips, like the reciprocal relations similar to the observations made by Ingold and Bird-David.

Spirits are considered as active agents and wild animals in this hunting zone are believed to be owned by a mountain spirit, *golon. Golon* is the most important spirit for hunters and this mountain spirit is believed to live on the high mountains and in thick forests. People believe that *golon* is the one who 'supplies' animals to the hunters so when there is a successful hunt, an offering has to be made to *golon*. If not, *golon* gets angry and could cause accidents to both hunters and consumers of the hunted animal, and may cause severe illness to either the hunter or his family members. Hunters have duties, responsibilities and rights, which need to be followed to let *golon* offer the animals to hunters. One of the duties of hunters is to address the animals in a proper way with special names. Wild animals have two names: one is the Idu Mishmi name that are used when they are in the village and other is the name that hunters know and use only during hunting, an exclusive secret knowledge that only hunters have.

Secret Codes of Hunters

During the hunting trip, hunters follow a 'moral code' of conduct, for example, getting angry, abusing or cursing someone, as well as swearing, is strictly avoided. Hunting is considered a risky activity and, therefore, cracking jokes or ridiculing someone is against the rules. If proper conduct is not followed, hunters believe they could face accidents or suddenly fall sick during the trip. There are unique code words for animals which only hunters know and use during hunting, especially in the high mountains (Table 1). It is important for hunters to have knowledge of these codes; not knowing them would have negative consequences. Hunters who do not know these code words are advised to be silent and not call out incorrect names, which could anger the spirits. Animals have unique names that should be used during hunting trips, for example, *aala* (musk deer) will be called *tambe aaroku-chi,* which means meat of the high mountains. The secret code names for animals also indicate the kind of habitat and forest types in which the animals are found that reflects hunter's knowledge of the landscape.

Table 1
Code Words for Animals Used by Hunters

English Names	*Idu Mishmi Names (Idu)*	*Hunter's Codes*
Goral	Aamee	azo chi (the one on rocky slopes).
Takin	Aakrun	ambeka chi (tambe-meat, kachi-big). The one with big meat.
Musk deer	Aalaa	tambe aaroku chi (tambe-meat, aaro-high mountain, ku-place). Meat of the high mountains.
Wild boar	Aamme	enabolon (enambo-nose, lo-long). The one with long nose.
Barking deer	Maanjo	tambre-shu (shu-small). The one with small meat.
Serow	Maaren	aazo-chi/ama-dro (ama-tree name, dro-two horns).
Bear	Aahun	ikku-zongon (meaning not clear).
Monkey	Aame	aadichi (aadi-above). The one who lives on the trees.
Satyr tragopan	Peba	apipa-chi (apipa=leaves). The one who lives near leaves.
Sclater's monal	Pidi	aaron chi pra-a (aaron-mountain). Bird of the mountains.
Himalayan monal	Chendan	kaanei (colour).
Blood pheasant	Cheekhoo	brunshu (brun=leg, shu-red). The one with red legs.
Tiger	Ketrebo	ketrebo-stripes.
Snake	Kanlon	kanlon-long.
Elephant	Enonohoya imina gila/chunlaa	enonohoya-both sides, imina-tail, gila-chunlaa (having). The one having tail on both sides.

After a successful hunt, the hunter performs a ritual *(aanphun aangi)*. This ritual symbolizes making a payment in the form of meat and a piece of metal to the spirit *golon*. '... *hum ko duum dena padta hai*', said a hunter, which translates to 'we have to make a payment or pay a price'. A small piece from the ear of the hunted animal, inserted into a bamboo fork, is planted on a nearby tree or on the ground. Using a *dao,* the hunter scrapes the brass metal *(aanphoodi/paao yute/seekhi yute*) over the dead animal and recites a chant, which roughly translates as:

> 'This animal has been killed. When I come again, please give more animals. One who rears the animal, let more animals be produced. Give us more animals whenever we come again. We have given you the payment, do not disturb or harass the one who eats this meat and the one who hunted this animal. The restrictions will be observed and do not follow us and watch us whether we did the right thing or not. Do not disturb us'.

Fresh meat is carried back if hunters are within a day's trek from the village but the meat is smoked if the hunters are far from the village. Meat is smoked over a make-shift platform in the forests. Carrying fresh meat is heavy, therefore smoking helps to make the meat lighter and easier to carry. Smoking also prevents the meat from rotting if the distance to the village is great and it can then be stored for longer periods of time.

When the hunter returns home, there is a restriction on things he can or cannot do for five days, but only if it was a successful hunt. There are taboos on eating onion *(elompran)*, garlic *(eloni)*, mushroom *(akupi)*, a herb called *marsana* and fermented soyabean *(aadulo chhin)*. Men stay in a separate room and sex is forbidden. They are not allowed to receive water and tea prepared by women who are menstruating. Hunters avoid attending funerals and avoid washing clothes. Wildmeat is cooked in a separate room (men's room – the first room of the house) or in a separate shed outside the house. Only men participate in cooking this meat and there are also separate utensils for cooking wildmeat. The animal skulls are mounted on the walls of the men's rooms. Displays of wild and domesticated animal skulls are a common sight amongst the Idu Mishmi (Figure 2). Wild boar, takin, serow, goral and asiatic black bear are some of the animals whose skulls are mounted on a neatly made bamboo frame which is found in almost every rural Idu Mishmi house. Animal skulls and jaws of animals are symbols of hunting and sacrificial rites. They are carefully arranged on the skull board. Skulls remind hunters of special events related to hunting or slaughtering of animals. There is a spatial separation between domesticated animal skulls and wild animal skulls. Two wooden poles (*amuni*) separate wild and domesticated animals. It is believed that a spirit (*ashu-andro* – spirit of the house) resides on this wooden pole, who keeps an eye on people's behaviour and the observation of the taboos. Animal blood collected during slaughtering of animals is applied on the skulls making the skulls black in appearance over a period of time. Men take pride in the skull board and maintain the skulls by cleaning and applying blood on them. Women are forbidden from touching these skulls. They are not even permitted to walk near the board and as a practice women who are menstruating take a detour around the hearth to go to the next room, rather than walking past the skulls. Women's menstrual blood might be considered to be the blood of life, as opposed to the blood of death spilled in hunting. Therefore, they should not be in contact with each other. There is separation of men and women, domesticated and wild animals, wild animal meat and domesticated animal meat.

Figure 2

Display of Wild Animal Skulls in an Idu Mishmi House

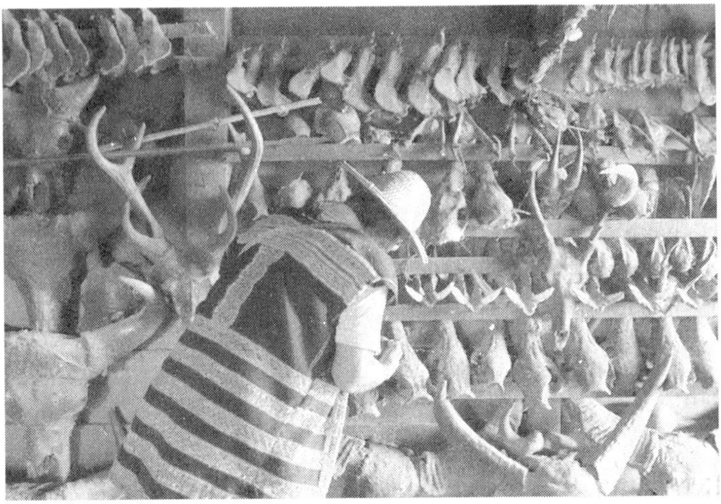

Idu Mishmis observe a separation between the notions of the domesticated and the wild. The spirit that own wild animals is different from domesticated animals. Mithuns roam freely between forests and village but their skulls are displayed separate from wild animal skulls. Therefore, they are considered domesticated animals. Mithuns are associated with male power and men take care of them and they are used in slaughtering during ceremonial sacrifices. Relationship between animals and male identity is prominent among the Idu Mishmis and this is displayed in the way the men maintain the wild animals, as well as the way mithun skulls are maintained. While hunting of some animals is permitted, provided one follows the taboos, there is a restriction of hunting of animals such as tigers and hoolock gibbon. Killing a tiger is the worst crime a man can commit and a strict taboo is observed not only by the hunter and by his family members but also by the entire village. The reasons for this is because according to Idu Mishmi mythology, Idu Mishmi and tigers were born to the same mother and were siblings, the tiger was the elder brother and the human, the Idu Mishmi, was the younger brother. This myth and why the Idu Mishmi are forbidden to hunt tigers was told to me by an *Igu* from Etaabe village:

> One day, a younger brother hunted a deer and left the deer with his elder brother and went to the jungle to collect firewood. On his return, he was terrified to see his brother eating the meat raw. He told his mother that 'his elder brother is a tiger. If he can eat the raw meat, then one day he will eat me too'. This became a serious concern that the tiger could be dangerous.
>
> A plan was made by their mother to have a competition between the two brothers. The one who crossed the river and reached the other side of the bank first would kill the other. Tiger decided to swim across the river, whereas the Idu Mishmi took the bridge. The tiger was the first to reach the bank. When the tiger was about to come out of the river, however, the mother threw an ant nest on the tiger's body to

prevent the tiger from winning. To get rid of the ants, the tiger went back to the water and scratched itself on a rock. The Idu Mishmi, meanwhile, reached the bank and shot the tiger with an arrow. Thus, the tiger died and its body floated in the river and was swept away to a faraway place. After several years, a bird saw the bones of the tiger scattered on the riverside. The bones were white and bright under the sunlight. The bird thought these were eggs and sat on them. It is believed that the large bones became a tiger. From the tiny bones, emerged leopard, leopard cat, clouded leopard and civet cats. This is a story of a tiger being born again and therefore tigers are not killed.

According to the Idu Mishmi, tigers could be only killed or trapped when there is a loss in property or for personal safety. If a tiger is killed, an elaborate ritual *(taamaamran)* over five days is conducted with restrictions on both the family members and the villagers. There are five clans (*meme, umpo, mena, mischi and misiwo*) of Idu Mishmis who are exempted from performing this ritual. Members of these clans are believed to be the descendants of the first priest of Idu Mishmi, *Sineru,* therefore, they do not have to perform this ritual but killing of tigers is still a taboo for them.

Women and Wildlife Hunting

Women are forbidden from wildlife hunting but they indirectly follow certain regulations and observe taboos to ensure success in their husband's hunting attempts. Hunting is avoided when the wife is menstruating. Once the men are out for hunting, women eat only in the evening when the men would have probably reached their destination. Eating food before would lead to failure in hunting. While the hunters are away, no rituals are held at home. Performing a ritual would mean the slaughter of a chicken and hence the spilling of blood. Since no blood may be spilled at home when the hunters are away, therefore, when women are menstruating, men avoid going hunting.

There are some general rules that women follow with respect to hunting. They are not permitted to touch guns and arrows when they are menstruating. Women are prohibited from eating wild meat, mostly of large mammals and pheasants. However, I was offered wildmeat. As I do not belong to the Idu Mishmi group, I was exempted from these prohibitions. The only wild meat that Idu Mishmi women are permitted to consume are fish (*anga*), birds (*pra*) and farm rats (*kachingo*). If women eat meat of mammals or pheasants, they observe taboos *(angein)* until the new moon phase. The major taboos include not washing clothes, not eating garlic, ginger and mushrooms. However, the younger women do not seriously follow these restrictions.

A strong link to menstrual blood is expressed through these taboos that segregate all aspects of hunting (hunting trips, weapons, food, animal remains) from menstruation and sex. The taboos place the blood from menstruating woman and the blood of hunted animals opposite to each other. Mixing of these bloods is seen as very dangerous and, therefore, menstruating women or their contact with weapons is prohibited.

Although the wild animals and domesticated animals are seen as separate, their worlds are interlinked in the Idu Mishmi society. Wild animals hunted are believed to be offered by the spirits; Idu Mishmis, in return are obliged to offer domesticated animals to the spirits in exchange for the wild animals. Chickens, pigs and mithuns are slaughtered during rituals (e.g. healing rituals and funerals) in the family or at the village level. Animals, in the Idu Mishmi world provide an important link in creating social relations. Like a social contract, spirits also enter social relations with human beings. Mithuns are offered as bridewealth during marriages and reproduction. Live animals are also offered to the deceased during funerals. Chickens and piglets are buried with other things in the tomb. Idu Mishmi funerals are elaborate[6] and it is believed that once the deceased reaches the 'other world', he/she needs these animals to be reared in the new world. Social relations with spirits are mediated through blood of animals, either through slaughtering of domesticated animals or by hunting of wild animals.

Domesticated Animals

Domesticated animals that Idu Mishmi rear are pigs (*ili*), mithuns (*sha/saa*) and chicken (*eto*). They are reared for meat, for trade and for ceremonial slaughtering. Pigs are always stall-fed in a separate section either below the bamboo house standing on stilts or adjacent to the house in pens (*ili apa*). Mithuns are never stall-fed but let out in the nearby forests to roam freely. There are gates to prevent them from entering the villages. Chickens are kept in a compound attached to the house. Idu Mishmi's engagement with domesticated animals (mithuns, chickens and pigs) and subsequent slaughtering during rituals is part of a complex system of their association with certain spirits. Of these domesticated animals, mithuns are considered important and play a vital role in the local cultures of Idu Mishmi as well as among other indigenous groups of North-East India.

Mithun: A Ceremonial Cattle of the Idu Mishmi

Mithun (*Bos frontalis*) is a semi-domesticated cattle and a descendent of the guar, the Indian bison (*Bos gaurus*). Mithun are not found truly in the wild, though some animals have become feral and can be found roaming in the wild. It belongs to the bovine family and is widely distributed in the hilly areas from the Arakan Hills and Chin Hills of Burma (Mayamar) through the Chittagong Hills of Bangladesh, North-East India and Bhutan. In northern Yunnan, it is called *drung, dulong* or *gayal* (Simoons and Simoons, 1968). This is the most prized and culturally valued domesticated animal in the region where they are found. This is true not only for the Idu Mishmis, but for all other cultural groups of North-East India.

Mithuns are reared for purposes of slaughtering during ceremonies (marriages, funerals, political gatherings) and as payment as fines, but not for milk or ploughing. Mithuns are never stall-fed but are left out in the forests and reared under free ranging conditions. Mithun play a crucial role in exchange of wealth between relatives (during marriages and conflict resolution) and during ceremonies for dead or propitiation of spirits. The slaughtering of mithuns as offerings to spirits is considered the most significant form of exchange deemed possible between humans and spirits and this renders it the sacrificial animal par excellence (Aisher, 2005). During the *Reh*[7] festival, shamans chant hymns (*shacha*) when a mithun is sacrificed. The hymns tell about the origin of mithun and help to lead the soul of the slaughtered mithun to the place of its origin. For a ritual like *amraseh* (to cure illness, for protection of family, overall peace and prosperity), pigs and chickens are usually slaughtered, which are less prestigious as sacrificial animals than the mithun.

Mithuns indicate status for the owner and are used as bride wealth during weddings. Mithuns are economically a valuable animal each costing around ₹ 40,000–50,000 (650–750 USD). The wealth of a person is gauged by the number of mithuns he owns. Women do not own mithuns. Wealthy Idu Mishmi men can afford to give more bride wealth and have more wives.[8] According to the customary law, willful killing of mithun, similar to killing tigers, is a serious crime, equivalent to murder and there is a heavy fine of 3–5 mithuns on the accused (Chaudhuri, 2008). When needed, mithuns are used to pay fines and settle disputes. Mithun heads were used as a currency for bartering any item in the past (Cooper, 1873: 190). Skulls of wild animals were not used in the same way as domesticated animal skulls. The owner of mithuns constantly maintains contact with the animals by providing them with salt.[9] Men walk into the forest or village periphery with a bag of salt and call 'Ho! Ho! Ho!' One by one mithuns appear from the forest and lick the salt from owner's hand or from the pile of salt left on the rocks. Owners can identify their mithuns by the slit marks made on the ear lobes. Salt is offered to mithuns to inculcate loyalty. Salt, in both the cases, is a metaphor for 'being loyal' to the provider of the salt. After sacrificing, mithun skulls with the horns intact are placed on the sacred skull board in the first room, similar to the wild animal skulls.

Idu Mishmi's Relation with Animals

The relationship between humans and spirits is acknowledged through rules and regulations in the form of fear and respect and mediated by blood. This fear is manifested in the way wild animals, their meat and their skulls are treated. There seems to be a strict separation of wild and domesticated animal skulls on the board. Skulls of domesticated animals and wild animals are never displayed together but placed apart with the separation of a border pole (*amuni*). Mixing of meat from wild animal and domesticated animal is also seen as a taboo, therefore never cooked together.

Similar to what Bird-David (1990) say about Nayakas, among the Idu Mishmi, there is a 'process of exchange' between the spirit world and humans in the form of reciprocity (Bird-David, 1990). *Golon* is the most important spirit for long-distance hunters like the musk deer hunters and is believed to be the caretaker of wild animals (animal master). *Golon* should be respected so that they will continue to provide wild animals to hunters and in exchange, hunters make a payment in the form of metal and a small meat piece from the dead animal. Like *golon*, there are other spirits that offer health and wealth on a reciprocal basis. For example, *aasaan* is the spirit who looks after large trees and the forest near villages. Cutting these large trees may annoy these spirits. In general large trees are not cut unless they are used for house construction. People cover the stumps of a chopped tree with mud and trees to prevent *aasaan* from seeing it. There are trees that should not be cut with out performing rituals. People act in accordance with the obligation to give, to receive and to pay. For example, an act of reciprocity is followed when the meat is shared. The person who shoots the animal gets the head. The rest is shared with others. Idu Mishmi have strong ethics when it comes to sharing of both domesticated animal meat and wild animal meat. During the *Reh* festival, meat is widely distributed to relatives and guests, similarly during weddings and funerals; sharing of meat between villagers is crucial. Therefore wildlife hunting or slaughtering domesticated animals are taken seriously. A complex network of exchanges exists between these two worlds in which slaughtered domesticated animals and hunted wild animals are part of this exchange process. This exchange process resonates with Ingold's work (1986) among the Cree Indians that slaughtering and hunting activities such as these are important to keep the 'world renewing process' going and helps to continue the circulation of energy. If certain taboos are not observed, there could be disruption in the circulation of energy causing illness, death, bad harvest and hunting failures.

The relations of the Idu Mishmi with animals are undergoing transformation because of the changes in their socio-economic situation. Cultural taboos, which were believed to prevent over-hunting of animals, are being eroded due to the changes in the belief system. Idu Mishmi who convert to Christianity do not follow hunting taboos. For example, those who have converted stop displaying animal skulls in their huts and have abandoned the ritualistic way of worshipping spirits, however, they continue to hunt. Idu Mishmi who are inclined to the Hindu groups have stopped slaughtering mithuns and some even stop eating meat. Those who are converted look down upon the Idu Mishmi beliefs as primitive practices. The changing Idu Mishmi-animal relations also need to be seen in the light of wildlife conservation practices brought in by the conservation NGOs and the State Government.

Wildlife Conservation

Wildlife hunting is an age-old practice in Arunachal. For people who live in and around forests, wildlife is an important resource – food, additional income, and as cultural practices. Hunting in North-East India is also a traditional leisure activity for various tribal communities, politicians and bureaucrats also take part in modern day hunting (Aiyadurai, 2011). I have met doctors, engineers and school teachers who participate in hunting, among not just Idu Mishmi, but in general among other indigenous people in North-East India.

However, the Indian Wildlife Protection Act, 1972 (GoI, 1994) prohibits hunting[10] of virtually all large wildlife. The main objectives of the act are (a) Prohibition of hunting of wild animals, birds and plants (b) setting up and management of national parks and sanctuaries (c) control of trade and commerce in wildlife and wildlife products. The Indian Wildlife Protection Act is a comprehensive law for protecting India's biodiversity and it prohibits hunting of any species, as well as trade in trophies, animal parts and their derivatives. A complete ban on hunting of wildlife species has affected the livelihood of many communities in India (Dutt, 2004; Gadgil and Malhotra, 1998). The law was created in response to the rapid decline of India's wildlife and in response to international pressure on forests and wildlife conservation. With the creation of these protected areas, the subsistence activities of the local people were deemed illegal; for example, according to the Act, inside a national park,

> No person shall destroy, exploit, or remove any wildlife from a National Park or destroy or damage the habitat or any wild animal[11] or deprive any wild animal or its habitat within such National Park except under and in accordance with a permit granted by the Chief Wildlife Warden and no such permit shall be granted unless the State Government, being satisfied that such destruction, exploitation, or removal of wildlife from the National Park is necessary for the improvement and better management of wildlife therein, authorizes the issue of such permit. No grazing of any livestock shall be permitted in a National Park and no livestock shall be allowed to enter except where such livestock is used as a vehicle by a person authorized to enter such National Park.

In remote areas such as North-East India, however, hunting still continues, largely due to its linkages with local customs (Aiyadurai, 2011). The awareness of these laws on the ground is extremely low and in even places where people are aware of this law hunting continues because people do not see hunting as unlawful and take pride in hunting. The North-East region of India was cut off from the rest of the country for decades. Lack of road connectivity and basic infrastructure has made this region immune to active governance for decades and therefore, implementation of laws has been rather weak. In addition to this, due to lack of economic alternatives or any other means of sustaining livelihoods in the region, people continue to hunt and trade wildlife parts to earn extra cash (Aiyadurai et al., 2010; Hilaludin et al., 2005). Setting up of protected areas has been one of the major approaches to conserve wildlife. Arunachal's forest department has set aside large tracts of land for conservation as national parks and wildlife sanctuaries. There are eight wildlife sanctuaries, two national parks which are also designated as tiger reserves in the state. The forest department's engagement with the local communities for wildlife conservation has been slow and for a long period, this was not a priority for the government. NGOs (World Wide Fund for Nature, Wildlife Trust of India, Nature Conservation Foundation) have taken an active role in conservation and have set up sites for research and conservation inside protected areas, viz. in Pakke Tiger Reserve and Namdapha Tiger Reserve.

Commentary

Over the last few decades, there has been a serious concern globally over wild animal extraction and research that indicate that hunting is leading to the extinction of wildlife populations (Bennett and Robinson, 2001). Places such as

Arunachal have been subjected to a growing academic interest among ecologists and conservationists recently. Wildlife research increased in the region, partly, because of including the region within the Eastern Himalaya 'biodiversity hotspot' (Myers et al., 2000). Conservation laws and NGOs consider local people to be harmful to the wildlife species in their areas, and natural resource extraction by local people to be unsustainable, resulting in the decline in forest cover and wildlife population (Datta et al., 2008; Hilaludin et al., 2005). Community-based conservation projects have been implemented in the state to wean hunters away from hunting, as well as awareness programmes and the setting up of schools and health programmes to encourage local communities to participate in conservation programmes (Datta, 2007). For places such as Arunachal where the relation between local people and animals is complex, and where people are dependent on the animals and forests resource for daily subsistence, any conservation measure needs to take into account the people's attitude to natural resources, especially people-animal relations. There have been no sociological studies of these community-based conservation projects to examine the impact on the ground.

How the local people react to the conservation efforts by the state, NGOs or the biologists emerge from their relations to animals and this required detailed examination. The cultural linkages of the Idu Mishmis to the natural world and their subsistence-based livelihood, place them in opposition to the approaches of the state's conservation practices. In this chapter, I explored the Idu Mishmi's relations with animals and spirits and how Mishmi's social world is part of a complex human-animal-spirit cosmology. Understanding taboos reflects Mishmi's world-view where animals and spirits are seen as part of their world and it is necessary to engage in exchange processes with them through reciprocal relations for the well-being of the Mishmi society. I focussed on their hunting rituals and taboos and how these practices are in conflict with the laws.

The visiting wildlife researchers gather information about the tigers, takin, bears, their habitats and their prey, but not adequate information about people's beliefs and perceptions to the animals and forests. With the increase in the presence of state and conservation NGOs in Dibang valley, one needs to enquire if the local sociocultural concerns and indigenous knowledge of the wildlife and forests are incorporated in both research and conservation programmes, so that wildlife conservation works for both wildlife and local people.

Appendix 1
List of *kheenus* (Spirits)

Golon	resides in high mountains
Beka	dwells in rivers and lakes
Asa	dwells in high and huge trees
Amra ji	causes the landslides and gorges
Khepa	dwells in deep forests, caves and deep gorges
Athru	strangles woman during birth
Asa-shu	moves around the villages at night
Mitu-sipa	guardian of animals
Ambhu	responsible for blood dysentery
Emo	responsible for epilepsy
Ithrie	responsible for respiratory troubles
Chidi	responsible for leprosy
Wha	responsible for gangrene
Apomo	responsible for bodily diseases
Irushu	responsible for accidental fire in the house
Apimishu	spirit of land
Andro-zinu	spirit of the house
Manu	spirit of agricultural land

Source: Lingi, M. (2011). Origin of Idu Mishmi, *Reh Souvenir*, Roing

Appendix 2
Kinds of Traps

Traps	*Species Targetted*	*Materials*	*Images*
Sekhimbyaa	Wild pig, bears, barking deer	Metal wire, bamboo	
Aayembya	Pheasants, musk deer	Wires, bamboo	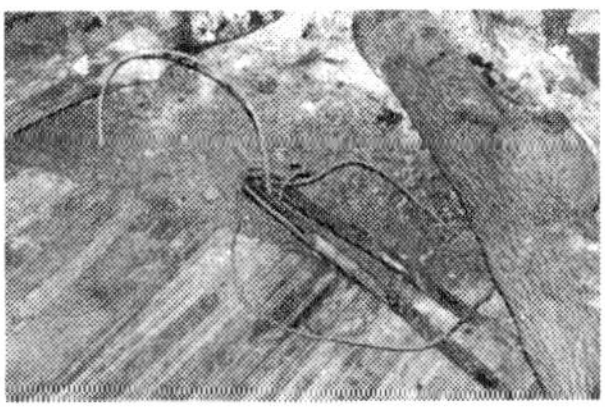

Cont'd...

...Cont'd

Athombra	For ground dwelling birds, specially for pheasants	Plant fibre, nylon ropes	
Singrimbra	Large and small birds	Metal and bamboo	
Drepran	Rodents, birds	Stone, bamboo	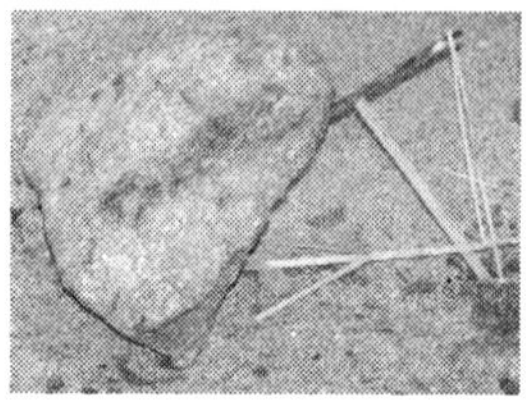
Aadadi/aadapo	Birds	Bamboo	
Boon	Bears	High altitude bamboo	
Koogi	Birds	Nylon rope, bamboo	

Cont'd...

...Cont'd

Adapo	Mainly rats		–
La	Large mammals	Bamboo, ropes	–
Thron-dra	Small mammals, monkeys	Logs, bamboo	–

Photographs taken in Dibanag Valley and Anjaw.
Illustration by Avinish Chauhan.

Appendix 3
Animals in Dibang Valley and their Local Names

Common Name	*Scientific Name*	*Idu Name*
Hoolock gibbon	Hylobates hoolock	aame epaan
Rhesus macaque	Macaca mulatta	aame
Himalayan musk deer	Moschus chryogaster	aalaa
Indian muntjac	Muntiacus muntjak	maanjo
Black barking deer	Muntiacus crinifrons	maanjo imbu
Sambar	Cervus unicolour	maachcho
Takin	Budorcas taxicolour	aakrun
Serow	Naemorhedus sumatrensis	maaren
Red goral	Naemorhedus goral	aamee
Wild pig	Sus scrofa	aamme
Red panda	Ailurus fulgens	aiminjini
Asiatic elephant	Elephas maximus	aantaan
Asiatic black bear	Ursus thibetanus	aahun
Sun bear	Helarctos malayanus	aahun tho
Asiatic jackal	Canis aureus	Maabun
Wild dog	Cuon alpinus	Apupru
Tiger	Panthera tigris	Aamra
Common leopard	Panthera pardus	aamra ipungoo/Aamra kichi
Clouded leopard	Neofelis nebulosa	–
Leopard cat	Prionailurus bengalensis	Aachango
Small-clawed otter	Amblonyx cinereus	Aawronron
Yellow-throated marten	Martes flavigula	Aakonkon
Civet sp.	–	Aapoee
Chinese pangolin	Manis pentadactyla	Aakrusoron
Indian porcupine	Hystrix indica	Aasonn
Himalayan crestless porcupine	Hystrix brachyura	Aali
Orange-bellied himalayan squirrel	Dremomys lokriah	Aadaa
Squirrel sp.	–	Aanache
Squirrel sp.	–	Aadaka
Flying squirrel sp.	–	Kaame
Himalayan rat	Rattus nitidus	Kaachigon
Bat sp.	–	Aaphun

Appendix 4
Items in Hunter's Kit

Items	*Idu Names and Remarks*
Gun	aagere
Cane backpack	entonn
Bamboo basket with lid	boiyyon
Tarpaulin	earlier people stayed in cave now use tarpaulin for making tents
Bullets	ipitaa
Metal piece	aanphoodi /paao yute /seekhi yute
Match box	aamikhe. In earlier days, flint stone (aalondo/aamise) and plant fibre (aalunso) from aalombo tree was used to make fire
Machete	eyenchen/dao
Quiver	elaann aann
Quiver lid	eroti
Arrow	epitaa
Bows	elipra (mrayata)
Poison	mra (aconite)
Rice	kebra
Salt	pra
Chilly	inchi
Tea leaves	phla
Rice beer	yiu in bamboo tube
Bag	akuchi

Notes

1. Species like musk deer and black bear are hunted for the musk deer pod and gall bladder respectively. These are in demand in the international market for their use in the traditional Chinese medicine. Meat is locally consumed and shared among the villagers but sometimes sold in the market if the village is closer to the town or the village has good road connectivity.
2. Some hunters develop trusted partnership with other hunters and tend to carry out trips only with them. For example, Angeche, my host and a medical doctor (earlier posted in Anini, and now based in Roing) made several successful trips together. Compatible working relations and mutual trust help in planning the trip as both have the knowledge of the routes and know each other's strengths and weaknesses.
3. *Tola* (10 gms) is a unit to measure gold and musk pods are also measured in the same unit.
4. *Marwaris* are traders from Rajasthan who run businesses in Arunachal and other parts of North-East India. They frequently travel in and out of the state and engage in trading in animal parts like musk pods.
5. In Anjaw district, Idu Mishmi reported that men from Myanmar give leg-hold metal traps to the local people for trapping otters.

6. A small hut like structure is prepared in the burial site where the deceased is laid on the bed, covered with a blanket. A small shelf is filled with food, alcohol, clothes, utensils, lantern, matchbox, salt, torch light, rice, millet and things that will be required for the deceased to start a new life. Live chickens and piglets in a bamboo cage are buried along with other items.
7. *Reh* festival is celebrated to worship '*Nani Inyitaya*'. All Idus are believed to be the children of *Nani Inyitaya*. *Reh* is held at a personal capacity and at the village level. Nowadays, the festival has become institutionalized and celebrated from 1st–3rd February. At a personal level, Idus believe that one *Reh* ritual should be carried out to get Nani Inyitaya's blessings once in a person's lifetime.
8. Mishmis are polygamous. Men are allowed to have more than one wife.
9. Cattle, both wild and domesticated, have a strong appetite for salt. In the wild, locations of salt-licks are permanently imprinted in their memory and they return to these locations when they require salt. Mithun calves are fed with salt by the owners when they are born and as adults, mithun either return to the village for salt or the owners frequently visit them in the forests to feed them salt. It is also a way of creating loyalty and bond between owners and mithuns.
10. Hunting here means capturing, poisoning, snaring, or trapping of any wild animal.
11. Wildlife refers to non-domesticated animal species, including all plants, fungi, and other organisms that grow or live wild in an area without being introduced by humans. 'Animal' includes mammals, birds, reptiles, and their young ones, and in case of birds and reptiles, their eggs.

References

Aisher, A. (2005). 'Through "Spirits": Cosmology and Landscape Ecology among the Nyishi Tribe of Upland Arunachal Pradesh, Northeast India', PhD Thesis, University College London, UK.

Aiyadurai, A. (2011). 'Wildlife Hunting and Conservation in Northeast India: A Need for an Interdisciplinary Understanding', *International Journal of Galliformes Conservation*, 2: 61–73.

Aiyadurai, A., N.J. Singh and E.J. Milner-Gulland (2010). 'Wildlife Hunting by Indigenous Tribes: A Case Study from Arunachal Pradesh, Northeast India', *Oryx*, 44(4): 564–72.

Bailey, F.M. (1912). Report on the Work of the Dibang Column – Mishmi Mission (1911–1912), IOR/MSS/EUR F 157, 304 (d). British Library, London.

Baruah, T.K. (1988). *The Idu Mishmis*, Directorate of Research, Government of Arunachal Pradesh, Itanagar.

Bennett, E.L. and J.G. Robinson (2001). *Hunting of Wildlife in Tropical Forests: Implications for Biodiversity and Forest Peoples*, World Bank, Washington, D.C.

Bhattacharjee, T.K. (1983). *Idus of Mathun and Dri Valley*, Directorate of Research, Government of Arunachal Pradesh, Shillong.

Bird-David, N. (1990). 'The Giving Environment: Another Perspective on the Economic System of Gatherer-Hunters', *Current Anthropology*, 31(2): 189–96.

Bouissac, P. (2010). *Semiotics at the Circus*, De Gruyter Mouton, New York.

Chaudhuri, Sarit K. (2008). 'Plight of the Igus: Notes on Shamanism among the Idu Mishmis of Arunachal Pradesh, India', *European Bulletin of Himalayan Research*, 32: 84–108.

Cooper, T.T. (1873). *The Mishmee Hills: An Account of a Journey Made in an Attempt to Penetrate Thibet from Assam to Open New Routes for Commerce*, H.S. King and Co., London.

Datta, A. (2007). 'Protecting with People in Namdapha: Threatened Forests, Forgotten People', in G. Shahabuddin and M. Rangarajan (eds), *Making Conservation Work: Securing Biodiversity in This New Century*, Permanent Black, New Delhi, pp. 165–20.

Datta, A., M.O. Anand and R. Naniwadekar (2008). 'Empty Forests: Large Carnivore and Prey Abundance in Namdapha National Park, North-east India', *Biological Conservation*, 141(5): 1429–35.

Dutt, B. (2004). *Biodiversity, Livelihoods and the Law: The Case of the Jogi-Nath Snake Charmers of India*, Wildlife Trust of India (WTI), New Delhi.

Franklin, A. (2002). *Nature and Social Theory*, Sage Publications, London.

—— (2006). *Animal Nation: The True Story of Animals and Australia*, Universty of New South Wales Press, Sydney.

Gadgil, M. and Malhotra, K.C. (1998). The Ecological Significance of Caste: In Social Ecology (ed R. Guha), pp. 27–41. Oxford University Press.

GoI (1994). *The Indian Wildlife Protection Act, 1972* (as amended upto 1993), 2nd edition, Natraj Publishers, Dehradun.

Hilaludin, R., R. Kaul and D. Ghose (2005). 'Conservation Implications of Wild Animal Biomass Extractions in Northeast India', *Animal Biodiversity and Conservation*, 28(2): 169–79.

Ingold, T. (1986). *The Appropriation of Nature: Essays on Human Ecology and Social Relations*, Manchester University Press, UK.

—— (1994). 'From Trust to Domination: An Alternative History of Human-Animal Relations', in A. Manning and J. Serpell (eds), *Animals and Human Society: Changing Perspectives*, Routledge, London and New York, pp. 1–22.

—— (2000). 'From Trust to Domination: An Alternative History of Human–Animal Relations', in T. Ingold (ed.), *The Perception of the Environment: Essays on Livelihood, Dwelling and Skill*, Routledge, London and New York, pp. 61–77.

Knight, J. (2004). *Wildlife in Asia: Cultural Perspectives*, Routledge/Curzon, London.

—— (2005). *Animals in Person: Cultural Perspectives on Human-Animal Intimacy*, Berg, Oxford.

Mainprice, F.P. (1945). Tour Diary of F.P. Mainprice, ICS, Assistant Political Officer, Lohit Valley, November 1943–May 1945. The British Library, London.

Manning, A. and A. James Serpell (1994). *Animals and Human Society: Changing Perspectives*, Routledge, London.

Mitchell, J.F. (1883). *Report (Topographical, Political and Military) on the North-East Frontier of India*, Superintendent of Government Printing, Calcutta, p. 367.

Morris, B. (2000). *Animals and Ancestors: An Ethnography*, Berg, Oxford.

Myers, N., Mittermeier, R.A., Mittermeier, C.G., da Fonseca, G.A.B., and Jennifer Kent (2000). Biodiversity Hotspots for Conservation Priorities, *Nature* volume: 403, pp. 853–58.

Oma, Armstrong (2010). 'Between Trust and Domination: Social Contracts between Humans and Animals', *World Archaeology*, 42(2): 175–87.

Simoons, F.J. and E.S. Simoons (1968). *A Ceremonial Ox of India: The Mithan in Nature, Culture, and History*, University of Wisconsin Press, Madison, WI.

Tanner, A. (1979). *Bringing Home Animals: Religious Ideology and Mode of Production of the Mistassini Cree Hunters*, St. Martin's Press, New York.

Vidyarthi, L.P. (1963). *The Maler: A Study in Nature-Spirit-Man Complex of a Hill Tribe in Bihar*. Bookland Private Limited, Calcutta.

Willersley, R. (2007). *Soul Hunters: Hunting, Animism, and Personhood among the Siberian Yukaghirs*, University of California Press, Berkeley.

7

Aspects of Marriage System of the Idu Mishmi Tribe of Arunachal Pradesh

JUSTINA UMBREY AND RAZZEKO DELLEY

Marriage has never been static monolithic institution. Overtime the role of man and women within marriage has changed. Social views on multiple wives, interracial relations and divorce has changed. Yet certain elements of the institution of the marriage have remained relatively constant for centuries. For instance, marriage has always entailed more than a mere contract. Marriage involves not just the couple, but extended family members, non-blood relations, etc. Edmund Leach (1955) argued that no one definition of marriage can be applied to all cultures.

The cultural definition of marriage in a society clearly establishes the boundaries of the social duties, rights, privileges and legal protection of the groups of kin involved when a man and woman enter into a marriage relationship. Typically, marriage is viewed in most cultures as an agreement, indeed a legal contract, between different kin groups. This agreement, or contract, may go on in time even though one, or both, of the marriage partner dies. A substantial part of the definition of the marriage relationship in many cultures is concerned with the exact ways that rights to property and services are transferred between the kin groups of the husband and wife. This concern almost always is focussed on keeping or obtaining an equality, or balance, of such rights and property between kin groups represented by a wife and husband.

Bertrand (2009) believes where a marriage is fruitful and both parties to it are reasonable and decent, the expectation ought to be that it will be life long, but not that it will exclude other sex relations. A marriage which begins with passionate love and leads to children who are desired and loved ought to produce so deep a tie between a man and woman that they will feel something infinitely precious in their companionship, even after sexual passion has decayed, and even if either or both feels sexual passion for someone else.

Bertrand (2009) sees that for a civilized man and woman to be happy in marriage is possible, although number of conditions must be fulfilled. He believes that, there must be a feeling of complete equality on both sides; there must be no interference with mutual freedom; there must be the most complete physical and mental intimacy; and there must be a certain similarity in regard to standards of values (It is fatal, for example, if one values only money while the other values only good work). Given all these conditions, he believes marriage to be the best and most important relation that can exist between two human beings. If it has not often been realized hitherto, that is chiefly because husbands and wives have regarded themselves as each other's policemen. If marriage is to achieve its possibilities, husbands and wives must learn to understand that whatever the law may say, in their private lives they must be free.

Marriage is traditionally a religious ceremony and it is more of a sacred duty rather than a matter of personal convenience or arrangement. Traditionally marriage was a sacred duty towards family and the community and there was no recognition of personal factors, interests and aspirations of the parties to the marriage. The modern concept wherein marriage is considered as a contractual obligation between the parties to the marriage and which cherishes around the fulfilment of personal goals of mutual adjustment and material gains in life.

Most of the Idu Mishmis are settled in Dibang Valley and Lower Dibang Valley districts of Arunachal Pradesh. A few have settled in Lohit and some other in eastern part of East Siang district of the state. They are broadly divided into Mithus and Midus according to the way they pronounce the Idu language while speaking.

Idu Mishmis call themselves as '*Kera-aa*', meaning 'children of *Kera*' where *Kera* is regarded as a remote ancestor of the tribe. In later part, the Ahoms and the Britishers first divided them into Idu Mishmis and Bebejiya Mishmis. Midus and Mithus were named as Idus and 'Bebejiyas' respectively. Thus, as the time passed, whole tribes were known as Idus. The word Idu originated from the word 'Midu'.

The Institution of Marriage

The institution of marriage is an important aspect of sociocultural set-up in every society. The Idu Mishmis are not exception to this. The institution plays an important role in reflecting the culture of the people and assuring the continuity of the society. Among the Idus a person is considered incomplete without marriage. The one who fails to marry is seen as socially inferior and a failure in life. Polygyny is a matter of pride for a man who practices it. The man who has more than one wife is considered having greater capacity in terms of control over a large number of family members and in terms of wealth to feed them.

Marriage in the Idu Mishmi society is not an isolated phenomenon. It is embedded in other aspects of life like religion. The man and woman who remain unmarried during lifetime are believed to descend after death into a place called 'Akungo-alo'; an underworld full of dense jungle.

Myths and Legends of Marriage in the Idu Mishmi Tribe

According to the myth of the Idus, the first marriage took place between *'Arume Mili'* and *'Atome Liru'*. *'Maselo Zinu'*, the creator, first created *'Arume Mili'*. According to the myth, *'Arume Mili'* conceived by exposing herself to the wind, and in the meantime she got married to *'Atome Liru'*. They gave birth to *'Thro Liru'*, the mother of the whole humanity. Many children were born to her; first son was *Ano*, the forefather of *Meechas* (non-tribals), the second son was *Assa*, the forefather of other tribes and then *Kera* the last son, the forefather of the *'Kera-aas*,' the present-day Idu Mishmis.

Idu Mishmi families are patriarchal in nature. The females in the household except the mother have no distinct voice in the marital affairs. After the consent of father and brothers of the girl, marital bond is established. *'Yaku-bri'* is a term equivalent to the word marriage in English. The word, distinct in itself, means marrying a woman. The whole meaning of the marriage itself is marrying a woman, as a wife. Nobody calls *'Meya-bri'*, marrying a man because the whole marriage process is initiated actively by the male side. Passive role is played from the side of the girl. After the marriage, wife is expected to be loyal to her husband in every aspect.

Abechi (The Process of Negotiation) and *Yaku-Bri* (Marriage)

The Idu Mishmi community is a network of relations related by kinship, the consanguinal and afinial kinship are given equal value. Therefore, the paternal uncle and maternal uncle are equal in the relation and so are their children. They practise clan exogamy in their marriage system. One is expected to marry an *'Achimi'*, non-relative and not an *'Ana'*, relative. Marriage usually takes place only when the bride and the groom descend from clans unrelated to each other on both paternal and maternal sides. One has to examine all the branches of kinship, generation by generation.

'Abeya', the negotiator, plays a major role before and after the marriage. The negotiators are those persons who have knowledge about the ancestors of the people. They are expert in tracing and examining generation to generation of the people; they are good orators and pursuers. A negotiator is paid handsomely for the task he undertakes. The negotiator should be able to solve the problems or disputes, which arise during the whole marital process. During the post-marriage also, the negotiator is the one who undertakes the task, for example, in case of divorce. During the process of divorce he is the one who plays the major role in making it successful or unsuccessful. The negotiators are, in most cases, the persons who have blood relationship with both the families. He is a middleman who also should have cordial relation with the family of the bride.

The negotiators in some cases are more than one but often it is only one who is appointed as a negotiator. They are sent from the side of the boy to the parents of the girl. It is he who negotiates, persuades and makes the marriage possible.

Negotiators in most cases approach to the parents of the girl indirectly. He first gives hints and after the purpose of his coming is disclosed, he approaches directly. In most cases rumour plays an important role. The parents come to know about the proposal before the arrival of the negotiator. It depends on the diplomacy of the negotiator how he tackles the situation. His diplomatic skill is put to test during the whole marital process.

It is not necessary for the physical presence of the bride and the groom during the negotiation or during the agreement and establishing of marital bond. One can receive the information of his or her marriage from other places, miles away from his home. After the agreement, mithuns and pigs are given to the parents of the girl from the side of the boy. Mithuns and pigs are sacrificed and community feast is held in the village of the girl. From then, both the boy and the girl are declared as husband and wife. However, after the marriage, bride remains in the house of her parents usually for a year or more. The husband, however, is permitted to visit her whenever he intends to. In most cases the *Abeya* or the negotiator on behalf of the groom fixes the date for the bride to leave for the house of her in-laws but in some cases the bride herself fixes the date. In some cases if both husband and wife like, they quietly settle. This practice however, is not held in high esteem in the society.

'*Thrutuga*' or elopement is also the way, a boy or a girl may opt for. A boy and a girl elope when the lovers feel that their clan members will not approve them marrying each other. The elopement is opted when the lovers are related to each other through kinship. For elopement, a groom is made to pay heavy penalty to make him realize the gravity of the crime he has committed.

After the marriage, if the bride is reluctant to accept her husband and if she is obstinate regarding her stand then the husband and his clan members opt for harsh step '*Yaku-Ango*', carrying away the bride forcefully. However, this step is taken, in most cases, by taking into confidence the father and the brothers of the bride, and assuring them during the whole process that they won't harm the bride.

Iyu Ena (Rituals)

The rituals are an important part of the marriage in the Idu Mishmi society. It is these rituals, which determine the well-being of the generations yet to come.

During *Abechi, Alobi-Amalo* also takes place, in which the groom takes the oath that, 'now that I've bought you, you will forever remain mine and till seven births we'll be one.' The husband after few years of marriage will send the *Abeya* (the negotiator) to his wife's place to inform them that soon *Echi-Chi* will take place and a date is fixed. This particular period is also known as '*Echi-Chi Aba-Ala*', as it is believed that the women always goes in search for new clan and identity, by losing its own identity.

If the groom had decided to bring the bride, he has to observe certain taboos; failing to observe them would lead to fatal accidents.

These fixed months are considered to be the tenderest period for both the husband and the wife. During these periods they should be alert and take care that they are not involved in any activities which may cause harm to them. Therefore, the phrase, '*Echi-Chi du-me biyando*' and '*Yaku-aa atu-me biyando*' matches perfectly with the tenderest period of the spouses. During these period if they are not careful enough, bad luck may befall upon them as it is believed that during this particular time evil omen keeps accompanying them. Therefore, if they fail to take precaution, either of them has to face death. In some of the cases the wife, soon after reaching the place of her husband, finds him dead either killed by wild animal or had an accidental death. In other cases the bride may die during the journey to her husband's place.

After the bride has been brought into the house, the groom has to offer chicken to all the relatives of the bride. After *Echi-Chi*, if the groom does not offer chicken to the guests from his bride's side, it is believed that his wife will suffer from *Eto-Bruso*, a neurological related disease. Therefore, offering chicken to his bride's relatives is of high priority.

The consumption of the meat, which is forbidden to woman, is tabooed for the groom and his clan members in the houses of the bride and her clan members for the rest of their lives. They can eat the flesh of the minor creature like fish, birds and mountain rat. The consumption of the meat is considered fatal for the unborn child. If any member from the groom's side does not abide by the norms, its consequences can be seen directly in the child. It is believed that the child starts eating up its own fingers. Such cases occur unknowingly and are rectified so that it does not happen again in the future. Another belief is that there will always be tension among the grooms clan.

When the bride leaves the house of her parents, she is followed by members of her clan. Except her parents and real brothers, every one can follow her.

Before leaving for the house of her in-laws, at the very outskirt of her village, an *Igu*, priest, makes '*Larou*' (a sort of small gate). The gate is made of plant *Epo* (Saccarum spontanum). The priest hands the bride *Ichi-Chi-Atobra* (a walking stick for proceeding towards the house of her husband). She is directed to walk by taking it in any of her hands. The priest chants the hymns and the bride has to pass through the '*Larou*', the gate. The followers, those who do not suffer from any diseases, also pass through it. Those who suffer from any diseases and ailments are forbidden to pass through this gate as it is believed that the diseases may follow the bride. The priest invokes the spirit, '*Gollo*'. The priest chants hymns to appease other spirits, as well, that may disrupt the journey of the bride. After invoking and appeasing the spirit '*Gollo*', priest appeases '*Bruvu*', the spirit of water. Then the priest chants hymns to appease spirits like '*Milee-Mewe*', the spirit which makes the couple impotent, '*Alutu-Awete*', the spirit which makes the people disabled, '*Lai-Laka*', the spirit of the path, 'Assa', the spirit of the jungle, '*Arru*', the spirit of the epidemics, '*Gu-wa*', the spirit of the skin diseases, *'Apu-Chedi'*, the spirit which causes leprosy, *'Amoti-Anave'*, the spirit which causes disorder in the nervous system like epilepsy, *'Annu-Arey'*, the spirit which causes chicken pox and small pox, *'Niko Nara'*, the spirit in the resting place on the way, etc. These spirits are appeased for the fact that these spirits should not possess the bride and disrupt her way to broom's house.

When the bride is about to reach the village of her husband, then the negotiator, the *'Abeya'* hides the *'Ichi-Chi-Atobra'*, the walking stick of the bride. The place of hiding of the walking stick is kept secret as it is said that tampering of this stick may bring evil to the unborn children in future and they may die.

The bride after reaching the destination stays for the whole night in *'Alonga'*, the first room of the house where males reside. She stays whole night with the people who have accompanied her. It is taboo for her to go out the entire night even for excreting and she observes it. Excreting and urinating is considered bad omen for the family and in future doom may fall on the family.

After her arrival in the house of her in-laws, she is forbidden to go out of the village and even within the village, she is forbidden to venture into others house for at least five days. As she is new to the village, it is believed that, the spirit of dwelling house may be hostile towards her. Before the expiring of the taboo, a priest is called for *'Aribi'* ritual which is done to ward off evils and for her well-being. The priest in this ritual appeases the same spirits which were appeased during *Larou* ritual. In this, a fowl is sacrificed especially to appease the spirits of the house like *'Atita-Amrawu'*, *'Ashu-Andro'* to accept the bride as she has become the part of the family. The priest also appeases *'Manu'*, the spirit of the agricultural land to accept her and give access to the agricultural land, crops and not to disrupt her.

Lyu and *Araa* (The Involvement of Cash in the Marriage)

It is not known when the money was introduced in making payments during marriage. But it seems that as the pigs and mithuns were for the father and the brothers of the bride, it was necessary to give something to mother as she customarily does not eat the meat of the pig or the mithun. Actually, the cash is meant for the mother of the bride. In case where the bride's mother had died, the cash goes to the father or the brother.

When a marriage is fixed, the groom pays some amount in cash and kind called *'Lyu'* to the parents of the bride and it is not fixed. It varies from individual to individual or according to the circumstances. If the clan of the groom had offended the clan of the bride in the past, then a heavy amount is asked for the damage done to the family and the clan. Though such a case is very exceptional, in most of such cases, it is not asked because it is considered that the gap between the families are being bridged by the marital bond. In case of elopement where the clan of the bride is made to feel offended, a heavy amount is demanded as penalty by the clan of the bride. In the case of the marriage in which the clan of the bride has no reservation, besides a pig and a mithun a minimal amount ranging from ₹ 5,000 to ₹ 10,000 is asked by the clan of the bride. The pigs and the mithuns given by the groom are sacrificed and it is shared by the members of the village of the bride. In most cases number of mithuns and pigs is more than one.

The gifts in return are brought by the bride while coming to the house of her in-laws. The gift in cash and kind which are brought by the bride are not fixed. It depends on the individual and it varies. In most cases, the gifts exceed the amount given by the groom during the marriage. These gifts are given by her parents and brothers and also the assets which the bride has earned by herself in her parental house become part of this gift.

However, these gifts are given only in the cases where bride leaves for her in-laws with the consent of her families. In case of elopement such gifts are not paid back. The amount whatever is brought by the bride in cash and kinds are made public.

The amount paid by the groom is returned when the marital bond is broken. The marital bond breaks in case of the death of the bride or the groom; in the circumstances where both are reluctant to accept each other as the spouse and in cases where one of them is obstinate and reluctant to accept the other as a spouse, despite pressure from both the clans. The amount '*Da*', is not returned in case of death of one of the spouse if they have any children. If the marital bond breaks without the fault of both the bride and the groom due to cases like tracing of relation based on kinship in between them then the amount, 'Da' is same as the amount paid by the groom. But, if one of them breaks the bond then he/she has to pay penalty for it. In the cases where groom is the reason for the breaking of the bond then he has to part with some of the amount which he has paid to the family of the bride during the marriage. The cases in which the bride breaks the bond, in such cases she is charged double of the amount by the groom as penalty. Such cases where bride rejects the groom is a prestige issue for the clan of the groom and is considered as an insult inflicted upon the clan by the bride.

When the clan members of the bride follow her to the house of the groom, some amount in cash is paid to them called 'Aberu'. There is no fixed amount; it varies according to the financial position of the groom.

When in future the couple celebrates *Reh* festival then also 'Ameta' is paid to the clan members of the wife. Ameta is a *Reh* gift, which is paid in cash and kind by the host of the festival to his relatives.

The Social Aspects (Clan Cooperation in the Marriage)

After the marriage, the husband as well as his clan members should not use filthy language against the people belonging to the clan of his wife. The same principle should be followed by the clan of the bride with that of the clan of the groom for the rest of their lives.

The people of both the clans advise parents of both the bride and the groom, and give opinion regarding the marriage. They help to trace from various sides and examine if there is relation based on kinship or not. They examine thoroughly, generation to generation, so that there should be no room for any controversy.

During the arrival of the bride the clan members of the groom contribute chicken, rice beer and other eatable. They also help financially if needed.

Some Other Aspects of the Marriage in Idu Society

Sororate and levirate are permissible in Idu Mishmi society. It happens in case of death of either bride or the groom. In other cases when the bride does not prefer the groom or vice versa they marry either the sister of the bride or the brother of the groom. Like this, marital bond is established only if both the families agree for such a bond.

After the death of his father, one is permitted to marry his stepmother if she has no relation based on kinship with her husband's son. A son may have relation based on kinship from his mother's side to his stepmother. In cases of relation, the marriage does not take place.

Traditionally, in the past, even a father-in-law can marry his daughter in law after the death of his son. This is socially sanctioned when the man dies before the arrival of his groom in his house. The marriage happens in the circumstances; (a) where after the death of the groom there is none to heir in the family to inherit her and also if he dies before establishing physical relation with the bride. After the physical relation is established between the bride and the groom, then the daughter-in-law is considered equal to his own daughter by the father-in-law. Such a marriage is possible only when the parents of the bride agree for it. Aforesaid two cases, though are permitted in the society, were rare in the past and presently no one in the community practises it.

In Idu Mishmi society, one can marry anyone except that, one should not be related to each other based on kinship from both consanguinal and afinial sides. It is followed as much as people can trace the past relation from generations. If anyone traces any relation in the past and if it is proved, one falls into difficult situation.

Widow marriage is permitted in the Idu Mishmi society. Marrying a widow is seen as one's sympathetic attitude towards the widow; giving her emotional support and also taking care of the orphans. Widow marriage in most cases happen within the people of her husband's clan. If none of the clan of the deceased husband marries the widow then the society does not hold the clan in high esteem. They are refuted in debates and other social gatherings. If none accepts from her husband's clan then she can go for others, taking into confidence by the clan of her deceased husband and her clan. Minimal amount is paid by the new husband to the clan of the deceased husband.

Traditionally, Idu Mishmis practised tribe endogamy in their marriage system. Even today, tribe exogamy is very rare. It is considered equal to marring someone out of the tribe and marrying an 'Apo' (slaves). Marrying them are considered inauspicious and considered slur on the whole clan.

Idus believe that one who marries out of the tribe, after death descends into 'Atita-Apra-Pa'. In this part of underworld is believed to be full of snails and slugs. So marrying someone out of the community is very rare, and it is rarer in case of males. According to the myth, the mother of humanity *'Thobri Liru'* divided her sons and daughters into various tribes and races. She further assigned them various roles as various tribes and races. And she forbade whole of them not to intermingle in future. Therefore, it is considered going against the will of the mother of the humanity. Extra marital affairs are not permitted. The paramour has to pay huge penalty for such deeds.

Present Scenario and Conclusion

Minimal change can be seen in the marriage system of the Idu Mishmis. Hitherto, almost most of the systems are still practised, the main problem arises when the people related to each other through kinship decide to be partners in their life. Still one faces stiff opposition from his and her clan when such cases arise. In some cases, the pressure of both the clan results in success and the boy and the girl are made to abandon each other. There are also some liberal cases shown by both the clans. In some cases, despite opposition, couple marry each other in the court and again by traditional way. Such a step taken by the couple and their family are accepted by both the sides of the clan, after they pay the required penalty for it to both the clans. Many cases are also there in which despite opposition the parents of both sides agree to the marriage of their children. However, huge penalty is demanded by the people of both the clans and they are made to pay it.

Still, marrying outside the tribe is very rare. Especially males, in very exceptional cases go for this marriage. Involvements of money in most cases are minimized due to awareness brought among the people. Nowadays, most of the parents even take their children into confidence regarding their marriage.

Acknowledgement

This paper is a revision of the original papers titled,

1. 'Some aspects of Marriage System of the Idus of Arunachal Pradesh', published in '*Marriage and Culture: Reflections from Tribal Societies of Arunachal Pradesh*', (Vol. I), edited by T. Mibang and M.C. Behera. Mittal Publications, New Delhi (2006: 89–98).
2. 'Marriage Practices in Idu Mishmi Society', published in *Marriage in Tribal Societies: Cultural Dynamics and Social Realities*, edited by T. Mibang and M.C. Behera, Bookwell Publication, New Delhi (2007: 115–24) by Razzeko Delley.

References

Bertrand, Russell (2009). *Marriage and Morals*, Routledge, Oxon.

Goyal, R.P. (1998). *Marriage Age in India*, B.R. Publishing Corporation, Delhi.

Leach, Edmund (1955). *Polyandry, Inheritance and the Definition of Marriage*, Man 55, pp. 182–86.

Williams, Thomas Rhys (1990). *Cultural Anthropology*, Prentice Hall, New Jersey.

8

The Great Fire and the Creation Myth

The Oral Tradition of the Idu Mishmis of Arunachal Pradesh

RUMO METO AND TARUN MENE

The Idu Mishmi tribe[1] is mainly concentrated in two districts viz. Lower Dibang Valley and Dibang Valley District of Arunachal Pradesh. Besides, they are also inhabited in small pockets in East Siang (Aohali village), Lohit (Tezu), Upper Siang (Singa) Districts of Arunachal Pradesh. They are included as a part of the larger constellation of the Mishmi group which includes Digaru and Miju Mishmis also.[2] Culturally, Idus are very much distinct from the rest of the two which are reflected in various aspects of their day-to-day life and social structure as well as value systems. Idu Mishmis are popularly known as the 'Chulikata Mishmis' because of their distinct hairstyle, perhaps this nomenclature is given by the people of the plains (Bhattacharjee, 1983: 13) with whom Idus had trade relations. Dalton (1872: 18) reported them as Midhi people and mentioned that they are greatly detested and mistrusted by their neighbours, the Abors and Tains and they are much dreaded by the Saudiya population in consequence of the prowling expeditions to kidnap women and children.

The migratory route is not clear; however, some light has been thrown on the topic by various researchers on the basis of oral history on the Idu tribe. For example, Bhattacharjee (1983: 13) believed that they must have come from the triangle of Burma where innumerable tribal groups of similar culture used to live in widely dispersed areas between Salween Mekong and Yangten. Baruah (1960: 7–13) in a similar fashion traces the original homeland of some clans such as *Inni-la Pon* of Mele clan, *Amriti* of the Taraon Polo and the Idu Pulu clan who migrated to the present place following the courses of Ilyu or Lohit rivers. He finally concluded that Idu's migrations took them through Tibet. Undeniable that the Idus have followed the various river courses such as Lohit or Illuh, Dri, Mathu, Ithun, Taloh, etc. from some ambiguous location and settled in various parts in the present vast political territory of Arunachal Pradesh as mentioned above. But looking at their 'total culture' it is adequate to ascertain that they must have spread out from a particular puddle, gradually at different time period following one after another. Their dialectic synonymies with Taraon Mishmi dialect also suggest that both the tribes must have been a homogenous group in the remote past and later on, due to some historical reasons they gradually diffused following different river courses. Subsequently, their social formation came to be known as Idu Mishmi and Taraon or Digaru Mishmi. Furthermore, it is interesting to see that the Idus remained and maintained themselves as a distinct cultural group but the Taraon Mishmi, in the process of their migration and contacts, assimilated themselves with the Kaman Mishmi which is well reflected in their social cultural, political, economic and religious aspects but their dialectic distinctiveness suggests that their process of assimilation took place somewhere in the remote past.

Origin of Myth

Transcription of myths relating to the origin of the Idu Mishmi people varies enormously which is reflected in various writings.[3] Elwin (1958: ix) rightly put it that 'In all tribal areas, there is a great divergence of ideas, especially in the realm of folklore, mythology and religion: stories and the names of gods and heroes vary from place to place; the same informant may even pronounce a word, or use a name differently on two successive days. This is inevitable in a region where there is no fixed deposit of doctrine, no sacred books to carry tradition from one generation to another, and where the repositories of knowledge are human beings exposed to the inspirations of their dreams and fancies.' Similar syndrome, one may find in the mythologies of the Idu Mishmis which is reflected in various writings.

All the versions of Idu mythology particularly in relation to the origin of mankind on earth begin with the initial stage of *Inniyala-Phi*, literary meaning 'fire on the earth', whereby the whole living and nonliving things on earth were completely burnt down and destroyed. The second or the after burnt phase starts with the gradual processes of recreation and re-evolution of all that was destroyed by the great fire. It is here in this stage that we find the names of various legends to whom Idus regard as Supreme Being. Some represent *Arume Mili* to be the lone survivor of the devastating fire and making union with *Asi-Anjoru* replenished the earth with all what we have today (Dele, 2006). Bhattacharjee (1983: 14–15) similarly noted that only six could have survived the devastating fire and from among them one *Arungomili* recreated the existence of all the living and nonliving things on the earth, including man. Baruah (1960: 69) stated that god *Anya* created human beings and other species at the direction of supreme god *Inni*. Linggi (2000) also touched upon the topic highlighting three versions. In the first one he mentioned *Eto Mili* who were hiding under *Ibri-Po* and *Ata-Po* (Banana tree) during the devastating fire and saved herself and thereafter filled the earth with life. In the second version, he talks about *Etothro-Liru* and *Dondo-Liru* to be the creator of life. In the third, he mentioned that the union of *Anyome* and *Ekomu*, who were father and daughter, recreated life on earth after the great fire destroyed everything. Pulu (1977: 69–70) also wrote about *Erayi* and *Ekomu,* who were brother and sister, restored the earth with life out of there union.

In this article, the author presents the following version of the creation of man on earth collected from his own fieldwork.

> As per the myth, once there was a massive fire on the earth (*Inniyala Phi*)[4] which started from Inniyala Witi, a mystical place away from the Idu inhabiting location. As a result, the whole earth came under great fire and everything was burnt down and devastated. Only one woman, Arume Mili, could survive hiding herself under the eight layered walls of Banana tree (Ibri-Po and Ata-Po). She realizes herself alone went to Muduako, a place other than human world, where one Asi-Anjoru, an ancestral shaman, was living. In the course of her wandering she felt a desire for procreation. Having no knowledge she sat on the hill top with her legs apart removing her garments. In the mean time, Asi-Anjoru in the form of wind went into her womb and as a result she conceived. To her surprise, she proceeds to query to Asi Anjoru about how she was impregnated. Responding to her Asi-Anjoru gave her the reason that it was the wind that impregnated her. Thus, Arume Mili first gave birth to a female child and named her Lopome Mili. Later on she got married to one Lomome Leru who was from Kandi Ati, other than human world. Their union first gave birth to the Sun, Moon, Stars, thundering and lightning, Beka (Cobra), Amraze (a unique admixture of man and tiger). They also gave birth to spirits like Golo, Apa-sa, etc. diseases like leprosy, cancer, chicken pox, etc. Then they also gave birth to all the human races of the world and their last progeny are believed to be Tudu and Tolo. From Tudu the Idu Mishmi has descended and from Tolo the Chinese appeared.[5]

Almost in all the versions, it is observable that the entire earth was first engulfed by fire which foraged from *Inniyala Witi,* a mystical place and destroyed everything including human beings on earth. Subsequently, various legends replenished the earth with almost everything that exists today including men and spirits, celestial bodies like the sun, moon, stars, etc. Unlike Adi tribe, Idu Mishmi folktale does not talk about *Nothingness (keyum* in the beginning but reflects that everything was pre-existent on earth. It is only the incident of fire (*Inniyala Phi*) that destroyed all life on earth. Therefore, the Idu folktale does not narrate how life itself originated on earth but how few lives escaped the great fire and repopulated the earth.

Furthermore, there is mention of many godly places, other than human world, such as *Inyila-Ati, Kandimo, Mudukoh,* etc. which were occupied by the mythical ancestral shamans. For example, *Andijuru* who came down from *Mudukoh* after the devastating fire and he, in the form of wind, conceived *Arume mili,* the lone survivor of the devastating fire, who helped in procreation of entire living and nonliving things on the earth. Considering this, it is likely that the Idu version of the myth represents two different categories of the world of which the first was occupied by the supreme beings and were beyond the reach of common human beings and the other is human world or where the Idus are today.

As stated above, many supernatural figures helped in restoring the human world after the great fire on earth, it is here that these supernatural beings also gave birth to celestial bodies like sun, moon, stars, etc. At this point, if we analyse the two phases, i.e. the initial phase of 'Fire on the Earth' (*Inniyala-Phi*) and after burnt phase in which everything was created by the various supernatural beings including celestial bodies like sun, moon, etc. then it is convincing that Idu's conception of a supreme being is not the sun which is marked today but is something beyond it whose character and activity is shrouded in the mist of antiquity.[6] Elwin (1958: 48–49) informed that there was no Moon at the beginning but there were two Suns who gave light and heat to the world. *Epanja* was the father of the Suns and their mother was *Lanbbai*. Similarly, Dele (2006) went on saying that '*Apanje* and *Lammai* were the parents of Sun and Moon.' Therefore, the Idu notion of a Supreme Being is not the physical object that is portrayed nowadays in the form of the Sun but something akin to metaphysical and spiritual and eternal in nature and beyond the vision and reach of common man.

Conclusion

From the above discussion it may be cogently concluded that the versions of origin myths in relation to mankind and other living things among the Idu Mishmis varies substantially, which is evident in various narratives. However, one similar view observable is that it is only in the after burnt phase that all the living and nonliving things gradually evolved and the celestial bodies like the sun and moon, etc. were created by various legends and therefore, for many Idus it is convincing that both Man and Sun are in the single line of descent, created by the same progenitor and for which the present notion of *Inni*, the Supreme Being, is not the physical Sun but something supernatural and uncanny beyond that.

Notes

1. Both the terminologies 'Idu' and 'Mishmi' have no concrete and specific meaning in Idu language. Baruah (1960: 98) mentioned that 'the word Idu is most probably a distortion of the word Midu which means inhabitant of Idu valley and is the name for only one section of the people'. It is here to mention that Idus may be categorized into three groups as per their dialectic variation and in few words, which are *Mindri, Mithu* and *Midu*. Most of the *Mindri* speaking Idus inhabits the present Upper Dibang Valley District around Dri and Mathu river valley. The *Mithu* inhabits both sides of the Ithun river valley. The *Midu* speaking Idus are mainly found in lower foothills and lower valleys of Mishmi Hills. So most probably, Midu speaking Idus of lower foothills and valleys first came in contact with outsiders and only from their dialectic nomenclature 'Midu' the term 'Idu' was coined to designate the tribe. As I put it, Mithu speaking Idus inhabits Ithun Valley, Baruah (1960: 11) designated the same Idus of Ithun valley as *Bebejiyas*, again the term which has no concrete meaning and origin in Idu language. And for the term 'Mishmi', Bhattacharjee (1983: 13) suggested that there is no clarity of origin of the term, though largely believed that it has been coined by the people of plains of

Assam to designate the tribe. Dimso Manyu in his PhD thesis mentions how the nomenclature Mishmi was derived from the phrase *Misa Misi* used by the plain people to designate those hill tribes who supposedly carried their trade on deceit and lies. The Britishers' mispronunciation of the phrase *Misa Misi* morphed into Mishmi. Further, one may find that Idus refer themselves as *Kera-Aa*. Here *Kera* is believed to be a name of ancestral forefather and *Aa* stands for children and thereby meaning children of Kera.

2. The Miju Mishmis are now popularly called Kaman and Digaru Mishmis as Taraon. Their dresses are so similar that one can barely distinguish them, though Idu Mishmis are quite distinct in this regard. However, one distinguishing feature of the Mishmis is their hair style (Dutta Chaudhuri, 1978).
3. See writing of Elwin (1958), Baruah (1960: 7–10), Pulu (1977: 69–70), Bhattacharjee (1983: 14–33), Miso (2004), Mene (2005), Dele (2006), Lingi and Mekola (2000), Linggi (2000), etc.
4. *Inniyala-Phi* literary means 'fire on the earth'. However, the exact source of this fire is not spelt out by Shaman or people alike. For some, it is a volcanic eruption and for others it is the scorching heat that gave birth to this fire.
5. Information was collected from Jinje Mega, Age 80+, Sex-Female, Ango Mimi, Age 90+, Ache Mimi (Shaman) 40+, all from village Ashali, Roing Circle, Lower Dibang Valley District during the preparation of M.A. Anthropology dissertation on Reh Festival of the Idu Mishmis Tribe of Arunachal Pradesh.
6. Similar notion was put forward by Ering (2004) and Rukbo (2004) in regard to Donyi-Polo faith and practices of Adis of Arunachal Pradesh.

References

Baruah, T.K. (1960). *The Idu Mishmis*, Directorate of Research, Government of Arunachal Pradesh, Itanagar.

Behera, M.C. and S.K. Chaudhuri (1998). *Indigenous Faiths and Practices of the Tribes of Arunachal Pradesh*, Himalayan Publications, Itanagar, Arunachal Pradesh.

Bhattacharjee, T. (1983). *Idus of Mathu and Dri Valley*, Directorate of Research, Government of Arunachal Pradesh, Itanagar.

Blackburn, S. (2002). IIAS Newsletter 29, November.

Borang, K. (2004). 'Philosophy of Donyi Polo', in T. Mibang and S.K. Chaudhuri (eds), *Understanding Tribal Religion*, Mittal Publications, New Delhi.

Chaudhuri, S.K. (2008). 'Plight of the Igus: Notes on Shamanism among the Idu Mishmi Tribe of Arunachal Pradesh, India', *European Bulletin of Himalayan Research*, 32: 84–108.

Chaudhury, S. and D.K. Duarah (2004). 'Religious Beliefs and Institution of Priesthood among the Tribes of Arunachal Pradesh', in T. Mibang and S.K. Chaudhuri (eds), *Understanding Tribal Religion*, Mittal Publications, New Delhi, pp. 19–34.

Dalton, E.T. (1872). *Descriptive Ethnology of Bengal*, Asiatic Society of Bengal, Calcutta.

Dele, R. (2006). 'Myth and Legend in the Idu Mishmi Society', Unpublished Dissertation submitted to AITS, Rajiv Gandhi University, Itanagar.

Dutta Chaudhuri, S. (1978). *Arunachal Pradesh*, Lohit District Gazetteer. Shillong: Government of Arunachal Pradesh.

Elwin, V. (1958). *Myths of the North-East Frontier of India*, Directorate of Research, Government of Arunachal Pradesh, Itanagar.

Ering, O. (2004). 'Philosophy of Donyi Polo', in T. Mibang and S.K. Chaudhuri (eds), *Understanding Tribal Religion*, Mittal Publications, New Delhi.

Linggi, B. (2000). 'Inyi-La Phi Taju (Creation of Mankind)', in *Seminar Report on Traditional Systems: Change and Continuity among the Idu Mishmis*, The Idu Cultural and Literary Society, Roing.

Linggi, L. and I. Mekola (2000). 'Divination', in *Seminar Report on Traditional Systems: Change and Continuity among the Idu Mishmis*, The Idu Cultural and Literary Society, Roing.

Mene, T. (2005). 'The Reh Festival of Idu Mishmis', Unpublished Dissertation submitted to AITS, Rajiv Gandhi University, Itanagar.

Miso, Rajiv (2004). 'Priesthood among the Idu Mishmis', Unpublished Dissertation submitted to AITS, Rajiv Gandhi University, Itanagar.

Pulu, J. (1977). 'Two Mishmi Tales', *Resarun*, 76.

—— (1999). 'Reh Festival of Idu Mishmi', *Resarun*, XXV(2): 81–89.

Rukbo, T. (2004). 'Donyi-Polo Faith and Practice of Adis', in T. Mibang and S.K. Chaudhuri (eds), *Understanding Tribal Religion*, Mittal Publications, New Delhi, pp. 73–86.

9

The Writing System of the Idu Mishmi Language

An Introduction

MITE LINGI

'Put people in chains, strip them, plug up their mouths; they are still free. Take away their job, their passport, the table they eat on, the bed they sleep in; they are still rich. People become poor and enslaved, when they are robbed of the tongue left them by their ancestors: They are lost forever.'

Ignazio Buttitta, in *Our Creative Diversity* (UNESCO, 1995)

The Writing System: A Carrier or a Barrier

Since written literature in our vernacular appears beyond our scope at this stage of our time, we could start with some socially pertinent questions. The Idu Mishmi way of life; how has it been passed down to us orally so far and how do we pass it on to our children in an affected time where the oral transmission is threatened by dilution? May be, we could begin by renewing some relevant but obvious questions.

1. How has the Idu Mishmis communicated across time and space in absence of a writing system?
2. Can oral literature carry the burden of the 'collective memories' of a community? If so, then is the present Idu Mishmi generation equipped with the required wherewithal of memory to carry the baggage of the past traditions orally? Doesn't the present generation look haggard even without possessing the simple art of the oral tradition, leave alone the collective memory?
3. How has the Idu Mishmi community or for that matter any tribe of Arunachal Pradesh carried on its social memory through the oral transmission?

4. In what could be clustered as 'the Idu Mishmi way of life' come all sorts of cultural, ethical and ethnic values, the extension of which must surely contain all notions of freedom as practised down the line since time immemorial. The pertinent question here is whether the development of a writing system will usher in a means to rewrite our little histories and store them for posterity, rather than just soothe the pride of our collective conscience as the bearer of our traditions.

The Idu Mishmi Language Development Committee (IMLDC)

The Idu Mishmi Language Development Committee (IMLDC) was constituted with the aim of preserving and promoting the Idu Mishmi language. The present members of the IMLDC include:

1. Shri Jimi Pulu
2. Shri Hindu Meme
3. Shri Rajkumar Keche
4. Shri Yona Mele
5. Shri Apomo Linggi
6. Dr Mite Lingi

The Idu Mishmi Language Development Committee (IMLDC) is a subcommittee of the Idu Mishmi Cultural and Literary Society (IMCLS), the apex body organization of the Idu Mishmi tribe. The IMLDC has been entrusted to realize the long standing societal vision of having its own writing system. To achieve the long-term goal of introducing the Idu Mishmi writing system in the Idu Mishmi inhabited areas, the IMLDC undertook the organizing of threefold task initially.

A Paper Trial

The IMLDC is under the process of examining the previously attempted Roman script. This mainly involves the work on the International Phonetic Alphabets (IPA) use to represent the sound system of the language; consonant and vowels, tone marking, nasalization and so on. The local resource persons are met on regular basis in the process. The paper trial will be a document to help the committee in recording the decisions and also the reasons for making those decisions.

A Trial Primer

The IMLDC visits schools and villages. These visits are made in order to collect materials for printing of the preliminary study materials such as primer, books, etc. at a later stage.

A Draft Dictionary

The IMLDC undertakes the task of visiting villages and meeting local people to collect materials for compiling a Draft Dictionary. The members collect photographs of flora and fauna while also collecting special words. The first Draft Dictionary of the community is awaiting publication.

Historical Background

In the year 1997, an NGO by name *Idu Ekobe Kebange* (IEK) was formed by Shri Laeta Umbrey, ex-Member of Parliament (MP) and Shri Jimi Pulu, Deputy Director (Research), Government of Arunachal Pradesh which had the sole purpose of developing a writing system for the Idu Mishmi language in roman script. The IEK had the following committee members:

1. Chairman – Shri Laeta Umbrey
2. Vice-Chairman – Shri Jimi Pulu
3. Secretary – Late Khumba Tacho
4. Treasurer – Shri Kelo Pulu
5. Joint Secretaries:
   (i) Shri Kotige Mena
   (ii) Shri Khindiko Mega
   (iii) Shri Robert Rondo
6. Members
   (i) Shri Matheim Linggi
   (ii) Shri Eri Tayu
   (iii) Shri Retra Umpo
   (iv) Shri Yime Mega
   (v) Smt NaSiya Mena
   (vi) Dr Mite Lingi

The IEK began a series of correspondence with the Central Institute of Indian Language (CIIL), Mysore, MHRD, the premier institute of Indian languages. In response to the persistent appeal of the IEK, the CIIL sent R. Elangayan, a linguist to Roing, the district headquarters of Lower Dibang Valley. He stayed at Roing for three months to work with IEK, after which Shri Jimi Pulu went to the CIIL to undertake the task of digital sound recording of the vocabulary besides obtaining preliminary training at the institute for three months. R. Elangayan came back to Roing and prepared the draft of a writing system which was released on the occasion of the Central *Reh* Festival in 2003.[1] The IEK released a trial book titled 'Idu Ekobe Alonzo' to raise the awareness level among the general public. The objective was to develop the Primers. The demise of R. Elangayan spelled a gap period. In the meantime, IEK had decided to visit the places and go to the Idu Mishmi people, and in the process conducted classes at the following places:

1. Cheta Central Reko, Roing.
2. Town Club Hall, Anini, Dibang Valley.
3. Govt Higher Secondary School, Roing.
4. Govt Secondary School, Korunu, Lower Dibang Valley.
5. Govt Secondary School, Desali, Lower Dibang Valley.

At this point of time, the Volkswagen Foundation of Germany sponsored the Potsdam University, Germany and Delhi University to document two endangered languages of India. The CIIL recommended the Idu Mishmi language of Arunachal Pradesh and the Khamiyang language of Assam for the documentation. In December 2003, Professor Caroline and Professor Gilsvert came to Roing along with Professor Subbha Rao of Delhi University to make a preliminary survey of the Idu Mishmi language. The survey report is known to have been submitted to the Volkswagen Foundation of which the Idu Mishmi community is still all ears to learn about. The repeated appeals to the Linguistics department, Delhi University by Shri Jimi Pulu, the then Language Officer failed to obtain any responses.

The Idu Mishmi community lost a great social worker in the form of Shri Khumba Tacho at this stage. Late Khumba Tacho was the spirit behind the movement of the language team. With his demise the wheels caught rust and the progress halted abruptly. A lot of work remained unfinished and so all the heads turned towards the CIIL once again. In the year 2010, once again at the behest of IEK, Shri G.D.P. Shastri, a linguist and the head of the Minority Languages, CIIL came to Roing. Around this time the IEK and the IMCLS came together to form the Idu Mishmi Language Development Committee (IMLDC). A four member team went to CIIL in Feb, 2012 to work on the script. Shri G.D.P Shastri retired from his job in 2013 and the task remained unaccomplished once again.

A chance meeting of Shri Jimi Pulu and Dr Mite Lingi in the month of February 2015 brought in Dr Roger Blench, a linguist and the Trustee of the Kay Williamson Educational Foundation, Cambridge (UK) into the unfinished saga of the Idu writing system. Dr Roger offered his expertise and the IMLDC saw it as providential. He worked with the IMLDC for a week, from 19 to 26, February 2015 to be precise and brought out a proposal for a writing system for the Idu Mishmi language. He said that Idu language could have its own writing system within a period of two years if the community meant it. As promised he came back to Roing on 30 November 2015 to rework on the proposal. He stayed the whole month of December, redrafted the proposal and helped the language committee compile a Draft Dictionary. The Draft Proposal as well as the Draft Dictionary is ready to go public. With the local Member of Legislative Assembly (MLA) Shri Mutchu Mithi standing firmly behind the development of Idu Mishmi language, the team is in confidence now of having our own writing system any day.

Conclusion

All the languages of Arunachal Pradesh are oral as we never had a time or place conducive to the development of writing system. If a writing system is the means of recording, thereby preserving a language how is it that we heard no cry of urgency? Or are we still hoping to save our languages using English and Hindi? Are we really comfortable? May be the government of the day fears the daunting task of bringing about a consistency if all tribes have their own writing systems. Will a multicultural and multilingual landscape as Arunachal Pradesh allow the writing system to be a sociopolitical necessity or will it be pursued by the elite few? The world may be getting smaller but only a writing system, by acting as the repository of our oral literature, will give us the desired prestige to make our presence felt. At the end of the day, it is the speakers of a native language who can revitalize the language and for this a writing system seems to be the only known means.

Note

1. *Reh* is the main festival of the Idu Mishmi community which is celebrated on 2nd and 3rd February annually. The Central Reh Festival is of recent origin which basically aimed at .... .

10

Attempts to Write the Idu Mishmi Language and a Proposal for a Modern Orthography

ROGER BLENCH

The Linguistic Situation in North-East India

The states of North-East India, known informally as the 'Seven Sisters', are a region of high linguistic diversity. Because of their geographical location, their populations align more with South-East Asia both culturally and in terms of language affiliation. Even within the region, Arunachal Pradesh is notable for both the number of languages and the high level of differences between them (Blench and Post, 2013). However, for political reasons, research and literacy development in the state remains at low levels. Arunachal Pradesh borders Tibet, and the Indian State claims to fear invasion from China, based on a major border incident in 1962. As a consequence, gaining access has been difficult and permits cover only short periods; so academic research on Arunachali languages has been limited.

Ironically, the Indian Government has long sponsored research on languages and cultures of Arunachal Pradesh, via the Museum and Institute, based in Itanagar. This goes back to the *panchsheel* policy of Jawaharlal Nehru, where he declared that the Adivasis (a rather ambiguous term for ethnic minorities in India) were to be 'cherished'. Despite scepticism from the minorities themselves, the government has funded a significant research effort in both linguistics and ethnography. The consequence has been a stream of publications, printed locally, which do not pass through a grid of external review. The linguistic volumes in particular are very much to a format, which is (in theory) to assist Government Officers in communicating with indigenous populations. Because these programmes are designed by Hindi speakers, they often use Hindi script in addition to Roman characters and are suffused with mainstream Indian cultural concepts.[1]

Separately, there has been some involvement from more mainstream Indian linguists. The Central Institute of Indian Languages (CIIL) based in Mysore, has also sent individual researchers to produce monographs on regional languages. These are almost invariably produced without reference to any previous work and are often not locally available. Again, they do not appear to have passed through any review process. Quality may kindly be described as variable. Individual churches, especially the Baptists, based in Shillong, have also sponsored orthography development, but a weak linguistic background has meant that these efforts have been broadly unsuccessful.

Until recently, these developments rather bypassed the indigenous populations, who have not really felt any need to write their languages. The small percentage who were literate usually wrote in Hindi or English. However, this situation has begun to change rapidly. As a consequence of globalization and increasing access to education, more children pass through the educational system and are beginning to go on to university. Their perception that the very alien culture of mainstream India is being forced on them becomes stronger. Broader information streams from the internet and television, make more obvious both the uniqueness of their cultures and the threat to their values from the waves of dross pumped out by the mainland media. At the same time, mobile phones and the possibility of texting and communicating through Facebook have become more widely available since about 2008 onwards, providing a much stronger incentive to develop a 'script' (as an orthography is locally known).

On the question of orthographies, the position taken by existing official publications from the Indian side is rather unclear. They appear to want to encourage writing languages in both Roman and Devanagri script, but a clear distinction between phonology and orthography is lacking. Primers and other reading and writing materials or indeed any formal programmes are absent. Chinese-language publications are strictly academic and set out a proposed phonology, but their purpose is not to help people read and write, especially in view of the small numbers of speakers on the Tibetan side of the border. They are generally not available on the Anglophone regions.

Indian Government policy on minority languages is somewhat ambiguous. In principle, minorities have a right to education in their own language, although this is mediated by education acts in individual states. In practice, this is more likely to be implemented where a language has an existing script and written tradition, as is the case for many larger regional languages. It is widely believed that once a minority can demonstrate it has a 'script' in use, funds will become available for the printing of primers and other teaching materials and the use of the language in primary education.

This situation has not gone unnoticed by outsiders, especially mission-oriented linguists. Christianity has made an impact in some parts of Arunachal Pradesh, although traditional belief remains strong. An institutionalized form of indigenous belief, Donyi-Polo, is widespread among the Tani peoples, and this acts as a barrier to wholesale conversion. As a consequence, attempts to develop orthographies have been conducted at a distance, for example by inviting speakers of minority languages to come to Assam and record material for analysis outside Arunachal Pradesh. Since these results are never published, the analyses only exist in samizdat form. This material is further discussed below, but it is safe to say that without backup from a literacy programme its impact has been minimal.

This background suggests the importance of conducting fresh linguistic field studies and assisting with the development of orthographies directly where the language is spoken rather than at a distance. Given the unreliable results from trying to analyse phonology at long range, the potential to circulate digital data and subject hypotheses to wider scrutiny is essential. This chapter[2] describes the situation of Idu, one of the 'Mishmi' languages in Arunachal Pradesh, covering its geography, existing literature, basic phonology, and the prospects for developing a consistent orthography which can be used by the community. It also describes briefly the complex problem of register in this language.

The Mishmi Peoples

The term 'Mishmi' has been used in the travel literature as far back as the early nineteenth century to refer to three distinct peoples and languages, the Kman [=Miju], Tawra [Digaru] and the Idu. The numerous variant names and spellings are detailed below. All of these peoples live in the north of Arunachal Pradesh, bordering Tibet and Myanmar, and all have villages across the frontier. Mishmi is a cultural classification; while Idu and Tawra languages are apparently related, Kman is quite different. Despite this, the Tawra consider themselves as closely related to the Kman and distinct from the Idu. This local ethno-classification has had an important impact on linguistic publications.

The Idu are also known as Chulikata [=Chulikotta, Sulikota], Midu [=Ida, Midhi, Nedu], Yidu Luoba, Lhoba [Chinese terms]. It is unfortunate that the ISO code [ckt] is based on the pejorative term Chulikata, now discouraged. The earliest reference to the Idu language is in Brown (1837). Some material can be found in Campbell (1874) and Konow (1902). The only significant publications on Idu from the Indian side are the pre-linguistic Talukdar (1962), Jatean Pulu (1978) and Jimi Pulu (2002a, b). Their main value is as elicitation guides, although the centralized Hindu-mainstream thinking that dominates its semantics, means they need to be treated with caution. Idu has also been described from the Chinese side [under the name Lhoba, Luoba], notably in Sun et al. (1980), Ouyang (1985), Sun (1983a, b, 1999) and Jiang [江荻] (2005).

Idu Settlements

The Idu originally seem to have been extremely scattered and publications such as the Lohit District Gazetteer (Dutta, 1978) record numerous settlements with a single family. However, the linguistic geography of the region was changed dramatically by a major earthquake in 1950 which struck the area of the Dibang Valley, causing considerable destruction. A flood following the earthquake also damaged existing settlements in the plains area and indirectly led to the establishment of Roing as a regional centre. The consequence was that many Idu and some Tawra villages in the Upper Siang were permanently depopulated. Households came down from the hills and settled in the fertile plains of the Brahmaputra. This was complicated, since there was significant prior settlement by both the Assamese and Nepalis, who had been relocated following military service. New villages were established and there was a switch to a rice growing culture more characteristic of the Assamese, which also changed Idu culture in important ways through contact with large-scale cultures and languages. Table 1 shows the locations of the Idu in India and China.

Table 1

Locations of the Mishmi People

People	*India*	*China*
Idu	NW Dibang District	SE Tibet, Zayul County, one village

Sources: Bradley (p.c.) and Ethnologue (Lewis et al., 2016).

Table 2 presents the population figures given in Ethnologue (Lewis et al., 2016) which are drawn from Indian and Chinese Government census figures.

Table 2

Mishmi People, Population Estimates

People	*India*	*China*
Idu	11,000 (2001)	80

These seem improbably high, given the small size and number of villages. Most local estimates suggest there are 4,000–5,000 current speakers of each language. Estimating competency remains a major issue, with a large percentage of younger people only having a passive knowledge of the language.

Sociolinguistics

The region is poorly described in the anthropological literature. There are passing references in the early travel literature (e.g. Wilcox, 1832; Rowlatt, 1845; Griffith, 1847; Brown, 1850; Young, 1907; Hamilton, 1912). Dalton (1872) is the first description of the main parameters of Idu life covers their social organization and 'warlike propensities' and his striking illustrations are not so dissimilar from village scenes today. The anthropological overview by Mills (1952) focusses heavily on kinship systems. Two monographs published in India describe the Idu, Baruah (1988) and Bhattarcharjee (1983) and these contain valuable descriptive material. The present volume should improve this situation.

If speaker numbers are in the few thousands, then the Mishmi languages are threatened but not critically endangered, between 6 and 7 on the EGIDS scale. Adults in peri-urban areas are often heard bemoaning the ability of youth to speak the language properly, and indeed, Hindi and English (and even Nepali) can be heard in houses around the town. Nonetheless, children in rural areas seem to be fluent speakers. There is no good information about the status of Chinese and Tibetan among Mishmi speakers across the border.

An issue which is not entirely resolved is the amount of internal variation in the Mishmi languages. Idu was certainly traditionally divided into 'Upper' and 'Lower', although the difference between these was quite small, according to examples cited. However, the 1950 earthquake threw the existing situation up in the air rather literally and 'Upper' households moved to the plain. As a result there is a significant variation between speakers even in adjacent households, mostly in the articulation of fricatives and affricates and palatalization of nasals. This does not seem to be the case with Tawra and Kman, where speakers from different villages usually have identical pronunciations. In addition to everyday speech, Mishmi languages have a striking feature, the existence of multiple registers, whose status is harder to evaluate. These are described in more detail in Spceialized Language Registers.

Classification

The first alignment of the Mishmi languages with a phylum is Brown's (1837) inclusion of these languages in 'Indo-Chinese'. Konow (1902: 614–41) provides more analysis although his material seems to be derived entirely from earlier sources. These languages were ascribed to a 'North Assam' group of Tibeto-Burman, for which no comparative evidence was presented. This has essentially been accepted and repeated in numerous subsequent classifications (see Blench and Post, 2013 for more detailed discussion). It is generally recognized that Idu and Tawra are related and this subgroup has been given the name Digarish, based on a river name applied to the Tawra. There is no doubt that these languages share many typological features with Tibeto-Burman, but this hardly constitutes proof of membership of the phylum. Evidently, the classification is only marginally relevant to the development of an orthography, but at present a cautious approach to the affiliation of Idu is recommended.

Phonologies

Overview

One the features that argues against the closeness of the Mishmi languages and the problem of trying to develop a 'one-size fits all' orthography is the differences in their phonologies. Idu is by far the richest, both in terms of vowel contrasts and modified consonants. The descriptions of vowel length and nasalization in Jatan Pulu (1978) and Jimi Pulu (2002a, b) are inaccurate, undermining the basis for an orthography. In this section, a summary phonology is given, which can be compared with the orthographic proposals outlined in Proposed Orthographies.

Idu

Idu consonants are shown in Table 3.

Table 3

Idu Consonants

	Bilabial	*Labio-dental*	*Alveolar*	*Retro-flex*	*Palato-alveolar*	*Palatal*	*Velar*	*Glottal*
Plosive	p, p^h b	–	t, t^h d	–	–	–	k, k^h g	–
Fricative	–	–	s, s^h [z]	–	[ʃ]	–	–	h
Affricate	–	–	ts [dz]	–	tʃ, tʃʰ, dʒ	–	–	–
Nasal	m	–	n	–	–	ɲ	ŋ	–
Flapped	–	–	r	–	–	–	–	–
Lateral	–	–	l	ɭ	–	–	–	–
Approximants	w	–	–	ɽ	–	y	–	–

Idu has a small subset of long or doubled consonants both in initial and medial position. Doubled initial consonants seem to be/mm/and/ll/, which are illustrated in the following contrasts;

llō	Warm	lō	to purchase
mmə̄	New	mə̀	old
mmò	to hide	mō	to bury
rrā̀	leave field fallow	rā	sharp

Doubled consonants in word-medial position are/mm/, /ll/, /tt/ and /ɽɽ/.

/s/ and /ʃ/ appear to be in free variation in many words, and are probably not to be considered distinct phonemes. However, in loanwords, such as /sini/ 'sugar', the original alveolar sound is conserved. The voiceless fricative /z/ appears in some words, for example *azu* cobra sp. or *ibizu* 'pika'. However, it is in free variation with both the affricate [dz] and the palatal affricate [dʒ]. Some speakers prefer [z] for particular words, so it may well be acceptable to write it as part of the alphabet, but it is unlikely to be a distinct phoneme.

Aspiration is the most common form of consonant modification and can be applied to all voiceless consonants. Thus;

/p^h/, /t^h/, k^h/, /$tʃ^h$/, /s^h/

/p^h/ is part of a consistent aspirated series, but is sometimes heard in free variation with [f].

Only/p/, /p^h/ and /b/ can be labialised in Idu, and this is uncommon. The following consonants can be rhotacised;

/p^r/, /p^{hr}/, b^r/, /t^{hr}/, /d^r/, /$ʃ^r$/, /k^r/, /k^{hr}/, /g^r/, /m^r/

One of the more perplexing issues in Idu phonology is the variation in palatalization, labialization and rhoticization, i.e. whether –y, –w or –r is articulated after a consonant. Many words seem to vary from one speaker to another and even within the speech of one individual. Although there are dialect differences between 'Upper' and 'Lower' Idu, this is apparently not one of them. There is a definite tendency for younger speakers to drop these consonant modifications, for example, saying *nopu* instead of *nyopu* for 'breast'. It is usual in writing systems to prefer the older, more conservative forms, but this remains an issue for discussion.

Vowels

The vowels of Idu are shown in Table 4.

Table 4
Idu Vowels

Vowels	*Front*	*Central*	*Back*
Close	i [ĩ]	–	u [ũ], [ụ]
Close-mid	e [ẽ]	–	o [õ]
Open-mid	–	ə, ə̣	[ɔ]
Open	–	a [ã] a̤	–

Idu has contrastive long vowels. However, some Idu words have two vowels of the same type following one another which are pronounced separately. Examples are;

à.ágrà	basket for baby
à.átò	loom part
è.écè	dao

All vowels in Idu can also be nasalised and vowel length contrastive. The following long nasal vowels have been recorded.

/ãã/, /ẽẽ/, /ĩĩ/, /õõ/, /ũũ/

No examples of nasalised long schwa /ə/ have been recorded. The retracted vowels show length but no nasalization.

In at least one example, a triple-length nasalised vowel has been recorded. This illustrates the probable genesis of long vowels in Idu, through intervocalic consonant deletion. The 'long' form is;

jōlòlõ̀ looking like an owl

However, the usual form is;

jȭ.õ̀õ̀ looking like an owl

The first õ is separated from the õõ by an audible break, presumably reflected the change in tone level. Nasalization has spread leftwards across all syllables, reinforced by the prior intervening consonants being laterals.

Apart from ordinary and nasalised vowels, Idu also has retracted vowels, where the lower jaw is pulled inwards at the moment of articulation. Two vowels have been recorded with this articulation, /ə̣/ and /ụ/. Only /ə̣/ is common. For ease of reading, retraction is noted throughout this document by underlining rather than the IPA symbol. The phonemic status of the schwa is shown by the pair;

khə̰	faeces	khə́	to satisfy
ícíkhə̰́	small		

/ə̰/ can be long, as in;

ánjìgrə̰ə̰ wild plant sp.

The nature of retracted vowels which are not part of an ATR vowel harmony system is disputed and Moisik et al. (2012) have recently proposed a new mechanism to explain them.

Idu has a single creaky vowel which only occurs in a single context, followed by a palatal (Table 5);

Table 5

a̰y Sequences in Idu

Idu	*Gloss*
ā̰yē	be irritating
ā̰yē	strip kernels from maize
à̰yē	poison
à̰yà	daughter
à̰yèbə̰̀	ritual
māà̰y	serow

Idu has abundant ay-sequences with a non-creaky vowel, but as Table 5 suggests, these are never followed by -e, which suggests/a̰/ is conditioned by the following mid-front vowel.

Tones

Idu has three contrastive tone heights, like its neighbours, Tawra and Kman, but unlike most regional languages. In this it resembles some of the Naga and Kuki-Chin languages. Rising and falling tones are absent on single segments and are only associated with VV sequences. The three level tones are marked as follows;

High	´
Mid	¯
Low	`

A macron (¯) over a vowel is thus mid-tone and not length.

The following are examples of minimal triplets, demonstrating the three contrastive tone heights.

Buy	ló
White	lō
drill, make hole	lò
smoke s.t. on a tray	kù
Grains	kū
go on journey and return on the same day	kú

Existing Literature and Proposed Orthographies

Formal Orthographies

The first formal attempt to develop an orthography for Idu followed a visit by linguists from the CIIL (Central Institute of Indian Languages). It is not clear what analysis was undertaken but a trial primer was published (CIIL, n.d.). This made use of what may tactfully described as unlikely conventions, including @ for schwa and doubled vowels for high tone. A storybook including songs and narrative pieces on Idu life was published using these conventions but is now extremely rare (Figure 1).

Figure 1
Idu Storybook

Christianity among the Idu does not yet have a high profile, but missionaries from other regions of NE India would like to see a bible translation undertaken. Funded by Living Word, Shillong, the Baptist Church of Nagaland began a project to translate the New Testament around 2000. To develop an orthography for Idu, they employed a Mizo missionary with some knowledge of linguistics. No formal phonology was undertaken and the basis for the orthography is thus unclear. Figure 2 shows the title page of the Gospel of St. John, published in a trial edition in 2013. This incorporates some rather counter-intuitive orthographic conventions, including the use of 'x' for nasalization. It omits the schwa, retracted vowels, long vowels, tones and other features of Idu which might be considered necessary to successful reading and writing. The consequence has been a sort of polite revolt inside the congregation, who are currently in discussion with the non-Christian literacy committee concerning a more effective orthography.

Figure 2
Gospel of St John in Idu

A curious addendum to these efforts at an orthography for religious purposes is Mega (2013). The cover is shown in Figure 3. This was apparently commissioned by the Bible Society of India although this is not evident from the book itself. Mega is concerned that 'This gives us reason to ask why all those efforts did not bring much fruit as it was expected'. This is a review of the existing systems and a proposal for a revision, heavily illustrated with colour images, apparently

Figure 3
Cover of Bible Society Reading Book

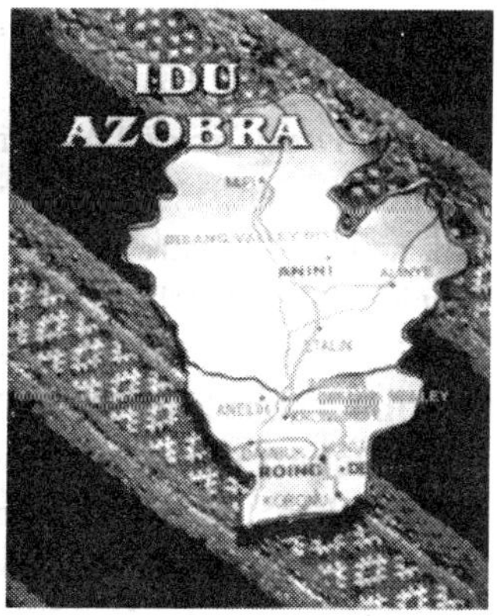

drawn from the internet. The revision has some curious features, including the omission of aspirated consonants on the basis that they 'need not be listed as they do not create any unnatural sound'. Mega (2013) marks 'stress' (apparently tone), nasalization, 'rough breathing' (perhaps retracted vowels) and 'rough nasal'. As he gives a single example of each sound in transcription it is difficult to compare this with a more mainstream account of the phonology. The reasons for producing this book are unclear but it has not been accompanied by any programme of dissemination, and has inevitably fallen by the wayside. There is more than a possibility this is an expression of inter-church rivalry among Protestant groups.

Texting, Facebook and Other Informal Orthographies

As may be clear, all these attempts to develop orthographies have failed, for lack of clear phonological analysis, coherent orthography proposals and follow-up. This was of limited interest to the communities until the later 2000s, when access to mobile phones and the internet became more widespread, at least in the plains areas. The potential to communicate via texting and Facebook became exciting, especially as written Hindi skills are far less developed than informal spoken varieties. The consequence was the development of *ad hoc* and somewhat inconsistent orthographies which could be typed without recourse to special characters. As writing systems, these work because the content is fairly predictable and the vocabulary is small. Tone and some of the more exotic consonants and vowels are not written, nor is length marked consistently. These surface in a small number of public signs (e.g. Photo 1 which shows the Idu language sign above the parade-ground in Roing).

Photo 1

Idu Public Signage in Roing

Source: Author Photo.

The existence of informal writing systems which work within a specific context creates a dilemma for linguists. Clearly their existence helps encourage the principle of reading and writing, but the absence of background analysis makes developing consistent teaching materials difficult or impossible. However, it is important to make a compromise with informal systems, and one principle is that use of special characters is excluded. This is an important change, since the availability of computers with Unicode character sets has encouraged the use of common IPA characters such as 'ŋ' in recent orthographies. The former difficulties of printing now bypassed, a more IPA-like direction seemed a good way to go. However, although mobile phone character sets do include some upper ASCII characters, the time wasted in seeking these out, means that typing is much quicker with the ordinary keyboard set. Orthography design must take on this new reality or risk being ignored.

Orthography Proposal for Idu

Table 6 shows the main consonants of Idu with the most usual way of writing them. The difficult consonants, where a writing solution is still under discussion, are marked with a shaded line.

Table 6

Writing Idu Consonants

IPA	*As in*	*Gloss*	*Written*	*Hence*
p	pà	to cross	p	pa
p^h	p^hálá	tea	ph	phala
b	bùɲì	yesterday	b	bunyi
t	tì	to cover	t	ti
t^h	t^hù	bite	th	thu
d	dò	suck	d	do
tɕ	tɕĩ́	to rot	tc, ts, cy	tcin, tsin, cyin
k	kə̱̀	rice	k	kə
k^h	k^hògá	dispute	kh	khoga
g	gə̱̀	to carry	g	gə
h	hă	eat	h	ha
s	sá	bridge	s	sa
ʃ	ʃù	red	sh	shu
tʃ	tʃí	acquire	c	ci
$tʃ^h$	$tʃ^h$ì	to walk	ch	chi
dʒ	dʒámì	yak	j	jami
z	ádʒù	cobra sp.	z	azu
m	má	black	m	ma
n	ná	painful	n	na
ɲ	ɲà	dance	ny	nya
ŋ	ŋá	I, me	ng	nga
r	rò	arrest	r	ro
ɽ	ɽí	boil	rh	rhi
l	lò	white	l	lo
ɭ	íɭù	eight	lh	ilhu
w	wá	cancer	w	wa
y	yù	beer	y	yu

Five of the Idu vowels correspond to English vowels as in Table 7 and can be written that way:

Table 7

Idu Cardinal Vowels

IPA	*Example*	*Gloss*	*Written*
a	à	child	a
e	è	to do	e
i	ìì	to live	i
o	ò	to shoot	o
u	ù	to pluck	u

The two other unmodified vowels are /ɔ/ and /ə/. These can be written 'oh' and 'ə').

/ɔ/ is very rare and a practical orthography may be able to dispense with it.

toh	tɔ̄	to row

/ə/ is extremely common and can be written using the standard IPA symbol.

gədu	gə̄dū	tapioca
ngə	ŋə̄	to saw
kə	kə̀	paddy
brə	brə̀	to swallow

The only common retracted vowel is/ə̠/ which can be written 'ə̠'

ngə̠	ŋə̠̄	sickness
gə̠	gə̠̄	to carry
hə̠	hə̠̄	honey
ilikhə̠	ìlīkhə̠̀	soil, earth

The single breathy vowel /a̤/ can be written 'ah' but it may be that speakers will automatically insert breathiness in the restricted phonological context.

ahye	ā̤yē	be irritating
ahye	à̤yē	poison
ahya	à̤yà	daughter
maahy	māà̤y	serow

Tones may need to be written to distinguish particular pairs or minimal triplets, such as in the examples in §2. At present testing will need to be done to establish the most practical strategy for tone-marking. Normal practice with three-tone systems is to leave mid-tone unmarked, as in the transcriptions in this paper.

Specialized Language Registers

General

A particular feature of language among the Mishmi peoples is the parallel registers used for specialized purposes. These range from shamanic chants, which are incomprehensible to speakers of everyday language, to mourning and humorous registers, understood by everyone. They include a language used by hunters while engaged in hunting, an angry register and vocabulary only used in poetry. Some of these are sufficiently different from everyday language, as not to be comprehensible to someone unfamiliar with them. Hunting and poetic language are substitution languages, where ordinary lexemes are replaced by new and unfamiliar items, but the syntax and morphology is preserved.

Shamanic language is more complex, since it includes elaborate periphrastic expressions, and fixed expressions which do not always conform to ordinary usage. The angry/mediation register includes shifting tones a level higher than normal speech and the use of complex replacement phrases that emphasise parallelism. These registers can be summarised as in Table 8;

Table 8

Registers of the Mishmi Languages

Register	*Characteristics*
Hunters	Spoken during hunting. Names of most animals and some common lexical items substituted either by periphrastic expressions or lexemes of unknown origin. Mostly unknown to speakers who are not hunters.
Shaman	Shamans are required to recite lengthy chants in a language generally not understood by everyday speakers. Common lexemes replaced by complex expressions, but also unusual syntax. Some replacement lexemes understood by mature adults.
Mourning	A series of fixed replacement expressions used in mourning. Reported for Idu
Angry/mediation	A series of lexical replacements used in mediation in disputes between individual households or clans. Can also be used in angry speech. Reported for Idu

None of the languages are 'secret' in the sense that speakers are unwilling to discuss them. However, public knowledge of them is extremely patchy, especially among young people, and it is clear that further research is required to define their status more exactly. If register is a 'variety of a language used for a particular purpose or in a particular social setting' then what happens in Mishmi goes rather beyond this. Certainly in terms of comprehensibility, the language of hunters and shamans are distinct languages.

Hunters' Language

The use of a specialized language spoken by hunters while engaged in the hunt was first reported in Sun (1999). Sun only provides a short table of examples of hunters' terms and interestingly, no animal names, which are at the core of this practice. To give an example of the substitutions typical of this system, Table 9 gives the ordinary and hunters' names for key animal species in Idu.

Table 9

Idu Names for Animals in Hunters' Language

Species	*Idu*	*Hunters' Name and Gloss*
Bear, generic	áhũ̀	*àmbrè njɔ̀ɔ́tɔ̀* 'wild huge and awkward' (walks from side to side)
Deer generic	mànjò	*áphú ácì* 'from the field' (deer come and eat crops in the night)
Deer, musk	álá	*ámbéshù* 'small animal'
Goral	ámì	*àjùshù* 'deep and high gorge small'
Serow	máyè	*àmàdrɔ̀* 'split in two' (because it has a divided hoof)
Thakin	ákhrù	*àmbrè kàcì* 'animal big'
Tiger	àmrá	*áŋgócì* 'from the highlands' *áŋgó* = montane region.
Wild pig	ám^{w}é	*ɛ̀nàmbɔ̀n dì* 'nose sharp'

Although all the hunters' names were eventually etymologised, even the components of their names are sometimes rather obscure and arcane words, only known to older people. It seems that this is not a fixed lexicon, as hunters' names for animals in the Hunli area were significantly different from those recorded in the plains.

The Language of Shamans

Shaman's chants are easy to record but complex to transcribe. The typical chant may last for many hours, performed by the bed of a sick person, and since the chants are learnt by rote, not even the shaman may be able to gloss every line. As an example of the language used, below are two expressions for the squirrel *ada* in Idu. The word-by-word glossing is as explained to me, but some words do not correspond to everyday speech. 'Tree', for example, is normally *asimbo* not *asi*, and the way of expressing 'above' and 'below' are also different.

asi	iŋgu lo ne	ruya	ə̱iga
tree	below the branches	noise	one who
asi	ngu pu nɛ	mra	ə̱iga
tree	top	stomach pain	one who

At this point, it can only be said that a great deal of more work is necessary to make definitive statements about all features of this language.

Can a Successful Orthography be Designed?

What will it take for an orthography to be accepted?

The discussion above makes clear that none of the attempts to develop an orthography for the Mishmi languages have been successful. The phonology has not been analysed according to modern methods, a document setting out the relationship between phonology and orthography not prepared and the community not consulted. Most of all, there has been no mechanism for a follow-up. In the past, speakers may not have been strongly motivated to develop a writing system, but this has changed, in part due to the desire to communicate via texting and the internet, but also due to an increasing awareness of cultural loss.

This situation can now be remedied in part. Phonology and orthography documents have been developed, and committees have been formed for Idu and also Kman. E-mail has made it possible for discussions for amendments and changes to be made at long distance and more regular visits can be made in person. However, the existing use of the Mishmi languages for texting has the implication that an orthography which requires special characters may struggle for acceptance. The next step is, therefore, to ensure that the writing conventions are genuinely accepted by the community rather than by a few enthusiasts, and that test versions of reading and writing books are circulated and evaluated.

Representing Language Registers

All the Mishmi languages have additional registers apart from everyday speech. Research on the nature and extent of these is in early stages, but so far there is no evidence of distinctive phonology, so these will probably not require any new conventions in the writing system. However, the language of shamans in particular is full of expressions whose etymologies are unclear. Decisions will need to be made about word breaks and other matters. However, this can safely be postponed until orthography is established for everyday speech.

Conclusion

The chapter describes the status, terminology and degree of documentation of the Idu language, spoken in Arunachal Pradesh, NE India, and to a much lesser extent in Tibet. It is probably more endangered than is suggested by the Ethnologue, in part because the figures may reflect the populations of towns said to speak indigenous languages but in reality dominated by major South Asian languages, such as Hindi, Assamese and Nepali. It is likely that Idu has no more than a few thousand fully fluent speakers, with several thousand more semi-speakers and similar numbers claiming ethnic identity, but unable to speak the language. Although language use in committed homes remains vigorous, there has been a highly significant loss of specialized terminology, particularly ethnoscientific. Many terms for the natural world are increasingly unknown to speakers in a multilingual environment. However, there is now a lively interest in writing these languages.

Notes

1. It is unclear why one might want to say 'the elephant is the largest of animals' in a region where there are no elephants.
2. I would like to thank Dr Mite Linggi and other members of the Idu community for assistance in the field and subsequent discussion over the internet. More developed versions of this talk were given at the Max Planck Institute, Nijmegen on 8 May 2015 and at the Meeting of the Consortium for the Prehistory of the Eastern Himalayas, Sydney on 21 August 2015. I would like to thank the audience on all these occasions for their comments and discussion. A community presentation on Idu orthography was given in Roing on 27 December 2015, and a second presentation on the project as a whole in Tezu on 29 December 2015.

References

Baruah, Tapan Kumar (1988). *The Idu Mishmis*, Government of Arunachal Pradesh, Itanagar.

Bhattarcharjee, Tarun (1983). *The Idus of Mathun and Dri Valley*, Government of Arunachal Pradesh, Shillong.

Blench, R.M. and M. Post (2013). 'Rethinking Sino-Tibetan Phylogeny from the Perspective of Northeast Indian Languages', in Nathan Hill and Tom Owen-Smith (eds), *Selected Papers from the 16th Himalayan Languages Symposium*, Mouton de Gruyter, New York, pp. 71–104.

Brown, N. (1837). 'Comparison of Indo-Chinese Languages', *Journal of the Asiatic Society of Bengal*, 6: 1023–38.

—— (1850). 'Aborigines of the North East Frontier', *Journal of the Asiatic Society of Bengal*, 19: 309–16.

Campbell, G. (1874). *Specimens of Languages of India: Including Those of the Aboriginal Tribes of Bengal, the Central Provinces, and the Eastern Frontier*, Bengal Secretariat Press, Calcutta.

CIIL (n.d.). *Idu Ekob@ Al~ozo*, no place of publication but Roing.

Dalton, E.J.T. (1872). *Descriptive Ethnology of Bengal*, Asiatic Society of Bengal, Calcutta.

Dutta, C. (1978). *Arunachal Pradesh, Lohit District Gazetteer*, Government of Arunachal Pradesh.

Griffith, W. (1847). *Journal of Travels in Assam, Burma, etc.*, Calcutta.

Hamilton, Angus (1912). *In Abor Jungles: An Account of the Abor Expedition, the Mishmi Mission and the Miri Mission*, Eveleigh Nash, London.

Jiang, Di 江荻 (2005). 义都语研究 *Yidu Language Research*, 民族出版社 Nationalities Press, 北京 Beijing .

Konow, Sten (1902). 'Note on the Languages Spoken between the Assam Valley and Tibet', *The Journal of the Royal Asiatic Society of Great Britain and Ireland*, 34(1): 127–37.

Lewis, M. Paul, Gary F. Simons and Charles D. Fennig (eds) (2016). *Ethnologue: Languages of the World*, Nineteenth edition, SIL International, Dallas, Texas. Online version: http://www.ethnologue.com.

Mega, Amuta (2013). *Idu Azobra*, s. l.

Mills, J.P. (1952). 'The Mishmis of the Lohit Valley, Assam', *The Journal of the Royal Anthropological Institute of Great Britain and Ireland*, 82(1): 1–12.

Moisik, S.R., E. Czaykowska-Higgins and J.H. Esling (2012). 'The Epilaryngeal Articulator: A New Conceptual Tool for Understanding Lingual-laryngeal Contrasts', in A. McKillen and J. Loughran (eds), The Proceedings from Montreal-Ottawa-Toronto (MOT) Phonology Workshop 2011: Phonology in the 21st Century: In Honour of Glyne Piggott, *McGill Working Papers in Linguistics*, 22(1): 1–15.

Ouyang, Jueya (1985). *A Brief Introduction to the Luoba Language*, Nationalities Press, Beijing.

Pulu, Jatan (1978). *Idu Phrase-book*, Directorate of Research, Government of Arunachal Pradesh, Shillong.

Pulu, Jimi (2002a). *Idu Mishmi Proverbs and Sayings*, Directorate of Research, Government of Arunachal Pradesh, Itanagar.

—— (2002b). *A Handbook on Idu Mishmi Language*, Directorate of Research, Government of Arunachal Pradesh, Itanagar.

Rowlatt, E.A. (1845). 'Report of an Expedition into the Mishmee Hills to the N.E. of Sudyah', *Journal of the Asiatic Society of Bengal*, 14(2): 477–93.

Sun, Hongkai (1983a). *A Brief Introduction to Idu (Luoba) Language* [In Chinese], Mínzú Yuwén 6, Mínzú Chûbanshè, Beijing.

—— (1983b). *The Languages of the Peoples of the Six River Valley Region and their Genetic Classification* [In Chinese], Mínzú Xuébào, Yunnan People's Publishing Company, Kunming.

—— (1999). 'On the Himalayan Languages of the Eastern Himalayan Area in China', *Linguistics of the Tibeto-Burman Area*, 22: 61–72.

Sun, Hongkai et al. 孙宏开 孙宏开 (1980). 们巴，珞巴，僜人的语言 *Menba, Luoba, and Deng Peoples' Languages*, 中国社会科学出版社 China Social Sciences Press, 北京 Beijing, pp. 174–231.

Talukdar, G.C. (1962). *A Phrase Book in Idu*, P.C. Dutta, Shillong.

Wilcox, R. (1832). 'Memoir of a Survey of Assam and the Neighbouring Countries Executed in 1825–6–7–8', *Asiatick Researches*, 17: 314–469.

Young, E.C. (1907). 'A Journey from Yunnan to Assam', *Geographical Journal*, 30(2): 152–80.

11

Festival and Emerging Social Reality

A Study of the Idu Mishmis of Arunachal Pradesh

TARUN MENE AND SARIT K. CHAUDHURI

Generally, festival symbolizes collective performances, often centring on certain ritual operations. A festival may have multiple connotations involving both sacred and secular dimensions and can also be perceived as an agglomeration of multiple folk genres, viz. dances, songs, chanting, myth, ritual offerings, feasting, etc. Most importantly it reveals manifested and latent aspects of cultural values and intricate social relationships in a given community. Thus, sometimes, it is said that festivals are the external expansion of social behaviour.

William Henderson (1866) observed that, 'festivals held by the primitive peoples consisted of collective magic or religious rites for propitiation of evil spirits and invocation of friendly supernatural powers and were held on such occasions as the admission of new members to a tribe, disposal of the dead; and preparations of fisherman for the catch, hunters for the these and warriors for battle. A communal meal was usually a part of the festival. The development of agriculture was accompanied by new festivals, also consisting of magical religious rituals, in connection with the seasons, especially with the virtual equinox and the winter solstices. Planting and harvesting were important festival occasions. Thus, it may be said that most of the festivals of the world developed out of magico-ritual practices. And according to some social analyst a ritual is an enactment of a myth. Thus, we may conclude that behind a festival there may be a myth. So, originally the festivals were exclusively religious. In the present context also, it may be said most of the festivals are still associated with religious observances' (cited by Datta et al., 1994: 151).

Scholars like Jacob Grimn, Max Muller, Andrew Lang, Wilhelm Mannhendt, James Frazer, and so on have made attempts to link primitive beliefs and magical rituals with the modern festivals. It is as well assumed that the tradition of the modern festivals emanated from the beliefs and magical ritual of the ancient communities. The ancient communities performed those magical rituals to make the days grow longer, to expel severe cold, to appease deities of the field and forests as well as sky and water. They also performed magical rituals to satisfy the rain-god or to appease the deadly deities of diseases and to please the malevolent dead and to appease the village ghosts as well. Even the ancient communities solemnized those magical rituals to promote fertility (Smith, 1972).

Festivals form an essential aspect of all cultures of the World. Most of the societies, whether primitive or folk or elite or modern, have their own festivals and these are celebrated in one form or the other. Regarding the people of Arunachal Pradesh, most of the ethnic groups are the follower of animism and most of their festivals are associated with agriculture. Festivals like *Moh-Mol* of Tangsas, *Dree* of the Apatanis, *Nyokum* of the Nyishis, *Mopin* of the Galos and *Chindang* of the Sajolang (Miji) are related to agriculture. There are some other festivals also, such as *Sangken* of the Khamptis and the Singphos, which is related to their religious faith (Buddhism) yet some are related to mark the New Year and so on. There are some festivals meant for peace and prosperity of the family and clan with religious elaboration and animal sacrifices.

Thus, precisely we may say that festival not only provides entertainments and social festivities to people, they also serve as an integrating force for the entire community. Most of the festivals co-occur with the activities of the people throughout the year. May be distinct in their outlook, festivals also serve to satisfy one's mental and spiritual needs, which ultimately builds their spiritual world and also reveals latent aspects of cultural values and intricate social relationship. For the reason, festivals are often regarded as the mirror of the society. They are not merely reflections of religion or belief system but many other aspects also. With this backdrop, the *Reh* festival of the Idu Mishmi tribe of Arunachal Pradesh is made the focal point of the present chapter.

The Meaning of *Reh* Festival

The word *Reh* is closely associated with the term '*Rae*' meaning 'invitation.' It is observed that for the celebration of *Reh* festival a rope called *Tayi* is distributed to all relatives and other associates, carrying the meaning of invitation, similar to modern day invitation cards. Thus, by inviting all, a successful *Reh* festival is celebrated. This festival is celebrated in two forms nowadays; one is traditional way of celebration at individual level and another at community level. The former is basically celebrated involving clan members, matrimonial relatives and people from the village only while the latter is celebrated at community level involving all the members of the community on a particular date of a calendar year with the arrangements of all possible modern elements, such as modern dance and music, fashion shows, goods and garments stalls, etc. In such type, there is very minimal representation of the traditional aspects. In this work, focus is on the traditional form of *Reh* festival, and its different aspects.

For the Idu Mishmis, *Reh* is the only festival which brings joy and pleasure to people. It is in this festival that the whole clan members of the *Reh* organizers gather on a common platform which serves in creating a strong relationship and kinship bonds. Further, for a successful celebration, it is the villagers who get the full credit for their participation in various activities.

With the operation of the festival which lasts for four nights and a day, there are certain activities related to exchanges of gifts (*Aagite, Aagiioro, Ameta)* and system of offering of security deposits (*Adda*)[1] and returning of security deposits (*Anda-da)* in the form of cash and animals which display people's sense of mutual understanding, cooperation and reciprocity. There are various kinds of ritual performances by the shaman (*Igu*) followed by observance of taboos. Such ritual performances are basically meant to appease both the benevolent and malevolent spirits and thereby to achieve peace and prosperity. These mark the religious aspects reflecting myth, folklore, tales, and elaborated belief system.

Origin Myth of the *Reh* Festival

As per the myth of the Idu Mishmis, *Reh* festival was first organized by a slave named *Apijuru*. Once when *Apijuru* was sitting in the agricultural field, looking after the crops, he saw some people coming. They were people belonging to a group called '*Inyiambribri*' who were returning from a hunting expedition to a place called *Zahiwu-Arow*. Coming in contact, *Inyiambribri* people offered *Apijuru* with some piece of their hunt. He was also suggested that if he wants more meat then he can proceed to *Zahiwa-Arow* to collect the leftover meat, the head of the *Beka* (the river serpent). To this suggestion, *Apijuru* enquired the way to reach the place and *Inyiambribri* people instructed *Apijuru* with some clues to follow. He was told to trace the cut marks in the jungle and to follow the course by keeping his eyes on the slashed wild banana plants (*ebi-ata*). *Apijuru* was also instructed to look for a place where bird *Pishu* is flying in abundance. Following all the hints, *Apijuru* finally reached *Zahiwu Awro* and there he finds the chopped off head of the *Beka* which the *Inyiambribris* had left. Finding his share of meat, *Apijuru* started chopping the head of *Beka* and while chopping the head apart he founds a glittering object called *pidi* (diamond).

While returning home, *Apijuru* brought the *pidi* with him, hiding it in his wearing. When he reached home he severely fell ill with fever. *Apijuru* sensed that it was the effect of the *pidi* so he took it out and hid it in the thatched roof. But the heat of the *pidi* was so strong that thatched roof was about to catch fire on many instances. Thereafter, he kept on changing the hiding place. He hides the *pidi* in different trees like *'Atombo', 'Eka-bo', 'Irumbo', 'Elambo'*, etc. But these trees also felt the heat of the *pidi*. *Apijuru* went for another hiding place and hid it in the river bank and water. These made sands shiny and the fishes that came in contact with the *pidi*, their scales also became shiny. *Apijuru* again searching for safer place to hide the *pidi* in a place called *andomo*. There, the *Aroh* (otter), *Ahu* (bear) and *'Amra'* (tiger) came in contact with the *pidi* and as a result their skins, bones and organs become shiny and more valuable.

Then *Apijuru* hid the *'pidi'* at a place called *Towpoka*. Here the peacock came in contact with the *pidi* and got the shine from it. The feathers of the peacock began to shine. The radiation of the '*pidi*' also came into contact with '*Aro*' (*coptis teeta*) and it became a valuable medicinal plant. In this way whatever things came into contact with the *pidi* became valuable. At last, *Aala* (musk deer) consumed the *pidi*.

In his attempt to hide the *pidi*, *Apijuru* wandered to many places and in due course of time he gathered all the valuable items like skin of the otter, tiger, tooth of tiger, *coptis teeta*, etc. and sold it to the '*Amis*' (the Tibetans). After selling all these valuable materials, he got in return utensils from them. On the way back to his place, *Apijuru* encountered with a musk deer running nearby the jungle. To have the mask deer, he made a trap and hunted down the deer. While operating the hunt, he found the *pidi* again which was there in the navel of the musk deer. After getting the musk of the deer *Apijuru* returned to his house which was a cave. Reaching the cave, he stored all the utensils there and again went to the people and asked about the *pidi*. He reached out the *Ami* (Tibetans), *Yusipu-Ponjame* (northern people probably the Chinese), *Iniya-tupu* (the Nagas), *Ami Mosa* (Adis) and *Taya* (Taraon Mishmi) but none of them claimed the *pidi*. Lastly, he meets *Ami-asa* (people of the plains) whom he sold off the *pidi*. And in return he received money and clothes from them. However, coming back to his place, he remained sick most of the time. So he approached *Anjoru*, a shaman and he diagnosed the cause of his suffering as due to the *Pidi*. *Anjoru* suggested *Apijuru* to perform ritual by sacrificing some animals and feeding the people. *Apijuru* began his *Reh* festival ritual. *Apijuru* was a slave and he had no relatives. Therefore, he offered *Yu* (rice beer) and pig as *Ameta* (gift offered to the material relatives and in laws) to the trees *Achumbo* and *Engabo* as his father and mother. In this way, *Apijuru* performed the *Reh* festival by sacrificing a pig only. The master of *Apijuru*, *Annyime-Menga* after knowing the festival conducted by *Apijuru* decides to conduct *Reh* festival. It was he who sacrificed Mithun in *Reh* festival and conducted the festivals in a massive manner by inviting all his relatives.[2]

The Structure and Organization of the *Reh* Festival

The structural aspects of the festival could be well perceived when we see the various activities related to preparation and organization of the festival. To organize an individual *Reh* festival one has to undergo long preparations. Some activities may take six to eight long years and some take only few months and weeks. These activities require both individual efforts as well as group activities. There are some which are gender and age specific. Some activities are followed by rigid taboos and some do not. Below is a discussion on various stages of preparation which helps us understand the overall structural features of the *Reh* festival.

Adda

When a person decides to organize a *Reh* festival, he starts offering security deposits in terms of cash and animals to other individuals who are actually organizing the *Reh* festival and this is done only in that particular occasion. He

offers as many times he is capable of and to as many individuals in as many villages where such individual *Reh* festival is organized. He stops this process of offering, the moment he feels satisfied with his security deposits. This system of offering is called *Adda* which is a clear indication that one has started his preparation for organizing *Reh* festival in the near future. One of the important features of this system is that it is done only by a married male member of the society and done on the occasion of someone's *Reh* festival only and not on any other occasion. Such offering may include cash, one or more mithun (*sa*) or pig (*illi*), rice brew (*yu*), smoked fish (*angaku*), smoked wild rat (*ashaku*), paddy (*keku*), millet (*eka*), maize (*ambo*), etc. It is done only by the married male member of the society, since he has matrimonial relatives who play a crucial role in realizing a successful *Reh* festival and also they are the ones responsible for creating a network of relationships and also help in exchanging gifts and presentations (*Agite, Agiiro, Ameta,* etc).

Ha-Thru

The term *Ha-Thru* conveys the mean counting of animals, especially of mithun and pig which are sacrificed for the purpose of *Reh* festival. If one decides to conduct the festival, he declares it by performing *Ha-thru* which is generally performed a year prior to the actual celebration. During its performance, villagers are called upon and feasting is done. However, ritual activities are not performed.

Mranno-Che

For food items like rice, millets, maize, chilly, ginger and other vegetables, cultivation is done almost for three to four seasons prior to declaration of *Reh* celebration. These involve clearing of jungle, sowing of seeds, harvesting of crops, etc. which can be collectively termed called *Mranno-Che*. The productions are especially used for the festival and are stored in storehouse called *Aka*. In the process of cultivation, the villagers are obliged to help the concerned person and family.

Rehgusi

In the *Reh* celebration, shaman (*Igu*) plays a pivotal role. Generally, the organizer of the festival himself selects a shaman for ritual performances. However, there is a system called *Rehgusi*, whereby a person requests the organizer for a deal or contract in selecting a shaman who would be engaged in the festival. In such a case, the organizer may come down to an agreement and hand over the deal to a person of his choice, who may be a shaman or a non-shaman. If he is a non-shaman, he offers mithuns or pigs as security deposit (*Adda*) to the organizer which is expected to be returned when the person (the non-shaman) celebrates his festival. For this deal, he gets in return a presentation called *Regusi-ne.* In case of a shaman, he gets the rewards for his duty and also recognition in the society. His reward includes animals and cash which is called *Igu-Gru* or *Reh-Gru.* After the completion of festival, the shaman has to observe taboos which is equally applicable to non-shaman also who had taken the contract of *Rehgusi.*

Illiprochu and Saprochu Ade

When one declares to organize *Reh* festival, he domesticates one mithun called *Sa-prochu* and a pig called *Illi-prochu* at least for one or more years. However, such domestication of animals does not have any especial purpose but one must keep both for the feasting purpose. Along with these, two numbers of fowl called *Etowur* and *Etopo* are also reared only to sacrifice in rituals called *Apo-nah, Apoh-nu* and *Apoh-tee.* In addition to this, a person can keep sufficient number of mithuns, pigs and poultries as per his capacity to feast the gathering.

Anda-Asi

This means asking of security deposits (*Adda*), i.e. cash and animals, from the individuals with whom one has deposited his securities during the time of their *Reh* festival. Thus, by doing so he gets back all his deposits (*Adda*) prior to his actual celebration. In fact, *Adda* and *Anda-da* are system of mutual reciprocity of security deposits which circulate within the larger network of individuals who are actually organizing and those who are planning to organize in the near future. Since *Reh* festival involves a large gathering of people, all preparations are done keeping in mind the sufficiency of all the requirements. Thus, when a person offers security deposits, it is called *Adda* and when one returns back it is called *Anda-da* and the process of asking back of security deposits is called *Anda-Asi.* In case if someone fails to return the security deposits for any reason, he and his family are socially looked down upon. In case of death of the person with whom the security was deposited, either his wife or his son or any other close relative is expected to return back the same amount. Sometimes, disagreement arises between persons over quantity, size, age, or number, etc. of the security deposits. This occurs when records are not properly kept and such a case is solved in mutual understanding with the interventions of senior members. Also there are instances where a person asks his deposits without organizing the festival. In such a case he is considered a failed person and also socially looked dawn upon.

Hawe-Anji

This preparation is related to food items gathered from the agricultural field. The harvested crops are put into process for making them final for consumption, which includes sundry, grinding, husking, storing, etc. These entire processing of edibles are collectively done both by the male and female folks of the village. Finally, all items are properly stored in the granary (*Aka*).

Yu-phe

This is an important activity in which all the villagers gather and prepare rice brew (*yu*) at the *rehko*, the particular house where the *Reh* festival is supposed to be organized. Generally, this preparation is done one to two months prior to the actual days of festival. On this occasion different types of rice brew are prepared called *Yu-ara, Yu-andro, Yu-nyi*[3] to serve the mass gathering. For the villagers one mithun and a pig are sacrificed for feast.

Asha Dra and Anga Ru

Asha Dra, meaning 'trapping of wild rats' and *Anga Ru* meaning 'catching of fish' in the river. For this purpose, groups of young male folk from the village collectively extend their helping hand. The process ends when it is sufficiently collected and generally it ends a month prior to the actual days of festival celebration. Various types of traps such as *depra* (trap made of flat rock), *giripra* (trap made by bamboo), *aadapo* (trap made by bamboo), *athombra* (trap made of rope), etc. are employed. After trapping rats they are smoked. In the same way fish are also collected from the river with the help of trap made of bamboo (*tha*), channeling the river into numbers of small and narrow streams and thereafter, catching the fish. After collection they are smoked and stored. These collections are meant for the food items especially prepared for the female folks and for the presentation as gifts to female relatives who come to attend the festival.

Sa-lo and Maji-lo

Sa meaning mithun and *Maji* meaning buffalo, are the most important animals because in the absence of these animals a festival is never considered as *Reh* festival. Therefore, as many as the number of these animals are sacrificed, one's festival is considered a success and the person as rich and wealthy in the society.

Apart from animals gathered from his *Adda*, the organizer may buy these animals from others, one to three months in advance. Generally, close relatives are engaged for the purpose. Thus, buying of animals for feast is one of the important parts of the preparation.

Tayi-la

After the completion of all the above preparations, the organizer sends invitation to all his clan relatives, matrimonial relatives and also to persons with whom his securities are deposited. This invitation is called *Tayi* which is about one feet long rope having numbers of knot as indicative of dates. Each knots of a rope denote a day. With the passing of day a knot is cut off. The remaining last two knots represent the starting or the first day of the festival called *Andro-puh*.

The distribution of invitation is one of the most important tasks as it requires listing of people to be invited in the festival. Usually, senior and knowledgeable persons of the clan are consulted in making of this list. The effort of the organizer is not to miss any member, no matter how far one resides, because it becomes matter of great emotions for someone if missed out and not invited. Usually, distribution of *tayi* is done within fifteen to twenty days in advance.

Anda-so

On this occasion, a platform or chang (*Anda*) is constructed in front of the house just five to six days prior to the actual days of celebration. On this platform all the important activities takes place, such as reception of the guest, chopping of meat, offering and receiving of security deposits (*Adda* and *Anda-da*), receiving of presents from female relative (*Agite*), gift presentation to matrimonial relatives (*Ameta*), etc.

Apart from the construction of platform, storerooms for keeping meat (*Sa-aka*), basketry works (*Andronga-apu*), pigsty (*Illi-Api*), construction of altar for animal sacrifice (*Sa-Khundu*), bamboo tubes (*yu achoka*), etc. work are done.

The collection of firewood, bamboo for various purposes, collection of green vegetable (*Ahona*), leaf for food packing (*Alana*), etc. are done in full swing during this period. In this time one or two mithuns or pigs are sacrificed for feast. Rice brew is part of this entire process. In the evening time, the organizer prepares rice brew especially meant for ritualistic purposes which are *Yu-agi, Yu-andro, Yu-ayu, and Yu-manu*. He prepares these various types of brew in the *Alongga*[4] when all the guests depart after completion of all the activities. Preparation of these brews is followed by strict taboos. However, these brews may be prepared on the day of *Yu-phe.*

The Celebration Days: Activities and Ritual Performances

The traditional individual *Reh* festival lasts for five days. The first day is called *Andropu*, which is followed by *Eyani* (second day), *Iyili* (third day), *Illirumuni* (fourth day) and *Etonu-che or Aru-haa* (fifth day).

Andropu, the First Day of the *Reh* Celebration

After all these long preparations, the celebration starts with gathering of villagers and clan people at the place of celebration (*Reh-ko).* The sacrifice of animals and fowls are seen in full swing. Various ritual performances of shaman go through-out night and day which lasts four nights and a day. Rituals are important part of the *Reh* celebration because without the involvement of ritual performances the celebration is not at all considered as *Reh* festival but simply called *Hasa-ha* meaning 'dry and meaningless celebration'.

The first day of festival celebration is called *Andro-pu*. It starts with the gathering of the villagers and clan relatives who take part in various activities early in the morning. As a host, both women and menfolk of the village and clan relatives get busy with their respective work. Females prepare rice brew and varieties of food items. Menfolk, on the other hand, get engaged in slaughtering of animals like pig, mithun and its chopping and cooking activities. The organizer of the festival (now onwards called as *mengga*) and his wife (called as *Susili)*, look after all the guest and invitees and also on the activities in process. Well experienced and knowledgeable senior clan relative accompany the *mengga* during entire days of celebration. On this day the shaman (*Igu*) arrives for the first time and starts rituals like *Mealata, Akuasa, Akuto, Mipi-Ayuthree, Andro-Mrayu La, Yu-Andro Bhru, Andro-Nah,* etc. These are the rituals of the first day. Flow of invitees and guests continues the whole day and night. On arrival, the invitees and guests are greeted by the host and villagers. Presentations (*Agite*) either in cash or in kind to the *mengga* from his female relatives, offering security advance (*Adda*) and returns of security deposits (*Anda-da*) in the form of cash and animals take place on this platform. To keep record of all these exchanges, a person is entrusted by the *mengga* as *Agiiro Thrayiga*. This record includes person's name, village, amount or quantity of *Adda* and *Anda-da*, presentation of gifts (*Agite*), etc. This record is properly maintained. The list of presentations (*Agite*) from the female relatives is crucial as *mengga* would return his part of gifts to his female relatives called *Agiiro* on the third day of the festival, which includes smoked fish and birds. All the guests and invitees are entertained with food and rice brew.

Eyani, the Second Day of the *Reh* Celebration

The second day of the *Reh* celebration is called *Eyani*. Ritual starts early in the morning which includes *Aro-Mriyee-Azo, Lopho-Ayuthri, Sa-Cha, Mengga-Ayuthri, Khundu-Dro, Aru-Emoto, Sa-Eyu-Athu, Sa-Mraba-Atu,* etc. Exchange of gift (*Agitey*) and presentations (*Agiiro*) and *Adda* and *Adda-da*, etc. continues till evening and these are recorded by the *Agiio-Thrayiga* (record keeper). Gathering of guests and invitees are at the maximum on this day, so maximum number of mithuns are sacrificed at the altar called *Sa-khundu/Sa-rumpo*. The head of the sacrificed mithuns are gifts for all the cousins of the *mengga*.

On this day, another form of gift presentation called *Ameta* is made by the *mengga*. This presentation is made to all the maternal uncles, father-in-laws and brother-in-laws which may include live pigs and cash. These are made as a mark of respect and have a strong relationship with the *mengga*.

Iyili, the Third Day of the *Reh* Celebration

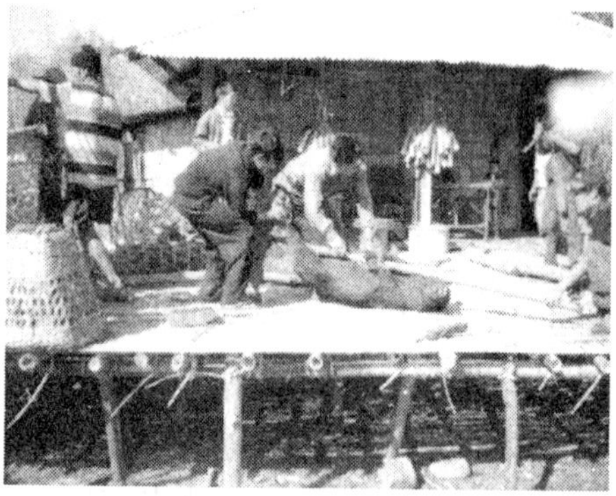

The third day of the *Reh* festival is called *Iyili*. Preparation of food and meat items starts early in the morning as most of the guests depart on this day. The day is significant as the maximum number of pigs are sacrificed on this day and the head of the sacrificed pigs are distributed among the maternal cousins of the *mengga*. On this day, *mengga* presents a special gift to his entire female relatives called *Agiiro* (bundle of smoked fish or smoked wild rats and birds). This presentation by *mengga* is given to those who have offered him gifts (*Agitey*) either in cash or in kind. This process of giving and receiving presentation between the relatives during the festival is a mark of respect, support and for strong clan bondage.

In the evening hour, after the departure of the guests, there will be an early dinner. Shaman continues various rituals like *Illi-Ache-Ajee, Illi-Eyu-Athu, Yuru-Su, Alerupisi or Cheta-Ru, Andra-Pro-Nah*, etc. which starts early in the morning and lasts till late night.

Illi–Ru-Muni or *Aru-go*, the Fourth Day of the *Reh* Festival

The fourth day of the festival is called *Illi–Ru-Muni* or *Aru-go*. People present on this day are from the village itself, and may be a few guests. Feasting continues and rituals start early morning which include *Adeh, Apoh-Nah, Apoh-Nu, Manu-Che,* etc. In the evening when the shaman chants the *Adeh* ritual, two male members dress themselves as a couple and display an act related to myth regarding the origin of paddy among the Idu Mishmis.

Etonu-che/Aru-haa, the Fifth Day of the *Reh* Festival

This is the concluding day called *Etonu-che* or *Aru-haa*. On this day, two fowls are sacrificed to forecast the future of the family members and of the house. Another fowl is sacrificed inside the granary by the shaman to appease the spirit of granary and of the food grain called *Manu*. The main purpose behind this ritual is

to appease the spirit *Apasha* and *Manu* for abundance of agricultural production for the family.

After the completion of all these rituals, the shaman departs to his house. He is offered rewards in terms of cash, meat and animals for his duty. The *mengga* and all his family members undergo strict taboos for another ten days, beginning right from the concluding day. The taboo includes restriction over offering/lending money, attaining funeral rituals, restriction on consumption of mushroom, wild animal's meat, washing clothes and garments, inter-village movement of the entire family member, etc.

Changing Perspective

It is fact that the cultural norms and values prevailing in any society govern the life and activities of an individual. These cultural values are transmitted from one generation to another since time immemorial. However, in due course of time cultures undergo changes as society moves from one phase to another. In tune with this background, the below discussion has tried to highlight the changes related to *Reh* festival of the Idu Mishmi.

For the last three and half decade a new form of *Reh* festival came to existence which has been celebrated simultaneously with the traditional form. This may be termed as community based celebration of *Reh* festival. This new form of festival is annually celebrated on a fixed date, i.e. on 2nd to 3rd February of every calendar year, in almost all the Idu Mishmi village. It was on 1st February 1968, the then Additional Deputy Commissioner, Anini, I.P Gupta, for the first time made a history by inaugurating the central form of *Reh* festival on community basis at Roing now the Headquarters of Lower Dibang Valley District. It was celebrated at a particular place calling it as Central *Reh* festival and representatives were from the entire Idu Mishmi villages. This initiation was stressed by some local personality of that time like Ita Pulu, Ature Linggi, Lango Linggi, Sole Linggi, Indru Mena, etc. with a philosophy of creating community feeling among the Idu Mishmi.[5]

Looking at the structural, organizational and functional aspects of these forms of *Reh* festival, it is quite clear that both the forms of *Reh* festival serves and fulfills different needs and motives for the Idu Mishms. If we have a close look both reveals a wide variation in its overall aspects. The structure of traditional form of *Reh* festival is undoubtedly a clan based festival and has no calendar like fixed date for its celebration. It takes a long preparation and moreover, the recognition for a successful celebration goes to a particular individual. He is responsible for all the arrangements and has the authority over all activities. It is celebrated for four nights and a day and the involvement of ritual activities starts right from the very first day and lasts till the closing day with scores of fowl and animal sacrifices. The exchanges of securities deposits and offering of securities deposits (*Adda* and *Adda-da*), presentation and receiving of gifts (*agiite, Agiiro, Ameta*) are the most important part of traditional form of festival.

But in case of central and village based community *Reh* festival celebration, such aspects are absent. For its organization, a committee is formed called central *Reh* committee or *Reh* committee and executive members are selected. For the celebration all the requirements such as rice brew, animals and fowls, food items, etc. are purchased from local villagers as well as from the market with donation money from every individual Idu Mishmi households and from the public leaders. It is celebrated for only two days and rituals are short and precise and last only for few hours. In the central form, chief guest and other dignitaries are invited for opening the festival. Flag hosting ceremony is observed by singing *Reh* song and flag song.[6] These new forms of festival include many new elements such as modern means of entertaining programmes like film song and dances, fashion shows, beauty contest, opening up of garment stalls, wine stalls, book stalls, sports competition like volleyball, etc. These multiple incorporation of modern elements by the locals has given birth to a new outlook of the festival which in fact, does not cover the real and aesthetic meaning of traditional *Reh* festival. The overall stress is for the eyes of others, neglecting the interest, sentiment and views of young Idu Mishmi generation. There exists a gap between the young and older generation due to various reasons and as a result the age-old norms and values and culture knowledge do not transmit to the younger generation. However, it is, as well, important to note that this community based *Reh* festival helped exposure of the community as a whole and *Reh* festival in particular worldwide and facilitated the Idu Mishmis in crossing the local boundaries. It also acted as a platform in bringing the whole community under one umbrella reflecting community solidarity and asserting a strong ethnic identity.

Similarly, it is also important to see the changes that have been observed in the traditional form of *Reh* festival. Not many but some of the important observations are like incorporation of modern calculus in record keeping, involvement of cash, foreign liquor, religious conversions, etc. has its role to a greater extend.

Conclusion

Festival is an agglomeration of human, sociocultural and religions aspects. That is why festival is sometimes referred as the mirror of a society. *Reh* festival of the Idu Mishmi reflects many aspect of the family or clan in particular and community as a whole. This festival also reflects various types of exchanges and gift presentations based on mutual reciprocity and social significance. For the celebration of the festival, one has to undergo a long preparation. It is celebrated for four nights and a day during which many activities are performed.

Many scholars and researchers held a common view point that most of the festival of the world developed out of magico-ritual practices and still most of the festivals are associated with religious observances. This viewpoint is clearly observed in the *Reh* festival of Idu Mishmis as it is strongly associated with various religious performances and associated myths and folklores, including ritual dance and performances. Various sacrifices are done in order to seek blessings, fortunes and lifelong peace and prosperity from gods and goddesses and spirits.

Change is inevitable and with the passage of time tribal people, in general, are passing through different phases of transition for multiple factors. This has a tremendous effect on the festivals of most of the tribes and *Reh* festival of the Idu Mishmis has its taste as discussed above. In the process many of its sacred and secular aspects have altercations and providing space for new elements. These are not only promoting community solidarity in a phase of social transition and in a state of traditional-modernity continuum but also talks about the stirring issue of identity of particular tribal community in the context of modern sociopolitical realities, perhaps an unavoidable state of affairs in a multi-tribe state like Arunachal Pradesh. Most importantly this new form of *Reh* festival today articulate the cultural identity as well as evolved aspirations of the Idu Mishmis who are in the path of transition.

Acknowledgement

The paper is a revised version of the original paper titled, 'Festival and Emerging Social Reality: Perspectives on the Idu Mishmis of Arunachal Pradesh' published in *The Oriental Anthropologist,* Vol.10 No. 1: 33–51, January–June 2010 by Tarun Mene and Sarit K. Chaudhuri.

Notes

1. Many scholars, including the present authors, have written on the *Reh* festival previously and mentioned the *Adda* system as 'Offering of Loan'. In this paper, the authors have rather preferred to define the system as 'Security deposits' because the term 'Loan' has different connotation and meaning which, to the author, do not imply the existing practice of *Adda* system in the *Reh* festival. The term 'Security deposits' has been used here which seems closely related with the *Adda* system as it implies a secured deposit of cash and animals to someone in an expectation that the same quantity or amount be returned and is not made in lieu of profit making or making demand for more than what has been deposited. It is done based on mutual insurance and mutual resiprocity which is free from the terms derivatived of the concepts 'loan', such as, 'interest' or 'time bound obligations'.
2. Informant: Ache Mimi, Shaman, Ashali village, Roing. Interview date: 7 January 2006.
3. There is no taboo regarding drinking of *Yu-ara* but there is restriction over drinking of *Yu-nyi* for few persons. A person cannot drink this brew if the *Reh* organizer is *Aluda*, meaning person belonging to family and clan of the enemy. It is believed that if one drinks this brew at *Aluda's Reh* then he would become mentally retarded in near future and cannot be treated by any shaman or by any other means. Drinking of the *Yu-nyi* is also restricted to '*Ashome*' meaning widow and '*Apolo*' meaning the widower. They drink only '*Yu-ara*', which is taboo free. If someone wishes to drink *Yu-nyi*, it is first purified by the shaman.
4. In a traditional Idu Mishmi house, there are generally three to four different apartments each having a hearth. The first one or the entrance room is called *Alongga.*
5. Another interesting aspect was the keen interest evinced by the local people. They took the initiative and organized the entire show in a perfect manner, all by themselves. The local people contributed about ₹ 5,000 in cash besides other

contributions in kind. This is indicative of the fact that the local people have regained confidence in their cultural heritage and realized the importance of celebrating their traditional festivals in a befitting manner. The NEFA administration has given a grant of ₹ 5,000, for the celebration of the festival.

6. The Flag song was composed by late Ahuki Pulu and the *Reh* song was composed by Sipito Miso, Buddhi Linggi, and Lolita Menjo.

References

Bhattacharjee, J. (1983). *Idus of Mathu and Dri Valley*, Directorate of Research, Government of Arunachal Pradesh, Itanagar.

Baruah, M.K. (1988). *The Idu Mishmis*, Directorate of Research, Government of Arunachal Pradesh, Itanagar.

Bose, M.L. (1997). *History of Arunachal Pradesh*, Concept Publishing Company, New Delhi.

Chakravarty, L.N. (1989). *Glimpses of the Early History of Arunachal*, Directorate of Research, Government of Arunachal Pradesh, Itanagar.

Datta, B., N.C. Sarma and P.C. Das (1994). *A Handbook of Folklore Material of North-East India*, ABILAL Publishing, Guwahati, Assam.

Dorson, Richard M. (1972). *Folklore and Folklife: An Introduction*, University of Chicago Press, Chicago and London.

Elwin, V. (1958). *Mysths of the NEFA*, Directorate of Research, Government of Arunachal Pradesh, Itanagar.

—— (1959). *A Philosophy for NEFA*, Directorate of Research, Government of Arunachal Pradesh, Shillong.

Gopalakrishanan, R. (1994). *Arunachal Pradesh*, Omsons Publications, New Delhi.

Henderson, William (1866). Notes on the Folklore of Northern Scotland and the Borders, London.

Simon, I.M. (1977). 'A Note on the Language of Arunachal', *Resarun*, 76, Directorate of Research, Government of Arunachal Pradesh, Itanagar.

Smith, Robert Jerome (1972). 'Festivals and Celebrations', in Richard M. Dorson (ed.), *Folklore and Folklife: An Introduction*, University of Chicago Press, Chicago and London, pp. 160–72.

Vidyarthi, L.P. and B.K. Rai (1976). *The Tribal Culture of India*, Concept Publishing Company, New Delhi.

12

Cultural Epidemiology of Malaria among the Idu Mishmis of Arunachal Pradesh

EVA UMPO

Globally, malaria remains a menace. Malaria is threat to more than 40 per cent of world population. An estimated of 219 million cases are reported annually worldwide leading to 6,60,000 deaths, with Sub-Saharan Africa (SSA) accounting for 90 per cent of the case (RBM, 2002; WHO, 2000). According to Malaria Report of WHO (2000), in South-East Asian region, 10 countries are endemic to malaria, around 1.6 billion people are at some risk and one billion people are at high risk. Around 2.5 million malaria cases are reported annually from South-East Asia, in which India alone contributes 52 per cent of the total number of cases.

Malaria is major public health concern in the North-Eastern states of India. It is noteworthy that these states are known for malaria endemicity that account for 10 per cent of the country's total malaria cases reported. Of the various vectors, *Plasmodium falciparum* in particular contributes 11 per cent of the disease burden due to malaria. Arunachal Pradesh is considered to be highly malaria endemic. Very few studies have been conducted in India and particularly in North-East India such as Arunachal Pradesh.

With so much information available on malaria, not all has been known about the disease from the very elementary to the highly technical. Malaria's cost to human and social well-being is enormous. Because of the seriousness of the problem, the World Health Organization (WHO), the United Nations Children's Fund (UNICEF), The United Nations Development Programme (UNDP), the World Bank (WB), and the Roll Back Malaria (RBM) have joined hands in malaria control effort worldwide, but it did not achieve its objectives up to the mark. The failure of efforts can frequently be blamed on the lack of adequate consideration given to the social and behavioural aspects of malaria control (WB, 2010). As human behaviour is much influenced by sociocultural factors, such as, social organization, culturally defined social roles and cultural belief about disease, all play important role in the observed variability in the disease, whether it is intentional or not. Often, the etiology and appropriate prevention and treatment actions are influenced by the social and cultural factors. Therefore, human behaviours do affect health promoting and disease preventing activities. And accordingly, the present chapter is aimed to provide a better understanding of the process through which social and cultural factors affect the biomedical burden as well as social burden of malaria in the Idu Mishmi community through anthropological perspective. It is an attempt to explore the cultural influence over disease which is better known as Cultural Epidemiology, based on which the present work has been framed. It has followed an interdisciplinary approach using anthropological methods to address the priority questions for malaria control.

It is observed that a considerable gap remains between correct scientific knowledge and the accepted practices and beliefs about malaria held by many of the Idu Mishmis of the Lower Dibang valley district of Arunachal Pradesh. There exists a relationship between malaria and the local perceptions about disease causation and its related problems among the Idu Mishmi tribe. According to Indian Council of Medical Research (ICMR) report, Lower Dibang Valley district falls under the 'high risk malaria zone' and as such malaria continues to pose a serious threat to public health and is endemic predominately with *Plasmodium falciparum* (PF) infections. The Kolkata edition of *The Telegraph* (3 July 2010) carried an article reporting that malaria stalked the flood-hit in the Lower Dibang Valley with Administration finding it difficult to battle. Month long health camps were conducted in different parts of the district and of the 3,960 blood samples tested, 364 contained malaria parasite. Despite the governmental and people's efforts, there is no visible achievement so far in the area in controlling and reducing the menace of malaria. In order to address these issues, the present work is focussed on social and cultural aspects to mitigating the problems of malaria disease among the Idu Mishmis of Lower Dibang Valley district of Arunachal Pradesh.

Methods, People and Area of Study

The Idu Mishmis are one of the major tribal communities living in Dibang Valley, Lower Dibang Valley, Lohit, East Siang and Upper Siang districts of Arunachal Pradesh for centuries. They are Indo-Mongoloid racial stock and belong to Tibeto-Burman group of languages. The population of the Idu Mishmi is around 10,000 as per 2001 census record. They are endogamous with clan exogamy as a rule. Monogamy is common but polygamy is also practiced. Nuclear family exists alongside vertically extended families. They are patriarchal and inheritance is traced through male line only. Rice is the staple food item supplemented by millet, maize and local pulses. They are fond of local beer which is locally known as 'Yu'. Lower Dibang Valley district, the area of present study, has an area of 3,900 sq km. The altitude of the district is 390 m above the sea level and the climatic condition of the region is moderate in nature with cold winter and highly humid in summer.

The study was carried out in the Lower Dibang Valley district of Arunachal Pradesh and the target population was the Idu Mishmi community. The study focussed more on social and cultural approach to understand the existing malaria problems. Focus Group Discussion (FGD) and In-Depth Interviews (IDI) with community members and health workers were conducted. FGD and IDI were done separately. First round was FGDs and the result from this round was used in the second round of data collection, which consisted of the (IDIs). Not less than 15 FGDs were conducted. Each (FGD) consisted of not less than five individuals and discussions were done separately for men and women. Questionnaire/schedule was also applied for collecting information. The data collection was carried out in the months of June, July and August 2016 when the frequency/cases of malaria are reported to be very high.

Etiology of Diseases

People from different culture have their own understanding to label disease differently and do not see diseases from the same perspective as biomedical practitioners do. Among the Idu Mishmis also causes of diseases are explained from dual approaches. In ethno-medical literature these are termed as Personalistic and Naturalistic approaches. Personalistic medical system is something in which illness or disease is believed to be caused by the purposeful intervention which might be a supernatural being (a deity) or a god, or a non-human being (such as a ghost, ancestor or evil spirit) or a human being (a witch or sorcerer). Whereas in Naturalistic medical system illness is explained in impersonal systemic terms and sensate agents play no role. In this system health conforms to an equilibrium model where the basic body elements – the *humors* in western medical system, the *yin* and *yang* in Chinese medical system and the *dosha* in Ayurveda medical system – are in the balance, appropriate to the age and condition of the individual health. When this balance is upset either from inside or outside, the body by natural forces such as heat, cold or sometimes emotions, illness follows. As like other diseases, people in different societies hold a variety of beliefs about the cause and transmission of malaria, which vary according to cultural education and economic status and have direct consequence on both preventive and treatment seeking behaviours.

The Idu Mishmis believe that in one's life, people may come across many sufferings and miseries. They divide the degree of sufferings and miseries in their own understanding. In their chart of sufferings, *Aruya* comes at the first place. Murder and other intentional and unintentional miseries are put together under *Aruya* and is the worst thing that could happen to anyone's life. It consists of many sufferings like murder, accident and various forms of suicides. Second place in the chart of sufferings comes *Ahroshu*. *Ahroshu* is also known as *oho phri* meaning 'fire accident'. These two, *Aruya* and *Ahroshu* in Idu Mishmi's chart of sufferings is said to be something which brings sudden loss and miseries. People with disease and illness may live for a while – shorter or longer – but not with *Aruya* and *Ahroshu*.

In the third place comes *Amo*. *Amo* in English means 'epilepsy'. Epilepsy is considered as one of the most dreaded disease. It is believed that one should not utter the word *Amo* and even discussion is avoided because people do not know when one may fall into the trap of *Amo*. So among the Idu Mishmis *Amo Ambre* is not discussed mostly. In their language, malaria is known as *Ahade/Ahade Ango*. The word malaria was an unknown word to them until the introduction of modern medical system during mid 20th century.

Etiology of Malaria

According to present research, it is well found that even today many Idu Mishmis don't make any relation between mosquito and malaria disease. Few believe that *Ahade* and malaria are same but many don't agree. Though there are lots of similarities between malaria and *Ahade* but many believe that in case of malaria, people often lose their lives but in case of *Ahade*, there are fewer who die. This is the sole reason for which they consider *Ahade* and malaria to be two different forms of disease. But if we compare the symptoms of both, we find many similarities like, episodic shaking, chills to intense fever to drenching sweats. In both the cases, infected individual may have symptoms often associated with flu involving fever and something periodic that mimic other diseases which make diagnosis difficult. Convulsion is observed in both cases. But in many cases fever and unstable varieties of symptoms, such as convulsion, are frequently not associated with malaria.

The severity of malaria is not the same everywhere. Accordingly, there are four different malaria endemic regions (Institute of Medicine, 1996: 33).

1. *Holoendemic*: Intense year round transmission where the population's level of immunity reaches a high level after early childhood.
2. *Hyper endemic*: Hyper epidemic seasonal transmission where the level of immunity offers little protection from diseases no matter the age group.
3. *Mesoendemic*: Malaria transmission is high with low level of immunity offers little protection.
4. *Hypo endemic*: Limited malaria transmission with little or no immunity to the parasite among the population.

The Idu Mishmis believe that *Ahade* is caused by the 'water spirit' which is called *Ahade heta*, the spirit of water. They believe that *Ahade heta* is very good looking and describe it as *Apashuhandu la unji* which means something that is mesmerizing. However, in many cases, people do not believe the water spirit as a sole agent responsible for malaria. This section of people believes that excessive exposure to sun in daytime and sudden change in climatic conditions cause *Ahade Ango*. Some agrees that consumption of bamboo shoots and citrus fruit are reasons of *Ahade*. And yet some believe that drinking of cold or chilled water in summer can cause *Ahade*. This shows that Idu Mishmis have their own way of explaining the causes of *Ahade* which in many cases are different from the modern medicinal and scientific explanations.

There are also two ways of explanations related to *Ahade* disease-causing and its result. It is believed that one may fall ill of *Ahade* if *Ahade heta* watch over or invigilate them and if *Ahade heta* touched them then the person is sure of his death. In the first case, the person will go through *Ango* (fever), from episodic shaking chills to intense fevers to drenching sweats but the person will not die. In the later case, it is certain that the patient will die.

To them, not all the sources of water cause *Ahade.* The water bodies where *Ahade heta* dwell are identifiable and are avoided. Following are some water bodies that are believed to have *Ahade heta* and hence are prone to *Ahade* (malaria).

Chisi Chera: Damp area with spring as a source of water. In such water body, water doesn't flow but is stable and dammed and is warm unlike flowing water which is cold and flows continuously.

Whudipa: *Whudipa* means meadow which is believed to be the zone of *Ahade.*

Ebupa: It means grassland with bamboo plants. It is considered as malaria precinct.

Episa: *Episa* means spider like webs which indicates an evil web surrounding the water bodies consisting *Ahade.*

Eluthrubru: Tributaries carrying *Ahade heta* (malaria spirit) from one place to another through the water bodies.

Endupa: Area with frequent rainfall is called *Endupa*. They consider *Endupa* as an existing zone which spreads *Ahade ahare*/malaria spirit.

They believe *Ahade*/malaria spreads from two directions. First one is from the *Eluthrubru* which means water tributaries with *Ahade ahara*/malaria spirits. Not all the water bodies are considered as *Ahade ahara*/malaria spirit existing body. Idu Mishmis believes that if a place is marshy with springs as a source of water and which is stagnant and stable, such type of water body is believed to be warm and contaminated. To them these are indications of *Ahadeahara* existing water bodies. If someone takes bath or drinks water from it, they get into the trap of evil spider web, which they called *Episa*. To them, *Ahade*/malaria is explained from Personalistic approach. In some places water bodies also possess *Ahade ahare* if it is surrounded by bamboo plants which they called *Ebupa.* Along with bamboo plants, meadows (*Whudipa*) and any place with frequent rainfall (*Endupa*) are considered as an *Ahade*/malaria dwelling areas. They believe that wherever such water body flows having *Ahadeheta,* it spreads *Episa*/malaria web and whoever comes across those places with malaria spirit, they become victim of *Ahade*/malaria disease.

Secondly, they believe that *Ahade* spread from the plain region. And as such they consider that any plain area where there is no Idu Mishmi population is *Ahade* or malaria zone. They also believe that *Ahade* as seasonal and active during summer only. Idu Mishmis do not prefer to visit plains during summer as they fear they may become victim of *Ahade*/malaria. They prefer going to plains during winter month of December, January and February. Even in their own land they do not go to *Boda* (forest) during summer. For this reason, activities such as hunting, trapping, fishing, etc. are also preferred during winter season.

Among the Idu Mishmis, shaman (*Igu*) plays an important role. If there is occurrence of high cases of malaria in any particular village then people expect a shaman to eradication or to ward off *Ahade*/malaria from their land. There is a belief that shaman cast away this dreaded disease to the land of non-Idu Mishmi places. In the four Vedas of the Hindus also, malaria is referred as 'a disease most dreaded affliction, king of disease'. The Chinese referred to it as 'mother of fever'. But Idu Mishmis' belief about malaria is different. Since *Ahade* is associated with the plains and non-Idu Mishmis region, many a times they come out with funny jokes related to *Ahade* (Malaria). For example, they ask their fellow villagers, like, 'Did you meet *Ahade's* father or *Ahade's* mother while returning back from plain?', 'Did you get physical intimacy with someone in plain?' Even some crack jokes saying, '*Ahade* (malaria) is the proof that you had physical intimacy with someone in the plains'.

Physical and SocioCultural Factors Enhancing Malaria Transmission

The studied area is very much influenced by many risk factors ranging from physical environment, health care system and socio-economic conditions that influence malaria causation and transmission. Physical environment play an essential part in the epidemiology of malaria. The maximum temperature of Lower Dibang valley is 40°C during summer and the average temperature recorded in this region during winter range from 15° to 21° Celsius. During monsoon, the temperature in this region is between 22°C to 30°C. This temperature range plays an important role in the development and affect the life cycle of malaria parasite. It influences the malaria with its favourable climatic temperature.

The rainfall varies between 450 centimetres to 80 centimetres and because of this heavy rainfall many mushy area get formed. Moreover, heavy rainfall also leads to rich vegetation mainly bamboo and other grasses. This act as a favourite ground for breeding of Anopheles mosquitoes. As the studied place lie in the lower belt, relative humidity affects malaria transmission through its effect on the activity and survival of mosquitoes.

Also, the housing condition has been suggested as one of the potential risk factors for spreading malaria vector. The house design is one of the significant factors which enhanced malaria transmission. Studies has revealed that living in a concrete house with brick and plaster walls along tiled roofs are in a better advantage to reduce malaria transmission compared to poor housing type. Maximum houses in Lower Dibang Valley are made of bamboo/wood pillars, bamboo split walls and dry leaves roof which give easy entry to the mosquitoes. When it comes to sanitation it has been observed that because of age-old habits and poverty some Idu Mishmis still practice traditional kind of toilets in which outlet directly lead to the pigsty below the house. In the house each room has at least a window facing towards the poultry yard or pigsty. Window towards the pigsty also gives easy entry to mosquitoes.

Since rice is a staple crop of the community their mainstay is agriculture. Though slash and burn is the most common method of agriculture of the community, but wet rice cultivation is done extensively in the study area which lies in the foothill and plains region. That is why, one of the main link found between malaria and agriculture in the wet cultivation is irrigation. Irrigation is extensively used for the cultivation of paddy, wheat, etc. in the study area.

Treatment Methods

Many studies reveal that traditional treatment method may often be the first way or line of treatment for malaria. The studies in major parts of the world also reveal that the use of herbal remedies in the treatment of malaria is widespread. Different treatment method depends on different etiological explanation for malaria. For instance, where malaria is thought to be of supernatural origin, treatment is usually within the domain of traditional medicines. Idu Mishmi treats *Ahade* in many ways. One of the important ways of treating *Ahade*/malaria is *Angoshayu* or *Ahadeshayu*. *Ango* mean 'fever', *sha* means kind of 'net or trap' and *yu* mean 'to pull out.' Basically it means 'to pull out the thread of fever from human body.'

Angoshayu is a healing process to get rid of the *Ahade* (malaria) from the body of the patient. The fever in the body is believed to exist because of *Ahade*/malaria. The whole process of *Angoshayu* starts with the chanting of *Igu* (shaman). The *Mengi* (patient) sits besides *Igu* throughout the *Angoshayu* ritual. He does this ritual without the help of any assistants (*Tamroh*), does not perform ritual dance or wear the *Igu* costumes. He sits in a particular spot and continues his chanting, having few moments of breaks from time to time. Along with his chanting, *Igu* beats their sacred instrument (*Ripu*) in a rhythmic way. After chanting for a while he comes closer to the *Mengi,* holding a piece of charcoal in his hand. He puts the charcoal over the head of *Mengi* and wipes it gently over the head of the patient. It is believed that in doing so a shining thread like substance comes out from the head of the *Mengi*. This shining thread is comparable with a spider web (*Episha*). The thread is believed to be very thin, so the shaman has to be very careful while removing it from the head of the *Mengi*. In case if it is broken midway, then the *Ahade*/malaria remains in the body of *Mengi*. In order to remove the thread, one has to perform a similar ritual again. So the *Igu* (shaman) slowly moves the charcoal in an attempt to roll the threads coming out of the head. *Igu* also puts the charcoal over the knees and repeats the same process over and again to relieve the patient from his sufferings and acute joint pain. So by removing all the thread from body, the Ahade/malaria is cured totally.

After the removal of this fine thread, a small pebble is collected from the water body where the patient, prior to his illness, had his bath or had drunk water. Believers say that this water body has supposedly resulted in *Ahade*. This pebble is kept in a hearth and it remains there until Ahade/malaria is cured completely. It may be mentioned here that in order to treat sickness, some shamans take a course on spiritual healing or else patients may look for various ethno-medicine from plants from the local experts. The extracts of available plants and animals are applied in the form of juice, powder, paste, etc. Sometimes fat of animal, bird or snake is applied directly to the affected area.

There are many other ways of treating *Ahade*/malaria. One way of treating *Ahade*/malaria is by using a particular snake called *Boshombo*. *Boshombo* is believed to be a blind snake that mostly eats rats. They believe that *Boshombo* snake gives a shock that enables the patient to get cured from Ahade. In a family, if someone is suffering from Ahade/malaria for a long time and not recovering, then one goes to the jungle to find Boshomo snake. They cover the *Boshomo* with the leaves and give it to the person suffering from *Ahade* (malaria). They ask the mengi (patient) whether he/she is hungry or not; if the patient asks for the food, they give him *Boshomo* as if it is something to eat. When the *Mengi* (patient) removes the leaves and finds it to be snake the patient screams aloud in fear and gets shocked. In this situation, sometimes the patient even forgets that he was sick with malaria. In many cases, people even run here and there. It is also believed that sometimes even people with acute illness get shocked and stand still for few seconds. So the Idu Mishmi believe *Boshombo* shock in many cases help malaria get cured.

Case Study

This is a case of an aged woman named Jani Mega of Asali village, Roing, the district headquarters of Lower Dibang Valley. She is 80 years old and had suffered from Ahade/malaria thrice in her lifetime. When she was at her parental residence, she never suffered from Ahade/malaria. But all the three episodes of malaria were at her husband's residence. When she first arrived in her new village she noticed everyone was suffering from Ahade/malaria, even the animals like dogs and cats were suffering from Ahade. She suffered Ahade/malaria when she conceived for the first time. As she was under severe sickness of malaria she didn't even remember how she gave birth to her first child. During the day of delivery she was suffering from acute Ahade with high fever and convulsion. The high convulsion was very severe that she even didn't realize the acute pain. It lasted for almost another two years. In the second instance, Ahade lasted for almost two years. In the third, she suffered for seventeen months. She believes that after the third time she never suffered of Ahade again. She never tried any medicine or other alternatives to cure Ahade. According to her, she got cured of malaria (Ahade) only after her encounter with a snake. During her third episode of suffering, she went to a nearby jungle to collect firewood. While collecting her firewoods, she accidentally fell down on the ground and lying there she realized that something is moving on her chest and neck. It was a snake. Out of fear she screamed aloud and ran away. After sometime she realized that her fever and convulsion become less intense and almost disappeared from her body. Back home, everyone was surprised to see her. After that incident she never encountered Ahade/malaria again in her life. According to her, it has been now about more than fifty years that she never encountered Ahade (malaria) again. To her, snake therapy is the perfect solution to do away with Ahade/malaria.

Modern Method Verses Local Methods of Treatment

According to modern medical system if a person is detected with malaria then they have to go through the complete anti-malaria medicines separate for both *Plasmodium falciparum* and *Plasmodium vivax*, as we all know both *Plasmodium falciparum* and *Plasmodium vivax* have separate ways of medications. Many times people get confused with the Plasmodium species. In many cases it has been seen that within the middle of the course they discontinue the medicine,

Many reasons have been put forward: some stop medications in the middle of the course, may be, because of improvement in health, which leads to incomplete treatment. Some stop medication during the middle of course due to bitterness of Quinine. In many cases it has been seen that immediately after the discontinuation of malaria medication they start with traditional way of medications like *Ango sha yu/Ahade sha yu, Bosombo/*blind snake shock and other implementation of ethno medicinal practices like using of biles of Fish, Porcupine, Bear, Monkey, Snake, Chicken, Musk deer, etc. They even use the meats, skin and bones of Bat, Swift, Otter, Chameleons, etc. and in herbs and plants they frequently use *Coptis teeta, Cherodendruma, Curcuma aromatica, Paederafoetida*, etc. Many respondents gave countless negative and positive views regarding the bed net acceptance, but mostly negative views. Many of the respondents think using of bed nets treated with insecticide cause them suffocation and itching.

There are many factors which influence heath seeking behaviour including the local beliefs about diseases, accessibility to health care providers, cost and attitude toward health care providers (both western and traditional healers). Before coming in contact with the modern medical system Idu Mishmis' attitude toward *Ahade*/malaria was altogether different. At that point of time they do not see *Ahade*/malaria as very serious illness. In many cases, whenever someone gets *Ahade*/malaria they come up with funny jokes.

Case Study

Simpi Melo, female, aged about 45 of Asali village suffered from malaria for more than ten times. In one case she was bedridden for three months. For complete three months she was in acute condition of Ahade/malaria. She even lost her hair completely. According to her account, once she recovered from it after the consumption of earthworm soup given to her by an *Igu*/shaman. However, she encountered Ahade/malaria many a times even after consumption of earthworm soup. Few years back also she suffered from Ahade/malaria and went to health clinic for checkup where she was detected with Ahade/malaria. She was given medicines and following the advice she started her medicine course. She said that she accepted modern medicine not as a choice but just because many people have started using it. However, she couldn't complete her medicine course as she believes that Ahade can be never be eradicated through modern medical system. She and many other respondents, especially the 50+ age group, have a strong inclination towards the traditional ways of curing.

It is found that majority of respondents have some factual information about malaria, its causes, transmitting agents, its treatments, etc. At the same time, there are some sections of people who are unaware of it. Though they are unaware of what causes malaria but they go to health clinic, no matter how late it is or whether or not complete the treatment course or whether they combine the treatment methods (traditional or clinical). Many of them also consider that drinking contaminated water, exposure to sun and sudden change in climate, consumption of citrus and bamboo shoots, drinking of cold water during warm sunny days, etc. leads to malaria. When asked about the common signs and symptoms of malaria, they pointed out, such as, high temperature/fever, loss of energy, convulsion, vomiting, sweating, headache, body pain, loss of appetite, chill, etc. The most important result of all the discourses of these discussions is that people do not make any connection of malaria with mosquitoes.

The treatment methods can be separated into three different categories (McCombie, 1996; Ahorlu et al., 1997) as follows; (a) Self-treatment or home remedy including both herbal, traditional treatment and/antibiotic use, (b) Traditional technique, and (c) The allopathic or western medical sector, including hospital, clinic, dispensaries, private practitioner and village workers.

According to survey done among the Idu Mishmis the existence of 'hierarchy of resort' is observed as same reported by McCombie (1996) who worked among Colombians. Target population often uses a combination of self-treatment, traditional medicine and more than one clinic or health care provider. Similarly, Idu Mishmis also use medicines like chloroquine along with plant remedies. It has been observed that if someone gets ill, first they take the patients to a shaman (*Igu*) for healing called *Angoshayu*. If the patient recovers, it is followed by another ritual of one night called *Ahayhe*. If the patient does not recover then only the patient is taken to the nearest health centre for immediate treatment.

According to modern medical system if a person is detected with malaria then they have to go through the complete anti-malaria medicines separately for both *Plasmodium falciparum* and *Plasmodium vivax* as both have different ways of medications. However, in many cases in the study area, it has been noticed that in the middle of the course many discontinue their medicines. Many reasons are put forwarded for giving up these medications, such as, improvement in health, bitter taste of Quinine and more often, shifting to traditional way of medications like *Angoshayu*/*Ahadeshayu*, *Bosombo*/blind snake shock, including the use of ethno-medicines like bile of fish, porcupine, bear, monkey, snake, chicken, musk deer, etc. meats, skin and bones of bat, swift, otter, chameleons, etc. Also herbs and plants are frequently used, such as, *Coptis teeta, Cherodendruma, Curcuma aromatica, Paederafoetida*, etc.

In many cases, it is also found that the severity of illness was reported due to the practice of hierarchy of resort in which they take on multiple treatments at a time. As one treatment fails they take recourse to another way. As rightly said by Yeneneh et al. (1993) in case of a hierarchy of resort, it is the perception of the great majority of people in countries throughout the world that most illness should first be treated at home, and when such treatment fails and the illness persists or worsens, should other type of therapies be sought. When people employ a hierarchy of resort as treatment for malaria, home treatment usually comes at first as line of protection. According to McCombie (1996), many times home treatment may, of course, result in incorrect or incomplete treatments or dosage and it may also cause delay in taking a severely sick person to health facilities in time.

In the study area it is also found that the malaria related medicines and prescriptions are freely in circulation from one family to another within the village. In many instances, it is observed that an old prescription of a malaria patient is referred for another person. Similarly, in many families of malaria patient, medicines remains half used for various reasons. These medicines are also dispensed to another person without any consultations with the doctors. Many families also keep medicines in stock for immediate use. These are done without diagnosing and laboratory tests of *Plasmodium vivax* or *Plasmodium falciparum*.

In the target population when people encounter with fever, firstly they go for self-medication by taking *Paracetamol* or *Nemuslide*. *Paracetamol* tablets belong to a group of medicine called *Analgesics*. They used it for relief from pain and feverish condition such as headache, toothache, cold, joint pain and period pains. According to the finding it is seen that households keep a few tablets in stock. Only when the condition worsens, they take the patient to the hospital. Many respondents have interesting opinion towards malaria and its treatment. For example, they believe that any bitter edibles contains cure for malaria. This notion may be because of the bitter taste of chloroquine. Likewise, there are many substances which are better and are used as a traditional malaria medication, like Coptisteeta, biles of snake, fish, etc.

Conclusion

Malaria is one of the dishonourable diseases affecting people worldwide and India alone contributes 52 per cent of the total number of cases in the South Asian region. It is major public health concern in the North-Eastern states of India like Arunachal Pradesh. The present study is focussed to understand and explore the local perceptions of malaria among the Idu Mishmi tribe of Lower Dibang Valley district of Arunachal Pradesh. The study basically aims to provide the linkages and the processes through which social and cultural factors affect the biomedical burden of malaria, better known as Cultural Epidemiology, by applying anthropologic approach and methods.

In Idu Mishmi language, malaria is known as *Ahade/AhadeAngo* and interestingly the study reveals that many Idu Mishmis, especially in the rural area, do not realize any connection between mosquitoes and malaria. To them *Ahade*/malaria is explained from personalistic approach. We may convincingly conclude that though malaria is very much a vector borne infectious diseases, its transmission and preventive measures are linked with local cultural and social conditions of the community. Similarly, the present study establishes that belief system, healing processes, use of locally available traditional medicines, ways of life, material culture, etc. of the Idu Mishmis have largely contributed in both controlling and encouraging and shaping their attitude towards malaria. Further, to address this disease at community level, one needs to understand the issue from the local point of view. For example, how people respond to such disease, their beliefs and practices that hinder in acceptance to modern treatment, etc. So, it is very pertinent to understand the local perception of the disease and their understanding of causation and treatment in order to achieve success related to various Public Health Policies, which are often targeted towards rural communities such as the Idu Mishmis of Arunachal Pradesh.

References

Abyan, I.M. and A.A. Osman (1993). 'Social and Behavioral Factors Affecting Malaria in Somalia', *Social and Economic Research Project Report*, WHO, Geneva, pp. 1–28.

Ahorlu, C.K., S.K. Dunyo, E.A. Afari, K.A. Koram and F.K. Nkrumah (1997). 'Malaria-related Belief and Behaviour in Southern Ghana: Implications for Treatment, Prevention and Control', *Tropical Medicine and International Health*, 2: 488–99.

Bruce, L.J. (1988). 'History of Malaria from Prehistory to Eradication', in W.H. Wernsdorfer and I. McGregor (eds), *Malaria Principles and Practice of Malariology*, Churchill Livingston, Edinburg.

Chipwaza, B., P.J. Mugasa, L. Mayumana, M. Amuri, C. Makungu and S.P. Gwakisa (2014). 'Self-medication with Anti-malarials is Common Practice in Rural Communities of Kilosa District of Tanzania', *Malaria Journal*, 13: 252.

Deobankar, R.B. and N.D. Palkar (1990). 'Magnitude of DDT Resistance in Anopheles Culicifacies in Maharashtra State', *Journal of Communicable Disease*, 22(1): 77.

Desowitz, R. (1991). *Malaria Capers: Tales of Parasite and People*, W.W. Norton and Company, New York.

Espino, F., L. Manderson, C. Acuin, F. Domingo and E. Ventura (1997). 'Perception of Malaria in Low Endemic Area in Philippines: Transmission and Prevention of Disease', *ActaTropica*, 63: 221–39.

Gessler, M.C., D.E. Msuya, M.H. Nkunya, L.B. Mwasumbi, A. Schar, M. Heinrich and M. Tanner (1995). 'Traditional Healers in Tanzania: The Treatment of Malaria with Plant Remedies', *Journal of Ethno Pharmacology*, 48: 119–30.

Heggenhougen, K., V. Hackethal and P. Vivek (2003). *The Behavioral and Social Aspect of Malaria and its Control*, UNDP, World Bank, WHO.

Institute of Medicine (US) Committee on Malaria Vaccines (1996). *Vaccines Against Malaria: Hope in a Gathering Storm*. Russell PK, Howson CP, (eds) Washington (DC): National Academies Press (US).

Jombo, G.T., M.E. Mbaawuaga, D.P. Akaa, D.O. Alao, J. Etete Peters, J.S. Utsalo, E.E. Okwori, J.T. Akosu and A.E. Etukumana (2010). *Sociocultural Factors Influencing the Control of Malaria in North Central Nigeria*, Benue University, Nigeria.

Krotoski, W.A., W.E. Collins, R.S. Bray, P.C. Garnham, F.B. Coqswell, R.W. Gwadz, R. Killick, R. Sinden, L.C. Koontz and P.S. Stanfill (1982). 'Demonstration of Hypnozoites in Sporozoite-Transmitted Plasmodium Vivax Infection', *American Journal of Tropical Medicine and Hygiene*, 31(6): 1291–93.

Lines, J. (1994). 'Trends, Priorities and Policy Direction in Control of Vector-borne Diseases in Urban Environments', *Health Policy and Planning*, 9(2): 113–29.

Martens, P. and L. Hall (2000). 'Malaria on the Move: Human Population Movement and Malaria Transmission', *Emerg Infect Dis*, 6(2): 103–09.

McCombie, S. (1996). 'Treatment Seeking for Malaria: A Review of Recent Research', *Social Science and Medicine*, 43(6): 933–45.

Metta, E., H. Hasima, F. Kessy, I. Hutton and A. Bailey (2014). 'We have Become Doctors for Ourselves: Motive for Malaria Self-care among Adult in Southeastern Tanzania', *Malaria Journal*, 13: 1–249.

Mutheneni, S.R., M. Upadhyayula and K. Nising (2014). 'Malaria Prevalence in Arunachal Pradesh', *Am J Trop Med Hyg*, 91(6): 1088–93.

Mwanje, L.F. (2013). *Knowledge Attitude and Practices on Malaria Prevention and Control in Uganda*, Report Submitted to Communication for Development Foundation Uganda (CDFU). Available at: http://www.musphcdc.ac.ug.

Mwenesi, H. (1994). *Mothers' Definition and Treatment of Childhood Malaria on the Kenya Coast*, Social and Economic Research Progress Reports, World Health Organization, Geneva.

Mwenesi, H., T. Harpham and R.W. Snow (1995). 'Child Malaria Treatment Practices among Mothers in Kenya', *Social Science and Medicine*, 40: 1271–77.

Neville, C.G. (1990). 'Malaria in Sub Saharan Africa', *Social Science and Medicine*, 31(6): 667–69.

Oaks, S.C. Jr., V.S. Mitchell, G.W. Pearson and C.C.J. Carpenter (1991). *Malaria: Obstacles and Opportunities*, National Academy Press, Washington, D.C.

Okonofua, F.E., B.J. Feyisetan, A.A. Davies and Y.O. Sanusi (1992). 'Influence of Socioeconomic Factors on the Treatment and Prevention of Malaria in Pregnant and Non-pregnant Adolescent Girls in Nigeria', *Journal of Tropical Medicine and Hygiene*, 95(5): 309–15.

Roll Back Malaria (RBM) (2002). What is Malaria? Available at: http://mosquito.who.int.

Srinivas, B. (2015). Malaria in India. Available at: http://www.malariasite.com/malaria-india/

Subarn, P., S. Dendoung and N. Dendoung (2001). 'Social and Cultural Aspects of Malaria', *Southeast Asian J Trop Med Public Health*, 32(4): 727–32.

Targett, G.A.T. (1991). *Waiting for the Vaccine*, John Wiley and Sons, New York.

Upadhyayula, S.M., S.R. Mutheneni, S. Chenna, V. Parasaram and M.R. Kadiri (2015). 'Climate Drivers on Malaria Transmission in Arunachal Pradesh, India', *PLoS ONE*, 10(3): e0119514. doi: 10.1371/journal.pone.0119514.

Vundule, C. and S. Mharakura (1996). 'Knowledge, Practice and Perception about Malaria in Rural Communities of Zimbabwe: Relevance to Malaria Control', *Bulletin of the World Health Organization*, 74(1): 55–60.

World Bank (2001). *Malaria on the rise, children most vulnerable: World Bank, WHO, UNICEF, and UNDP call for much more action in the fight against malaria*. News release, 2001/302/AFR.

World Health Organization (1997). *Control of Tropical Disease: Malaria Prevention and Control*, WHO, Geneva.

—— (2000). *Twentieth Report*, WHO, Geneva.

Yeneneh, H., T.W. Gyorkos, L. Joshep, J. Pickering and S. Tedla (1993). 'Antimalarial Drug Utilization by Women in Ethiopia: A Knowledge–attitudes–practice Study', *Bulletin of World Health Organization*, 67: 763–72.

13

Funeral Traditions of the Idu Mishmi Tribe of Arunachal Pradesh

S. SIMON JOHN AND MAYA PULU

Ritual practices, one of the important aspects of Intangible Cultural Heritage (ICH), have been a focus of study for long. Edmund Leach (1968) suggested that the term 'ritual' should be applied to all 'culturally defined sets of behaviour,' that is, to the symbolical dimension of human behaviour as such, regardless of its explicit religious, social, or other content. For Leach, such behaviour should be regarded as a form of social communication or code of information, and analysed in terms of its 'grammar'. Ritual is thus treated as a cognitive category. Eliade (1987) mentioned that 'rituals' are those conscious and voluntary, repetitious and stylized symbolic bodily actions that are centred on cosmic structures and/or sacred presences. Verbal behaviour such as chant, song and prayer are included in the category of bodily actions. Even more fundamentally, ritual is intentional body engagements in the paradigmatic forms and relationships of reality. As such, ritual brings not only the body but also that body's social and cultural identity to the encounter with the transcendental realm. By conforming to models or paradigms that refer to the primordial past and that can be shared by many people, ritual also enables each person to transcend the individual self, and thus it can link many people together into enduring and true forms of community. Ritual draws into itself every aspect of human life, and almost every discipline of the social sciences and humanities has something to say about it. The body is evidently more important in religious experience than is often thought of.

Rituals are orally transmitted from generation to generation and play a significant role in tribal culture. Generally, most of the rituals are associated with religion, life cycle ceremonies and agriculture. Funeral rituals, the last rite of human beings, play a significant role in the life cycle ceremonies of every culture. Among all the life cycle rituals, the funeral rites are significant because it deals with afterlife of the deceased person and well-being of the survivors. Almost all the traditional societies in the world follow a set of practices, customs and beliefs associated with death and funerals. These funeral rites and customs are concerned not only with the mourning, preparation and disposal of the body, but also with the well-being of the survivors and with the persistence of the spirit or memory of the deceased. The various methods used for disposal of the body are linked to religious beliefs, climate and geography, and social status. Burial is associated with ancestor worship or beliefs about the afterlife; cremation is sometimes viewed as liberating the spirit of the deceased. Almost in all traditional societies, the corpse is prepared in some prescribed way before it is finally laid to rest. The funeral practices and rituals vary between cultures, and between religious affiliations within those cultures. A number of customs, beliefs, rituals, mourning, lamentations, narratives, chanting and performances are closely associated with funeral rites. The customs, beliefs, practices, observances, taboos, performances associated with death are deeply associated with particular religious beliefs, and also have important psychological, sociological functions for the deceased as well as for the survivors.

Arnold van Gennep (1960) in his classic book, *The Rites of Passage* discussed different kinds of life cycle ceremonies and the significance of those rituals. He pointed out that, when the activities associated with such ceremonies are examined in terms of their order and content, they can be distinguished into three major phases: separation, transition, and incorporation. He said that 'regeneration' is a law of life and of the universe: the energy which is found in any system gradually becomes spent and must be renewed at intervals in the social world through the rites of passage. He also explained in detail about the funeral rites and stated that funeral rites vary widely among different peoples and that further variations depend on the sex, age and social position of the deceased.

Smith (1974) stated that funeral is only the first of a series of mortuary rites conducted on behalf of the spirit of the deceased. Although the funeral has taken place, the spirit is still an unstable, dangerous and polluted being that needs to be appeased and purified by a further series of rituals because the purification is a gradual process that ought to be accompanied by a regular series of rituals over a certain period of time. Namihira Emiko (1985) has stated that mortuary rituals function as devices to eliminate or diminish the pollution of death and finally recover a state of purity. According to Emiko, the pollution of death may be diminished by both the passage of time and the series of rituals, but the series of rituals is more important than the time taken to purify the pollution of death because pollution cannot be fully purified only by the passage of time. He further states that many factors have a bearing on the mortuary ritual: the religion of the deceased or of their family, the age at which the person died, their gender, their social status, the family's economic circumstances, and whether the death was a suicide, a miscarriage, an abortion, an accidental death, or even a violent death.

With this brief understanding, this present chapter is an attempt to study and document the funeral traditions of the Idu Mishimi tribe of Arunachal Pradesh. The Idu Mishmi tribe of Arunachal Pradesh inhabit the districts of Dibang Valley, Lower Dibang Valley, Lohit district and a few pockets in the vicinity of East Siang and Upper Siang district. Empirical data for this study is collected through fieldwork by following the triangulation research methodology, i.e. observation, interview and audio-visual documentation.

Death, Shamans and Rituals

Origin: Myth of Death

In times immemorial, a man known as Sineru went to a village where he was summoned to stop the prevailing epidemic. Sineru was not confident that he would come back alive. Therefore, he planted an *egambo* tree in his yard and asked his mother, wife and children to look after the plant. He also left *ishuru*, a bird, to communicate with his family. One day *ishuru* brought a message of death of his child. But Sineru thought it would be better to serve the people because a child can be obtained later on. The next time, the bird brought the message of his wife's death and Sineru preferred to stay and thought he could remarry. Then one day, *ishuru* brought the message of the death of his mother. Sineru's heart was broken, since he cannot get back a mother in his life again. He returned to his place and went to Athuka, a place through which every soul passes and he tried to locate if his mother's soul was passing through or not. After reaching home he hired Iruliru for chanting *anja* (mourning song) at the place to call back his mother's soul. But Iruliru was unsuccessful in the attempt. Therefore, Sineru himself, holding *kalinta tothobra* (herb) in his hand, chanted *yah* continuously for five days. By virtue of his chants, his mother came back. But instead of earrings in her ears, she carried earth worms (signifying the grave). Sineru's second wife could not accept the form in which his mother came back. She drove her away with *aabripa* (a loom stick). Sineru was worried about this. Then an owl came and sought to keep the mother under his care.

Some days later, when Sineru came and enquired about his mother, the owl replied that she might have fallen in the mountain. Sineru enquired about this from other birds but they replied that they had never heard such sounds of falling. Sineru then saw some hair at the mouth of the owl, and a housefly came flying out. The housefly began doing all the activities which Sineru's mother did during her lifetime. He confirmed that the owl had eaten his mother. He became depressed since his mother could not come back in human form. He started chanting and wished that if his mother came back, the fish would begin climbing trees and rats would grow long teeth like tigers. Since all these were impossible, his mother never came back from the land of the soul. Since then, the *Igus* (shaman) chant all the words which had been recited by Sineru to stop the dead from coming back.

Shamans and Funeral Rituals

The funeral ritual practices of Idu Mishmis are unique in nature and generally performed for three to five days depending on the nature of death. The Idu Mishmis believe in afterlife and that after death, life is transformed from the materialistic world to the divine world, i.e. the land of the soul which is referred to as *Asiãlõko. Igu*, the shaman, plays an important role in funeral rituals and performs a number of rituals, dance and music, and offerings in the house of the deceased continuously for days and nights together. Several customs, practices, taboos, beliefs, offerings, oral narratives, dance and music are associated with this funeral ritual.

Igus are of two kinds. The first is highly experienced and officiates in rituals like *Yah, Reh, Amra-sey,* etc. in which they need to be in full sacred costumes. The junior *Igus* act as medicine men and perform rituals like *Ayi, Atare, Alluthru,* etc. Sacred dress and ornaments are part of *Igu* and they use costumes like *Amrala, Rẽpu, Awẽto,* etc. in various ceremonies. Without the costumes, the *Igus* are considered incomplete. The costumes are kept with great care by the *Igu* in their houses in *Apito.* Among them, the principles of leading a better life exist in the form of sacred chants and hymns, mythology, rituals, customs and practices, origin narratives, etc. The hymns and chants are sacred, and a member of the community is expected to abide by it from birth to death. The chanting of the hymns vividly describes the great relationship of man with nature. The survival of the tribe till today is due to their understanding and belief of spiritual connection with Mother Nature. These chants and rituals are performed by the *Igu* and he is considered master of all supernatural sprits. In Idu Mishmi community, both men and women can become *Igu* and they both play an important role in the society. Certain important rituals like *Amar-se* (which is performed to protect family members from the evils), *Brõchana* (graveyard dance), *Ya* (ritual to guide the soul to the super natural world) and *Brõfri* rituals are performed by elderly *Igus.*

Whenever deaths occur in the village, the relatives of the deceased go to the *Igu*'s house and inform him about the death and request him to come and perform the rituals. As soon as the priest gets information, at night, he starts chanting from *andaku* (drawing room of house), in order to find out the cause of the death. He tries to find out which evil spirit had killed the man/woman, which evil spirit or ghost had crossed the boundary (*lãrõ*), and eaten up the person. After knowing the cause of the death, he sleeps at night in his house and the next morning he gets ready to go to the deceased's house to perform the rituals. The *Igu* wears his traditional sacred dress and ornaments and takes several sacred objects and musical instruments along with him when he goes to perform the funeral.

Before leaving his house, the *Igu* performs a chant and invokes the chief of the evil spirits and invites the spirit to accompany him. It is believed that the other spirits may attack his house when he goes to perform the funeral rituals. Therefore, he chants, cuts a *tothro* plant (bamboo), blows the horn, and locks the house and leaves. After invoking the spirits, he should not go back to his house,

Figure 1
Igu in His Sacred Dress

and if this rule is violated, it is believed that the spirits will destroy his house. Normally, two persons assist *Igu* in rituals. Therefore, *Igu* chants for the assistants also in order to protect them from the evil spirits. On reaching the house (where the person had died), the assistants help the *Igu* in his rituals. They make sure that menstruating women do not touch the sacred items, nor prepare any food for the *Igu*.

Iguthrõ refers to hosting the *Igu* in a special way. A few persons are deputed to look after the special needs of the *Igu* for the rituals. On hearing about death, close relatives bring mithun, pig, hen and local rice beer (*yu*). These relatives prepare food – young girls/women serve *yu* to the guests, while young men/women or elderly women/men serve food. Some guests may refuse to eat food in the house of the deceased, so one of the neighbours is requested to host it. For this purpose, a special structure known as *lãrõ* (made of bamboo) is prepared. This structure is semi-circular in shape and built away from the house. The food has to be served from the *lãrõ*, and the one serving should neither cross the *lãrõ* nor touch the guest. If by mistake, he/she touches the guest, he/she has to attend the full death ritual ceremony.

Funeral Practices

There are a number of rituals and practices connected to the funeral among the Idu Mishmis. These are discussed below.

Brõto: Construction of Grave

Brõto refers to the construction of a new grave for the deceased person. It is usually constructed by relatives and neighbours. Normally, the size of the grave is about six feet in length and the depth is about five metres. After digging the grave, walls are made of bricks on the four sides and the flooring is done with cement. Once done, it looks like a well constructed furnished room with bed, wardrobe, etc. Sometimes, the interior is also decorated with wall papers.

Figure 2
Offering of Things Inside the Grave

As soon as a person dies, the corpse is washed and clothed with new traditional clothes. The body is in extended position with hands crossed over the chest with folded palms. Before the burial, the dead body is placed in *ãloñga* or *idriku* (refers to

Figures 3 and 4

Offering of Piglet and Hen Inside the Grave

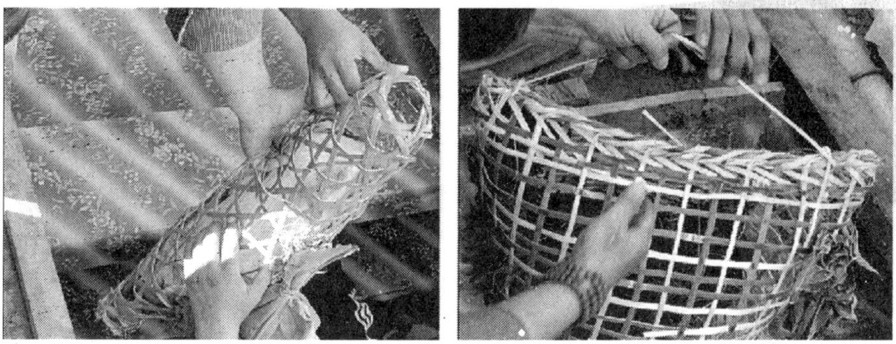

Figures 5 and 6

Relatives with Offerings Placed Inside the Grave

the place where skulls are displayed in the house). Here, the body is laid on a carpet, on which two or three large bed sheets, or a mattress is placed. The direction of placement is according to the direction of the house. Normally, the dead body is kept opposite to *idriku* where the heads of hunted animals are displayed.

Coins and paper currencies are placed in the palm of the deceased person. It is believed that the deceased person will buy water in *ãlõchiko*, the world of the dead. *Alõanini*, the owner of *ãlõchiko*, will not give water unless he is paid money and therefore, the relatives offer money to the deceased person.

They also offer bamboo leaves to use in the world of the dead in order to chase away flies and insects. If he was a hunter or murderer or possessed a gun, one of his relatives will first fire the gun in the air through a window. This is known as *ãsõkata*. It is believed that the people and animals that were killed (by the dead man) would be waiting to take revenge on him. So the gun is shot to give warning to the vengeful souls.

If the dead person is poor then an arrow is shot in the air, and then the gun is shot in the air outside the veranda before the body is carried to the graveyard. One shot is fired in the graveyard too.

Figures 7 and 8

The Deceased Placed in the Grave, and the Grave Being Closed

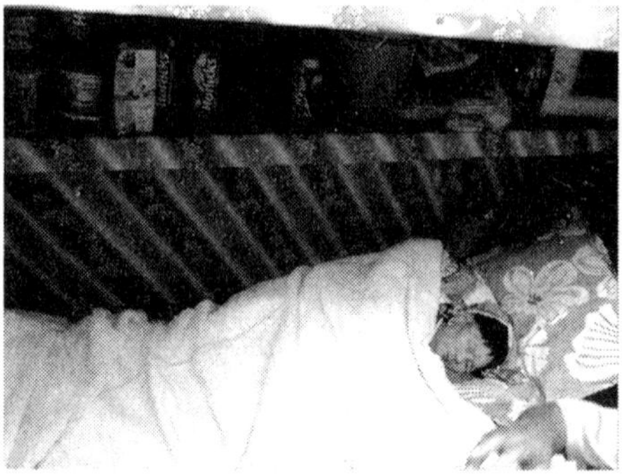

Figure 9

Igu Performing Funeral Ritual

If the death is normal, the *Igu* comes with *tothro* plant, chants and puts the plant in *andaku* (veranda of the house). Before entering the house, he goes to a specially made hut (*Atita Akõpra*) to perform the rituals the whole night. The assistants accompany the *Igu* and perform on the *gerambu* (small drum) and blow the *ajiru* (buffalo hornpipe). The host gives some money to the *Igu* to perform the rituals. The *Igu* chants and performs the rituals for the whole night without sleeping. During the rituals, he communicates with *mrega* (the soul) and the time of the communication depends on *Igu*. It may be early in the morning or midnight, before burying the corpse. This ritual is called *Abrĩgĩ*. Some *Igus* conduct this conversation with the soul after burial and before the performance of *Brõchna* (the graveyard dance).

Abrĩgĩ is performed before the burial. When *Igu* performs *Abrĩgĩ*, one of his assistants sits behind and plays the *kãlĩto* (flat gong). This gong should not be performed continuously, but at regular intervals. Everyone present there maintains silence when the *Igu* performs *Abrĩgĩ*. Otherwise, it is believed that because of the noise, the soul will not have a proper conversation with the priest. During *Abrĩgĩ*, aged men and women who know the language of *Igu* sit near him and listen to the communication carefully. Many people do not understand the priestly language; however, they sit and listen to the conversation.

Alimbrõ is performing on the gong (*kãlĩto*) after the burial. Here too, as during the performance of *Abrĩgĩ*, everybody maintains silence.

Post-Burial Rituals

The time of burial depends upon the family members. If the relatives have to travel a long distance, then the burial time is based on their arrival. Before taking the dead body to the grave, all the belongings of the deceased are taken to the graveyard and arranged in the newly constructed grave. Then the corpse is carried away along with a mattress to the graveyard. Those who carry the corpse make a peculiar sound like '*hooooo* ...', and hearing the sound, others make way for them. The relatives also give a certain amount of money to the persons who carry the corpse. The relatives follow the corpse to the graveyard and place the corpse inside the newly constructed grave. Generally, the corpse is kept in a lying position on the new bed in the east-west direction, and all the new items like crockery, wardrobe, etc. are kept inside the grave. After this, they close the top of the grave with concrete or wooden platforms.

After the burial, they all come back to the house of the deceased and the *Igu* performs *Alluthru* (purification ritual). This ritual is primarily to purify the persons from the evil spirits. Whoever enters the dead person's house cannot go back without doing *Alluthru.* Here, the *Igu* chants and touches the person's body or head with bamboo leaves to drive away the malevolent spirits. Everyone has to stay in the house till the priest performs the final *Alluthru* in the house.

Figure 10
Alluthru Being Performed

Figure 11
Mrabakhusu Being Performed

After *Alluthru*, the *Igu* performs *Amra se* in order to protect family members from the evils. Generally it is performed throughout the night. In the ritual of *Ali brula* the *Igu* invokes the souls of all the family members and he checks who is in danger from evil spirit, also checks what bad tidings would befall them. He asks the souls about their problems, and it is said that he comes to know who is going to die a natural or unnatural death in that family or in the village.

After *Ali brula*, *Igu* performs *Mrabakhusu* in the house. In the ritual of *Mrabakhusu* the *Igu* wears all the ornaments, and accompanied with musical instruments, he chants all the history of Idus and tells the story of Sineru, and invokes the supernatural spirits. After performing *Mrabakhusu* the priest takes the *tothro* plant with him, chants for the protection of his assistants and musical performers who are going to perform *Brõchana* (the graveyard dance).

Brõchana is performed by the *Igu* in the graveyard after the burial. During this ritual, the *Igu* gives food to *mrega*, the soul of the deceased, and tells that he is not alive anymore, and that is why he is giving food at the graveyard. The *Igu* tells the soul not to come back to the world of the living. Then he offers rice beer to the soul and says that he may come back to the human world when stone is rotten and when bamboo reaches the clouds. It implies that the soul should never return to the world of the living. The *Igu* also lays down the condition that the soul may return to this world only when the colour of the *evina* leaves disappears. The *ewuoo* bird cannot fly very high, and lives on the ground. *Igu* cuts off one claw of the bird, buries it in the ground, and tells the soul that it may return only when the bird is able to fly above the big trees in the forest. He warns the soul that if it tries to come back in the form of a rat, or *ejikru* (a small bird), it will be eaten up by the house ghosts *Aasu, Andro, Eru, Anda*. He further states that the soul may return only when the tiger stops roaring. This ritual of *Brõchana* generally lasts for more than three hours.

Figure 12
Igu Performing Ya Ritual

Ya ritual is performed in the deceased person's house by the priest. It is performed to guide the soul to the supernatural world. The primary difference between *ya* and *brõchana* is mainly the difference in the duration of chants. In *Ya* the chants continue for three nights and in the case of *Brõcha*, it is only for two nights. It depends on the family member to do only *Brõchana* or to perform *Yah*. Here, the *Igu* feeds the soul and guides the journey of the soul from the entrance of the house through several mountains which is called *Mabra*. He describes a number of places on the journey of the soul and guides the soul properly to its place. During this journey, wherever hills are encountered, he provides a ladder to climb and where rivers occur, he provides bridges to cross the rivers. The *Igu* guides every step of the journey of the soul till the soul reaches its destination.

There are certain restrictions for *Igu* who perform *Ya* ritual. Restrictions for those days are that the *Igu* should not eat any kind of mushroom, onion, or garlic; he should not go near the weaving areas, nor wash clothes. He should not take food prepared by menstruating women, and he should stay away from sexual relationship. If *Igu* performs *Ya* for the first time in his priestly service, then he has to follow the restrictions for ten days in his house. If it is the second time, then he has to follow the restrictions for nine days. If it is the third time, then he has to follow the restrictions for eight days, and so forth.

In the ritual of *Ayukhishu* the *Igu* narrates many stories about different types of bamboos like, *aruto* (big size bamboo), *abrato* (small size bamboo), story of *ewena* leaf and story of *ayumbra, angroashothrula,* etc. After this, the priest performs *Mrabayo,* in which he narrates the history of Idu Mishmis and he guides the soul to the dead world crossing different types of *mabra* (mountain) and gives food to the soul whenever they reach different *mabras.*

In the ritual of *Nathrutamro Mrayawete* the *Igu* chants for the people who helped during the funeral ceremony in cooking, serving, digging the grave, who offered things to the deceased person, etc. in order to protect them from the spirits. It is believed that sometimes the spirit will go along with these people and therefore this ritual is performed to protect them.

In *Lominã* the *Igu* chants in order to send away all the bacteria and bad diseases like cancer, and leprosy from the house by calling all the supernatural powers. This will protect the family members from all bad diseases.

In *Andomorõto ritual, the soul is guided by the Igu* beyond the *Andomo,* and on the way, a river has to be crossed with the help of a boat. As an enactment, the *Igu* bargains with a boatman in order to carry the soul across the river. After they cross the river, the *Igu* through his chants returns to the living world. After crossing the *Andomo,* the soul can rest at any place in the vast expanse of territory of the after world. In this ritual, the soul of the deceased is to be symbolically sent across the river, therefore one person acts as a boatman by wearing an Assamese towel on his forehead and another person tells the boatman, 'one person is going with lots of luggage and animals'. The person who tells the boatman should be very cautious while explaining and answering the boatman's queries because it refers to the dead person's soul. By mistake if he says, 'many people are going', then it is believed that some more deaths will occur in reality. He should clearly state that one aged male is coming or aged female is coming or young boy or young girl, or baby girl or baby boy. One other person acts as if he is bargaining with the boatman about the charges for the boat and the boatman replies in Assamese. It is important to note that the person who acts as bargainer should not act the same role in other death rituals for a year. If he violates this rule, it is believed that he will die.

In the ritual of *Ashothõ,* the family members sit in a line and the *Igu* will suck each individual's forehead or stomach of family member with *kãlĩta* (herbal plant root) in his mouth; and the *Igu* also places a feather of a rooster on the hair of each family member. This is performed to purify the members of the deceased's family.

Asa jĩ is performed at the end of the death ritual ceremony. Here the *Igu* carries *aweto* (the headgear) in his mouth, or sometimes a live rooster, and with a sword in his hand, drives away the evil spirits from that place. This ritual is performed in *alonga* or *edriku* of the house. After chasing away the spirits, the *Igu* goes outside the house and kills the rooster with his mouth, drinks the raw blood, and takes out the liver.

The next morning, he throws the *tothro* plant from where he had cut it. He throws the plant where no one can touch it, and leaves the house to depart for his own house. The family members of the deceased offer rice beer, *aku*, rooster and other meat to the *Igu*. Taking all these, the *Igu* leaves for his house and on the way, far from the house of the deceased, he makes *lãrõ* (boundary made of bamboo) and invokes all the powerful spirits, whom he invoked earlier. There he offers them food, rice beer, *etola*, and *aku* and requests the spirits not to follow him to his house and sends them to their own places.

Thereafter, after a gap of some months, *Brõfri* is performed. This ritual has to be performed within one year of the funeral. In this, the family members perform the same rituals that they had performed earlier during the funeral. They make a similar kind of grave and bury beer, different types of seeds, rice seeds, clothes, vegetables, and bamboo baskets. The close relatives of the deceased and the members of the community take part in this ritual and the host holds a feast for all the people with food and drinks. This ritual concludes the funeral rites of the Idu Mishmis.

Discussion and Conclusion

The above-mentioned ritual practices are generally performed during normal/natural death. However, there are some minor differences in rituals in certain kinds of death. When a baby dies in the mother's womb or within ten days of birth then the father or the mother places the infant in a small basket (*agra*) and hangs it from a tree which is situated a little away from the village. Generally, this is done secretly. During this kind of death, both the mother and the father maintain certain restrictions for five months. It is believed that when a child dies, the soul lingers on the earth for a certain period, roaming aimlessly and feeding on the sap or little trees and bushes to satisfy its hunger and thirst. After some time, it dissolves into thin air. But if a baby dies in ten days time, then they perform the death rituals similar to that of adults. However, young girls/boys and unmarried men/women are not allowed to attend the funerals because if they do it is believed that the same kind of death may befall them in future.

When a husband or wife dies, then the surviving spouse follows certain restrictions. They should not eat banana, sugarcane, squirrel, birds like *pidi* (peacock) and *peba*, fish, or any other big animals like tiger, bear, deer and monkey. Even garlic, onion, and sweet potatoes are not allowed to be eaten. When a priest dies, first they close the eyes and mouth, and wash the dead body of the priest. They shake the priest's *amrãla*, blow the hornpipe, and play the musical instrument *rẽpu;* one screams '*hooooo* ...' aloud, while one plays the small drum. After this, they perform the rituals by calling other priests to the deceased's house.

In unnatural deaths, the *Igu* uses the *ashowuu* (small branch of tree) in every chant and in *Anja*. The *Igu* holds it in his hand or hangs the branch with a rope while performing the chant. Different types of unnatural death rituals are seen – suicide, murder, fire accident, death in water, etc. If the dead is a female, then ritual performance is done for four days. *Alluthru* concludes the rituals. So, on the fourth night, everyone has to spend one night in the jungle. In the same way, on the death of a male, on the fifth night they have to stay in the forest. Boundary protection (*lãrõ*) is made by the priest with bamboo. For this, they make a structure out of *apito* bamboo which is found only in the hilly area or from *aruto* bamboo which is available near rivers or at the edge of the village. Here, they sacrifice raw eggs and place the broken shell over a bamboo sliver or throw a stone and cross the structure. But menstruating women cannot cross this structure; they have to go by its side after throwing the stone or bamboo sliver. In an unnatural death, *Alluthru* is not performed before the end of the funeral rituals, but in normal conditions *Alluthru* can be performed prior to it. In the case of a murder, before washing of the body and closing of eyes and mouth, the hornpipe is played. One plays the *rẽpu*, one other shouts '*hooooo* ...' into the ears of the deceased, while some others play the small drum. On the dead body, they sacrifice a bear and then burn it. Even in the graveyard, they practice the same.

There are some restrictions in offering goods while burying in the grave. When a woman dies, a weaving loom is not allowed to be buried along with the corpse. It is believed that if one does so, then the deceased person will cut the survivors. If a male person dies, then they do not bury the locally made rain coat (*elebe*), but they burn it. Before burying the hat (*apõtolo*) of the deceased, they make a hole in it and it is believed that in the death world there will be rain all the time where he or she goes. It will create a problem if the hat is put in the grave during cultivation as it will spoil all the grains in the death world. Again, when an *Igu* dies, the headgear (*ãwẽtõ*) is not buried if he did not have the power of *ãrosiyato* (i.e. to fly). If such an *Igu* is buried with the headgear, then he cannot walk and run away from the *alõanini* (the owner of the underworld) who would imprison him and make him a slave. It becomes very easy to catch the priest when he is not able to fly.

The Idu Mishmis believe in a place of confession (*adege*), where the dead confess whatever they did during their lifetime and how they lived on earth. There are different *adege* for different persons. If the person has performed *Reh* in his life time, then the soul will go to *Remo Adeanuli Adege* for confession; if a person has committed murder then his/her soul will go towards *Athurõ echachi Metrõ ayãmko Adege*; if a person was a hunter, then the soul will go to *Arũgo-Adepõlo?*. After confession in *adege,* every soul goes towards the death world known as *Mudu-ãlõkõ*. After this they go to the final death world which is known as *Asiã lõkõ.* The poor or the rich have a similar fate; their souls go to the final death world. But the servant has a different death world which is called *Etadi-aichi Adepothũ.* Here, the servant's soul confesses everything what he/she did in his/her life. The soul of those who had sexual relationship with servants will also go to the servant's death world.

All the beliefs described above, ritual practices and narratives clearly reflect the traditional world-view of death among the Idu Mishmis. These funeral rites and customs are concerned not only with the mourning, preparation and disposal of the body, but also with afterlife of the deceased person, the well-being of the survivors and with the persistence of the spirit or memory of the deceased. Idu Mishmis strongly believe that there is a life for human beings after death and therefore, they bury the deceased person in a well constructed room and offer all the required things like bed, blankets, crockery, fan, TV, grains, piglets, hen, money, dress, umbrella, ornaments, etc. to the deceased person, believing that these things are required for the afterlife. The funeral practices of Idu Mishmis not only deal with burial and afterlife of the deceased person, but also with the well-being of the survivors. The main function of the *Igu* is to perform rituals in order to direct and drive the deceased soul to the underworld and make sure that the spirit will not come back to the living world. These rituals involve chanting, music, dance, offerings, etc. The shaman also performs rituals like *Alluthru* to purify the survivors/people who took part in the funeral ceremony. It shows that the spirit of the deceased person may affect the survivor and therefore, they believe that they have to get purified through rituals. These belief systems, rituals and narratives are orally transmitted from generation to generation.

However, in the modern social-cultural context, these practices and belief systems are gradually losing their value due to several reasons. One of the major reasons is religious conversion. A considerable number of religious conversions took place among the Idu Mishmi tribe particularly from indigenous faith to Christianity. Those who have converted do not follow the traditional practices associated with festivals, agriculture, or life cycle ceremonies including funeral ceremony. In Christian funerals, the church priest plays an important role, and not the *Igu.* The priest prays and sprinkles holy water on everyone in the name of Jesus and prays for the soul to rest in peace and also for the well-being of the survivors. Again, *Anja* is an integral part of funeral ceremony and it cannot be performed by everyone. Nowadays, only a few elderly people know how to perform *Anja* in funerals. The present generation is not aware of *Anja* and its function. There is a change in the construction of the grave also. Earlier, they dug the grave and covered it with wood which can be used for agriculture after a certain period, but now they build the grave with cement and bricks which becomes a permanent structure. As a result, the agricultural land is also reduced.

In modern days there is a huge demand for *Igu* to perform the rituals, but there are few *Igus.* The younger generation is not interested in becoming an *Igu* because of the modern education and employment, and there is no formal institution to learn the knowledge of *Igu.* The death ratio of the existing *Igus* is also very high due to alcohol and health problems. As a result, the knowledge of performing rituals and their functions are slowly disappearing from the society. Traditionally, the family that hosted the rituals offered a rooster or some special portion of the sacrificed pigs or mithuns to the *Igu* as remuneration for his service. Nowadays, they give cash payment to the priest, and the amount of money depends on the financial status of the person. At times they receive up to ₹ 20,000 or more. Therefore, the poor are unable to afford the expenses towards funeral rituals. It is believed by the Idu Mishmis that the changes occurring in traditional belief systems, rituals and practices harm the society and as a result several unnatural deaths are happening in Idu Mishmi society today.

Acknowledgement

The paper is a reprint of the original paper published as 'Funeral Traditions of the Idu Mishmi Tribe of Arunachal Pradesh'. In *Humankind*, Vol.–11, 2015, pp. 81–98.

References

Eliade, M. (1987). *The Encyclopedia of Religion*, Vol. 2, Macmillan, New York.

Hall, E.T. (1977). *Beyond Culture*, Anchor, New York.

Hyunchul, K. (2012). 'The Purification Process of Death: Mortuary Rites in a Japanese Rural Town', *Asian Ethnology*, 71(2): 225–57.

Leach, E.R. (1968). 'Ritual', in D.L. Sills (ed.), *International Encyclopedia of the Social Sciences*, Vol. 13, Macmillan, New York.

Namihira, Emiko (1985). *Pollution*, Tokyo: Tokyodo.

Smith, Robert, J. (1974). *Ancestor Worship in Contemporary Japan*, Stanford: Stanford University Press.

Taylor, L.J. (1989). 'Cultural Constructions of Death in Ireland', *Anthropological Quarterly*, 62(4): 175–87.

van Gennep, Arnold (1960). *The Rites of Passage*, University of Chicago Press, Chicago.

14

Underestimation of Suicide

A Study of the Idu Mishmi Tribe of Arunachal Pradesh

TARUN MENE

Suicide remained a major concern for various scientific intellectuals worldwide. In recent decades research on suicide and suicidal behaviour has expanded and preventing and reducing suicidal behaviour are now important targets of the World Health Organization (WHO) which estimates that worldwide, about one million people die by suicide every year. This represents a global annual suicide rate of 16 per 1,00,000 people. In addition, the suicide attempt rate is about 10–15 times more frequent than the suicide rate. These suicide estimates are based on national mortality statistics, with suicide rates ranging from zero suicides per 1,00,000 people per year in countries such as Egypt, Haiti and Honduras, to more than 30 suicides per 1,00,000 people per year in Belarus, the Russian Federation and Lithuania (Tøllefsen et al., 2012: 1).

Asia suicide alone contributes as many as 60 per cent of the world's suicides, so at least 60 million people are affected by suicide or attempted suicide each year. Despite this, suicide has received relatively less attention in Asia than it has in Europe and North America (Hendin et al., 2008a: 1). On the other hand, a crucial challenge in studying suicide in Asia is the availability and quality of suicide data for monitoring and surveillance. For approximately 20 per cent of the population, suicide data are not available. In countries where data are available, there are problems of underestimation due to inaccurate ascertainment and delay in reporting suicide deaths (Chen et al., 2012).

As a result, the magnitude of the problem is unknown in some Asian countries (Hendin et al., 2008a: 1). Similar suicide studies in the west have raised questions and debated on the accuracy and hence the value of official suicide statistics for one reason or another, for example, Sainsbury and Jenkins, 1982; Simpson, 1950; Giddens, 1978; Whalen, 1964; Walsh et al., 1990; Cantor et al. 1997; Fusé, 1997; etc. Some psychologists also doubt to an extent that they dismiss their usefulness and reject the validity of all statistics on the subject (Powell, 1958).[1] It is also substantiated that the non-inclusion of deaths occurred as a result of complications of suicide attempts in the statistical methods makes the official data unreliable and inadequate (Simpson, 1950: 659).

Suicide in India

In India, research on suicide and suicidal behaviour has received less attention despite good proportion of population being under threat of suicidal death. Only about 25 per cent of deaths in India are registered and only about 10 per cent are medically certified. Studies of large scale verbal autopsy of all deaths in rural regions reveal that the suicide rate in the rural areas is three to four times higher than that reported by the government, so the official suicide rate reported in the country is probably significantly lower than the actual rate (Hendin et al., 2008b: 10; Saddichha et al., 2010: 57; Gajalakshmi and Peto, 2007).[2]

The available suicide estimate in India is based on National Crime Records Bureau (NCRB) and these report fewer suicide deaths (about 1,35,000 suicide deaths in 2010) than estimated by World Health Organization (1,70,000 in India). This NCRB's suicide estimates has also been questioned on the ground of its reliability because they are based on police reports, and suicide is still a crime in India, which might affect the veracity of reporting (Patel et al., 2012). Thus, it is reasonable to expect suicide statistics, despite the inaccuracies, to have heuristic value in Indian context. And for all these reasons the suicide mortality estimates for India is rated poor to fair in the World Health Organization (WHO) rating system (Hendin et al., 2008a).

It is estimated that 1,35,585 persons lost their lives through suicide in India during the year 2011, with an increase of 0.7 per cent over the previous year's figure (1,34,599). The number of suicides in the country during the decade (2001–11) has recorded an increase of 25 per cent. The official report adjusted suicide rate for India at 11.2 per 1,00,000 populations. The overall male : female ratio of suicide for the year 2011 was 64.8 : 35.2. The proportion of suicide victims who are boys: girls suicide victims (up to 14 years of age) was 52 : 48. Youths (15–29 years) and lower middle-aged people (30–44 years) were the prime groups committing suicides. Among the specified causes, family problems, illness and love affairs were the main cause of suicides (NCRB, 2011).

Among the Indian states, West Bengal has reported the highest number of suicides, accounting for 12.2 per cent, of the total, followed by Tamil Nadu (11.8%), Maharashtra (11.8%), Andhra Pradesh (11.1%) and Karnataka (9.3%). These five states together accounted for 56.2 per cent of the total suicides reported in the country (ibid.).

However, the age-specific and sex-specific death totals, rates and risks, as well as the mode of suicide in India's diverse sociodemographic populations, are not well understood (Patel et al., 2012: 2343). Vijayakumar (2010) reviewed fifty four articles on 'Suicide' published in the *Indian Journal of Psychiatry* (IJP) from 1958 to 2009 but none of the article cites or relates the problem of suicide in North-Eastern states of India. Besides, there are several studies in India, but not a single scientific inquiry into the problem of suicide in the North-Eastern states. Though, there is a relative paucity in publications on suicide in India, by and large, suicide as an area of research remained aloof from the preview of scientific intellectuals in this part of India.

Such negligence has contributed to our partial and limited understanding of suicide and suicidal behaviour of the population of the North-Eastern states which is dominated by the tribal. The North-East Indian states have merely about 2.9 per cent share to the total suicides in India, but interestingly, these very states represents, on the one hand, India's highest rate of suicide (Sikkim with 45.9) and on the other, the lowest rate among the Indian states (Manipur 1.2) (NCRB, 2011).

Official Statistics

Considering the perdurable scientific speculation into the problem, and impediment of reliability and underestimation of available suicide statistics in India and worldwide, the present study examines the existing official suicide estimate according to NCRB report and state police reports in respect of Arunachal Pradesh (AP) and its two districts, viz. Dibang Valley and Lower Dibang Valley. These data were then compared with the data on suicides acquired by the researcher from the fieldwork among the Idu Mishmi tribe of the Dibang Valley and Lower Dibang Valley districts. This helps us in validating the reliability of official data and addresses the issue of underestimation of completed suicides in the study area, and of the Idu Mishmi tribe in particular.

A community-based study of the article further aims at ascertaining whether the cases of Idu Mishmi suicides were included in the existing official suicide data. The result of the present study would be noteworthy, and reliable quantification of the suicide deaths is timely, keeping in mind that the Government of India's Twelfth Five-Year Plan (2012–17) includes strategies to tackle chronic diseases and mental health (Patel et al., 2012).

AP which has reported 134 cases of completed suicide in 2011, comparatively lower percentage of suicidal deaths among the Indian states, accounting for only 0.1 per cent of the total suicide in the country. Out of this total, 99 are males and 35 females with 9.7 per 1,00,000 population rate of suicides and the state is ranked in 21st among the Indian states. The age groups of 15–44 is found to be a vulnerable group with regards to suicide, followed by 45–59 age group. About 42.5 per cent victims in AP were young (15–29 years) as compared to the national average of 35.4 per cent. As to the cause of the suicides, the maximum number of cases were categorized under 'unclassified' and 'other causes', which means the evidence is incomplete or else no verification of death has been done at all.

As for their profession, good numbers of individuals were found to be housewives and self-employed (others) followed by persons engaged in the service sector (both government and private) and students. As for their marital status, the married outnumbered the unmarried, and there was no report of widowed and divorcee suicides. A combined 70 per cent of suicide victims had attained primary, middle and matriculation education and 24.6 per cent had no education. Hanging (71.6%) remained the most preferred method of suicide (NCRB, 2011).

The data on district-wise trends of completed suicide in Arunachal Pradesh reveals a total of 1,023, from 2001 to 2010.[3] Among the 16 districts, Papum Pare district topped the rank with a total 219 suicidal deaths, and the highest was recorded in 2010 with 39 cases in the city itself (cases of suicidal deaths in the rural areas were not recorded). Next is Lohit district with a total of 210 cases, and highest occurrence was witnessed during 2007 with a total of 53 cases. These two districts are followed by West Kameng (135 cases), East Siang (110 cases), Changlang (93 cases), West Siang (88 cases), Lower Dibang Valley (67 cases), East Kameng (49 cases), Tirap (44 cases), Lower Subansiri (35 cases), Upper Subansiri (28 cases), Tawang (27 cases), Kurung Kumey (14 cases), Upper Siang (10 cases), Dibang Valley (07 cases) and lastly, Anjaw district with only one case (Office of the Deputy Inspector General of Police (DIGP), Crime Branch, Itanagar, 2011).

However, it is necessary to highlight that the data provided for 2009 reported only 98 cases, which differs from the data in the NCRB's, 2010 report, which showed 110 completed suicides in AP (NCRB, 2010). And, as of 2010, the data may vary because the data of NCRB are collected by the State Crime Records Bureau (SCRB) from the District Crime Records Bureau (DCRB) and sent to the NCRB at the end of the year (Table 1).

Table 1

Incidences of Suicide in Two Districts of Arunachal Pradesh

S. No.	*District*	*2001*	*2002*	*2003*	*2004*	*2005*	*2006*	*2007*	*2008*	*2009*	*2010*	*Total*
1.	L/Dibang Valley	13	17	8	7	2	–	3	2	4	3	59
2.	Dibang Valley	–	–	3	–	–	4	–	–	–	–	7
3.	Arunachal Pradesh	111	114	81	79	70	129	129	110	98	102	1,023
4.	Arunachal Pradesh	111	114	81	79	70	129	129	110	110	131	1,064
5.	Idu Mishmi	12	2	6	7	3	7	3	10	6	6	62

Sources by Row: 1, 2 and 3: State Crime Branch, DIGP Office, Itanagar, AP.
4: National Crime Record Bureau 2001–10.
5: Field-data.

Suicide in Lower Dibang Valley and Dibang Valley

The official data of the incidence of completed suicides for 2000–10 in Lower Dibang Valley and Dibang Valley reveals 74 cases of suicide that had occurred in the two districts. The age groups 15–29 and 30–44 remained the most vulnerable to suicide. The highest occurrence is witnessed in 2001, 2002 and 2003 with a total of 13, 17 and 11 respectively (Table 2).

Table 2
Age and Suicide (2000–10)
Lower Dibang and Dibang Valley Districts of Arunachal Pradesh

Year	*Age Group*					*Total Cases*
	Upto 14	*15–29*	*30–44*	*45–59*	*60+*	
2000	–	3	5	–	–	8
2001	–	7	5	1	–	13
2002	–	7	8	2	–	17
2003	–	3	8	–	–	11
2004	1	1	5	–	–	7
2005	–	1	1	–	–	2
2006	–	2	1	1	Nil	4
2007	–	–	3	–	–	3
2008	–	–	2	–	–	2
2009	–	2	1	1	–	4
2010	1	1	–	1	–	3
Total	2	27	39	6	–	74

Source: State Crime Branch, DIGP Office, Itanagar, Arunachal Pradesh.

As the present article examines the available official suicide data and its reliability, to ascertain whether the cases of suicide that had occurred among the Idu Mishmi tribe were registered, the cases of completed suicides registered in three police stations in the Lower Dibang Valley District, viz. Roing, Dambuk and Hunli police station, were also accessed from the office of the Superintendent of Police (SP), Roing, the district headquarters, for 2000–2010.[4] However, to our utter dissatisfaction and for some unknown reason, the data revealed only 42 cases of completed suicide and another seven cases of unnatural death by other means registered with the authorities, which evidently contradict the data of 67 cases for Lower Dibang Valley district as provided by the office of the DIGP, Itanagar.

Further, as a revealing fact, out of these 42 cases, only two cases, a suicide pact[5] of Idu Mishmi suicides were found to be registered at the local police station. The case took place in Desali village in Lower Dibang Valley district in April 2002. The victims reported were Roki Miso, a 25-year-old male, and Indirani Kechee, a 22-year-old female.[6] Another three (two males and one female) were reported from the Adi tribe,[7] and the remaining cases were of non-locals. Maximum numbers were reported from the 10–29 age group. Hanging (32 cases) remained the preferred method, followed by ingestion of poisonous chemical elements (9 cases) and by self-immolation (one case, female).

Suicide among the Idu Mishmi Tribe: Field Statistics (2001–10)

Table 3

Yearwise Incident of Suicide (2001–10) among the Idu Mishmi

Age Group	*2001*		*2002*		*2003*		*2004*		*2005*		*2006*		*2007*		*2008*		*2009*		*2010*		*Total*
	M	*F*	*M*	*F*	*M*	*F*	*M*	*F*	*M*	*F*	*M*	*F*	*M*	*F*	*M*	*F*	*M*	*F*	*M*	*F*	
10-19	1	2	–	–	–	–	–	1	–	–	–	2	–	1	1	2	2	–	1	1	14
20–29	1	2	–	1	1	1	1	2	1	1	2	2	1	–	3	2	–	–	2	–	23
30–39	2	1	–	–	1	1	1	–	–	–	–	1	–	1	1	–	1	–	–	–	10
40–49	–	–	–	–	–	2	–	1	–	–	–	–	–	–	1	–	1	1	1	–	7
50–59	1	1	–	–	–	–	1	–	1	–	–	–	–	–	–	–	1	–	–	–	5
Above 60	–	1	–	1	–	–	–	–	–	–	–	–	–	–	–	–	–	–	–	1	3
Total	5	7	–	2	2	4	3	4	2	1	2	5	1	2	6	4	5	1	4	2	62
Grand Total	12		2		6		7		3		7		3		10		6		6		62

Source: Field study (2007–10).

Note: The registered case of suicide of Roki Miso and Indirani Kechee is not included in the above estimate.

Field Statistics

It is for certain that not all the cases of the Idu Mishmi suicides are reported or available in the official statistics. Suicide is neither considered a public health problem nor does any agency address this social menace (Table 3).

While generating the data, special efforts were made to identify all the suicidal deaths and the required information was obtained after conducting extensive fieldwork during 2007–10 in the study area at different time intervals. Household enumeration of the suicide victims was carried out following the interview method with structured schedule. The schedule contained both open and close-ended questions pertaining to data on name, age at death, sex, father/spouse name, details of family members, place of death, time of death, date of death, season, means adopted, material used, physical status of the victim, cause of death of the deceased as perceived by the family members, relatives, friends, neighbours, etc.

In a decade, from 2001 to 2010, a total 62 cases of suicide occurred among the Idu Mishmi which have gone missing from the official records (Table 3). Out of the total, 25 cases took place in Lower Dibang valley and 37 in Dibang valley district. The male suicide ratio for the two districts stands at 48 per cent, and the female ratio at 52 per cent. The age groups 10–39 remained the most vulnerable with a combined total of 47 cases. In this age group, female outnumbered their male counterparts.

Hanging remained the most common means of suicide, followed by drowning and ingestion of poison, like pesticides. Classified by marital status, 32 were unmarried, 26 married and four widowed. Persons engaged in agriculture and farming, self-employed persons and students were the prime groups.

The average annual rate of suicide is about 66.31 per 1,00,000 population, considering the total population of Idu Mishmi tribes based on the 2001 census report. The highest number of cases is noticed in 2001 and 2008, and on an average, six persons annually chose to commit suicide among the Idu Mishmi tribe (Table 3). A comparison of the data for completed suicides in the Dibang Valley and Lower Dibang Valley districts and the Idu Mishmi tribe has been presented in Figure 1.

Figure 1
Suicide Comparison

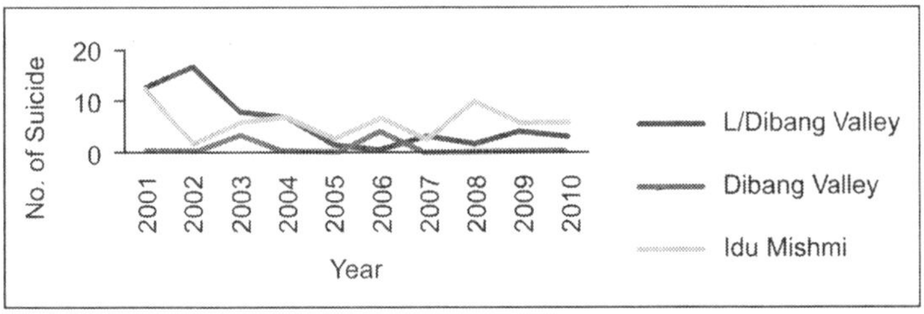

Sources of Data: State Crime Branch, DIGP Office, Itanagar, for the completed suicide in Dibang Valley and the Lower Dibang Valley districts and Fieldwork data of the completed suicide among the Idu Mishmi tribe.

Need for Intervention

Despite the data justifying suicide as a serious problem, there has not been a single scientific inquiry into the problem and there has been complete absence of any intervention programme. There is a serious lack of insight into the problem from the Government agencies as well as at an individual level. As a consequence of this, its impact is well reflected in the Idu Mishmi tribe, among whom the incidence of suicide is rather an internal matter of the community, which is negotiating with the situation as per its own traditional social norms or the so called 'Customary Law'.[8]

Among the Idu Mishmi, for example, a case had occurred in 2005 of a young 18-year-old girl, who was a student in Class 10. As per the information, the girl was in love with a boy who was her distant clan relative (cousin). But such a relationship is considered taboo and the Idu Mishmi society at large, generally denounces such a relationship between two individuals having blood ties.[9] Consequently, the societal custom lingered overhead and their relationship started to get sore. One day, in a shocking incident, the girl was found dead on her bed in her room, where she lived alone and an empty bottle of pesticide was found beside her.

Her death resulted in mixed notions of manifested suicide and voluntary suicide among the local residents. Suspiciousness and tenseness lingered for quite some time, and finally girl's family and clan relatives alleged that the boy was responsible for her suicide but not for homicide. Thus, quarrel between the two parties grew and subsequently the matter was resolved through *Abbalah* (traditional Idu Mishmi political council) and the boy's party compensated in the form of *Acheenu*[10] to the deceased family, which included 15 numbers of *Sa* (*Bos frontalis*), along with cash.[11]

In another case from Desali village in Lower Dibang Valley, a young student of class seven, aged around 13, hanged himself from a tree because he was beaten up at school by his seniors over some matter. He was so intensely angered and depressed that he left a suicide note where he wrote about the incident and also mentioned the names of his senior fellows whom he considered responsible for his suicide act. As a result, the boy's clansmen charged those seniors and the strife was resolved only after the compensation was made to the victim's family which included *Sa* (*Bos frontalis*) and cash.[12]

In both the cases, despite having in hand the Indian Penal Code (IPC) according to which all cases of unnatural deaths must be examined and their causes be ascertained, the agencies responsible remained inactive.[13] A timely intervention could have helped in understanding not only the suicidal behaviour of the Idu Mishmi in general, but also could have been a guiding factor and a source for the formulation of necessary prevention and intervention measures by targeting the high risk groups in a population. More importantly, registration of such cases could have been a reliable source of suicide data in understanding the overall suicide phenomena in the region and the state as a whole.

Dearth in Research

Karl A. Menninger in his foreword, writing in Shneidman and Farberow (1957), was of the viewed that

> few people realize that suicide is more frequent than murder and more easily predicted .... To the normal person suicide seems too dreadful and senseless to be conceivable. There almost seems to be taboo on the serious discussion of it. There has never been a wide campaign against it, as there has been against other less easily preventable forms of death. There is no organized public interest in it. There is very little scientific research concerning it.

More than six decades have elapsed and what Menninger had claimed seems valid to this day.

It is evident from the available data that in AP too, we do not find proper records or data of suicidal deaths. Those available with the Crime Branch, Office of the DIGP, Itanagar, do not provide clear and complete information required in understanding the problem of suicide in the state. The reasons put forward by the Police Officials for such discrepancies are, on the one hand, negligence being done on their own part, basically at district level, and on the other, under-or non-reporting of suicide cases by the family members or relatives because they fear the social and legal consequences associated with suicide.[14]

Further, it is astonishing to note that from the Government and from various Non-Governmental Organizations, there is no initiative yet to address the issue of suicides. In fact, such incidences are hardly recorded by the Government institutions like the police, district administration, etc.

The bulletins published by the State Government agencies such as Arunachal Pradesh Human Development Report, the District Socio-economics

Review, the Statistical Abstract of Arunachal Pradesh, etc. all carry a good number of cases of murder, dacoity, burglary, theft, robbery, kidnapping, riots, culpable homicide, etc. but nothing in relation to suicidal death. More importantly, the total cases of murder, attempt to murder, fatal accidents and non-fatal accidents from January 2001 to January 2010 were 780 cases in AP, whereas suicide alone contributed 1,023 cases during 2001–10 (Table 1).

Similarly, in the Lower Dibang Valley and Dibang Valley districts, a combined total of 29 cases were reported for murder, attempt to murder, fatal accidents and non-fatal accidents from January 2001 to January 2010, whereas death by suicide alone contributed 74 cases during 2000–10 (Table 2).[15]

Conclusion

Thus, it may be concluded that in India, and particularly in AP, suicide is under-emphasized and under-reported for a number of reasons, such as, lack of resources and competing priorities combined with inefficient and incomprehensible death reporting systems, family fear of social and legal consequences associated with suicide, etc. Previous studies in India and outside have drawn conclusions with the similar views, such as, Gajalakshmi and Peto (2007), Patel et al. (2012), Tøllefsen et al. (2012), Hendin and Phillips et al. (2008c), Walsh et al. (1990), Cantor and Leenaars et al. (1997), Sainsbury and Jenkins (1982), Chen et al. (2012), Chuang and Huang (2007), etc. And, as a result, there are serious concerns with regard to the official suicide estimates, its validity and reliability.

The present study has evidently shown that the reliability of the official estimate is subject to error from variation in defining – the data of the state crime branch mixes the cause of suicide with the method of suicide employed- and reporting cases – the kind of inaccuracies between the actual number of suicides and the figure officially reported. There is variation in reported suicide incidents at the state as well as at the district level. It explored and quantified the under-reporting of suicides among the Idu Mishmi tribe, talking about not only the prevalence of suicide, but also the vulnerability of a particular community with respect to suicide.

The study calls for establishing a suicide prevention agenda. Researchers and health professionals need to draw attention to the issue at the highest levels of the governmental (e.g. Ministry of Health). However, while reflecting the diverse range of cultural, social and economic backgrounds in the area, these strategies need to be innovative, and have low-cost support (both financial and in human resources) from major stakeholders such as government officials and policy-makers, health professionals, community organizations and police departments. Increasing awareness as well as public education campaigns may help address the stigma and comprehend the need for sensitivity to local traditions and values. This clearly requires a long-term approach, involving frequent consultation with local researchers and stakeholders.

Acknowledgement

This paper is a reprint of original paper published as, 'Underestimation of Suicide Deaths: A Study of Idu Mishmi Tribe of Arunachal Pradesh'. In the *Economic & Political Weekly*, December 28, 2013, Vol. xlviii, No. 52: 129–33 by Tarun Mene.

Notes

1. In this connection, Powell, in his footnote, noted Gregory Zilboorg (1936) saying, 'present-day statistical data deserve little if any credence .... However, statistics confined to the limited universe of a single community are not subject to the inaccuracies found on a national or international scale.'
2. H. Hendin et al. (2008b) referred to M. Bhat (1991). *Mortality from Accidents and Violence in India and China, Research Reports 91-06-1*, Center for Population Analysis and Policy, Humphrey Institute of Public Affairs, University of Minnesota, Minneapolis MI; L.T. Ruzicka (1998). 'Suicide in Countries and Areas of the ESCAP Region', *Asia Pacific Population Journal*, 13: 55–74; V. Gajalakshmi and R. Peto (2007). 'Suicide Rates in Tamil Nadu, South India: Verbal Autopsy of 39,000 Deaths in 1997–1998', *International Journal of Epidemiology*, 36: 203–07; A. Joseph, S. Abraham, J.P. Muliyil, K. George, J. Prasad, S. Minz, V.J. Abraham and K.S. Jacob (2003). 'Evaluation of Suicide Rates in Rural India Using Verbal Autopsies, 1994–99', *British Medical Journal*, 326: 1121–22; P. Jha et al. (2006). 'Prospective Study of One Million Deaths in India: Rationale, Design, and Validation Results', *PLoS Medicine*, 3: e18; A. Bose et al. (2006). 'Mortality Rate and Years of Life Lost from Unintentional Injury and Suicide in South India', *Tropical Medicine Internal Health*, 11(10): 1553–56.
3. The data was assessed in April 2011 from the office of the DIGP, Itanagar. Further, it was told to the researcher that prior to this period the data on suicide is in distorted form and for most of the districts suicidal data is not available or else not reported to them by the concerned district level authorities. Thus, the data is untraceable.
4. The official data of recorded suicide in the Dibang Valley District could not be assessed. However, back in the year 2007, it was verbally told to the researcher that there is no reported case of suicidal death at the Anini police station.
5. A suicide pact is an agreed plan between two or more individuals to commit suicide. The plan may be to die together, or separately and closely timed. The suicide pacts are important concept in the study of suicide, and have occurred throughout history, as well as in fiction.
6. The cause of suicide is not mentioned in the FIR but researcher's interview with the family members of Indirani Kechee reveal that both the suicide victims were in love affair. But as per the social norm of the Idu Mishmi it is a taboo relationship, for both were very close clan relatives. At the same time, Indirani Kechee was betrothed to another man, so her relationship with Roki Miso was also not appropriate. In fact, it was Indirani Kechee's adamant father who had legitimated the marriage proposal, ignoring her wish and consent. Gradually, their affair got public and at this, their clansmen cautioned them for their illicit and immoral intimacy. Constant fear and precarious situation rendered no space for peace in their life. Finding no way out, both, with premeditated mind, ingested sulphuric

acid that they stole from the school laboratory and died together at Roki's government quarter. A day later, they were discovered (Interview was done with Indirani Kechee's elder sister in December 2009, at Ashali village).

7. Adi Padam tribe was formerly known as Abor (unruly and savage) lived closely with the Idu Mishmi tribe of Lower Dibang Valley district. As a consolidated tribe it has number of subgroups like Padam, Minyong, Pasi, Karko, Simong, Millang, Bori-Bokar, Komkar, Tangam, etc. They are mainly concentrated in East Siang, West Siang, Upper Siang, in the foothills of Lower Dibang Valley districts of Arunachal Pradesh.
8. Unlike the cases here, in other parts of India, it is noticed that although police investigate the case, the 'panchayatdars', review the case before the final verdict is passed (Hendin et al., 2008b: 10). However, among the Idu Mishmis, the final verdict of a suicide case entirely depends on the family members of the victim, following traditional customs in the absence of police investigation and intervention.
9. In Idu Mishmi society, by custom, having a partner from either the maternal or paternal clan relations is denounced.
10. The term basically refers to a type of compensation made for breaching the norm of Idu Mishmi marriage system. Among the Idu Mishmi, it is taboo to establish any relationship leading to marriage within the larger network of consanguineal relatives. If such thing happens, the clan elders impose compensation, generally paid by the boy's party to the girl's party, in the form of *Sa* (*Bos frontalis*), pig and cash.
11. Interview with elder brother and maternal uncle of the deceased, February 2010.
12. Interview with cousin brother of the deceased, February 2010.
13. Under Section 306 and 309 of the Indian Penal Code (IPC), abetting the commission of suicide and attempt to commit suicide is regarded as an offence and the persons involved are liable for imprisonment (Hoshiarpur Police, viewed on 17 December 2007, http://hoshiarpurpolice.org/ipc.htm)
14. S.D. Varma (Sub-Inspector) and M. Chetry (Head Constable), Crime Branch, Office of the Deputy Inspector General of Police (DIGP), Police Headquarters, Itanagar (Interview 3 May 2011).
15. Data on murder, attempt to murder, fatal accident and non-fatal accident were accessed from the official website of AP Police, viewed on 22 July 2012, http://www.arunpol.nic.in/home/crime_stats_dst.htm

References

Cantor, H.C., A.A. Leenaars and D. Lester (1997). 'Under-reporting of Suicide in Ireland 1960–1989', *Archives of Suicide Research*, 3: 5–12.

Chen, Ying-Yeh, Wu, Kevin Chien-Chang, Yousuf, Saman, and Paul S.F. Yip (2012). 'Suicide in Asia: Opportunities and Challenges', *Epidemiol Rev*, 34: 129–44.

Chuang, H.L. and W.C. Huang (2007). 'A Re-Examination of the Suicide Rates in Taiwan', *Social Indicators Research*, 83(3): 465–85.

Fusé, T. (1997). *Suicide, Individual and Society*, Canadian Scholars Press, Toronto.

Gajalakshmi, V. and R. Peto (2007). 'Suicide Rates in Rural Tamil Nadu, South India: Verbal Autopsy of 39,000 Deaths in 1997–98', *International Journal of Epidemiology*, 36: 203–07.

Giddens, A. (1978). *Durkheim*, Fontana Press, London.

Hendin, H. et al. (2008a). *Suicide and Suicide Prevention in Asia*, World Health Organization, Geneva.

—— (2008b). 'Epidemiology of Suicide in Asia', in *Suicide and Suicide Prevention in Asia*, World Health Organization, Geneva, pp. 7–18.

Jha, P. et al. (2006). 'Prospective Study of One Million Deaths in India: Rationale, Design, and Validation Results', *PLos Med*, 3: e18.

NCRB (2010, 2011). *Accidental Deaths and Suicides in India*, National Crime Records Bureau, Ministry of Home Affairs, New Delhi.

Patel, V. et al. (2012). 'Suicide Mortality in India: A Nationally Representative Survey', *Lancet*, 379: 2343–51.

Powell, H. Elwin (1958). 'Occupation, Status, and Suicide: Toward a Redefinition of Anomie', *American Sociological Review*, 23(2): 131–39.

Saddichha, S., M.N. Prasad and M.K. Saxena (2010). 'Attempted Suicides in India: A Comprehensive Look', *Archives of Suicide Research*, 14: 56–65.

Sainsbury, P. and S. Jenkins (1982). 'The Accuracy of Officially Reported Suicide Statistics for Purposes of Epidemiological Research', *Journal of Epidemiology and Community Health*, 36: 43–48.

Shneidman, E. and N.L. Farberow (1957). *Clues to Suicide*, McGraw Hill, New York.

Simpson, George (1950). 'Methodological Problems in Determining the Aetiology of Suicide', *American Sociological Review*, 15(5): 658–63.

Tøllefsen, I. Maria et al. (2012). 'The Reliability of Suicide Statistics: A Systematic Review', *BMC Psychiatry*, 12: 9.

Vijayakumar, L. (2010). 'Indian Research on Suicide', *Indian Journal of Psychiatry*, 52: 291–96.

Walsh, Dermot et al. (1990). 'Do Statistics Lie? Suicide in Kildare and in Ireland', *Psychological Medicine*, 20: 867–71.

Whalen, A.E. (1964). 'Religion and Suicide', *Review of Religious Research*, 5(2): 91–110.

15

Sineru Monomyth

The Idu Mishmi Funeral Mythography

RAZZEKO DELLEY

On the third day of Idu Mishmi funeral ritual, the shaman starts escorting the soul of the deceased to the underworld. Before entering the underworld, they need to cross an eternal river of dead, *Kandi*. Elaborate arrangements are made on the bank of the river. The boatman is called, bargain begins for boat fare, the price is fixed, and thereafter, the shaman and the soul get in the boat and row towards *Andomo*, the entrance of the underworld. However, no living being can enter the underworld, only souls are permitted there. To enter the underworld, shaman's soul has to leave the body. All of a sudden the shaman collapses. His soul has left the body. Drums are beaten, horn is blown and cries are made to call back the soul of the shaman. Lingering or tarrying of the soul in underworld will be fatal to him. He may fall into oblivion or may be withheld there permanently.

After couple of minutes, the shaman rises slowly and resumes the funeral chant. As he has been to the underworld, the shaman has foreseen the calamities which are going to befall on the community and individuals. This stage is one of the most solemn and complex part of the funeral rituals. This solemn ritualistic process is founded upon the mythic quest of *Sineru*, the almighty shaman and cultural hero who originated the *Ya* ritual. The heroic journey of *Sineru* needs elaborate study. Therefore, in this chapter an attempt has been made to interpret the main mythological aspect of Idu Mishmi funeral oration and tries to unravel the cultural and psychological dimension associated with it. The study is based on the cultural hero concept of Joseph Campbell (1949) and archetypal hero theory of Carl Jung (1953).

The Light in the Darkness: Heroes in Society

In the first book of *Bible; Genesis*, there is a passage describing the duel between Jacob and an unseen rival. He fights with might and remains undefeated. At last his opponent addresses him and declares thus, 'your name shall no longer be Jacob but Israel, for you have striven with god and with men and have prevailed. Jacob later becomes the father of Israeli people' (6th and 5th centuries BC).

Numerous epics and myths like this biblical episode narrate the heroic struggle of heroes who are able to prevail by struggling against gods and men. The wrestling between Israel and God can be considered as an allegorical manifestation of hero striving against the unseen forces or fate and thereafter prevailing over it. Heroes dare to step in an irrevocable offensive unknown territory and liberate as well as encourage the people with their actions. They are human champions who shoulder the burden of the whole society and solve the mystery of the universe and restore order to the chaos and eliminate the torment of the endless darkness.

These heroes are recurring characters through literature and myth of all over the world and their heroic endeavours remain largely similar despite the different cultural context. Hercules and Boadicea, James Bond and Ulysses, Jason and Perseus, Scheherazade and Taliesin, Aladdin and Superman are all heroes who battle against the darkness that pose danger to their society. They may belong to different time and space and employ and wield different weapons against the darkness, but their basic narrative remains the same.

According to Campbell (1949), the hero is a human champion who struggles to understand the mysteries of the world and illuminates all the dark corners which cause fear and confusion. Moreover, the hero is also the person through whom God manifests himself to the world: the hero and the god are one self-mirrored mystery. It is only through the hero, the god is glimpsed and because god is the beginning, middle and end of all beings, it is through our manifestation of him in the hero that we are shown our divine, heroic potential. His action shape and structure the fate of a tribe or a nation. The heroic figure of a community also enables us to take a peep at the aspirations, hopes and beliefs of a community as heroes represent their ideal figures of their abstract virtues and notions. Therefore, hero sets an example to the humanity and makes them realize that the hero could be anyone of us, and that, we all could command the name Israel. All these aspects make the hero worthy of attention and study.

Joseph Campbell, Lord Raglan, Dorothy Norman and Jessie Weston, all agree that there is a fundamental heroic pattern among all the culture and can be pinned to a *Monomyth* (Pearson and Pope, 1981: 3). *Monomyth* now is inferred as a standard cross cultural hero, the recurrent structure within which all heroic myths operate.

Campbell (1949) divides these elemental patterns in three basic stages in the form of hero's quest: *Departure, Initiation* and *Return*. This pattern according to Campbell is a revelation of man's eternal struggle for identity in this universe.

In the first stage 'Departure', the hero leaves his worldly comfortable and familiar world and ventures into realms of unknown darkness. In the second stage 'Initiation', the hero undertakes mammoth tasks and faces grave ordeals. This is the stage where he has to prove his worthy character. In the third and last stage, 'Return', the hero brings the boons of his quest back for the benefit of his people and thereby, the fruits of his mission are shared by all the members of his community.

However, Campbell also observes that all the hero myth may not have all of these stages. Changes may occur in these heroic myths. Some myths may be devoid of some stages or a significant space and time may be devoted only to some specific stage.

Among the Idu Mishmis, *Sineru* is the most popular cultural hero and most revered one. He is invoked and deified in important ritual like in normal death of the people. He stands tallest among all the heroes and therefore, 'Sineru Monomyth' will unravel the deep psychology of the community who deify him.

Sineru Monomyth

Departure

This stages covers: (i) Heroics Traits (ii) Call to the Adventure and (iii) Supernatural Aid.

As in the Sineru myth: There once lived a very powerful Shaman called *Sineru*. As he was very powerful and popular, *Sineru* was called to different parts of the world by sick and destitute. Once he was called to Tibet. The epidemic was severe; thousands had died due to blood dysentery. Before leaving for Tibet, Sineru entrusted his confident Ishuru (the Hawk) to look after his family members. He departed leaving his mother, young wife and a son. Sineru had to remain in Tibet for several years. One day, the Hawk flies to him and says, 'Sineru, you are needed at home. Your son has died'. But Sineru had to remain in Tibet. He was entreated by the people not to leave his noble mission. He told the Hawk, 'I can get my children back if my wife and I procreate them. If my wife dies, I can re-marry and have a wife again. Here my task is not yet over. Therefore, I cannot leave this place.' Hawk flies back and Sineru continues healing people.

Several years pass by. One day, the hawk returns and breaks the news, 'This time your mother is no more.' This news shatters Sineru. He falls in deep grief. At last he deplores and utters in despair, 'If my son dies, I can procreate and have a son again. If my wife dies, I can re-marry and get a wife again but in no case, I can ever get a mother back once dead'. Thereafter, Sineru abandons his mission and departs for his home. He passes through the great mounts namely; *Iduba, Yuyua, Ipussi, Satilo, Leno, Alosle, Adege*. In the mount *Assimbra* he planted the seeds of *Maloh* and *Aeve* (Sago palm, plants used during funeral rituals). From there this plants spread to the rest of the world. At last, after reaching Athupopu, beneath a rock Sineru remorsefully grieves for five days. The loss of an affectionate mother was so grave to bear. Sineru at that time decides to redeem his filial duties by bringing back his mother from the underworld.

Departure is the first stage in which hero journeys away from the society. He may depart from the will of his own, or may be forced to depart from the comfort of the society. According to Pearson and Pope (1981: 17), hero has to depart because 'the potential for self-actualization and the heroic life is obscured from men as well as women by society's restrictive myths'. The hero breaches the status quo in his heroic quest. Sineru has to depart from the comfort zone of his family and society to Tibet, a country of different people as well as community in distress and chaos. His healing spiritual powers are put to test by the sick and destitute. This is the first stage of self-actualization.

Heroic Traits

Northrop Frye (1957: 33) classifies the heroes found in literature according to their type:

1. If superior in kind to both other men and to the environment of other men, the hero is a divine being, and the story about him will be a myth in the common sense of a story about a god.
2. If superior in degree to other men and to his environment, the hero is the typical hero of romance, whose actions are marvellous but who is himself identified as a human being. The hero of romance moves in a world in which the ordinary laws of nature are slightly suspended: prodigies of courage and endurance, unnatural to us, are natural to him, and enchanted weapons, talking animals, terrifying ogres and witches, and talismans of miraculous power violate no probability once the postulates of romance have been established. Here we have moved from myth, properly so-called, into legend, folktale, marchen and their literary affiliates and derivatives.
3. If superior in degree to other men but not to his natural environment, the hero is a leader. He has authority, passions, and powers of expression far greater than ours, but what he does is subject both to social criticism and to the order of nature. This is the hero of the high mimetic mode, of most epic and tragedy, and is primarily the kind of hero Aristotle had in mind.

Sineru, being a human and shaman fits into first and second characteristics. As a shaman, he can communicate with different energies of nature and therefore, he is above ordinary humans and being bestowed with spiritual power he is also responsible for the well-being of people, not only for his own community but also others. Despite his power, Sineru is a human and all the social conventions and taboos also apply to him. His heroic trait lies in his shamanic power and his generosity. He is also duty bound and even the death of his son cannot deter his noble mission.

However, another essential heroic trait of a hero is his courage to question the authority of social status quo. Sineru's heroism is manifested during his sheer disturbed moment. In this stage, he resolves to act against conventions and restriction of his society. He chooses the untrodden path and dares to step beyond the pale of society and question the authority of status quo. But the mission of Sineru is enormous the answer to question which he is seeking is beyond the human world.

The Call to the Adventure

In this stage, the hero, after confronting chaos and confusion has to make an appropriate decision. He should clearly see the task and resolve to attain the goal. However, his accomplishment, goal or findings is not only significant to him but also to the whole world. Sineru, after the death of his mother resolves to seek her back. He abandons the first call of healing people and decides to undertake a quest to the dangerous and unfamiliar domains, the underworld itself. Though he is unaware of the consequences of his quest to the society but it paves way for the foundation of a very important sociocultural set-up of his people.

Supernatural Aid

The hero during his quest receives supernatural aid in various forms. He may receive signs in his sleep or may be shown direction from different elements of nature like birds, animals and insects.

In this myth, Sineru is offered supernatural aid by birds like hawk, *Pethro* and *Pali*. They at different stages appear to give direction to the hero. Moreover, as a powerful shaman he can render services from the supernatural beings. His spiritual wisdom also shows him the way. The Idu Mishmis also believe that a shaman is always guided by powerful *Drowo* (tutelary spirit).

Initiation

Road of Trials

After reaching the outskirts of his village, Sineru orders the hawk to fetch a rooster from his house and see whether anyone is alive there. After a while, the hawk returns and informs him thus, 'There was only an old and decrepit woman who tried to shoo me away while clawing the fowl'. The young wife whom Sineru left several years back was now an old lady and only survivor in the house.

Sineru prepares *larou* (a spiritual gate) in the outskirts of his village and by crisscrossing his swords, sits down meditating for several hours. In trance he sees the soul of his mother in the underworld. Sineru reaches home and starts *Igu* (shamanic chants). After five days of shamanic ritual, the mother returns from the underworld. But she appeared in a very disgusting form. Her whole body was stinking. She had earthworm for a necklace and earrings. The mother unknowingly entered the room of Sineru's wife. She got frightened by seeing the horrifying figure and hit the mother with abripa (weaving shuttle).

After observing this incident, *Apholo*, the owl suggests to Sineru that her mother needs a good cleaning. And then he volunteers for the task, Sineru grants him the permission. The owl returns after couple of hours, but without mother. He tells Sineru, 'While I was cleaning your mother she fell down in the cliff *Manojuru* full of hovering *Pishus* and *Prawus* (species of red birds.)

Sineru worried, rushes to the great cliff *Manojuru* and dives into all the deep gorges and canyons exploring. But the remains of his mother were untraceable. During the flight he asks the flock of *pishus* and *prawus* (species of birds) about his mother. They had no idea. Later he asks the bird *pethro* and *pali*, they replied to him thus, 'everywhere we have been flying and drinking water from the different gorges of the great cliff *Manojurn* but we have not seen any sign of human being. Only when we met the owl we could smell abominable foul stench coming out of his beak.'

Now Sineru understood the whole matter. The owl had tricked him and devoured his mother. Sineru returns and summons the owl. The stinking beak confirms him of the doubt. He kills the owl and splits his beak wide open. But he only found a tuft of mother's hair from it.

Sineru's heroic quest is full of trials and ordeals. His call to Tibet, death of his son and ultimately his mother dying for second time are all part of the road of trials and ordeals which the hero has to endure. Heroic traits emerge in the form of overcoming all these setbacks and moving ahead in the quest. The heroes in their quest explore the deep mysterious caves and dungeons lurking with dangerous monsters and dragons. The Idu Mishmi world is unknown to deep caves and dungeons. However, high cliffs and deep unfathomable gorges in myth are equivalent to caves and dungeons. Therefore, Sineru here explores the high mountains, stiff cliffs and deep gorges full of dangers.

Return

Sineru once again gets into trance and tries to trace the soul of his mother. But it could not be traced. The soul had entered the deep chambers of underworld. Thereafter, Sineru embarks upon a journey to the underworld. After an arduous journey, Sineru reaches the bank of river *Kandi* (eternal river of the dead) on the entrance of the underworld. He pays boatman and crosses the river and gets into the underworld. After exhausting search, Sineru found his mother's soul in a remote chamber of the underworld. But to his dismay, the soul had transformed itself into a fly. After deep contemplation Sineru decides to return back. In deep anguish, Sineru at last declares 'my mother is no more in the form of my mother. She is no longer my mother in form or thought. Now she is just an insect, a fly, destined to fly around shrubs and bushes. Death has separated us. You are no more my mother. Now we have different world. Let's stay in our own world'. Saying thus, Sineru returns to the human world. After reaching his place Sineru begins the funeral ritual, *Ya*. He reminds the soul of his mother that, they are now beings of different world. He urges again and again never to return back in the human world. Thus, then started the funeral ritual *Ya.*

Beast of the Belly

Sineru is in beast of the belly when he reaches the underworld. The boatman is the guardian of the threshold. He needs to be paid handsomely, even today at the time of soul's journey; the Idu Mishmis enact paying the boatman. After crossing the eternal river *Kandi*, Sineru is in the unknown dark, dangerous and alien world. The funeral ritual enacting the quest of a shaman to the underworld suggests that the place is full of danger. A shaman may even forget to return or may be withheld there for eternity. There are also legends of shamans dying while making quest to the underworld.

Campbell calls this passage, a transit into a sphere of rebirth. Here, hero crosses his human threshold and gets into the unknown and would appear to have died. But the hero would be reborn as a transformed man. This transformation leads to hero's apotheosis. Passage into the beast of the belly is essential for a hero as he needs to get beyond the confines of the visible world and therefore, hero goes inward to be born again and resurrected as an enlightened one. Sineru also gains in-depth knowledge about dead and living in the underworld. This knowledge makes him a bigger hero which results into his apotheosis.

Apotheosis

Apotheosis is the stage in which the hero attains the divine status. For achieving apotheosis, the hero has to face his other side and become wiser. He has to confront and transcend his ego and move into the domains of eternal and become a resurrected man. This is the stage in which Sineru faces the biggest ordeal. After confronting the soul of his mother he is in a dilemma whether to accept the eternal law of nature or fall into maternal emotions. Therefore, the biggest conflict, which Sineru faces, is psychological one. He looks beyond the maternal love and accepts the law of nature. He overcomes his ego and realizes that the binary opposition of nature; life and death cannot be bridged. The super ego is conquered and the hero comes to terms with the eternal laws of nature. Sineru here attains the divine status by overcoming his ego.

Sineru, therefore, after gaining the knowledge of eternity chooses to return to the human world by leaving the dead in her place. Though she is affectionate and a revered mother but the eternal law of nature has to be obeyed. By sacrificing his own maternal love Sineru opts for the human world. Another heroic virtue of Sineru, that being the self-sacrificing hero emerges in this episode. Sineru's submission to the eternal law of nature is his surrender to the cosmos and therefore, he is also a world redeemer.

The hero's ability to transcend death is the most important task in human terms. The hero during the quest overcomes the powerful evil powers and attains the self-knowledge and lives with his people to tell his tale. According to Norman (1969: 11), myths of the heroes speak most eloquently of humanity's quest to choose life over death. This can be compared with what Freud calls struggle between *thanatos* (death drive) and *libido* (life drive). The hero embodies for the people the strife between *libido* and *thanatos.* He illuminates the lives of people and gives them strength and wisdom to face death and obscurity. The exemplary heroism of the hero enables the people to overcome the fear of death. This aspect of the hero makes him identifiable with libido. Therefore, the full growth of the hero demands that he needs to die and thereafter be resurrected to manifest the victory of *libido* over *Thanatos.*

The Ultimate Boon/the Hero Seizes the Sword

The hero in this stage takes possession of the treasure he had been seeking for. Though Sineru had been seeking the soul of his mother the ultimate boon is quite contrary. The ultimate boon or Holy Grail for Sineru is the knowledge and experience that leads to his greater understanding and reconciliation with forces of nature: living and dying. The ultimate boon, the sword he seizes is the knowledge of eternal truth.

Return with Elixir, Master of Two Worlds and Freedom to Live

The full round, the norm of the *monomyth*, requires that the hero shall now begin the labour of bringing the runes of wisdom, the golden fleece, or his sleeping princess, back into the kingdom of humanity, where the boon may redound to the renewing of the community, the nation, the planet, or the ten thousand worlds (Campbell, 1949: 193).

The rune of wisdom, the Golden Fleece which Sineru brings back into the kingdom of humanity is the eternal truth. He brings back the wisdom that life and death are binary opposites in this human world and unbridgeable. Thus, everyone must accept this eternal law of nature. This knowledge is a boon for the whole tribe for deeper understanding of mysteries over life and death.

Hero in this stage becomes the master of both the worlds as his understanding of time and being change significantly. He is now an enlightened one having knowledge about the eternal world and champion of things becoming, not of thing become, because he is (Campbell, 1949: 243). The quest draws to close as now hero has accomplished his mission, he as an agent of change and has brought the renewal of the world. Therefore, the heroic quest forces the hero to embark upon a journey to unknown realms during which he comes to understand himself and the world. The quest in the end leads the hero back to his people where he shares the new knowledge which he has acquired during the course of the quest.

Sineru: The Culture Hero

The difference between the warrior hero and culture hero is that, the warrior hero wields the sword of virtue and culture hero wields the sceptre of dominion. Both warrior hero and culture hero challenge the status quo and bring the change in society. However, the difference lies in their modus operandi and ultimate result. The culture hero introduces a new system, philosophy, inventions, scientific theories and other ways of life (Campbell, 1949).

Sineru is a culture hero because he is able to impart the knowledge of forbidden world through his power and dedicated pursuits. Though he commits mistakes but quickly learns from them and moves toward his goal. He undertakes dangerous quest to the underworld and tries to question the concept of death itself. During the quest, there is a development of thought process which equips him to overcome his ego. He is able to balance the personal emotion and eternal law of nature. For the sake of collective good he sacrifices his family life. Though he undertakes a dangerous journey, the change which Sineru bring upon his community is not out of battle and bloodshed. It is more to do with knowledge and wisdom: The knowledge to accept and endure the deaths of one's own and abide by the eternal law of nature. The new way of looking at life and death has far-reaching impact on the sociocultural set-up of his community.

Sineru's heroic ethic is his compassion, steadfastness and sacrifice. All these characteristics of his make Sineru an inspiring figure for the whole tribe. His heroism also lies in his pursuit for commitment. However, the biggest heroic ethic in him is his ability to overcome his ego for the eternal law of nature. And like a true hero he returns as an enlightened and resurrected one to share the runes of wisdom with his own people.

Conclusion

Heroic mythology reflects the aspiration of the community who narrates them. Campbell (1949: 238) asserted that, 'proper study of these myths can become an 'eloquent document of the profoundest depths of human character .... We have only to read it, study its constant patterns, analyse its variations, and therewith come to an understanding of the deep forces that have shaped man's destiny and must continue to determine both our private and our public lives.'

Heroic figures play vital role among the humans as discussed among the Idu Mishmis. They place themselves in the deep psyche and enable them to understand the relationship between themselves and the world. And by contemplating the heroes, they feel their presence which strengthens them to endure the realities of life. Heroes illuminate the world and overcome the darkness; the people are inspired by his action and dare to take heroic step in their life. They act as a rejuvenating agent of society. Apart from inspiring and enlightening, the heroes also validate the social arrangement, social norms and rituals. Many of the time, it is the cultural hero who is the architect of social foundation. Myth then becomes a way of thinking, way of reflecting and exploring ourselves. The symbol, sign and all the characters in the myth play a vital revelatory role about the thinking process of mankind. And heroes certainly play a central role. According to Jung (1953: 68), 'The universal hero myth ... always refers to a powerful man or god-man who vanquishes evil in the form of dragons, serpents, monsters, demons, and so on, and who liberates his people from destruction and death.'

What Jung (1953) is implying here is that, the fear of death and darkness among the people transcend time and space. Irrespective of race and culture, the fear of death, darkness and destruction influence the impulses and thought process of people. And this thought process forces them to share a desire for a hero who will play the part of saviour and guardian against death, darkness and destruction. The hero then is born out of this collective unconsciousness shared by everyone. Therefore, the hero myth follows a similar pattern all over the world irrespective of race and culture. As his central role is to free the humanity from the fear of death, the hero embodies life at its most significant and active period. And this characteristic makes him look like a god; the one who animates all life. The heroic archetype is also manifestation of our desire for truth and greatness, and therefore, he is the reflection of ultimate truth imbued with potentials of life The hero appeals to us and becomes a symbol of hope and aspiration by battling against our fear. And this aspect makes him our saviour and guardian.

All these aspects of archetypal hero as a symbol, affirm the profound impact of a hero on the collective psyche of humanity. Hero as a symbol positions himself in our deep psyche and influences impulses of both ecstasy and fear in us. No other symbol has the power to evolve in us different feelings like an archetypal hero. But most important of all is the hope which hero infuses in us. And this hope is the driving force of life. Despite all the earthly ills, heroes inspire the people to be good and righteous, brave, compassionate and strive for good of self and others.

References

Campbell, Joseph (1949). *The Hero with a Thousand Faces*, Princeton University Press, Princeton, NJ.

Carlyle, T. (1840). *Heroes and Hero Worship*, Ballantyne, London.

Firth, R. (1973). *Symbols: Public and Private*, George Allen and Unwin, London.

Freud, Sigmund (1985). 'Project for a Scientific Psychology', in M. Bonaparte, A. Freud and S. Kris (eds), *The Origins of Psychoanalysis: Letters to Wilhelm Fliess, Drafts and Notes: 1887-1902*, Basic Books, New York.

Frye, Northrop (1957). *Anatomy of Criticism*, Princeton University Press, Princeton, NJ.

Goldberger, A. (1965). *Visions of a New Hero: The Heroic Life According to Andre Malraux and Earlier Advocates of Human Grandeur*, Biblioteque Des Lettres Modrenes, Paris.

Jung, Carl (1953). *Four Archetypes*, Routledge Publications, New York.

Lash, J. (1995). *The Hero: Manhood and Power*, Thames and Hudson, London.

Norman, Dorothy (1969). *The/Hero/Myth/Image/Symbol*, New American Library, New York.

Pearson, C. and K. Pope (1981). *The Female Hero in American and British Literature*, R.R. Bowker, New York.

Rubenstein, A. (1998). 'Bearer's Dream: An Archetypal Symbolism in Fantasy and Science Fiction', Unpublished Thesis, University of Pretoria, Pretoria.

The Bible (2008). Authorized King James Version, Oxford University Press, Oxford.

16

Euthanasia among the Idu Mishmis of Arunachal Pradesh

Understanding Issues and Concerns of a Frontier Tribe

TARUN MENE AND SARIT K. CHAUDHURI

Derived from the Greek terms *eu* meaning good, and *thanos* meaning death, euthanasia is the act of bringing death to another person in a relatively painless way for reasons of mercy. It is generally defined as the intentional killing by act or by omission of a dependent human being for removing his or her suffering (Prabhu and Kalita, 2013). According to the dictionary euthanasia means, 'a gentle and easy death', but it is now used to refer to the killing of those who are incurably ill and in great pain or distress, for the sake of those killed, and in order to spare them further suffering or distress (Singer, 1993: 175). Euthanasia has historically been a common practice in many societies; it remains one of the most controversial topics today (Polacek, 2013). It came to be used in the last decade of the 20th century to mean a death that is perpetrated or accelerated with the help of medicine. The practice has drawn increased attention and discussion in recent decades as a result of advances in medicine and technology and a growing interest in human rights (Mystakidou et al., 2005: 96).

The definition of euthanasia as well as the interpretation of the terms like 'good death', 'dying with dignity', 'physician assisted suicide', etc. has been scrutinized ethically and critically and still has remained one of the biggest controversies of this decade (Bamgbose, 2004). For example, defining euthanasia as good death is not adequate because to die a natural death after spending many years on earth is equally conceived by many cultures as good death. Thus, the word euthanasia is ambiguous and better not to be defined but described. Such definitions, at the same time, are also not adequate because they often exclude the forms of euthanasia such as voluntary, involuntary and non-voluntary euthanasia.

Attempts have been made by many to classify euthanasia on the basis of the consent and on the basis of the action. On the basis of consent, that is, whether the patient is consenting or capable of consenting to death, we can differentiate euthanasia into three types – voluntary, non-voluntary and involuntary euthanasia. Voluntary euthanasia is when the person themselves feels their life is not worth living and thus request by the sufferer for euthanasia. Involuntary euthanasia is that when the competent person is not consulted and is against the will of the patient. Non-voluntary is that when the person is not competent to decide for oneself, for example, the person is demented. According to the way the euthanasia is practised, it is further classified into active and passive euthanasia. Active euthanasia entails the use of lethal substances or forces to kill a person, e.g. a lethal injection given to a person with terminal cancer who is in terrible agony. Passive euthanasia entails withholding of medical treatment for continuance of life, e.g. withholding of antibiotics where without giving it a patient is likely to die, or removing the heart, lung machine, from a patient in coma (Prabhu and Kalita, 2013: 47–48). However, passive euthanasia is no longer used as an expression especially in the dutch standard definition of euthanasia, because it is not considered euthanasia. What is required is the intention to end life. Cases in which there is no patient's request are also not considered to be euthanasia (Haves, 2001: 507).

Over the years, euthanasia has been a subject of much debate. The topic holds interest for a large number of stakeholders including physicians, anaesthetists, surgeons, nursing personnel, ancillary health-care staff, legal experts, theologists, journalists, community leaders and public at large, apart from psychiatrists (Punnoose and Sarkar, 2014). It is also argued on the grounds that every human being has a right to life, and a number of international human rights instruments assert this right to life. For example, the Universal Declaration on Human Rights (1948), the United Nations Charter (1945), European Convention for the Protection of Human Rights and Fundamental Freedom (1950), American Convention on Human Rights (1969) and the African Charter on Human and Peoples Rights (1981) are some of the instruments which explicitly and implicitly prohibit the unlawful taking of life. As a general principle of law, they stand for the protection of life (Bamgbose, 2004). Therefore, it seems that the debate on euthanasia from multidimensional perspective will continue to grow and for now it is certainly a difficult task to draw a general consensus for and against the act of euthanasia. Also a considerable number of studies concerning physicians' attitudes and practices regarding euthanasia and physician-assisted suicide have been carried out across the world. Since almost none of these studies have a common design, international comparison of factual findings is problematic. There can be little doubt that much of the trouble is due to inappropriate and too vague definitions of euthanasia and physician assisted suicide in many studies (Materstvedt and Kaasa, 2002).

Globally, countries like Netherlands became the first country in Europe to legalize euthanasia. Nevertheless, this was not legalized without strict conditions guiding it. It was followed by Belgian in 2002. In 1997, Oregon became the first state in the United States to decriminalize physician-assisted suicide.

Until recently, attempt to commit suicide under the Indian Penal Code (IPC) 309 was a criminal offence and was punishable by imprisonment or fine. However, in its recent decision, the Government of India has decided to repeal the said section, noting that attempt to suicide may be regarded more as a manifestation of a diseased condition of mind, deserving treatment and care rather than punishment (*The Times of India*, dated 10 December, 2014 issue). On the other hand, under the current Indian laws, euthanasia amounts to homicide by the physician and suicide by the patient. However, there are many who support for the legalization of euthanasia. For instance, recently, a Constitution bench of five Justices of the Supreme Court of India has issued a notice to states and union territories suggesting for a countrywide debate on the matter of passive euthanasia. This was in response to a plea by Common Cause, a non-governmental organization which called for allowing voluntary withdrawal of life support for persons with terminal diseases (Punnoose and Sarkar, 2014). Following this notice, in the Arunachal Pradesh State Legislative Assembly, the issue was raised by some legislature for a debate but it was not accepted by the State Government considering euthanasia as a century old issue (*The Arunachal Times*, dated 30 July, 2014 issue). Another example is of Aruna Shaunbaug versus King Edward Memorial hospital case in the Supreme Court of India in March 2011 (Prabhu and Kalita, 2013). Many bills proposing this action have been introduced in the Indian Parliament, but these have not been accepted. It must be admitted that passive euthanasia is being practised in India without it being legalized (Verma et al., 1999: 28).

It is against such backdrops that the present work seeks to look at the prevalence of the practice of euthanasia among the Idu Mishmi tribe of Arunachal Pradesh – one of the eighth North-Eastern states of the Indian Federation. The authors bring an account of the historical and cultural aspects of euthanasia as existed among the Idu Mishmi tribe of Arunachal Pradesh until recently. It addresses the practical issue of management in which the family members of the victim had to make difficult decisions when faced with a person expressing a wish to die. Focussing on the case study of different forms of live burial, the chapter has tried to understand how, when and why an Idu Mishmi desires for such distinct form of dying. The chapter has also tried to extract how the attitudes toward these practices have varied over time and space. This will also reflect broader social system and people's attitude towards death. Perhaps, in the entire North-East India, the Idu Mishmis are the only tribal group which practised euthanasia in its own uniquely rudimentary form, much before it came to be known to the modern world.

Locating the Tribe

The Mishmi tribe of Arunachal is divided into three subgroup: Taraon Mishmi, Kaman Mishmi, and Idu Mishmi.[1] Chiefly located in Lower Dibang Valley, Dibang

Valley and Lohit districts of Arunachal Pradesh, some of them also inhabit East and Upper Siang districts of the state. Culturally speaking, Idus are quiet distinct from rest of the two Mishmi subgroups which is reflected in various aspects of their day to day life and social structure as well as value systems. However, their dialect has very close affinity with that of the Taraon Mishmi. Idu Mishmis are popularly known as the Chulikata Mishmis because of their distinct hairstyle. It is widely believed that this nomenclature was bestowed upon them by the people from the plains with whom Idus have traditionally shared trade relations (Bhattacharjee, 1983: 13).

The prevalence of the practice of euthanasia (*Misi-muh* in the local parlance) among the Idus is widely recalled and recounted by them. In sharp contrast to the modern-day practice which is couched in medical and legal lingo, euthanasia enjoyed social sanction amongst the Mishmis on entirely practical considerations. In one such widely reported case, a certain Pietyi Mepo of Engalin village volunteered to be put to death. Sick of his illness, he requested his son and other family members to do the needful. A small stone house (*Ju*) was constructed with no ventilation which acted as a death chamber. After performing the necessary self-funeral rites and rituals, Mepo walked into the stone house and eventually died of suffocation.[2] The occurrence of the same incident is also noted in Baruah's study. Baruah locates the above incident in Ahui Valley in 1948, wherein Pietyi Mepo had volunteered for an end to his life. Before embracing death, Baruah mentions, Mepo had summoned all his close relatives over a feast as per the custom in order to see them all for one last time. Soon after the relatives left, Mepo entered into the stone structure, erected for the purpose of causing his death, never to walk out of it (Baruah, 1960: 57).

Baruah also records four other unrelated cases of infanticides in his study. However, these incidents were largely related to adultery among the Idu Mishmi. As he observes, 'adultery is viewed with great abhorrence and a woman is severely punished for it. It is considered dishonour for a girl to have an illegitimate child. So to avoid social castigation and disgrace, the child is put to death immediately after it is born. Of the four infanticide cases in the last twelve years, about which I have detailed information, one child was strangled, one buried alive, the third was abandoned in the jungle, and the fourth child was killed with drugs in the womb' (Baruah, 1960: 64). Although Baruah puts all the four cases under the blanket category of infanticide, the nature of each specific act could be seen as very different from the others, leading to very different outcomes. While the first case represents the classic case of murder, the second and third incidents characterize the act of involuntary euthanasia wherein the infants were buried and abandoned alive obviously without their consent. The issue of obtaining prior consent was simply out of question given the age of the victims. The fourth case, however, was a typical example of abortion

Prevalence of euthanasia among the Idu Mishmis has also been documented by other scholars. Bhattacharjee, for example, records the practice of burying a person alive in extreme cases of sufferings from incurable diseases. However, this would happen only after exhausting all possibilities of curing the diseased person by the Shaman (*Igu*). The final step would precede all the rituals of offering supper and drinks before accompanying the concerned person to the grave (Bhattacharjee, 1983: 138).

All the three dominant types of euthanasia, i.e. voluntary, non-voluntary and involuntary were found to be prevalent amongst the Idu Mishmis. Voluntary type include cases in which the concerned person invariably suffered from certain incurable diseases (at least in those days) like leprosy (*chede*),[3] cancer (*wa*), swelling of body (*Asha Agisi*), epilepsy (*Emo*), etc. Most of these diseases were conventionally linked to evil forces. Most of the non-voluntary cases of euthanasia included those people who suffered from certain abnormalities (*Atho/Kapa*), paralysis (*Ikhibi/asapucheyala*), tuberculosis (*Ithri*), etc. while involuntary euthanasia comprised of those who had become some kind of a burden, owing to the terminal nature of their illness, on those who were the caretakers but who had to helplessly assist involuntary euthanasia. The method used in assisting euthanasia among the Idu Mishmis is in sync with the prescribed custom of disposition of the dead among them. Since the dead has to be buried as per the prevailing custom, the same method is followed also in the case of assisting euthanasia. It is done in two distinct ways: one, in which a grave (*Bro*) is dug, and in the second case a stone structure in the shape of a small room (*Ju*) is erected on the ground which is then plastered with mud in order to block any passage of air. In the course of fieldwork, the prevalence of some thirty-six cases of different forms of euthanasia was traced among the Idu Mishmi community. For the purpose of this chapter, we zero in on only five of these of which two each are voluntary and non-voluntary while the last one is the case of involuntary euthanasia. These incidents occurred between the 1940s and 1970s in the Rango and Awahali villages of Lower Dibang Valley and East Siang Districts of Arunachal Pradesh.[4] In presenting these incidents below, we have taken utmost care to reproduce them verbatim as narrated to us by the interviewees. This is done as a conscious decision in order to avoid interfering with the flow of the narration. Hence, the reproductions below are being presented in the first person.

Cases of Voluntary Euthanasia

Case No. 1

I was 27 years old when I had witnessed the second incident of unnatural death in my life. It relates to the case of a 65-year-old woman, Jeelo Umpe of Rango village, whose unnatural funeral was arranged by her relatives on her persistent requests to put an end to her sufferings. It probably occurred 6 to 7 years after the 1950 earthquake which had badly devastated the region. Jeelo was a widow with a dumb daughter who was nearly half her age at the time of the incident. She was suffering from some form of edema, locally called *Asha Agisi*, for the last two years. Her situation had deteriorated to the extent that she had slipped into a permanently vegetative state. She could not even lie down owing to intolerable pain, as her body had swelled beyond imagination. The only way she could somehow manage to keep herself alive was by way of sitting in a constant posture at one given place with her hands holding a rope tied to the raft overhead. It was not at all easy for her to sit in this posture all through the day and night, as it was excruciatingly painful and became unbearable after some time. All this made her make up her mind to call it quits. Feeling absolutely hopeless about any possibility of recovery, she started pleading her relatives to kill her so that she could get liberated from the day-to-day torture that she had to undergo. At last, her persistence paid off with the relatives agreeing to give in to her request/demand.

Accordingly, a female Shaman (*Igu*) named Meli Molo was summoned from Amili village to perform the last ceremonial rituals. On the opening day of the two-day funeral ceremony, Jeelo herself supervised all the arrangements, requesting her relatives to make sure that everything was in place. The second day afternoon witnessed some protest from her dumb daughter who did not want her mother to die like this. However, given the fact that Jeelo herself was having bouts of emotional outbursts, requesting everybody to bring an end to her sufferings, the relatives had no option but to ignore her daughter's protests. After all the rituals were carried out, Jeelo was carefully wrapped in a blanket (*Badu*) and was taken to the burial ground. She was then gently laid down in the grave. Following the prevailing customs, different items supposedly required to live even after death was put in the grave alongside her body. Finally, Jeelo was made unconscious through the performance of a ritual called Agra-Lati which is similar to Dirge chant whereby, as per the belief, the soul of the person is overpowered to facilitate smooth burial. This is a ritual which is followed in all instances of euthanasia among the Idu Mishmis.[5]

Case No. 2

This relates to the case of Tudu Mimi of Rango village who was put to death in the late 1970s. He was just about 26 years old then. Orphaned by the death of his parents at a very young age, he was brought up by one of his uncles, Anati Mimi. Tudu was suffering from leprosy (*chede-che*). Except the face, his entire body had swelled with blisters all over, leading to unbearable pain. The same status continued for almost three months. His situation had worsened so much that he could barely move his body. More than wanting to put an end to his personal sufferings, Tudu believed that if he were to die a natural death he might pass the disease on to the other members in the family. Scared of such a prospect, he earnestly urged his uncle and others in the family to bury him alive.

Once his request was conceded, he became actively involved in overseeing the entire process of arranging his own funeral. He personally chose Khukta Mimi from Elope village to act as the Shaman for the funeral. Since I was myself a witness to the whole episode, I clearly remember how fearless Tudu was and relished his own funeral feast with much delight and contentment. What really struck me about him was his level of self-confidence and clarity about life which he summarized thus, 'I know nobody from amongst my ancestors would wish to have food and drink with me. Not even my father or mother, let alone other relatives. Hence, I wish to have my last supper with you all here this last day of my life. I do not want much to be offered to me in my grave as I will die soon after I am buried'. With such kind of philosophy, he truly enjoyed his food and drinks with others around him. After the feast got over, Khukta Mimi carried Tudu on his back to the grave in a large size basket (*Aagra*) which was especially knitted for the purpose.[6] As soon as the basket was lowered down, Tudu himself walked out of it and lied down on the bed inside the grave. Lying on the bed inside the burial, he repeatedly pleaded not to offer much to him as he is soon going to die, and he would not consume anything thereafter. However, he was offered some food and drinks as per the ritual before his burial was roofed with mud and boulders. No *Agra Lati* was performed in this case which is usually done in order to make the person unconscious before he/she is buried.[7]

Cases of Non-Voluntary Euthanasia

Case No. 1

It was my first experience of witnessing the incident of somebody being put to death alive. I was so very much amazed that it took me a while to understand its long-term implications. As far as I can recall, it happened exactly about two years before the Rango village was hit by an earthquake in 1950. Gali Umpe, who was married to Akhola Mimi with a son Bano and two daughters Dumaye and Emimeh, was physically challenged. Given her inability to reason out what is good or bad for her, she could not decide for herself as to what should be done with her.[8] Her condition demanded that she be looked after all the time by a caretaker from amongst the family members. Given her state of affairs, she was never left alone owing to the fear that she might unintentionally and unknowingly harm herself or others. On many occasions, she was prevented from causing self-harm and/or injury to others. Once she threw burning firewood onto the *Apo*,[9] where domestic articles like baskets are kept. It could have completely burnt the house if it had not caught the attention of a family member. Sometimes, she would defecate on the same plate she had had her meal minutes before. On one occasion, she removed the skull of a wild animal hung from the wall, and consumed it after roasting it in the fire.[10] Her acts led to increasing frustration and an overwhelming sense of hopelessness amongst the family members, not knowing what to do and how to make her calm herself down. After much deliberation and soul-searching, it was decided that it might be a better idea to help her die.

Resultantly, Ami Elapra, a female shaman from Ebuli village, was called upon for performing the funeral rituals. While Gali Umpe witnessed all the funeral-related activities on the first day, she could not make sense of it at all owing to her mental state. On being taken to burial the next day, she thought that she was being shifted to a new house where she would have to live in seclusion. I vividly remember her uttering these words angrily, 'If I am made to live all by myself in a separate house, I can very well do so. What do they think?' After reaching the burial ground, she walked into the grave and lied down on the bed continuing to repeat what she had said while being carried to the funeral site. Unable to comprehend the chanting of Anja (dirge chant) by her husband in the background, she queried, '*Aw eseya ni tro ... tro ... tro ... lazi ba*' (who is making sound like *tro tro tro*). On being told it was her husband, she remarked, '*oh! Akhola mo wela bala ne lazi we do*' (oh! Akhola is reciting it so sympathetically!). Finally, the funeral ritual came to an end with the chanting of *Agra lati* by her husband, which made her unconscious before being buried in the grave.[11]

Case No. 2

This was my first experience of witnessing somebody being put to death before actually dying. It relates to Mupi Mimi from Rango village who was in her late twenties and unmarried at the time of the incident. She had lost her mother as well as two younger brothers while she was a young child. Emiyu, her younger sister, was alive at the time she was put to death.

Mupi was born a normal child and was all fine until she became sick at a much later stage and developed some problem because of which she started behaving abnormally. She would often play with fire at great risk to herself and others. She once ate the skulls of wild animals after roasting it in the fire, an act which is actually considered a taboo for females. She was prone to committing such acts while she was alone at home. Her sickness continued for almost a year, eventually turning her into a vegetative state. Owing to her illness, she could barely move herself and had to remain constantly stationed in one place. Her father could not bear the sufferings of her daughter and decided in consultation with other members of the family to bring an end to her day-to-day angst and pain. Accordingly, Khuka Mimi, a male shaman from Elope Village was summoned to arrange her funeral with a view to putting an end to her life, in order to ease her of her sufferings once and for all.

This decision was initially not disclosed to others from the village. Hearing the howl and cry at her home, the villagers assumed that Mupi was finally dead. Ignorant of the actual plan, I too believed that Mupi was dead and I went and sat beside her body in order to perform dirge (*Anja*) as is usually the custom during funeral. I was completely shocked when I realized that Mupi was stealthily holding my right arm. I remember how I pulled myself back almost screaming in disbelief as to how could a dead person suddenly wake up to hold somebody's hand! I got back to normal state only on being told about the actual reality. Till then I had no idea whatsoever about what was going on. I had absolutely no idea about the existence of some such method of putting a live person to death. However, once the funeral process started and people started gathering, the real motive behind arranging the funeral was revealed to everyone. Since Mupi could not have been a part of the decision-making process about the end of her own life given her mental state, it was her father who had to take the final call with a view to bringing an end to her sufferings. Once the decision was taken, others could only join, as per the existing norms, in accomplishing the act in a peaceful manner.

Although Mupi was a witness to all the arrangements being carried out like gathering of the people, chanting of rituals (dirge), and preparation of food and drinks, she could not fathom the underlying motive behind it, as she was in a semi-conscious state. On the second (final) day of the funeral, the dirge chant (*Anja*) was performed by her father in the presence of the shaman, Khuka Mimi, before burying her in the grave.[12]

A Case of Involuntary Euthanasia

This relates to the case of 60-year-old Gimiya Mito, a deaf and dumb woman from Awahali village of East Siang district, who was otherwise quite sturdy and full of life. She along with other women agriculturalists from her village had once gone to the field in the early morning, as is the usual practice, for harvesting millet. Suddenly, Gimiya had bouts of diarrhea, making her so weak in the process that she could not even get up from the place till the evening. Her friends did try to help her, but to no avail. Initially, Gimiya kept assuring her friends that she would soon get alright and then she will collect and carry bamboo shoots and fire-woods for all. However, her situation deteriorated considerably owing to severe dehydration. To this, her friends got angry considering her as useless and slothful and there was no sign of recovery. Not knowing what to do, her friends decided to bury her alive. They went ahead with the process of live burial without bothering about performing funeral rituals which is otherwise invariably always followed by the Mishmis. They dug a grave and laid her down in it and covered it with mud and boulders. To this day, the women folk of Awahali village in particular are sometimes jestingly referred to as 'undertaker of live burial of men', as informed by the informant.[13]

Popular Perception of Euthanasia

Even though the term 'euthanasia' was unknown to most of its practitioners, the actually existing practice of putting out somebody's life while alive was very much in sync with what the modern term has come to signify in contemporary times. In line with the modern definition, the actual practice of the act in the universe of this study was very much in accordance with the principle of 'mercy killing'. The trigger for effecting euthanasia under the voluntary category was clearly the concerned person himself. It was only on the basis of a manifest request or plea from the sufferer that a subsequent decision to take recourse to what is today called euthanasia was taken by others in the family. Even in the cases of non-voluntary euthanasia covered in this study, the prime motivational factor was a general concern amongst the family members to cut short the lingering angst and suffering of the person. Other factors like lack of adequate medical aid and prevailing myths about the nature of the specific disease or illness one was inflicted with served only as retrospective or secondary explanations.

Based on in-depth interviews with a cross-section of people amongst the Idu-Mishmis cutting across age, gender, educational and occupational backgrounds, this section seeks to highlight the differing perceptions of people on the current raging debates on euthanasia. Interestingly and predictably, a majority of the interviewees had never heard the modern technical jargon, 'euthanasia', even though they had very definitive views on the efficacy of the practice which some of them had firsthand experience of witnessing at some point of time in their lifetimes.

An overwhelming majority of the elderly interviewees held very positive views about the practice, as they invariably empathized with those who were suffering from long-term incurable diseases.[14] As is evident from the observation of Jinge Mega, a 70-year-old woman, who had been witness to several cases of voluntary euthanasia:

> It is pitiful to see someone suffering endlessly from some prolonged incurable disease with absolutely no hope of recovery. What does one do in such a situation? It is better to concede to the plea of the sufferer to ease him/her of unending sufferings.

Such a view is representative of the general perceptions amongst the older people, as several women interviewees like Debiya Mili, Kiche Linggi, Timiya Mihu and many more, all in the age group of 70 plus held similar views. The views of their male counterparts like Diko Miwu and Emuko Miwu from Maroli village in Dibang Valley district in the same age group were no different, as they echoed the same sentiments of helplessness and unending sufferings. Recalling his father's direct involvement in five different incidents of voluntary euthanasia as an *Igu*, Diko Miwu shared his father's observation,

> ... when people themselves are asking to be buried alive owing to their unbearable anguish resulting from unending suffering, how could I shy away from performing my duty?

Their approval of the method adopted to put an end to the prolonged sufferings of people could perhaps be out of a deep-seated realization, given their own precarious old-age related problems, that it is perhaps better to embrace death than to suffer endlessly. The level of attendance in the funeral could also be seen as an indicator about the general social acceptability of the practice. Barring a few cases, most of the euthanasia-linked funerals invariably attracted a huge gathering, as the co-villagers not only approved of such a practice, but also extended all possible help in arranging them. Such unstinted support is clearly a reflection of not only the shared world-view, but also of the much needed unconditional compassion with the sufferer and emotional support to the family under duress.

Low level of attendance in a euthanasia-linked funeral is also popularly viewed, on the other hand, as an indicator of its unpopularity and social disapproval. As is evident from the testimony of Anoko Mega, a shaman from Cheta village, who was summoned to perform the death ritual of Sumi Menjo of Anaya village.

> I was not aware of the fact that the person I was summoned to perform funeral rituals of was still alive. I was told that the person was dead. I got to know about it only when I was half-way through with the rituals. Even though I did express my reluctance to continue, I could not stop the process, as Sumi Menjo's elder son requested me to do so. Poor attendance by the villagers in the funeral clearly revealed that there were many others like me who disagreed with the practice of killing somebody before natural death.

Another Shaman, Sipa Melo, from Aleney village located in Dri Valley of Dibang Valley District voiced strong reservations about its popularity and social acceptability,

> Such cases of unnatural death did not enjoy social sanction, as the decision to put an end to somebody's life was kept a closely guarded secret. Apart from the affected person who volunteered to die, only a few very close members of the family were involved in taking the final decision. In cases where the concerned person was not in a position to take an informed decision, it was invariably decided by a few core members of the family. Nobody else from the clan or the village was ever consulted. Moreover, the prevailing myth among the Idus that 'evil' disease (Khinu Hembe) like leprosy, epilepsy, tuberculosis, swelling, etc. could spread like an epidemic further contributed towards maintaining the veil of secrecy shrouding such a practice.

In sharp contrast to the perceptions of the older generation which invariably, albeit with rare exceptions, approved of the traditional modes of 'euthanasia' on grounds of mercy killing; the younger generation does not approve the practice in modern times and tend to look at the older practice more as a kind of necessary evil. Historical marginalization and geographical isolation of the region are seen as the major contributing factors for the prevalence of such practices by the younger generation.[15] As Sunil Mow, a practicing Idu advocate, eloquently observed;

> Most of the cases took place in the absence of medical and legal establishment in the region and were largely influenced and supported under the Idu sociocultural dimensions. But in the modern days, there are plenty of agents through which people's perception could be changed against misconception of diseases like leprosy and tuberculosis which were the root cause and are considered evil and untreatable by the Idu people. Now there are medical camps, resettlement camps, etc. in many parts of the nation where people with leprosy disease could be transported and could get medical treatment. If there is any case of euthanasia among the Idus in recent time than that must have been kept in secret or not publicized at large. Otherwise serious criminal case may be initiated against those persons who are involved in assisting such form of death even if it is voluntary.

It is important to note that in case of non-voluntary and involuntary euthanasia, the act of 'mercy killing' is kept as a closely guarded secret with only the very close family members being a party to the decision-making process. Others – from outside the family – have no clue about what is actually happening, and they participate in the funeral procession as they would ordinarily do.[16] The reason behind maintaining a veil of secrecy about such cases is that unlike the case of voluntary euthanasia, the motivating factor here is not mercy killing, but the back-breaking burden of caretaking of a person who happens to be in a vegetative state with no hope of ever recuperating from his/her present status. Poor material conditions may often combine with heavy emotional drain on the part of the caretakers in thus reaching a decision to get rid of the concerned person in order not only to relieve the sufferer but also equally those who have been hopelessly taking care at times for years together. The relatively old age of the sufferers along with the nature of incurable diseases (at least in those days) were other contributing factors in taking recourse to such extreme measures.

Discussion and Conclusion

While the prevalence of the practice of live burial among the Idu Mishmis in the past may not tantamount to the modern practice of euthanasia, it would certainly not be out of place to assert that what they actually practised was indeed very close to the modern practice, albeit in its own rudimentary form.[17] To draw a parallel between the two would thus not only be fallacious but overstretching the case a bit too far. What, however, does remain common between the two is the broader concern – to ease the last turbulent and trying days of the sufferer by facilitating untimely death.

The Idu Mishmis stand out in terms of being the only known community in India which practised an ingenious form of live burial. However, along with the practice, the role of the performers of the same – the Idus who held iconic status in the traditional world-view dominated by evil spirits (khinus) – is also on decline today.[18]

Contestations over ethico-legal issues are increasingly becoming sharper with the younger educated class raising several important questions about the efficacy of such a practice in modern times. Amidst a raging debate in India, as in other parts of the world, whether or not to allow a terminally sick person the right to die with dignity; the traditional Idu experiences do impel us to ask if they were not wiser than the modern-day skeptics!

Acknowledgement

The paper is a reprint of original paper published in *J. Indian Anthrop. Soc.* 51: 24–40 (2016).

Notes

1. Both the terminologies 'Idu' and 'Mishmi' have no concrete and specific meaning in Idu language. Baruah (1960: 98) mentioned that 'the word Idu, ... , is most probably a distortion of the word Midu which means inhabitant of Idu valley and is the name for only one section of the people'. It is here to mention that Idus may be categorized into three groups as per their dialectic variation and in few words meaning which are Mindri, Mithu and Midu. Most of the Mindri speaking Idus inhabit the present Upper Dibang Valley District around Dri and Mathu river valley The Mithu inhabits both sides of the Ithun river valley. The Midu speaking Idus are mainly found in lower foothills and lower valleys of Mishmi hills. So most probably, Midu speaking Idus of lower foothills and valleys first came in contact with outsiders and only from their dialectic nomenclature 'Midu' the term 'Idu' was coined to designate the tribe. As I put it Mithu speaking Idus inhabits Ithun valley, Baruah (1960: 11) designated the same Idus of Ithun valley as Bebejiyas, again the term which has no concrete meaning and origin in Idu language. And for the term 'Mishmi', Bhattacharjee (1983: 13) suggested that there is no clarity of origin of the term though largely believed that it has been coined by the people of plains of Assam to designate the tribe. Further, one may find that Idus refer

themselves as Kera-A. Here 'Kera' is believed to be a name of ancestral forefather and 'A' stands for children and thereby meaning children of Kera.

2. Notes and Queries, Man in India, The Anthoropological Survey of India, pp. 81–82.
3. For leprosy (*Chede*), the Idus had no medicine to cure. Even these day people in the interior places perceive leprosy as evil, communicable and an incurable disease. Sometimes, lepers are disposed off from the main dwelling to a separate hut at the periphery of village boundary. For example, Mecho Mimi of Anaya village was a leper who was transported to temporary hut adjacent to his main residence. Eventually, he died of leprosy naturally and after his death the hut was burnt down in an attempt to eradicate the disease completely. After the dead of a leper (by any means) his/her belongings are burnt down to ashes along with the house where the victim took his last breath.
4. As the introduction of education is a recent development in the region, people have no written record, particularly date of any incidences of euthanasia. Though some recent cases (three to five decades back) are still fresh in memory of some elderly Idus but that too have no written records. On the other hand, Idus prescribe it taboo in uttering name and sometimes even incidence of dead person. Such belief has helped in fading the memory of such incidences. It is here, therefore, the age of the informants, of their parents and the year of the great earthquake in the region, i.e. 1950 were taken roughly in calculating the year of the incidence. Sometimes, season as per traditional agricultural calendar is also used in calculating the month of the incidence.
5. The information collected from Jinje Mega, Age – 80+, Sex – Female, Village – Ashali, Roing and Ango Mimi, Age – 90+, Sex – Male, Village – Ashali, Roing.
6. It is said that wherever Khuka Mimi, the shaman, performs funeral ritual in case of the person who died of leprosy he used to carry the person alone, may be dead or alive, to the burial place. As per the Idu's perception it is the tutorial spirit of the shaman (dron) who directs him and gives power to do so.
7. The information collected from Jinje Mega, Age – 80+, Sex – Female, Village – Ashali, Roing and Ango Mimi, Age – 90+, Sex – Male, Village – Ashali, Roing.
8. As per the information, the victim was not mentally retarded during her early age but later, on reaching her old age she started abnormal activities which assured people that her mental status was not normal and considered her to be a mad lady.
9. The third shelf of the three-layered shelves above the fireplace found in every traditional Idu Mishmi household.
10. Eating of wild animal meat is a strict taboo for the Idu women and they never take it. For the male, eating of such meat is followed by taboos which may last for two to three days.
11. The information collected from Jinje Mega, Age – 80+, Sex – Female, Village – Ashali, Roing, Ango Mimi, Age – 90+, Sex – Male, Village – Ashali, Roing and Akusi Kechee, Age – 55+, Sex – Female, Village Ashali, Roing.
12. The information collected from Jinje Mega, Age – 80+, Sex – Female, Village – Ashali, Roing and Debia Mili, Age – 70+, Village – Ashali, Roing.
13. Information collected from lete Kichu Lingi, female, aged 100+ of Aball village, Roing. Note: There are reports of at least four cases of involuntary live burials among the Idu Mishmi where the victims were forcefully buried alive by the kin members due to varied reasons. In this section, only one case may be briefly discussed.

14. Notion mostly held by the elderly Idus like Shri Limu Meme, Age – 60+ of Kebali Village, Shri Ango Mimi, Age – 80+, Smti Jinje Mega, Age – 70, Smti Akusi Kechee, Age – 60+, Shri Andro Elapra, Age – 65+, Smti Dibia Mili, Age – 70+, Smti Junta Mene, Age – 55+, Smti Pema Meto, Age – 45+ of Ashali Village, Roing.
15. Views provided by Sumo Lingi, male 50+ of Mayu village, Lower Dibang valley district and Thuti Mili, male 45+ of Ashali village, Lower Dibang valley district.
16. The case of Mupi Mimi is an example which was even not known to informant Smti Jinge Mega who at that time was a participant in the funeral ceremony.
17. In order to have an idea of the complex healing mechanism and perception of diseases by the shamans in Idu Mishmi tribe of Arunachal Pradesh one can see article by Sarit K. Chaudhuri (2008) presented in the 20th ECMSAS in Manchester University, UK from 8th to 11th July on 'Igus of the Idu Mishmis of Arunachal Pradesh: Relocating Indigenous Healers and Healing Traditions of a Frontier Tribe of North East India' in the panel on Disease, Possession and Healing in South Asia convened by F.F. Ferrari and P. Srinivasan.
18. In spite of the dominance of the institution of shamanism in village life this institution is gradually losing its past popularity because of multiple reasons. The number of shamans has reduced to a great extent. In order to have a critical discourse on the plight of the Igu or shamans of the Idu Mishmis, read Chaudhuri's (2008) article on the 'Plight of the Igus: Notes on Shamanism among the Idu Mishmis of Arunachal Pradesh'.

References

Bamgbose, Oluyemisi (2004). 'Euthanasia: Another Face of Murder', *International Journal of Offender Therapy and Comparative Criminology*, 48: 111–21.

Baruah, T.K. (1960). *The Idu Mishmis*, Directorate of Research, Government of Arunachal Pradesh, Itanagar.

Bhattacharjee, T.K. (1983). *Idus of Mathu and Dri Valley*, Directorate of Research, Government of Arunachal Pradesh, Itanagar.

Chaudhuri, Sarit K. (2008). *Plight of the Igus: Notes on Shamanism among the Idu Mishmi Tribe of Arunachal Pradesh, India*, European Bulletin of Himalayan Research 32: pp. 84–108.

Have, H.A.M.J. ten (2001). 'Euthanasia: Moral Paradoxes', *Palliative Medicine*, 15: 505–11.

Materstvedt, L.J. and S. Kaasa (2002). 'Euthanasia and Physician-assisted Suicide in Scandinavia with a Conceptual Suggestion Regarding International Research in Relation to the Phenomena', *Palliat Med*, 16: 17–32.

Mystakidou, Kyriaki, Efi Parpa, Eleni Tsilika, Emmanuela Katsouda and Lambros Vlahos (2005). 'The Evolution of Euthanasia and its Perceptions in Greek Culture and Civilization', *Perspect Biol Med*, 48: 95–104.

Polacek, Kelly M. (2013). 'Euthanasia: A Guide to Sources', *Reference and User Services Quarterly*, 46: 13–19.

Prabhu, V. and Tanuja Kalita (2013). 'Ethics and Legality of Euthanasia in Indian Context', *EJAIB*, 23: 46–50.

Punnoose, V.P. and Siddharth Sarkar (2014). 'Euthanasia in India: Social Psychiatric Aspects', *Indian J. Soc Psychiatry*, 30: 77–79.

Singer, P. (1993). *Practical Ethics*, Cambridge University Press, Cambridge.

Verma, K., M. Mehta, B.V. Adkoli and V.K. Paul (1999). 'Ethics Perspectives from India', in Nimal Kasturiaratchi, Reidar Lie and Jens Seeberg (eds), *Health Ethics in Six SEAR Countries* Vol. I, World Health Organization, Regional Office for South East Asia, New Delhi, pp. 10–36. Available at: http://www.who.int/ethics/regions/en/searo_ethics.pdf. Accessed on 17 April 2014.

17

Women in the Face of Globalization

Observations on the Idu Mishmi Society of Arunachal Pradesh

JUSTINA UMBREY AND TARUN MENE

Society is never static and so are its institutions. Change is an everyday phenomenon, which brings about new challenges and opportunities in one or more aspects of any given society. Globalization is one of such changes which, in its literal sense, is a process of transformation of local or regional phenomena into global ones. It represents a combination of economic, technological, sociocultural, and political force of change.

It is being experienced in most parts of the world and in most aspects of an individual's life. Globalization cuts across geographical, social, cultural and economic boundaries, leading towards a larger integration of the world and facilitating interdependence, and thereby creates a 'global village' out of all cultures and civilizations of the world. Globalization covers several different processes that are occurring simultaneously. Some aspects of globalization are positive, but many aspects are negative. For example, the globalization of information through the internet has enabled more ideas and news to be exchanged between more people, resulted in breaking geographic isolation, and created a global platform for communication and connection between communities and individuals. However, its negative aspect has been the domination of one culture – the Western culture, specifically the US culture – over other cultures. It has resulted in the dominance of English language and the disappearance of many local tribal languages throughout the world. Globalization is set to displace diversity of local cultures to a unified global culture.

Corporate globalization, on the other hand, follows the principle of market fundamentalism, trade liberalization or free trade, which calls for the removal of all barriers of trade that are meant to protect the local industries, the environment, and even human rights. At the local level, globalization poses a serious threat to the local indigenous habitants. In the name of development, a good number of people are displaced from their traditional habitats, causing them much trauma. For example, studies show that between 1947 and 2000 globalization-driven developmental projects have displaced some 50 to 60 million persons (Fernandes, 2004). Studies also show that most of the displaced/project-affected persons are from assetless rural poor classes. According to one estimate, 55.16 per cent of them are tribal but some others peg it at 40 per cent (Bharali, 2006). Tribals are the worst sufferers since many development projects such as dams and industries are located in tribal areas.

Within this broader context, globalization as a process continues to be a serious threat to the economy and identity of women in general and tribal women in particular. There is a gender issue in the process of globalization since marginalized social groups like women are often found excluded from the discussions on the effects of globalization. It has, however, been evident that women in the developing countries, both as consumers and producers, are placed at a disadvantageous position under the new regime of globalization. The incidence of poverty among women is said to be increasing compared to that of men. Globalization has been blamed to have increased the incidence of unemployment and underemployment among women and has given rise to many forms of discriminations in the labour market (Fernandes, 2003). Some women might have gained better access to the labour market but the majority of them are staying locked in at relatively low levels of pay and skills, becoming increasingly discriminated against. Globalization also widens the wage gap between men and women and increases inequalities of income. For example, in Orissa (Odisha), some tribals got semi-skilled jobs in the NALCO unit at Damanjodi, Koraput district because a voluntary agency trained them in some skills. Otherwise, all the skilled jobs go to persons from the dominant castes (Fernandes and Raj, 1992). Most jobs given to the tribals, particularly women, are unskilled, often on daily wages. Women who work in the formal sector had the most arduous, repetitive, and insecure jobs due to lack of the required technical skills. Many of these working women are now forced to give up their positions as members of the permanent staff, and to become contractual employees. Female workers are also not paid wages according to their productivity. They are assigned to work under hazardous conditions causing health problems (Kumar and Shivalkar, 2002). Many women have migrated to the cities where they face tremendous problems of housing and sanitation (Sen, 1999). Women have become selective victims of globalization as working in the corporate establishments they are denied to form unions and so denied of their rights. Very often women are subject to verbal and physical abuse (Yogish, 2007). The manifestations of the globalization syndrome are to be seen in terms of increasing centralization of market and product, shifting from food crops to cash crops, and the predominance of monocultures where once there was bio-diversity. Women have lost their recognition for the work they used to do in the agricultural field (Sen, 1999). Growing numbers of crime against women such as physical harassments, rape, molestation, and human trafficking simply talk about the status of women in the modern context. Thus, the multiple drivers of change such as climate, globalization, land use, economic liberalization and migration have over the years become major development challenges, particularly in developing and least developed countries. More so, with the tribal women as they have been recognized as one of the most vulnerable groups from the impact of climate and other changes due to their socially constructed roles and responsibilities and relatively poor economic and political positions. At the same time, their relatively poor exposure to the external world controlled by the formal system pushes them to the peripheries of the polity. For example, displacement due to developmental initiatives pushes the tribals into its economy and society without adequate preparation. This causes deprivation of livelihood, economic impoverishment, and sociocultural marginalization.

This article discusses briefly the impact of globalization on the tribal women in the North-Eastern Region of India with special reference to Idu Mishmi women. The data of the paper is based on primary and secondary sources collected from field observations.

Globalization and Tribal Women in India: An Overview

Around 806.49 lakh of people are tribals in India out of which 394.11 lakh are women (GOI, NSSO, 2009–10). These tribal women are victims of globalization. Tribal cultures in general have a sensitive and organic relationship with the surroundings. It cannot be static but keeps changing according to the situation. As globalization impacts every facet of life in India, it affects the tribal communities more than the others, because the former's mineral and natural resources-rich regions are exploited unprecedentedly without any benefit for the tribals. So the tribal communities run the risk of greater marginalization than in the past (Fernandes, 2003). The development activities necessitate large scale industries and dams, which force the tribals to alienate their land. In the process, women lose their identity not only as bread earners but also as custodians of traditional knowledge. Women who had enjoyed a higher status in the tribal communities as custodians of the traditional knowledge, with loss of their traditional livelihood are forced to internalize the ideology of women's subordination and develop a new culture which strengthens patriarchy, as can be seen among many displaced tribal men and women in Odisha. With her status deteriorating, the woman often accepts the caste custom of the housewife eating last, after feeding the elders, her husband, other men and the children. In a context of shortages, girls and the housewife get very little food and are malnourished. Impoverishment also forces many young girls to go to middle-class families as domestic workers, as found among Adivasis in Odisha (Fernandes and Raj, 1992), Assam tea gardens, Jharkhand, and elsewhere (Fernandes and Barbora, 2002).

Due to lack of education and modern necessities they cannot always fit in the formal sector. With the loss of their economic status, most of the tribal women are forced to lose their traditional status in the society. Around the world, especially in the tribal communities, the role of women as wild plant gatherers, home gardeners, plant domesticators, herbalists, and seed custodians is well recognized. They played important roles in resource utilization, socio-economic roles and even physical roles in gathering, processing, and trading wildlife, agriculture and forest produce to outsiders. Following the current global phenomenon of climate change, tribal women face greater challenges in adapting to environmental change, because they do the majority of agricultural work and have limited access to other income-generating opportunities. In addition, they were also responsible for providing daily household commodities such as food, fodder, fuel wood, animal and fowl rearing, clothing, and shelter. Due to increasing hardship, women also face various health issues such as nutritional deficiency.

Tribal women's traditional activities were mostly forest dependent and agriculture based. As a result of globalization, the per capita land share of the tribals has shrunk and the lucrative forestlands moved far from the households. Thus, these women are no more able to provide for the needs of the village. Community ownership of land among tribals automatically held women as equal stakeholders in the land, raising their status in the society. However, due to commercialization and privatization of land, women in this society are no longer the beneficiaries in the land processes now (D'Souza et al., 2002). For example, dry and wet fields and terrace fields are being brought under private ownership among the Angami Nagas and Dimasa tribals.

With the market becoming an important element in defining social relations, the status of women spiralled downward in the social system. Earlier, women contributed to the overall economy, but by losing their traditional rights and status, men exercise control over the means of livelihood and thereby reducing the decision-making power of the women in the households (Fernandes and Barbora, 2002). With rapid urbanization, a transformation is seen in their distinct culture, dialects, and values. They migrate to different places in search of work, resulting in a weak social structure.

Many tribal women, such as Adivasis, have now become merely wage labourers found working in tea gardens, construction work under builders, in Border Road Organization, etc. Girl children and young women are forced to become domestic helps and work in exploitative conditions (Kumar and Shivalkar, 2002). Thus, globalization has victimized many tribals to marginalization and such number is immeasurable in real terms. Such marginalization has resulted in competition for limited resources amongst the tribes and thus gives rise to ethnic conflicts in many tribal areas, especially in North East India.

Status of the Idu Mishmi Women in the Changing Society

Arunachal Pradesh is predominantly a tribal state and it is the largest of the North-Eastern states of India. The total population of the state is 13,83,727 out of which 9,51,821 persons are tribals where females outnumber the males (2011, Census). There are 26 major tribes in the state with around 120 subtribes which present a myriad variety of culture and traditions. Out of these, the Idu Mishmi forms a distinct tribal community, earlier popularly known as 'Chulikatas', because of their distinct hairstyle. They are located predominantly in the Dibang and the lower Dibang valley districts of Arunachal Pradesh. They are estimated to be around 15,000 as per the census of 2011. According to Mills (1952), the Mishmi were full-time hunter-gatherers until recently. Today they are agriculturists; mainly shifting cultivators; but hunting and gathering continues to be an integral part of their life.

The society is patriarchal, and this determines the gender relations and is the cause of existence of various discriminatory practices against women. These practices may have had some functional attributes, but over the years the continuity of these practices has led to the display of male superiority behind the veil of customs and traditions (Behera and Basar, 2008). In fact, patriarchy is moreover getting stronger than in the past among the tribals. As a result, tribal women are being further marginalized. In the matter of marriage affairs in the Idu Mishmi society, traditionally, females were not permitted to have a distinct voice except the mother. The consent is asked only from the father and brothers of the girl to establish a marital bond. And after the marriage, a wife is expected to be loyal to her husband in every aspect. But such privileges are not there for women; they have suffered and suffocated silently under the patriarchal roof. Although this practice is still rampant in the society, but with the passage of time there has been a lot of changes, which the society is gradually accepting and listening to. Divorce is permitted by the traditional customary law, however, women without any progeny has to return the gift received during their marriage from the groom's party. A divorced woman loses her rights in her husband's property if she leaves her husband's house, but she retains all her personal belongings.

The practice of polygamy exists and has traditional sanctions. As said above, an individual with a feeling of superiority (physical or culture-sanctioned) becomes vulnerable to the forces of brutality and therefore, involves in violent activities, taking advantage of the helplessness of the powerless. Along with this, the custom of bride capturing also exists, but not in public. In this 21st century it's hard to believe that bride capturing is still practised, but the fact is that if consent is given by the parents and brother of the bride, there is no way she can escape. There are many instances of it, which proves that bride capturing though it's not rampant is still practised within the Idu society. In such cases, women are often tortured and become victims to violence. She is put to torture, physically, mentally, and sometimes sexually assaulted during the captive period in order to accept the marriage proposal. The practice of inheritance of a widow by a stepson or deceased husband's brother is allowed in the Idu Mishmi society. The widow's opinion about this inheritance is often unheard and neglected. They are often forced into accepting such marital bond with brother or stepson of her deceased husband. Very often, especially the brother-in-laws of the widow claims right upon her, vowing to support her and her children, although the widow refrains from accepting this new relationship she is ultimately made to accept it. This obviously is violence against women's right, as women in such a circumstance are considered as merely a commodity which can be bought or inherited. The miseries and pangs of women are often left unheard as the society believes these happenings to be inevitable. These further deepen the women's position in the society.

However, with the changing situation, educated women are now standing against such traditional atrocities and challenge the customs of male domination, for instance, 'Enjalu Menda Organization' is one of such organizations in Idu community which helps the women and children in raising their voice against domestic violence and provides justice to them, as well as helps them to fight against their plight. With the advent of modern institutions of law, there is a rise in awareness concerning rights and opportunities and women have begun to participate in various decision-making bodies such as Panchayat, village level councils, etc.

The traditional village political institution is called *abala*, which is arbitrary in nature. This institution is responsible in maintaining social order and deals with cases such as murder, assault, theft, land dispute, marriage dispute, etc. Women are not made members of this institution. Generally, it is assumed that women are responsible for the household affairs only. However, there are instances where women have played a significant role in administrative matters. Rondo (n.d.), informs that one Awunya Tayu, wife of Mingusi Tayu, was very popular and an expert '*Abala*.' She could solve the disputes relating to various issues including murder. There are frequent cases relating to women before the *abala*, such as case of adultery, marriage disputes, etc. and in such cases women are never victimized. It is observed that in case of adultery, generally no fine is imposed on the woman and instead, the whole responsibility is held against the male who must compensate for his actions.

In the Idu Mishmi society, different types of ownership exist, such as individually owned property, property owned in common by the lineage, clan, or villages. Generally, the immovable property goes to the male line, but there is no strict customary rule that restricts women to inherit such property. An Idu Mishmi woman can inherit what her parents acquire, but cannot inherit ancestral property. But with the changing land relation, women also have her share not only as a gift but also can ask for the land from their parents. It may be precisely said that in traditional Idu Mishmi society, women have substantial property rights.

Agriculture is the main subsistence economic activity of the Idu Mishmi and they practise both *jhum* (shifting) and wet rice cultivation. Women have larger role to play during the agricultural season, they play a decisive role in agricultural operations and they perform most of the agricultural operations; their contribution towards it cannot be overlooked. Women's role in agricultural activities and their hard work can be equated with that of men of the Idu society. They also take charge of the produce and are the custodians of seed and seed varieties. At the household level, they are responsible for providing daily household commodities, taking care and rearing of their children's as well as domestic animals. They play a wider role in fulfilling the basic needs of the house, i.e. through weaving, collecting firewood from the forests, wild leaves and fruits to feed the domestic animals, taking part in the foraging activities, etc. They play an important role in resource management as well – through their socio-economic and physical roles in gathering, processing, consuming and trading wildlife, agriculture and forest produce to outsiders. Thus, the position of women in Idu Mishmi society as a bread earner cannot be overlooked.

In the sphere of religion, involvement of women as shaman is quite distinct. They take part in almost all the religious events as specialists, and more often as participants. In their absence, it would not be possible for any religious ceremony to take place at all. However, with the globalization of religion, the impact of Christian missionaries can be seen in various aspects of the life of Idu Mishmi women. It has brought in both, positive as well as negative impact upon them. For example, Christianity forbids polygamy and other patriarchal social practices and also brought social emancipation by adopting modern education and giving priority to women's education. There is no strict rule in forbidding one from taking local brew, but with the religious conversion (to some Christian denominations) such practice is looked at as an offence. This has positive implications in terms of health and also with respect to moral principles. But then on the other hand, many of them have even restricted themselves from participating in the social events and adhering by the norms which it lays down for all; therefore the religion which they have embraced to some extent has been responsible in drifting them away from the society of which they are greater part and parcel. But on the other hand, the missionaries were more concerned about promoting Christianity and in due process the indigenous culture was left to suffer. Thus, globalization has brought both positive and negative impacts. On the negative side, globalization has created disparities by creating an imbalance in the generation of income, increasing gender gap, environmental issues, religious conversions, etc. It has brought people in contact with cultures from across the world which has resulted in adopting new cultures and neglect of one's own culture.

Like other tribes, the Idu Mishmis are passing through the phase of transition as a consequence of globalization. As compared to other tribes, Idu Mishmi women have been able to cope up fairly well with the process of globalization. They have gained greater access to the modern education system and health amenities with modern technologies. They have developed new avenues of leadership by forming NGOs, entrepreneurship, microfinancial institutions, etc. This has paved the way for establishing an expanded identity and awareness towards their rights.

In the urban areas, women have entered into quite a few non-traditional occupations such as running grocery shops, beauty parlours, computer work, tailoring, restaurants, etc. Their exposure to the outside world, rather than being caged in the four walls of their house, has changed their attitude and perspective towards the outside world. This gradual change and exposure has also given them a better chance for earning better income as well as to some extent has boosted them up for raising their voice against violence. These thought to be male activity is now being taken over by women, which can be said to be a direct impact of the changing market conditions due to the liberalization process.

By the virtue of their hard work, the Idu Mishmi women are producing cash crops, and have actively engaged in horticulture. They are known to outsiders for their excellent handloom and handicraft products. Traditionally, weaving happens to be a household activity for every woman, it is an important source of income for them. Weaving is an important tool in the hands of women of the Idu society, though the income earned through it is sometimes very meagre, yet it helps them in running their homes. But now there are many independent women entrepreneurs, specially working for the empowerment of women in handlooms and handicrafts. Microfinance institutions have emerged as a tool for bringing about economic prosperity to the rural economy. There are many SHGs and NGOs which are run by women in creating awareness of women empowerment and employment. Fashion and technology have also changed the attitude of many Idu Mishmi women. With the growing fashion industry in the country, they are at par with the global world and many are pursuing the profession. Self-employed women who own beauty parlours, or are engaged as tailors or in embroidery work in the urban areas are reported to be making profits.

Many Idu Mishmi women have received modern education in the last decades of the 20th and early years of 21st century. The importance of education within the society has been widely accepted and understood. This has resulted in a large number of Idu Mishmi women securing employment outside home. A good number of women have earned the position of civil services and other officer ranks in governmental establishment. Globalization has changed the role of women in society. Modern education has brought in tremendous change and better opportunity for the women of the Idu society and to a large extent has even changed their outlook towards their society and outside world. It has given Idu Mishmi society women such as Tine Mena, Maselo Mihu who have excelled in the field of sports and have represented the nation at global events.

The Idu Mishmi women have lived in a long political exile where they are separated from decision-making bodies. In the olden days, women performed subordinate role in sociocultural set-up and their role at social level was almost non-existent. Some customary laws forbid the law of inheritance to women. Women spent most of their time doing household chores, agriculture, and they were also looked down upon. But with the implementation of the Panchayati Raj System after 73rd Constitutional Amendment Act 1992, the political status of women in Idu Mishmi society has also improved to a greater extent. There are young women who are members of student unions and raise their voice on many social issues. There are many women Panchayat leaders who are working towards the overall development of the Idu Mishmi society. Though women are provided equal rights as men to vote and participate in society as leaders, decisions on matters related to women are often taken by the male members of the family. Along with the modernization, there are several new challenges before the community. For example, with the cross breeding of local women with the outsiders, the property rights of land have become a centre of discussion and a serious concern for the community. Thus, the traditional system on the right of women in inheriting land is in serious threat and seeks redefinition in customary terms.

Conclusion

In the era of globalization, far-reaching changes have been noticed in the traditional tribal societies in general and the Idu Mishmi society in particular. Such changes have no doubt deep impact on the women in tribal societies. There has been a drastic change in the role of women in traditional setting, but new generation Idu Mishmi women have come up a long way in asserting their rights and getting noticed, maintaining the significance of achieved status as an important part of women's identity.

The impact of globalization on different sociocultural, political, and economic aspects of the Idu Mishmi society, and the Idu Mishmi women in particular, has been mixed. In general, the Idu Mishmi women are at par with men; yet at the same time, certain aspects such as property rights to women, recognition of indigenous knowledge attributed to women need immediate attention and acknowledgement. Many challenges lie ahead; hence, the Idu Mishmi tribe certainly has to be prepared considering the future negative encounters and positive opportunities. In this aspect, the initiatives by the Indian Government such as 'Beti Bachao Beti Padaao' movement, women scholarships in the higher education also need larger public campaign. Keeping in mind the 2014 theme of International Women's Day, 'equality for women is progress for all', women in particular should be made a part of the decision-making body so that their issues and abilities are acknowledged and protected from being marginalized. There is an urgent need for identification of gender issues in the process of globalization and negotiating with the parties concerned to realize a well-formulated state policy for women as well.

Acknowledgement

This is a revised version of the original paper titled, 'Women in the Face of Globalization: Observations on the Idu Mishmi Society of Arunachal Pradesh', published in *Interview: An Interdisciplinary Journal in Social Sciences*, Vol. 2, No. 1, 79–89, 2015 by Tarun Mene.

References

Behera, M.C. and J. Basar (2008). 'Embeddedness of Violence in Inequality: Understanding Violence against Women in Patriarchal Tribal Culture with Arunachal Pradesh as Case Study', Paper presented at the 29th NIEHA Session at Dibrugarh University held from 6 to 8 November, Assam.

Bharali, G. (2006). 'Development Projects' Threat to Tribal Livelihood: Case Study', *Bulletin of Assam Institute of Research for Tribals and Scheduled Caste*, 1(XVI).

Bhuimali, A. and S.A. Kumar (eds) (2007). *Women in the Face of Globalization*, Serials, New Delhi.

D'Souza, A., K. Christina and N. Veronica (2002). *Status of Women in North-east India: A Comparative Study of Three Ethnic Groups in North-east India: Aka, Angami and Dimasa*, St Joseph's College, Jakhama.

Fernandes W. (2003). Challenges to Tribal Culture in the Context of Globalization. In Fr. John Desrochers (Ed.), Promoting Tribal Rights and Culture, NBCLC Series (pp. 29–39), Centre for Social Action, Bangalore.

—— (2004). 'Rehabilitation Policy for the Displaced', *Economic and Political Weekly*, 39(12): 1191–93.

Fernandes, W. and S. Barbora (2002). *Modernisation and Women's Status in North-East India: A Comparative Study of Six Tribes*, North Eastern Social Research Centre, Guwahati.

Fernandes, W. and S.A. Raj (1992). *Development, Displacement, and Rehabilitation in the Tribal Areas of Orissa*, Indian Social Institute, New Delhi.

Kumar, N. and S. Shivalkar (2002). *Impact of Land Alienation on Adivasi Women and Children*, Setu, Ahmedabad.

Mills, J.P. (1952). 'The Mishmis of the Lohit Valley, Assam', *The Journal of the Royal Anthropological Institute of Great Britain and Ireland*, 82(1): 1–12.

Rondo, J. (n.d.). Customary Laws of Idu Mishmi: A Profile. Retrieved from www.themishmis.com. Accessed on 22 October 2015.

Sen, I. (1999). 'The Impact of Globalization on Women', *Caritas India Quarterly*, 49(1): 23–25.

Sharma, A. (2005). *Impact of Globalization on the Women of Assam*, Report supported by National Commission for Women, New Delhi.

Yogish, S.N. (2007). 'Human Rights of Women', in A. Bhuimali and S.A. Kumar (eds), *Women in the Face of Globalization*, Serials, New Delhi, pp. 223–40.

18

Plight of the *Igus*

Notes on Shamanism among the Idu Mishmis of Arunachal Pradesh

SARIT K. CHAUDHURI

> The problem of religion in NEFA is a complex one, for the sudden impact and rapid development to which the people have been exposed is without precedent, and it is thus not easy to predict what their reactions will be. (Elwin 1957/1999: 207)

> ... tribal religion gives the people the power to reconcile themselves to the eternal emergencies of life. (ibid.: 214)

Locating the Idu Mishmis

Idus Mishmis are considered to be one of the major tribes of Arunachal Pradesh though their total number only amounts to 57,543 persons (as per 2001 Census, Government of India) located in the Upper Dibang Valley and Lower Dibang Valley districts of Arunachal Pradesh. They are sometimes included as part of the larger constellation of the Mishmi group, which also includes Digaru and Miju Mishmis.[1] Culturally speaking, Idus are to a large extent distinct from the other two which is reflected in various aspects of their day-to-day life and social structure as well as their system of values. Idu Mishmis are commonly known as Chulikata Mishmis because of their distinct hairstyle and perhaps this nomenclature was given by the people of the plains with whom Idus used to do trade (Bhattacharjee, 1983: 13). In a few colonial documents, some Idus were wrongly identified as a separate tribe called Bebejiya who were negatively portrayed (Needham, 1900; Allen, 1905; Cooper [1873], 1960/95).[2] Dalton (1872: 18) reported them as being Midhi people and mentioned that they were intensely detested and mistrusted by their neighbours, the Abors and Tanis, and they were much dreaded by the Saudiya[3] population due to the sneaky expeditions they made to kidnap women and children.

Bhattacharjee (1983) and Baruah (1960: 13–33) tried to textualize their origin and migration on the basis of various elements of oral narrative, while in his recent publications (2003–04, 2005) Blackburn touched upon this area and critically discussed their memories of migration and their journey compared to some of the tribes of Arunachal Pradesh.

Traditionally, an *Igu* represents the central icon in the arena of religious beliefs and practices in Idu society. Almost every major aspect of Idu life revolves around their *Igus* and its importance is reflected even beyond the sacred boundary, since they are involved in profane activities. For them, the key concept of spirit (*khinyu*) rules the world of the unknown, which may be benevolent or malevolent, while nourishing the concept of a Supreme Creator known as *Inni*.

'The Supreme God *Inni*, embodies the highest ethical conception reached by the Idus. Besides being the Supreme Creator of all things, he is the impersonal principle of justice, and the upholder of the moral order of creation' (Baruah, 1960: 69). According to Bhattacharjee (1983: 117), 'An Idu is constantly haunted by the spirits (*khinyu*) who abound in jungles, hills, shadowy recesses, rivers, gorges, cliffs as well as in the house and the village. They are dreaded as no one knows when and where one may fall into the trap. The spirits are the real masters of their fate. Any calamity befalling them is attributed to spirits'.

Idu mythology reflects this syndrome. Since the origins of the universe, man and spirits have been the progeny of the same forefathers. According to their beliefs, even in the world of the unknown, hierarchy still exists among the variegated deities who were responsible for the creation and the survival of the moral order of things (Lingi and Miso, 2000: 23). It is the *Igu* or shaman who works as the mediator between the Idus and their world of the unknown by performing various rituals, magic-religious acts and most importantly, by a unique dance assisted by some team members. The *Igu* has such pervasive influence in the whole social system that even today when their society is undergoing a transformation process most people still have a strong cognitive perception of the divine power of the *Igus*; an institution which has fallen into gradual decline.

Concept of the Shaman

Figure 1

Healing Dance (Sarit K. Chaudhuri)

According to the *Oxford Advanced Learner's Dictionary* (2000: 1176), a shaman is a person in some religions and societies who is believed to be able to contact good and evil spirits and cure people of illness. In general parlance, shamanism implies power possessed by medicine men and sorcerers who are used to controlling or manipulating spiritual forces for human ends. Eliade (1964: 3) contested such a notion and said that if the word 'shaman' is taken to mean any magician, sorcerer, medicine man, or ecstatic found throughout the history of religions and religious ethnology, we arrive at a notion at once extremely complex and extremely vague. He did not deny that a shaman is also a medicine man or magician but he emphasized that beyond that, a shaman is a psychopomp and he may be a priest, mystic or poet (ibid.: 4). According to him, shamanism in the strict sense of the word is pre-eminently a religious phenomenon which originated in Siberia and Central Asia, and the very word came from Russian, from the Tunguisic saman (ibid.: 4).

In the context of North-East India, the rise of shaktaism or tantrism out of the local shamanistic religions of the Indo-Mongoloids has been widely acknowledged by scholars (Bhagabati, 1998: 1). According to Stirn and Van Ham (2000: 95), 'By instituting the shaman, the peoples of North-East India created an expert who is able to establish direct contact with spiritual beings. This becomes necessary when an imbalance arise in the world. Such shamanistic insight into the world's interrelations and the ability to make direct contact with these forces distinguishes man from his fellow earthly creatures'. In the context of Arunachal Pradesh, which is an excellent example of religious syncretism, shamanism still plays a very important role among most non-Buddhist tribes, even though Christianity is gradually becoming a dominant reality in this Indian frontier region. Every tribe has its own nomenclature for religious specialists, though many scholars do not distinguish them in terms of priest or shaman.[4] But if we look at the functional aspects, then undoubtedly most of them can be conceptualized as shaman. This chapter attempts to understand this very phenomenon of shamanism in the life of Idu Mishmis and the plight of such shamans commonly called *Igu* in the contemporary context where society as such is undergoing a transition phase. They perform different types of rituals starting with life-cycle rituals, rituals related to health and sickness, for a good harvest, for successful hunting, for the construction of a traditional house and even to settle disputes, and especially with the aim of identifying the guilty person.

The origin of the *Igu* shaman is linked to the myth of the emergence of humankind itself. In short, a person called Inni Asili Mili gave birth to powerful priests, namely Sineru, Lomo Asili Mili, Lunjuru, etc. who are considered to be the masters of the different activities described below. According to Baruah (1988: 72), 'All sacrificial ritual is conducted by priests, of whom the Idus recognize two classes, the *Igu* or *Igu* Meme and the *Igu*-A. The former is a person of experience and dignity who officiates at a wide variety of ceremonies. The *Igu*-a is a trainee, not yet fully qualified, who is concerned with lesser rituals such as ascertaining the cause and cure of diseases. He is simply a medicine man, but capable of falling into trance. An *Igu*-A can become an *Igu*, if by his association with other experienced *Igus* or, through initiation by the spirits, he gains sufficient knowledge and proves himself capable of dealing with the powerful and malicious spirits'.[5]

It is believed that each *Igu* has a tutelary spirit known as *drawn* who guides him or her while diagnosing disease or performing various rituals. And it is this tutelary spirit whom *Igu* invokes while in a trance to guide him or her in the proper direction. Baruah (1988: 73) mentions 'I have been told that the tutelary spirit of a male priest is generally male, but occasionally, he may have a female tutelary also. Rukhu Meme of Aonli village, for example, told me that his tutelary spirit was a female, who visited him in trance when he presided over the more important sacrifices. A female shaman on the other hand always has a male tutelary spirit'.

In former times one was always careful while visiting the house of an *Igu* to ensure that the *Igu* was not disturbed as he or she may have been involved in spiritual acts or may even have been holding a dialogue with the supernatural powers. People avoided visiting such a house early in the morning.[6]

Some Popular Stories about *Igus*

Pai Miou once went out to hunt with four villagers in the jungle. They hunted a big wild buffalo but they did not have any matches with them to light a fire to roast the meat. Pai Miou noticed smoke coming from a mountain. So he sent his friends one after another to trace it but no one came back. He waited for a long time then he himself went to the mountain where smoke was coming out. He saw that a demon was roasting all his friends in a pan. Fuming with rage, he asked him to meet in five days' time. However, in the meantime he could not control his anger and he destroyed that mountain which led to the death of the demon.

There is another such story about the priest Gomti Alapro. Once he visited his cousin, also a priest, who challenged him and flew away carrying a pig on his back. Then Gomti Alapro also demonstrated his power by making a hole in a stone, placing it on his fingers and using the stone as a fan.

Arati Melon, a great priest from Anini, is said to have crossed the Dre River by walking along a fine thread.

Sondo Umpo is remembered for having flown from Kroling through Alapa around 2 a.m. in the dark to reach Mehao Lake.

Rano Mihu is reported to have travelled back to his village, a distance of ten kilometres in one month; he had to erect special obstacles (*laro*) everywhere to deter the spirit from accompanying him to the village. Although the Idus believe that those who have drowned in rivers are claimed by a water snake, it is also said that Rano Mihu was able to drag the snake out of the water with a tremendous pull. In fact,

Figure 2

Rano Mihu, One of the Famous Igu from Anini Circle (Sarit K. Chaudhuri)

people affirm that once he pulled out a thin black thread, which represented such a snake, from the Dri River near Ahunli village when a man accidentally slipped in and died.

Becoming an *Igu*

In Idu Mishmi society, *Igus* do not have any gender bias though the majority of *Igus* belong to the male group. There is awareness of hierarchy among the *Igus* and it is generally believed that female *Igus*, who are actually much fewer, are quite powerful and even more powerful than their male counterparts.

No one can become an *Igu* by virtue of a wish. Such spiritual power is transmitted as a gift of god, which may be reflected by some symptoms; mostly through abnormal activities. So a son or daughter of an *Igu* does not automatically become an *Igu*. On the other hand, a son of a non-*Igu* (*minga*) may become a powerful *Igu* by the grace of god. The hymns which an *Igu* chants cannot be understood by common Idus except for a few elderly people, as well as those who have assisted *Igus* for a long period of time while dancing or performing other rituals. Idus believe that if any *Igu* tries to teach such sacred hymns to his or her offspring against the wish of God to make him or her an *Igu*, then the trainee may even die.

The process of becoming an *Igu* is quite varied and many popular beliefs can be traced back to describing unusual events, such as sleeping on tree leafs, consuming human excreta and many other such acts. Apa Mega of Arenli village in the Desali circle recounts, 'I started playing the role of *Igu* in 1973 when Mr Das was Circle Officer at Desali. It was my sincerest wish to become an *Igu*. I used to chant again and again even when I was working. My friends also encouraged me to become an *Igu*.'

It is a matter of destiny as to who will become an *Igu* and with what status and to what degree. The Idu strongly believes that such a plight is determined while an individual is in their mother's womb. It is generally perceived that by pervasive training one cannot simply become an *Igu* by divine power. The very first instance of an *Igu* undergoing divination in his or her life is reflected in some abnormal acts which are beyond the comprehension of an Idu, such as wholeheartedly eating human excreta and instructing others to do so, lifting huge baskets containing 5 to 10 bags of paddy, etc. Such a situation may last a few hours and this period of divine transition is called *atombo*. Only then does one becomes *Igu* and is empowered to act as a mediator between human society and the gods, goddesses and spirits who control the world of the unknown. Indeed, Baruah (1960: 74) writes:

> Not everyone can be a priest. A man so destined should be born with certain signs, such as the umbilical chord around his neck at birth. Sometimes, the mother gets a prediction in her dreams that her child will be an important priest. A pregnant women, who dreams of caressing a child lying in a basket which is hung in the egamba or iu-amba tree expects that her child will be a priest. So does a woman who dreams of the bird praerru making its nest on the roof of the house. In such cases, when the child attains maturity, or sometimes even at an earlier age, he falls

> into a trance, and his soul travels to the spirit-world. There it becomes acquainted with the spirits and lives with them for a long time, thus becoming capable of conducting various ceremonies. Very often a man destined to be priest leaves his home at the beginning of a long trance, and stays in the jungle for several days till his soul comes back to him. At this stage he loses his senses and does unusual things. He may eat human excreta and regard the most delicious food as dirt.

While narrating his experience of becoming *Igu*, Yango Mow of the Angrim Valley said that when his mother fell ill, instead of calling the *Igu*, he took a *kalih* (herbal medicine/root used by an *Igu*) and sat outside his house on the verandah and began chanting hymns very quietly. As he chanted, many passers-by asked him what was he muttering about. As they came nearer, he hid the *kalih* in his lap. In doing so, he performed *aanyongo* and cured his mother. It was because of God's wish that he became an *Igu*. But after this incident he made no further attempt to act as an *Igu* because he felt that if anyone heard him they would laugh at him. Once he went with friends to build a house. After the house was built, when an *Igu* was needed, his friends told the owner that he was an *Igu*. On hearing this, the owner asked him to perform the *thruh* ritual (protection of a new house by sacrificing a hen). He was very nervous as well as shy, and was sure that he would be laughed at. He suddenly began in a very loud voice that startled everybody; they all burst into laughter. After a few minutes everything carried on smoothly. He was not even aware of what he was saying. At the end of the ritual everyone applauded him for his hymns. In this way he became a professional *Igu*.

Similarly, Buchu Tacho of Etabe village said that he became an *Igu* thanks to the blessings of the Almighty. He had no teacher. He learnt the chanting on hearing the *Igus* during rituals. During these rituals he was only a follower and he gradually developed *Igu* behaviour as well as learnt the art of chanting. He began as an *Igu* with the *meshala* ritual performed in the case of murder or disputes where a heavy fine is imposed. Indeed he was the person called upon to settle his own uncle's murder case. As he could not find an *Igu* to conduct *meshala*, he did it himself. Then he performed death rituals such as *broacha* and *yah* numerous times.

Smti Imuno Linggi from Anini narrated her experience of becoming an *Igu*. Her father was a renowned *Igu*, but he never encouraged his daughter to become an *Igu*, though villagers talked to her father about her *Igu*-like behaviour. When she came to stay with her husband, she began to develop some peculiar habits such as eating mud from the toilet, which is a sign that one is becoming an *Igu*. Seeing this, her husband's grandmother, herself a powerful *Igu*, encouraged her to become an *Igu*. Her grandmother started taking an interest in her but she didn't teach her any hymns or chanting because she herself had developed the spiritual power to chant the hymns. The chanting of hymns came to her spontaneously. She believed that self-acquired power and wisdom is worthier than learning it from a senior *Igu*. Her husband's grandmother made her an *Igu* by making her perform the *amraseh* ritual to protect all the family members of the house and grant them peace for the first time at their home. Her next performance was when she acted as *rehguh* during the *Reh* festival. She was nervous because it would be her first major ritual, which she had never imagined herself performing, and she was aware that many great *Igus* would be assembled to hear her. The one she feared most was an *Igu*, known as Towshi Miuli, who said that she would not be capable of chanting hymns, especially the *shacha*, the hymns that are chanted when a *mithun* or *sha* (*Bos frontalis*) is to be sacrificed. These hymns about the origin of the *mithun* are chanted while leading the soul of the *mithun* to its place of origin.

On her way to the village, she was so nervous that her hands trembled. She could not properly cut the bamboo which an *Igu* carries to perform *Reh*. She was unable to speak or look at the face of her followers. Then when she proceeded with the ritual and started chanting hymns they were all amazed. After listening to her hymns, Towshi Miuli showered her with praise regarding the fact that she knew all the hymns and rules for chanting during the *Reh* ritual. Hence she performed 23 *rehgus* and 15 *yahs*.

Odah Miwu of Maruli village revealed his experience of becoming an *Igu*. Since his boyhood he had always wanted to become an *Igu*. He took an interest in *Igus* and attended every ritual, though he understood nothing. Even with his friends he never played any other game than dancing like an *Igu* with undecipherable hymns that he had heard. He and his friends made the *Igu* costume by collecting the dried bones of monkeys and other animals. They also collected bamboo roots to carve into tiger jaws. After preparing this costume they would dance for hours. As he was well and truly an adolescent by then and his friends and relatives asked him to think seriously about becoming an *Igu* and advised him to train under some senior *Igus*. But he was not sure of his own capabilities or even of what he actually chanted while dancing.

Once it happened that a neighbour was suffering from *aya-thu* (food poisoning) and his friends forced him to perform *aanyongo*. He began chanting whatever came to mind. To his utter surprise, the man was cured. This was at the age of 18. After this he had a dream. Then after a few days there was an invitation from another village to perform *ayiih* (a ritual conducted to cure illness) for somebody who was suffering from *apomother* (a kind of illness where part of the body swells then starts itching and develops wounds which could be very dangerous). He was nervous because he did not know what to say. It was not like *aanyongo*, where one has to chant for only 20 to 30 minutes and no one actually hears it. For *aayih*, an *Igu* has to sit and chant for 12 hours. Moreover, there would be many people within earshot. On that occasion as well, he chanted whatever came to mind and the patient was cured. He then began believing in himself and felt that he could really become an *Igu*.

Apparently, although ideally shamanism is perceived as a gift of God, a few Idus have achieved the same aim by their sustained interest. It is even reported that one may become an *Igu* by assisting powerful *Igus* over a long period of time. However, Idus believe that generally speaking such *Igus* are less powerful and cannot perform all the necessary rituals. Bhattacharjee (1983: 121) reported, 'Not anyone can become a shaman even if he tries to be so. He must show some indication of being possessed by spirits and some definite sign of communication and understanding with the supernatural elements, which dominate the world of the Idus. He should also be well conversant with legends and history of the tribe from the beginning of creation and should name detailed knowledge of various ceremonial rites, otherwise his standing as an *Igu* will be held in ridicule'.

Igu Costume

In most tribes of Arunachal Pradesh, priests or shamans wear a special costume by which they are immediately distinguishable from the rest of the community. According to myth, the first *Igus* wanted special ceremonial clothes for ritual performances because they needed to acquire power and adopt different outlooks, which could only be done by wearing different clothes from those of commoners. The Almighty would send down power if they wore a special hairband and other items making up the *Igu* costume. Moreover, such a costume would protect an *Igu* from evil spirits. It is believed that *Igus* do not remain a common human being while performing rituals. By chanting hymns and tying the tail of a yak to his/her hairband, an *Igu* asks God to endow him or her with the power of the mountains where such animals are reared. Moreover, that is the place where the souls of the dead are believed to be taken.

The costume which an *Igu* wears during major ritual performances is composed of eleven items collectively known as *amralapoh*. It is the most sacred possession for an *Igu* and does not differ according to gender. Of course, some variations are to be noted in the size and shape of the costume's different components. This costume is kept outside the house in a handmade basket, which is placed on wooden poles or hung near the entrance door, or stored inside the storehouse. On seeing such baskets, one immediately recognizes the house as belonging to an *Igu*. Sometimes the drum, *gerembo*, beaten during the *Igu* dance by his or her assistants, is also kept hanging near the entrance of the house and symbolizes the presence of an *Igu* in that house.

Of the eleven components constituting the *Igu* costume, three of them, namely *etobih*, *etotih* and *athomambra*, are woven with a waist loom. The first and second garments are sleeveless coats. The third one, *athomambra*, is worn like a skirt but is completely different from traditional Idu skirt. Special skills are required to weave it though no ritual is required before or after completion of such special textiles.

Traditionally, *Igus* are not supposed to wear these garments unless an occasion for ritual performance and chanting actually arises, and no one can touch them. This is still considered to be completely taboo by most powerful *Igus*, though a few are not so strict about such taboos with regard to wearing the costume.

When an *Igu* dies, such clothing is rarely buried with him or her; it is sometimes sold with other items of the costume. It may be kept within the family in case a possible *Igu* may emerge in the future. In fact, many *Igus* get such costumes from other *Igus*. Before dying, they may decide what is to become of their costumes, and may even decide to donate them to some organizations for their preservation. For instance, Rano Mihu of Mihundo village decided to donate his costume to the Idu Cultural and Literary Society which has been set up to promote and preserve the Idu cultural heritage.

Igu's Day-to-Day Life

Figure 3

Component of Igu's Costume Hung from Neck or Igu's Garland Used During Ritual Dance (Sarit K. Chaudhuri)

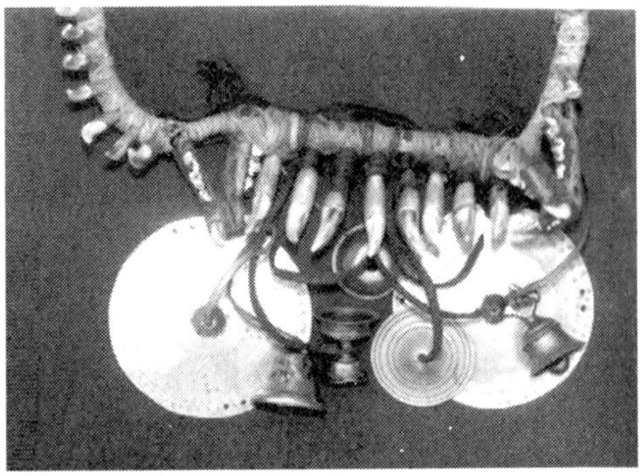

Traditionally, an *Igu* is supposed to undergo various restrictions throughout his/her life. Before performing any major ritual, an *Igu* has to abstain from sexual intercourse for a few days. He or she is banned from entering a house where people are engaged in dyeing cloth or yarn. An *Igu* is not allowed to drink rice beer prepared by a woman who is having her period. In case of symptoms like epilepsy where an *Igu* may fall suddenly unconscious during ritual performance, he or she is not supposed to eat chillies, onion, garlic, wash clothes or even sleep with his/her spouse. Similar restrictions over a more or less long period are applicable when performing *broacha, ekularuma, Reh* or *yah* rituals. To perform *impeh* which is a ritual for sunshine, an *Igu* has to avoid drinking cold water and for *aayiih* just a one-day ban is enforced on eating chillies; for *yuh-maru-yh*, i.e. to pray to the god of property and prosperity, a ten-day ban is observed on washing clothes, eating onion, garlic, fried vegetables, chillies and even sleeping with one's partner.

An *Igu* does not enjoy any special privilege in terms of economic activities, as he or she has to manage just like the other Idus. They need to cultivate their own land, *jhum* or irrigated, and join in some other related economic activities such as hunting, gathering, trapping, etc. This is reflected in their day-to-day lifestyle as well as their traditional house structure. However, with modernization and exposure to broader economic opportunities, a few *Igus* (only four in Dibang Valley district)[7] now work in government jobs.

Yet, ritual performance also has an economic dimension, since after completing a rite an *Igu* is supposed to obtain his or her share of sacrificial meat with some other food items as well as money from the house owner. The remuneration depends on many criteria, including the economic situation of the person at whose house the ritual is performed. However, it has undergone some standardization for the various kinds of rituals.

Igus in former times were much more rigid and whatever they demanded for worship or sacrifice, etc. had to be arranged by the family or individual concerned. Imuno Linggi (85 years), one of the oldest female *Igu*, mentioned that she got a big *dao* knife and a pig as remuneration. If she got money she would distribute it among her followers and she would even give away the pig on the spot where the *Reh* festival was performed. She had received sums ranging from one paisa to 100 rupees in payment throughout her lifetime. For performing yah, she received 50 to 60 rupees out of which she kept 10 to 20 rupees and the other 40 to 50 rupees she distributed to her assistants. During her early life, she could buy enough household articles and food items with one rupee. There was an ongoing stream of people at her home. Even when she was working in fields, villagers would come with her husband to invite her to conduct a ritual. It happened that she had to leave her agricultural work to attend to the ritual. She received a lot of encouragement from her husband.

Regarding the social or economic privileges, she mentioned that she received a lot of help from her family with household tasks, though farm work was left to her. She added that she did not receive any special privileges from the society or from her family. Though people accepted her as a great *Igu*, that did not make her life very different. The government as well as Idu society has not formulated any privileges for *Igus*. Moreover, she does not welcome any interference in their society from outsiders because she feels that the government is only poking its nose in, rather than helping them out. This is the reason why she has never caste her vote during elections. The only privilege that she enjoyed as an *Igu* was the remuneration that she received on conducting rituals.

On the other hand, Natu Prawe, a very elderly *Igu*, disclosed that by performing *broacha* in bygone days he used to get 300 to 400 rupees but that it has now increased to 3,000 to 4,000 rupees. By performing *amrasey, Igus* get 1,500 rupees, *yah* – 3,000 to 5,000 rupees and *Reh* just one pig.

Idus represent a patriarchal, patrilineal society where polygyny was quite a normal practice. Wealthy Idus have remained polygamous. If an *Igu* or non-*Igu* wishes to marry he can do so as many times as he likes. *Igus*, especially famous or powerful ones, are sought-after-grooms because of the high esteem society holds them in and of the spiritual power they possess as a mediator between human beings and the unseen powers. Many male *Igus* had a good number of wives who also earned money for their husband by weaving, collecting *Coptis teeta* (popularly known as Mishmi teeta),[8] rearing animals as well as doing their farm work. For each wife, they used to have a separate room in their traditional long house, a unique feature of their material culture that is fading out rapidly. Indeed, there is a general trend towards forming nuclear families and monogamy is emerging as the rule of the day. With exposure to education and other modern influences there is a new generation, which prefers new economic opportunities rather than their traditional mode of agriculture. And *Igus* are no exception to this.

Life-Cycle and Well-Being Rituals

Birth Rituals of a Newly Born Child

According to Idu mythology there was a man on earth called Anome Liwu who married a lady named Asili Mili. None of their issues were still alive, even though they had had many children. The priest advised both of them to arrange a ritual called *ah-tayeh* in which immediately after the baby's birth a name should be given to request that the almighty Nany-Intya-Maselo-Jinu provide protection to the newborn (Lingi and Miso, 2000: 29). He asked Anome-Liwu to bring *epoteh* and *ewethreh*, two kinds of grass, and placed them on the wall to symbolize fatherhood. The *ah-tayeh* ritual was performed accordingly and it was found that the child was born normal, healthy and free of all disease. Then the priest advised Anome-Liwu to nurture two cockerels called *Etohi* and *Yu-Awru*. At the same time, he prayed to Nanyi-Intaya-Maselo-Jinu, the invincible Supreme Creator, for the parents and newborn's well-being, then he blessed the child for long life and prosperity.

Nowadays, on the day a child is born, a fresh branch of bamboo leaves is planted at the entrance to the house or at the gate, which signifies that a baby is born at that particular house and generally people do not go to the house unless they are specially invited to the birth ceremony.[9] Then, according to Baruah (1960: 48), 'On the day after the birth of the child, the Iu-a-rru ceremony is performed, the priest offers rice-beer and two fowls as sacrifice to the gods, Asa and Asila-amide, who watch over little children, begging them to look after the new-born child, and to ward off the evil spirits coming near it. He then takes the names of the child's dead ancestors, and offers them blood and liquorice beer. He generally recites the following chant:

> Had there been no Gods, the rivers and the hills would not have existed. There are hills and rivers; and men live on the hills. The gods protect mankind. Let them now be pleased and take care of the new-born child and protect him. I am offering them rice-beer and fowls.
>
> The nuhi ceremony, which falls on the ninth day is a simple one. The priest invokes the household Gods, Asu and Andra, and prays to them to look after the child.

Rituals for Family Well-being

Among the great variety of rituals performed on different occasions in order to promote peace, prosperity and good health, *amyase* is very popular. It includes twelve distinct phases, each phase being identified by a specific name as mentioned by Lingi and Miso (2000: 25–27).

The *Igu* performs the very first phase (*achita wu*) in his own house before moving to the invitee's house. There, he prays to the almighty that no harm is done to invitee's family members. The second phase (*aku-tou*) marks its arrival at the invitee or patient's house where he ensures that the harmless spirits will not be disturbed by the ritual acts. During the third phase (*larwoh-ayuchru*), he narrates the origin of a sacred bamboo shrub called *abratoh*.[10] In the fourth phase *(larwoh mraba*), he tries to drive away evil spirits through an imaginary gate in different directions whereas in the fifth phase *(amrala ayusu*), he narrates the origin lore related to the sacred necklace (*amrulu*), one of the significant components of their costume. In the sixth phase (*ayenjo*), he tries to drive away evil forces that can cause epidemics or other diseases by using spiritual powers. The seventh phase is called *ipishu-lawroche*. Indeed, it is believed that the *Igu* may sometimes be unable to drive away evil spirits. In such an event, he tries to hide men's souls away in a place called *iwu loka* and women's souls in a place called *ambi loka* in order to provide full protection. In the eighth phase (*amyase*), the *Igu* builds a spiritual house for family members and an imaginary sty for the pigs by chanting. Then, he offers the blood of sacrificed pigs to appease the evil spirits and to bring good health, peace and wealth. In the ninth phase (*alth-bru*), he foresees the fortune of every family member: how long one will survive, how much property he will possess, how many children one lady will give birth to, etc. Then he continues to chant while praying to the god and goddess for protection, prosperity and good health for all the family. The tenth phase is called *amra-nah* where all the members of the family assemble in a particular place. Such a process is known as *agu-toh*. The *Igu* chants while dancing and sticks in the hair of each family member a feather from the chicken to be sacrificed. This will provide protection from evil spirits. The eleventh phase is called *ashanji* when the *Igu* drives out evil spirits from each room occupied by female members. He then drives back the spirit from the last room of the male members, known as *elonga*, and finally drives it out of the house or village with a warning not to return. In the concluding phase (*akuju*) the *Igu* foresees the possibility of a natural or supernatural disaster, which may befall the house or village in question and he/she advises them to remain alert in order to avert it.

Death Stories and Rituals

Tales or legends regarding death are very common among villagers. One goes like this:

> At the beginning of the world there was no death except in a place in Iniambrume. In Iniambrume, each death caused lamentation, which was followed by an elaborate burial ceremony. Everyone then went to Iniambrume when news of the death reached them so that they could offer their help. On returning to their village, they also decided to observe similar rituals. A rat was killed and a loud cry was raised for its death. The people from Iniambrume, on hearing the news of the death, came to the village, but only found that a ritual for the death of a rat was being observed. This greatly annoyed them and they left the place in a huff. They cursed them to death. Because of this curse, death followed, but soon after the dead came back to life.

Another story says:

> There was a man who had a wife. After her death the body was buried in a cave. The man again married. One day when he was out, his second wife stayed alone in the house. Suddenly his previous wife appeared near the place where poultry are kept. Though she looked like a living body yet her lips were covered with earthworms. She requested the woman to remove the earthworms so that she could regain the energy, which was in the worms. But the woman was frightened at her reappearance by the prospect of her coming back and thus becoming a rival. She took a stick and drove her away. After being driven out, the deceased women came to a place (Iphu-Ajoru) where a long tailed langur used to dwell. The langur told her that he could remove the earthworms from her mouth so that she could regain the strength. But the langur had another plan. Pretending to be her benefactor, he

> killed her and ate her body. When people returned to the village they heard the news of her disappearance and called all the *Igus* to track her down. The *Igus* went to the langur's den and asked him to produce the woman otherwise they would kill him. Thoroughly scared, the langur made a grunting noise in his throat and a small fly, which was the soul of the woman, came out and escaped. The *Igus* thought that there was no use catching such a small fly and let it go. [That is why till to date the Idus believe a soul never dies even after the death of the person]. To prevent the dead from coming back to life the other woman put a stone and the branch of a particular tree, which never rots, inside the grave. [Indeed, the Idus believe thereby the dead will never come back to life though its spirit travels elsewhere].

Whenever an Idu dies, the bugle (*ajuru*) made from a *mithun* horn sounds along with lengthy shouts, which symbolizes the message of death. In response, villagers start gathering and the *Igu* is called, either from the same village or from another one. Depending on his/her availability as well as the distance to be covered, an *Igu* generally appears on the same day, but he/she may even come the next day accompanied by his/her companions and with sacred bamboo twigs which the *Igu* plants at the entrance before entering the house. After accepting a drink, the *Igu* lifts the dead body onto a flattened wooden cot (*epra*) by wrapping it in new clothes. It is customary that whoever receives the message of death must come, and generally people bring new clothes or even some food items.

The final burial ceremony involves a lot of details and some taboos have to be observed while the body is placed inside the tunnel or graveyard. For instance, on such occasions weaving or even collecting firewood is not permitted. Special food is prepared and pork or other meat from sacrificed animals is specially offered to the *Igu*.

On the day, on which the dead body is laid in the grave, the *Igu* with his/her assistants performs a ritual dance by beating drums, blowing trumpets and smashing cymbals. This continues for at least two hours after which he returns to the house of the deceased. The *Igu* then again takes up his/her dancing and chanting punctuated with his/her typical body movements for a while before sitting down next to the sacred bamboo structure still chanting. No one can move from that particular place without permission from the shaman who performs certain rituals. Whenever anyone wants to move, he repeats the same rituals.

The *Igu* prepares a special structure called *amungo*, whereby two bamboo shoots are placed on either side of the path and split bamboo in the form of a bow is struck across the path to ward off evil spirits. Then he initiates a dialogue with the spirit while narrating in great detail the various journeys taken by the deceased before death to the world of the unknown. The *Igu* invites the spirits to tell them which path is to be followed, where steps have been laid, where ladders have been fixed and bridges have been made spanning rivers and streams. In the course of such a dialogue, the *Igu* strikes a sword (*ambrebi*) on the *amungo* which symbolizes that the evil spirits are driven out. The other half of the sword, which is visible, symbolizes the family's well-being. Then the *Igu* chants continuously requesting the spirits to move towards the grave where utility goods are kept. This continues till morning as he tries to send the soul to the land to where all his/her ancestors have gone peacefully and advises it not to return home again.

After completing this ritual, the *Igu* starts standing again in front of *amungo* while others line up behind the *Igu* holding brooms. While dancing, the *Igu* starts collecting these brooms and then throws them at the *amungo*. Any remaining leaves on the *amungo* are thrown away due to the continuous beating with the broom. This is to keep the dead body away from any contact with various insects. The *Igu* holds a cockerel and moves from one corner of the house to another chanting all the time and then places two swords in a crossed position. With a sword in his hand, the *Igu* and his/her followers move in different directions stamping the floor with their feet and continuously shouting in a particular tone of voice. There is a simultaneous blowing of trumpets and beating of drums. The *Igu* tries to catch imaginary objects with the help of sword and then throws them across the door while blowing over the crossed swords placed near the entrance. No one, even animal, is allowed to enter the room. The women and men of the house gather together and sit while the *Igu* swings a cockerel over their heads starting from one end to the other to the beating of drums and the crashing of cymbals. Then again the *Igu* starts drawing imaginary objects from different parts of the body with the help of sword. Just like in previous movements, these imaginary objects are blown across the crossed swords placed near the door. The *Igu* then sits near a cloth stretched over the floor, which symbolizes a river that needs to be crossed.

It is very interesting to note that villagers sit on either side of this laid cloth and start bartering with an imaginary boatman to cross the span of water with all their articles. As a result, arguments and counter arguments break out along with the cracking of jokes and laughter.

After settling on the fare in the form of leaves and bamboo sticks with the imaginary boatman, the river is crossed. The *Igu* then implores the soul not to appear even in dream, which is considered as a bad omen. The wide span of water is known as *kandemo*, which is not easy to cross. A sinner cannot cross the *kandemo*. To wash off their sins many sacrifices are required. If the *Igu* tries to send the soul across the *kandemo* without performing any elaborate rituals, then he will be struck by the wrath of a spirit and consequently death is sure to follow. After crossing the *kandemo*, the soul can rest in any of the places in the vast expanse of territory. In the east such a place is known as *nyomo ashiku*, in the west *nyimy ashiku*, in the north *nyoto ashiku* and in the south *ati ashiku*. After completing the rituals, people are allowed to take food (Bhattacharjee, 1983: 132–36). Bhattacharjee adds that after sending the soul safely across the *kandemo* the *Igu's* duty now comes to an end. He prepares to start for home. He is given fresh meat, which has been carefully kept separately. A large cockerel is also handed over as well as freshly-brewed beer in new jugs which have not been touched by others, along with rice, millet, maize, dried rats, fish and birds for the women of his house. The *Igu* then starts back to his village while his/her companions help to carry the heavy load of food stuffs usually enough to cover his/her needs for more than a month. Even before arriving in the village, a shaman will again propitiate the spirits. Bamboo twigs are planted on either side of the path and split bamboos, bent like a bow, are stuck in the ground along with a *dao* (knife). A cockerel is then sacrificed, its blood is sprinkled everywhere and its meat is roasted over a fire. Upon reaching the house, all the *Igu's* ceremonial items are kept outside and only foodstuffs are taken inside the house.

Illness and Cures

I had the opportunity of seeing an *Igu* from the Desali area in action curing a lady suffering from acute back pain along with pain in the abdominal area. I reached the house at night along with some Idu schoolteachers and I stayed there for 3 hours sitting just next to the *Igu* while I recorded his chanting for an hour. On entering I found that a good number of young and middle-aged Idu Mishmi males and a few females were sitting in a circle playing cards. And next to them just by the hearth was one Idu lady who was lying fully covered in a blanket. Her daughter, along with some other ladies, was sitting at her head and an *Igu* was chanting while beating his sacred instrument (*ripu*) in a rhythmic way. From time to time the *Igu* took a plant in his hand. All the while the lady was screaming in pain. She would touch some water kept in a small bowl near the fireplace, then rub her abdomen to bring some relief. After almost 40 minutes of chanting, the *Igu* took a break and sipped their local liquor from a mug. Then he started repeating the same kind of chanting.

He did not have an assistant. He did not perform a dance or even wear a typical *Igu* costume. But he sat in a particular spot and chanted continuously, taking a break from time to time. He was trying to drive out the evil spirit which had caused such sickness. On one occasion the lady sat up comfortably for a few minutes, then lied down again and took up her previous posture. Some elderly Idus from neighbouring houses called in and sat besides the *Igu* for some time and shared the local liquor. After almost two and half hours I left the house though this scene went on until midnight. Only then did the *Igu* leave. It may be mentioned here that in order to treat sickness, some shamans take a course on spiritual healings or even use various ethno-medicines prepared from plants, animals or other components.[11] Even in order to attend to a patient suffering from an acute or serious illness, the *Igu* may need his or her companions for the ritual performance.

Figure 3

An Igu: Igu Chanting to Heal Abdominal Pain of an Idu Woman in Desali Area (Sarit K. Chaudhuri)

Ethno-medicines and other Ritual Practices

As mentioned earlier, the Idus are great believers in spirits (*khiynu*), such as, *Golo*, the spirit of hills and mountains, *Ashan*, the spirit of the forest and burial grounds, *Apimi Shu*, the spirit of land, etc. Any form of illness is perceived as linked to such spirits. However, sickness is not always cured by propitiating and appeasing such a wide range of evil forces by dancing, chanting or sacrificing animals. It also involves the use of a large number of plants and animals available in the surroundings. With the passage of time, some such ethno-medicinal practices are now part of a collective wisdom shared by a good number of Idus. Many such plants and animals are available which are applied in the form of juice, powder, paste, etc. Some fat of animals, birds, and snakes is applied directly to the affected area or else animal bile is taken orally mixed with water.

Diseases are classified into six broad groups, most of which are only curable with the help of the *Igus*, though in some cases, commoners may also provide some medicines, which are made from indigenous substances. For instance, *aruru* are airborne or water-borne diseases, which are caught through contact; medicinal treatment is preferred for such cases. *Manu-mara* (skin or eye diseases), *apomo* (itching, swelling of the skin) can be also cured with common medicines known to Idus in general. On the other hand, *khinyu meko*, disease caused by spirits dwelling in houses, only curable through a spiritual healing process done by the *Igu* (Mitapo, 2000: 38).

Rituals and sacrifices are also associated with agriculture as well as with hunting. In the case of agriculture, a fowl is sacrificed in the name of *Malo* in order to produce a good harvest. Such a sacrifice is done by a shaman or even by the person whose land is to be cultivated. Similarly, before hunting, a cockerel will be offered to the forest deity called *Golo* and prayers will be said for a successful hunting expedition. However, one of the most significant Idu ceremonies is considered to be *Reh*: an elaborate ceremony performed over a four-day period in which the *Igu* remains the central figure along with his/her companions. There are different stages in the ceremony and at each stage the *Igu* has certain specific roles to perform. No doubt, every Idu dreams of performing such a ceremony at least once in their lifetime to ensure prosperity for the family, a bumper harvest and good health by driving out evil spirits. The *Reh* ceremony involves multiple implications in understanding social relationships, clan bonds, kinship ties, the economic situation of the person requesting the celebration and the oratory skill of the shaman performing the ritual dances and chants. Mention may be made here of the variations in the form of *Reh*, but it has traditionally remained essentially an individual celebration. However, since 1968, this has been turned into a community festival and performed centrally at Roing circle in Lower Dibang valley district. Since then, ICLS (Idu Cultural and Literary Society) has been trying to change this ceremony, especially the rules and regulations regarding sacrifices and expenditure, though its basic form including the involvement of a shaman and the core of the whole celebration has been maintained. In fact, the *Igus* like dancing and there is sometimes competitive spirit among the *Igus* to show off their dancing and chanting skills. This is gradually becoming the central attraction of the whole central *Reh* celebration. This symbolizes their identity in the context of an emerging social reality.

Plight of Shamanism

It is evident that the *Igus* play a pivotal role even today when the whole of society is undergoing a transition process. There are multiple factors which operate collectively among the tribes of Arunachal Pradesh, such as greater post-colonial administrative penetration, the emergence of a modernization process and exposure to wider world-views through mass media and interactions across ethnic boundaries. However, it is evident that the number of shamans is on a gradual decline in Idu society. Though it is strongly believed that one can become an *Igu* by the gift of god, at the same time some people have become *Igus* by virtue of their association with the great *Igus* as well as because of their strong willpower to learn the chanting. With the introduction of modern education and the availability of wider economic opportunities, up and coming young Idus, both male and female, are not greatly concerned about learning the shaman's language and they are even unwilling to work as *Igu's* assistants. Some people express the view that the modernization process and the market economy make people more outward looking, gradually destroying their sense of collective responsibilities. Hence, young Idus are not mentally ready to follow the strict lifestyle, which shamans are supposed to lead.

It is a well-known fact that *Igus* cannot lead a normal daily life as they may be called upon at any time to go to different parts of Idu-inhabited areas. It is true that they traditionally enjoyed great respect from society, but in the changing context they are no longer the preferred groom during marriage negotiations. A few Idus admit that today some shamans do not even follow the strict code of conduct they are supposed to maintain according to their traditional social system and that this itself has led to the critical situation the institution finds itself in. Some add that today people have become extremely corrupt and greedy and that such persons could never become *Igus*. On the other hand, some old members declare that the shaman institution will never die even though the number of shamans possessing great spiritual power is dwindling. They strongly believe that in the course of time powerful *Igus* will reappear; at least from the progenies of contemporary as well as past shamans.

To the question concerning the future of shamanism, *Igus* themselves came out with heterogeneous responses. Some of their views are expressed here.

Aprolo Mega from Arneli village commented, 'Nowadays I find that *Igus* are fast disappearing. Our children are busy with their studies and no longer want to become an *Igu*. I have often dreamt that somebody from my family was going to become an *Igu*. My son chants very well. I hope he may become an *Igu*'.

According to Giba Mow, 'Shamanism will never die because since creation, God has always bestowed his blessings on each successive generation and had created *Igus*. Present-day *Igus* are adopting more and more borrowed powers from other tribes. In order to preserve its pure form, we *Igus* have to teach young *Igus* if they want to'. He adds, 'An organization is needed to help the *Igus* of today's generation improve themselves. *Igus* should donate their remuneration to poor villagers. *Igus* who perform yah and rehguh should contribute because they get enough money'.

Natu Prawe noted, 'There is a vast difference between the *Igus* of the past and present. At present, they are Indianised, self-made *Igus* who do not follow the pure and ancient form of their art. One can become an *Igu* by writing down the related processes and by learning them, but that will not make him/her powerful. He has to be blessed by God and a miracle must take place within him. There will forever be *Igus* as long as Idu society continues to exist'.

Buchu Tacho declared, 'There will forever be *Igus*. But this depends on the will of God. There will be many more *Igus* in the future. After these, many will take the path that his son is taking at present. He is one of the leading *Igus* of today's generation. The situation will never decline or cease as long as society goes on existing'. He added, 'There is no need for an organization. Since time immemorial *Igus* have lived an independent life. If they are brought together, their ideas and powers may clash'.

Conclusion

Various intricate aspects of shamanism reveal how pervasive the role of the *Igus* is in the life of the Idu Mishmis even when their society is undergoing a transition phase. It may be mentioned here that Mishmis in general and Idus in particular are least effected by the Christian faith which has had a huge impact on most Tani tribes, such as the Adi, Nyishi, Apatani, Tagin, Hill Miri, etc. However, the heterogeneous voice of the Idu people reveals the ongoing dilemma concerning the future of the shaman institution. Many Idu elites who run the Idu Cultural and Literary Society (ICLS)[12] are apprehensive about the future of such an institution. They are consequently planning to textualize the whole genre of oral tradition related to their *Igus* so that they can use these documents to train new *Igus* or at least to set up their *Reh* festival or various other ceremonies. In fact, shamans constitute one of the core cultural markers of the Mishmi tribes which include the Idu, Digaru and Miju Mishmis.[13] Of course, ICLS is yet to make a major breakthrough in this respect. However, as a first step they have tried to develop their own script which they like to use for such documentation work. It may be further noted that shamanism is a dominant phenomenon among most tribes of Arunachal Pradesh. Nevertheless, with the emergence of Christianity as a dominant reality and due to the impact of the modernization process, it is loosing its sacred base amongst tribes in general, although it has not yet been completely wiped out from any of the tribes. It seems that as long as village life exists, shamanism will continue to survive, though it is bound to introduce some modifications for keeping in tune with emerging sociopolitical transformations in Arunachal Pradesh which may lead to a 'Third order reality'.[14]

Glossary of Main Terms

It may be noted here that because of the nasal tones in pronunciation, it is sometimes very difficult to get the exact spelling of Idu words even by the Idu scholars.

Aanyongo: ritual to detect the cause of illness.

Aayiih: ritual to cure sickness.

Ah-tayeh: birth ritual performed by shamans to protect newly-born from evil spirits.

Amrasey: ritual for the protection of entire family members from malevolent spirits and for peace, prosperity and good health.
Ambrebi: a long sword with a metal handle
Amralapoh: the costume which an *Igu* wears during major ritual performances, which is composed of eleven items.
Amungo: a bamboo structure made from jungle leaves (Eyuna) erected inside the house on the wall. This is supposed to be the boat by which shamans cross rivers to accompany the departed.
Apimi Shu: the spirit of land.
Apomother: a kind of illness, where part of the body swells then starts itching and develops wounds, which is potentially very dangerous.
Apomo: itching, swelling of the skin.
Ashan: the spirit of the forest and burial grounds.
Athomambra: skirt like costume worn by the *Igu*.
Ajuru: horn of a mithun which is blown during the death and amrasey ritual.
Brochah: death ritual conducted for one night to accompany the departed.
Dao: knife
Ekularuma: ritual related to dreaded diseases such as epilepsy, leprosy, etc.
Epoteh: a kind of grass used during the Ah-tayeh ritual.
Epra: a flattened wooden cot
Etotih: sleeveless coats worn by the *Igu*.
Ewethreh: a kind of grass used during the Ah-tayeh ritual.
Golo: the spirit of hills and mountains.
Impeh: a ritual to bring sunshine.
Khinu/khyinyu: both benevolent and malevolent spirits.
Khyinyu/Khinu meko: spirit dwelling at home.
Kandemo: a place with a wide stretch of water across which the soul accompanied by the *Igu*.
Manu-mara: skin or eye diseases.
Meshala: ritual performed in the case of murder or disputes where a heavy fine is imposed.
Iniambrume: a place where there was no incidence of death.
Reh: festival for a good harvest, peace, prosperity, good health.
Rehguh: shamans employed for their ritual performance in *Reh* festival.
Sha: mithun (*Bos frontalis*).
Yah: death ritual conducted for two nights to accompany the departed.
Yu-maru-yh or Yu-meu-ru: rituals to ward off the ill effects of spirits.

Acknowledgement

The paper is a reprint of the original paper titled 'Plight of the Igus: Notes on Shamanism among the Idu Mishmis of Arunachal Pradesh, India' published in the *European Bulletin of Himalayan Research* 32: 84–108 (2008) by Sarit K. Chaudhuri.

Notes

1. The Miju Mishmis are now commonly known as Kamans, whereas Digaru Mishmis are called Taraons. One distinguishing feature of the Mishmis is their hairstyle (Dutta Chaudhuri, 1978).
2. The Intelligence Branch of the Division of the Chief of the Staff, Army Headquarters, India, reported (1907: 181) that the Chulikattas are the largest and boldest tribe, while the Bebejias, occupying more remote areas, are known to be the least civilized and the source of violence in the plains.
3. During the colonial period, Saudia was a famous trade centre in the plains of Assam near the Brahmaputra River. This was the place where hill tribes of NEFA (North-East Frontier Agency) used to come down along distinct trade routes to barter, sell or exchange their indigenous products with the people of the plains. During the return journey they used to take back whatever they needed, such as salt, beads, clothes, iron implements, etc. Most annual administrative reports from Assam during the colonial period contain detailed accounts of such trade activities which British administrators encouraged and for which they had to draw up a distinct policy regarding trade in Saudia.
4. Chaudhury and Duarah (2004: 19–34) briefly reviewed the institution of priesthood in relation to the tribes of Arunachal Pradesh where they have given tribe-specific nomenclatures for priests or shamans. The People of India volume, which deals with Arunachal Pradesh, gives a brief ethnographic account of the tribes where one gets a basic idea about religious specialists (Dutta and Ahmad, 1995).
5. See also Bhattacharjee (1983: 121–22).
6. The situation is now far less rigid as I managed to visit many *igu* houses at different periods of the day and interacted with *igus* freely. Some of them allowed me to see and touch their costumes and even allowed me to take photographs.
7. Their names are Dindru Miri of Upper Dibang Valley and Rembu Linggi of Cheta village, Loda Meto of Mayu and Andro Elapra of Asali village. They work as peons in government offices.
8. Mishmi teeta is a creeper which generally grows in high-altitude areas surrounding the Mishmi hills and is of high medicinal value. This has remained one of the prime items of trade for the Mishmis. This famous plant is extremely bitter in taste.
9. See Lingi and Miso (2000: 29).
10. This particular bamboo is carried by the *igus* whenever they move to different houses for ritual practice. Such bamboo shrubs are found next to the house of the *igus*. Generally, they plant a branch of abratoh at the entrance of the patient's house and they place a few on the top of the roof to drive out evil spirits.
11. How the *igu* exactly performs the ritual and the whole course of events starting from the journey from his/her own house to the patient's house, then returning to his/her own house is narrated by Bhattacharjee (1983: 126–28).
12. Now the nomenclature is popularly called Idu Mishmi Literary and Cultural Society (IMCLS), the apex community organization and its Headquaters is based at Roing, Lower Dibang Valley.
13. My recent fieldwork in January 2008 among the Digaru and Miju Mishmis of Lohit district reveals that there are a lot of similarities between the Shamans of the Idus and the Digaru or the Mijus in terms of costume, ritual performance, symbols, etc.

though their dialects differ greatly. It may be mentioned here that some Idus may call upon shamans from neighbouring Mishmi tribes for healing purposes.

14. This was used by A.C. Bhagabati (2002: 47–50) in order to explain emerging Arunachali societies where one can find a combination of old and new elements of culture.

References

Allen, B.C. (1905). *Assam District Gazettiers*, Vol. 8, City Press, Calcutta.

Baruah, T.K. (1960). *The Idu Mishmis*, Directorate of Research, Government of Arunachal Pradesh, Itanagar.

Bhagabati, A.C. (1998). 'Indigenous Faith and Customs: Some Observations', in M.C. Behera and S.K. Chaudhuri (eds), *Indigenous Faith and Practices by the Tribes of Arunachal Pradesh*, Himalayan Publishers, Itanagar.

—— (2002). 'Social Structure in Arunachal Pradesh: An anthropological Overview', in R.C. Sundriyal, Trilochan Sing and G.N. Sinha (eds), *Arunachal Pradesh: Environmental Planning and Sustainable Development, Opportunities and Challenges*, GBPIHED, Almora, pp. 47–50.

Bhattacharjee, T.K. (1983). *The Idu Mishmis of Dri Valley*, Directorate of Research, Shillong.

Blackburn, S. (2003/2004). 'Memories of Migration: Notes on Legends and Beads in Arunachal Pradesh, India', *European Bulletin of Himalayan Research*, 25/26: 15–60.

—— (2005). 'The Journey of the Soul: Notes on Funeral Rituals and Oral Texts in Arunachal Pradesh, India', in Der Abschied Von den Totem, *Trauerrituale im kulturvergleich*, edited by J. Assamann and F. Michaels [as per original English version], Wallstein, Gottingen, pp. 1–35.

Chaudhury, S. and D.K. Duarah (2004). 'Religious Beliefs and Institution of Priesthood among the Tribes of Arunachal Pradesh', in T. Mibang and S.K. Chaudhuri (eds), *Understanding Tribal Religion*, Mittal Publications, New Delhi, pp. 19–34.

Cooper, T.T. (1995/1960). *The Mishmi Hills*, Mittal Publications, New Delhi.

Dalton, E.J.T. (1872). *Descriptive Ethnology of Bengal*, Asiatic Society of Bengal, Calcutta.

Dutta Chaudhuri, S. (1978). *Arunachal Pradesh, Lohit District Gazetteer*, Government of Arunachal Pradesh, Shillong.

Dutta, P. and S.I. Ahmad (1995). *People of India: Arunachal Pradesh*, Vol. 14, Seagull Books, Calcutta.

Eliade, M. (1964). *Shamanism: Archaic Techniques of Ecstasy*, Penguin Books, London.

Elwin, V. (1957/1999). *A Philosophy for NEFA* (4th reprint), Directorate of Research, Itanagar.

Intelligence Branch, AHQ, India (1907). *Frontier and Overseas Expeditions from India*, Government Monotype Press, Shimla.

Lingi, M. and T. Miso (2000). 'Rituals Practised by the Idus and Role of an Igu', in *Seminar Report on Traditional Systems: Change and Continuity among the Idu Mishmis*, The Idu Cultural and Literary Society, Roing.

Mitapo, S.J. (2000). 'Traditional Healing by Use of Herbs, Plants and Animal Products in Idu Mishmi Community', in *Seminar Report on Traditional Systems: Change and Continuity among the Idu Mishmis*, The Idu Cultural and Literary Society, Roing.

Needham, J.F. (1900). *Report of the Bebejiya Mishmi Expedition, 1899–1900*, Shillong.

Stirn, A. and P. Van Ham (2000). *The Seven Sisters of India*, Mapin Publishing, Ahmedabad.

19

Traditional Use of Indigenous Medicinal Plants

A Case Study on Idu Mishmis of Arunachal Pradesh

ATHUKO TAYU

By definition, 'traditional' use of herbal medicines implies substantial historical use, and this is certainly true for many products that are available as 'traditional herbal medicines'. In many countries of the world, a large proportion of the population relies on traditional practitioners and their armamentarium of medicinal plants in order to meet health care requirements. Although modern medicine may exist side-by-side with such traditional practice, herbal medicines have often maintained their popularity for historical and cultural reasons.

In the past before the introduction of allopathic medicinal technology, tribal people were dependent on the traditional medicines for healing their wounds, diseases and psychological treatment. Their forefathers transferred these practices to the present generation throughout the history and we benefit even today in the modern world. At present, some ailments are being cured through the traditional medicines derived from roots, barks, leafs, fruits, and flowers, etc. In general, Arunachal Pradesh is one of the hot spots for herbal medicines specially the area around the Himalayan belt. Due to the unscientific way of harvesting of indigenous medicinal plants some of the valued medicinal plants have been rooted out and extinct, and quite a few are now on the verge of extinction, as the forest areas in the state as a whole, and Idu Mismis dominated area in particular. It is necessary to cultivate medicinal plants in order to protect and insuring production in a larger scale. This will not only help our economic growth but also strengthen the ecology. Old traditions and practices should also be disseminated to the next generation on the importance of indigenous way of cultivation and its uses.

The natural flora and fauna used by a specific ethnic group in the form of medicine in curing and preventing different aliments and diseases are known as ethno-medicine. From time immemorial, indigenous people of different parts of the world have been gathering knowledge about these forms of medicine and medication, which has been handed down from generation to generation merely on verbal tradition. The art is not so compact today because of the allopathic form of modern medicine which is neither cost-effective nor having easy accessibility at remote villages of state or country.

Study Area

The study area is located in the North-Eastern part of state of Arunachal Pradesh where Idu Mishmis community is dominantly found (Dibang Valley and Lower Dibang Valley districts). Idus are also found in some pockets of Upper Siang and Lohit districts) (Figure 1). It extends between the latitudinal extent of 27° 45′N to 28° 60′ north latitude and longitude extension of 95° 5′ E to 98° 4′ East longitudes. It has a total geographical area of 13,029 sq km. The entire region is covered by hilly and mountainous topography except only for the few river valleys where the settlements and agricultural activities are large. The Dibang river drains the whole study area including numerous major tributaries like Angi river, Mathu river, Tallon river, Emra river, Ahhi river in the Dibang Valley and Inthu river, Ephi river and Eze (Deopani) river in the lower Dibang Valley. This study area is strategically located in an isolate and border district in the North-Eastern part of the state which is purely inhabited by a single tribe called Idu Mishmi, also known as Chaulikata-Mishmi. They have gained this nomenclature of Chaulikata due to their half round haircut by both sexes.

In Lower Dibang Valley, the Idu Mishmis are also dominantly found, though the entire district is also inhabited by Adi community in the lower parts. The Idu Mishmis of Lower Dibang Valley are agriculturally more advanced because of the both topographic and climatic factors. Topographically, it is situated in the

Figure 1

Map of Arunachal Pradesh and Proposed study Area (Shaded Lines)

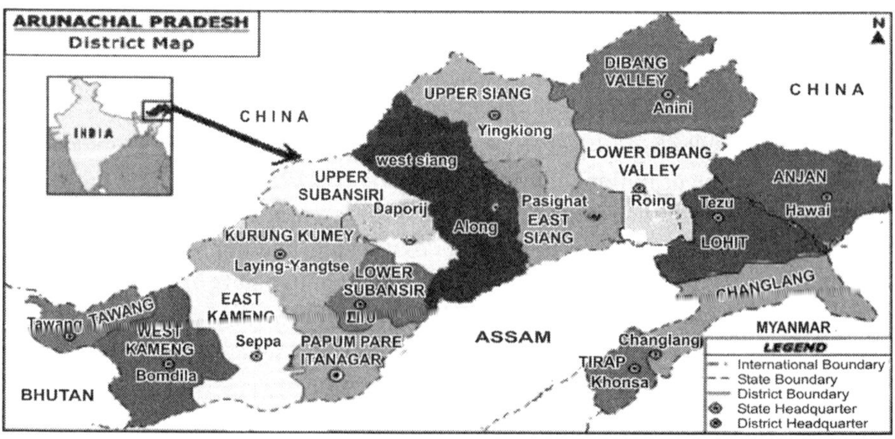

foothills and lowland plain areas where the soils are more fertile in nature. The whole study area is located between 200 metres to above 7,000 metres above mean sea level. Climatic condition is congenial for the cultivation with easy transporting and marketing access to the neighbouring state (Assam). Climatically, the lower foothills region is warmer than that of the upper mountainous region. Heavy rainfall occurs during the monsoon season blocking both air and surface transport communication.

The whole study area comes under Dibang Biosphere Reserve. The vegetation cover with thickly forested high trees and other shrubs is the common characteristics at the altitude between 500 metres and 2,000 metres. The region experiences heavy rainfalls due to the effect of monsoon as well as heavy vegetation. Tropical semi-evergreen to Alpine type of forest is found in this entire region. In the lower foothills, Coniferous type of vegetation can found. The whole region has been identified with many important medicinal plants and herbs, out of which few species have been used traditionally.

The study area is rich in wildlife species. Rare mammals such as Mishmi Takin, Musk-Deer, Red goral, etc. while among birds, there are the rare Sclater's Monal also called Mishmi Monal and Hornbills, etc. A flying squirrel, new to science, has been recently discovered in these districts. It has been named as *Mishmi Hills Giant Flying Squirrel Petaurista mishmiensis*. In 1991, Dibang Valley district became home to the Dibang Wildlife Sanctuary, which has an area of 4,149 km^2 (1,601.9 sq miles). At present, it includes Mehao Wildlife Sanctuary and many other restricted forests. These entire regions have very dense majestic flora and fauna environment and by taking the advantages of such congenial ecology the people have set up their economic activities for their sustainable development keeping with the present pace of development.

The Idu Mishmis are originally shifting (*jhum*) cultivators, hunters, fishing, and forest product gatherers. Shifting cultivation is the main occupation of the people of Dibang Valley, whereas in Lower Dibang valley permanent cultivation is done in the plain areas. On the whole, the community is still partly dependent on the forest products for the fulfilment of their sociocultural activities. The economic condition of this tribal people is still of subsistence with the natural resources in the form of edible, medicinal and trade products. On the contrary, the traditional methods of economic activities are slowly and slowly being replaced by the modern technologies. The agricultural products are produced in a large quantity by using various chemicals and fertilizers to feed the ever-increasing population. People engaged themselves in business activities as a part of their livelihood. So, the whole society is changing day by day with time and space which ultimately impacts on the sustainability of the environment. Due to its varied altitudinal range, the climate varies from place to place. In tropical region of the district, particularly in foothill areas like Roing, temperature rises up to 42°C during summer and subtropical regions like Anini, Dambuen, Angolin, Hunli and Desali, enjoy moderate climate during summer and have extreme cold during winter months.

Objectives

The objectives of the study:

1. To study the traditional uses of indigenous medicinal plants by Idu Mishmi tribe.
2. To identify the locally used medicinal species found in an around the study area.
3. To suggest the measures for protection and conservation of the indigenous medicinal plants.

Methods

In order to accomplish the objectives different modes or methods were applied to find out the results. Detailed survey was carried out in Dibang valley district for preliminary record with the help of Questionnaire and Interview method with the different elders of the population, area, land use, flora and fauna, climate and vegetation, etc. The main source was the interaction with senior citizens who gave the information on the different names of indigenous medicinal plants and their uses. The shaman (*Igu*) narrated about the linkage of diseases and healing process with the help of indigenous medicines.

The information about the types of medicinal plants used by the Idu Mishmis for various purposes was recorded along with their indigenous way of plant's identification. However, the information was gathered directly from the villagers including elders of different villages. During the survey it was found that local people closely related nature with regard to their ethnic beliefs, myth and in respect of medicinal plants in tribal society. From a general observation and a causal form of oral investigation with the elderly people of the area, it was found that the hope and scope of farming of ethno-medicinal plants by which the local farmers may improve their standard of living, not only in terms of income generation in the short run, but the practice as proved in the other familiar agro-climatic zones of the world that it could evolve into a healthy environment for the mother earth by minimizing the social cost as incurred by *Jhuming* and bring a larger benefit to the society as a whole.

Result

The present investigation revealed that the Idu Mishmi know over thousand usages of more than 500 plants, out of which this chapter reports 40 unique plants uses. These plants comprise herbs, shrubs, trees, climbers and grass. Usage of these plants mainly is to treat asthma, inflammation, disorders associated with lactation, poisonous bites, skin problems, stomach ache and tooth ache, etc. Sometimes, combination of two or more different plants is also administered. Materials of animal origin were also used along with the plants in a few preparations. The dosage forms include inhalation, oral administration and topical applications. Most of the ailments such as, stomach ache, urinary problems, jaundice and diarrhoea can be cured by oral administration while most of the skin diseases, wounds, body swelling, tonsils, hair growth, tumours, pneumonia, piles and encephalitis can be cured by topical application, while animal bites and muscular problems were treated usually by both ways. An attempt was made to convince and explain the importance of such species, which need to be preserved and sustained.

The below given Table 1 shows the different botanical/scientific and local names and their parts of use.

Table 1

Traditional Uses of Medicinal Plants

S.No	Botanical/Scientific Name	Local Name	Part of Use	Traditionally Used
1.	Asplenium nidus Family; aspleniaceae	Anjee-boo	Whole parts	Used as anti allergy and anti septic
2.	Actinodaphne oborata Family; lauraceae	Genah-boo	Leaf and stem	Fresh leaf and stem are used in curing cuts and wounds.
3.	Coptis teeta Family; ranunculaceae	Anroow	Roots	Treatment of fever and stomach problem and blood dysentery and anti-malaria agent
4.	Curcuma cesea Family; zingibraceae	Kanli-ta	Rhyzomes/ Roots	Specially used for psychological treatment.
5.	Cinamomum tamala Family; lauraceae	Tayinko	Leaf and bark	Leaves and barks are used in diarrhoea, cough and urinary diseases.
6.	Cirsium verutum Family; asteracea	Awise- mbo	Leafs	Hair cleaning and used as anti-dandruff
7.	Crossocepalum vitellinum Family; asteracea	Deya- mbo	Stem, leafs	Used in fever and urinary disorder
8.	Crawfurdia speciosa Family; gentianaceae	Ephe-mbra	Leaf and stem	Leaf and stem are used in cuts and wounds.
9.	Drymaria cordata Family; caryophyllaceae	Kape-mbrai	Leaf	Blood clotting and prevent leech to enter in the body.
10.	Epiremnum amplissimum Family; araceae	Apinaa	Leaf	Stem and leaves are used in cut wounds.
11.	Floscopa scandens Family; commelinaceae	Ebhi-mboo	Stem and leaf	Stem releases fresh jelly mucus which is used during blood clotting, leaves used in jaundice treatment.
12.	Gaultheria sps Family; ericaceae	Achamiyi	Whole plant body	Leaf part is used in cuts and wounds, and skin disease.
13.	Gynocardie odarata Family; flacoritiaceae	Aseka boo	Fruits, bark	Fruit is used as poison for insect; bark is also used as poisoning fish.
14.	Homolomena aromatic Family; araceae	Manzam-mboo	Rhizome, leaf, stem	Rhizome part is used as curing pig's skin diseases.
15.	Hydrocotyl asiatica Family: apiaceae	Eli-na	Whole plant body	Used as blood clotting
16.	Kalanchoe pinneta Family; crassulaceae	Ansi-bra	Stem, leaf	Leaf and stem are used in burnt part and blood clotting

Cont'd...

...Cont'd

S.No	Botanical/Scientific Name	Local Name	Part of Use	Traditionally Used
17.	Oxyspora paniculata Family;melastomataceae	Tanwe-na	Whole plant body	Used in bone fracture
18.	Paris polyphyla Family; liliaceae	Reta-pu	Rhizomes, root	Used as anti-anthelmintic tonic Lip balm
19.	Piper mullesua Family; piperaceae	Anho-Krayaa	Rhizomes, fruits, leafs	Rhizome and fruits are used in cough and cold carminative
20.	Poikilospermum raucleiflorum Family; cecropiaceae	Aun-bra	Leafs, twigs	Used as anti-allergy, jaundice.
21.	Plantago erosa Family; plantanginaceae	Aree-sapra-na	Leaf, stem	Stem and leaves are used in nerve injury and bone fracture.
22.	Raphidophora decursiva Family; araceae	Ange-gerubuu	Fruits, stem, leaf	Stem and leaf are used as antifungal and it is used in cut and wounds.
23.	Rhynchoglossum obliquim Family; gesneriaceae	Aru-mboo	Leafs, stem	Used in fever and common cold.
24.	Strobilanthes sps Family; acanthaceae	Praaku-naa	Leaf, stem	Leaves and stem are used in itching, blood clothing etc.
25.	Swertia chirayita Family; gentianaceae	Ebo-mbra	Whole plant body	Used in liver treatment disorder, cough, fever.
26.	Sepria Himalayana Family; rafflesiaceae	Tare-braa	Whole plant body	Used as antifungal, body itching.
27.	Tinospora cordifolia Family; menispermaceae	*Igu*-mboo	Stem	Used in fever and urinary disorder.
28.	Trichosanthes tricuspidata Family; cucurbitaceae	Eka-puun	Leaf, seeds, fruits	Leafs, paste is used in burnt part; seeds are used to reduce inflammation weakness of limb and ear ache. Fruit is used in epilepsy and leprosy.
29.	Zanthoxylum aromatum Family; rutaceae	Atha-naa	Barks, leafs, fruits, seeds	Seeds are used as aromatic tonic in fever, cholera. Stems are chewed for toothache, stomach disorder, powdered fruits is used in hepatic disorder.
30.	Zenthoxylum rhetse Family; rutaceae	Athmryan	Leaves, fruits, seeds	Leaf juice is used as healing joint pains. Powdered seeds are used in fever.

Source: Scientific name collected from different references and Local name from field study.

Discussion

The present study identified thirty ethno-botanical/medicinal plants species belonging to 25 different families and these plants are used as herbal medicines for treating various human ailments/diseases. Most ethno-botanical plants collected from Dibang valley are herbs, shrubs, trees, climbers, and some are epiphytes. The medicinal plants consist of two distinct, viz. areal part and underground parts, areal parts includes stem, leaf, bark, fruits, seeds and flowers. An underground part includes roots, rhizome and tuber. Some plants like *Raphidophora aromatic's* fruits and stems are used for curing different diseases; fruits used in curing epilepsy and stems used as anti-fungal and *Coptis teeta's* roots are used as anti-malaria agent and gastrointestinal disorder. Some other plants like *Gynocadia odorata's* barks are used for poisoning of fish. From the investigation it is observed that areal parts of the plants are more usable then the underground parts. Some of the plants like Epipremnum amplissinum and Asplenium nidus are used as whole plants in curing different diseases.

According to Idu Mishmi traditional experts no specific amount of medication is recommended for human ailments/diseases. But some precautions are referred to avoid overdoses. Normally, they provide medication and recommend two doses daily, i.e. morning session and evening session. They prepare some herbal plants which are directly applied on the cut and wounds, but some oral medication like Coptist teeta and other periporphyrisis are used after drying properly. After properly drying and grinding into powdery form, this powdery form is dissolved with appropriate amount of water; thereafter the precipitate is filtered properly before use. Medicine plants like *Plantango erosa* should be grinded properly and pasted in wounded regions.

During the field survey, scholar interacted with many local elderly people, including both male and female aged around 30 to 65 years from different parts of the study area. During the survey some of renowned or specialized in the traditional knowledge of medicinal plants were secretly interviewed. In fact, they did not reveal the names and application of medicines as part of their social taboos. The informant consensus to provide the knowledge of medicinal plants usage in Idu ethnic groups, results were ranging from different illness category. The informants were keenly interested to identify those plants which are generally used in gastrointestinal disorder and skin disease. It is because the local knowledge for diseases treatment depends on the availability of plant species during the occurrence of diseases in the particular area. This study reveals that, there was a significant knowledge between men and women. From the investigation it is found that the males are superior in the field of traditional medicines knowledge than the females. In Idu community very few persons acquires such knowledge of medicinal uses. It is because of certain taboos, like traditional beliefs and fear.

All the medicinal plants identified in the study area are all found as wild products. The traditional knowledgeable person collects those medicines as per their requirement. Some eminent herbs like *coptis – teeta* are cultivated in few areas like Acheson and Ahimro (Chepe village). There are more than thousands of medicinal plants which are highly economic as well as with medicinal values, but local people don't know the market value of such medicinal plants which they just collect for their domestic uses. Some plants are used for multiple functions; such plants are *Raphidophora discursive* species, their soft parts are eatable and leafs are used to cure several diseases like allergy and their rhizomes are used to cure gastrointestinal diseases. Another one is *Coptis teeta* which is used as anti-malaria, gastrointestinal diseases, stomach disorder, headache etc. Available plants found in the local habitat are *Plantango erosa, Piper mullasea, Curcuma cesea, Raphidophora dicursiva, Deascorea bulbifera,* etc.

Most popularly useful (indigenously used) medicinal plants of study area are:

1. Coptis teeta (Mishmi teeta)
2. Plantago erosa (Aree-sapra-na)
3. Curcuma cease (Kanli-ta)
4. Paris polyphylla (Reta-pu)
5. Aconite (Mra)

Measures for preservation of the existing medicinal plants as well as other flora and fauna species.

1. Need to inform the local people about the future value of the existing flora and fauna species.
2. Future economic value related education should be give to the local citizens.
3. The local medical practitioner should be rewarded in terms of case and kind and urged to impart his knowledge to the younger generation for future use.
4. The scientific farming system should be initiated by the government and other agencies to motivate the local citizens while keeping both valuable plants and ecology in a static balance.
5. And it is very necessary to approach the practitioner not to believe very rigidly regarding the medicinal plants species knowledge, healing process and uses, etc.

Conclusion

The recent survey reveals that the rich indigenous knowledge and usage of traditional plants are not recorded in written documents, which is very important to future generation. The survey also shows that the traditional knowledge of medicinal plants of Idu Mishmis is at high risk due to certain taboos. Certain taboos existed since time immemorial. Idu Mishmi tribe has numerous taboos regarding the killing of birds and animals, practice of healing wounds and diseases, etc.

Following are of the beliefs which are kept in mind during the process and healing hours:

1. They believe in loss of spiritual power of curing diseases, if they share their traditional knowledge of medication with other people, even with their own family members.
2. A kind of particular diseases may affect their own family member of practitioner.
3. The serious concern among the Idu Mishmi is that the younger generations do not following the use of locally found medicine (accept few cases). Discontinuation of this traditional methods and beliefs may result in extinction of all valuable knowledge in the near future.

4. After the performance of healing the practitioner should avoid certain food items like chillies, garlic, mushroom, fermented soybean, etc. and should not share the bed with spouse.
5. The family members (of practitioner) are restricted not to ask anything related to the medication by the patient as well as about the disease patient is ailing from.
6. Younger generations believe that their elders (medical practitioner) do not reveal the medicinal species including the process and their uses publicly. It could be the reason that our youth would not be able to maintain the valuable knowledge regarding the traditional knowledge and the healing values. (One of the youth respondent)
7. Other respondent argued that without knowing the economic value of these certain naturally found plant species how could it be possible to preserve them in natural condition. At a certain point of time it would die anyway.
8. Proper scientific research seems to be an utmost necessity to preserve the thousands of unexplored flora species within the range of Eastern Himalayan belt including this Mishmi Hills.

Keeping in view the major finding of the present study, it is concluded that the indigenous tribe like Idu Mishmis are one of the important users of the natural resources including medicinal plants. The whole unit of the study area is full of natural resources in terms of water, forest, minerals, etc. as environmental resources. As the whole region of Dibang Valley is covered with thick dense forest consisting more than hundreds of flora and fauna species which thrive in the entire region. The vegetation types mainly found in the whole region are subtropical evergreen forest and temperate belt in between 1,000 m to 1,800 m elevation, mainly in and around proposed study area. Besides this, the pine forest is covered above the altitude of 1,800 m. Alpine forest is found in the higher hills above an altitude of 4,000 m up to 5,500 m above the timber line. For major part of the year, the area is covered by snow and regeneration of plants activities is restricted for a few months till the snow cover is melted out. The main vegetation found in this region is of shrubs and bushes of very hard and strong growth which have adopted only in the very high altitudinal zone. The proposed study area is though mainly influenced by the subtropical evergreen forest and temperate belt, Bamboo forests which are conducive for development of temperate plantation and also the agriculture activities can be easily adopted. So, both the agriculture and horticulture development is taking place in this entire region.

The Idu Mishmis are well endowed with their natural resources in and around their surroundings. Historically, it is believed that this Mishmi people are well aware of physical and culture environment as they are part and parcel of nature since time immemorial. It is said that they are very inquisitive about their surroundings as it their mother of livelihood, e.g. this tribe performs some rituals and sacrifices of animals (dog, pig, cock etc.) in view of keeping their hazardless environment. So, their social belief and religious practice is directly or indirectly dealt with through nature.

References

Angami, A., P.R. Gujrel, P. Rethy, B. Sing and S.K. Kalita (2006). 'Status and Potential of Wild Edible Plants of Arunachal Pradesh', *Indian Journal of Traditional Knowledge*, 5(4): 541–50.

Benniamin, A. (2009). *Medicinal Ferns of North Eastern India with Special Reference to Arunachal Pradesh*, Botanical Survey of India, Arunachal Pradesh Regional Centre, Itanagar.

Bharati, C. (2005). 'Indian Cultural Heritage and Environment Conservation through Traditional Knowledge', *Mainstream*, XLVI(25): 1–5.

Bussman, R.W. and D. Sharon (2006). *Traditional Plant Use in Northern Peru: Tracking Two Thousand Years of Health Culture*, Rewamp Publications, New York.

Chauhan, N.S. (1988). 'Ethnobotanical Study of Medicinal Plants of Himachal Pradesh', in P. Kaushik (ed.), *Indigenous Medicinal Plants: 187–198*, M/S Today and Tomorrow's Printers, New Delhi.

Jain, S.K. (1813). *A Dictionary of Indian Folk Medicine and Ethonobotany*, Deep Publications, Delhi.

Kirtikar, K.R. and B.D. Basu (1934). *Indian Medicinal Plants*, Lalit Mohan Basu, Allahabad.

Nayar, M.P. (1996). *'Hotspot' of Endemic Plants of India, Nepal and Bhutan*, Tropical Botanic Garden and Research Institute, Polode, Thiruvanathapuramn.

Rau, M.A. (1974). 'Vegetation and Phytogeography of Himalaya', in M.S. Mani (ed.), *Ecology and Biogeography in India*, Dr W. Junk, The Hague.

Samant, S.S. and U. Dhar (1997). *Medicinal Plants of Indian Himalayan: Diversity Distribution and Potential Value*, Gyanodaya Prakash, Nainital.

Tiwari, L. (2003). 'Traditional Himalayan Medicine System and its Material Medication', in *History of Indian Science and Technology*. Available at: http://www.indianscience.org/

Warrier, P.K., V.P.K. Nambiar and C. Raman Kutty (1996). *Indian Medicinal Plants*, Vol. 5, Orient Longman Ltd., New Delhi.

20

Mehao Lake of Arunachal Pradesh

A Biological Treasure

BONI AMIN LASKAR, SAMIRAN ROY, KENJUM BAGRA AND D.N. DAS

Himalayan uplands are bestowed with innumerable lakes. The state of Arunachal Pradesh is located in the extreme east of India with an area of 83,743 km^2. The region is gifted with large number of lakes holding cold-water biotic resources, which have vast untapped potential for enhancement of fish yield and harbour a variety of commercially important cultivatable fish germplasm resources.[1]

The 'Mehao' Lake is situated in Lower Dibang Valley district of the state Arunachal Pradesh in India (Figure 1). The geographical position of the lake is 28° 8' 48.51" N Latitude, 95° 56' 9.33" E Longitude and 1,778 m above mean sea level. The lake is located within a protected area known as Mehao wild life sanctuary. The approach to the lake is via Roing, headquarters of the Lower

Figure 1

Map of Lower Dibang Valley District Showing Mehao Lake

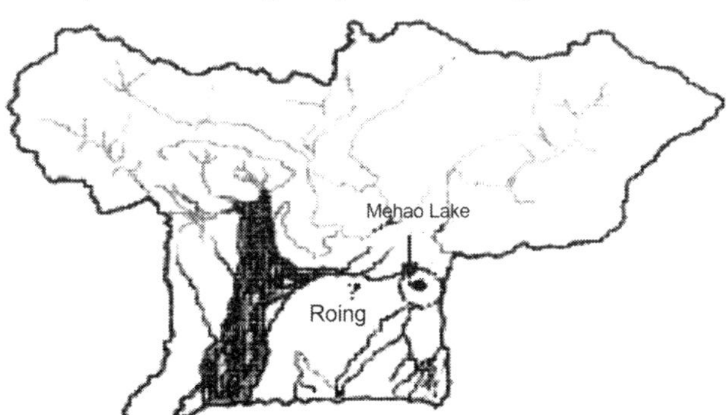

Dibang Valley district. There is no roadway from Roing to the lake but a trekking of around 15 km reaches the lake. The trekking continues on a riverside (named river Deopani) for about an hour and then goes upward for another one hour through a valley which ends at a stream. The lake has an apparent linking with the river by this stream. The stream trickles down directly from Mehao Lake through a steep cascade. After crossing the stream the trekking becomes more strenuous and the striding continues for an additional two hours to reach the Mehao Lake. The entry to the lake is from west to east direction.

Four periodical surveys of the lake were carried out and during the preliminary study a special attention was paid to explore the fish species availability. The collected fish specimens were identified following taxonomic keys.[2]

Scientific information on the water area and depth of the lake is not known. However, it has been estimated to be approximately 20.0 hectare. The lake has no any geometrically definable shape. The peripheral area of the lake also rarely contains soil. Mostly the undercut bedrocks, boulders and rocks form the periphery of the lake. There are much dense overhanging vegetation of trees, shrubs and creepers at almost 80 per cent of the lake's periphery. Due to this overhanging vegetation, thorough roaming around the lake is impossible.

The lake water is very much clear, drinkable and safe for life. During daytime the transparency of the water is visible up to chest height of an average tall man. The upper surface of the lake water is totally open and there is no floating vegetation in the lake. The open blue sky during day time gives a beautiful colour to the lake water. Some wild animals drink the lake water which is revealed from the observation of the presence of pug marks near the lake water. The lake water is a ground for some aquatic birds. The ducklings of some aquatic birds are visible during the month of February which indicates that the aquatic birds breed at some nearby area of the lake.

The lake is a home for large fishes like Brown trout – *Salmo trutta fario* (Plate 1), Chinese common carp – *Cyprinus carpio* and indigenous Chocolate Mahseer – *Neolissochilus hexagonolepis*. These three kinds of fishes have been transplanted to the lake during 1994–95 by the department of fisheries, Government of Arunachal Pradesh as told by the District Fishery Development Officer of the district. The common carps and chocolate mahseers were carried from a local lake at Roing called 'Sally Lake'. The review of literature shows that Chocolate Mahseer has been thriving well in Sally lake and established natural population there.[3,4] The seeds of the Brown Trout were brought from trout breeding centre at West Kameng district of Arunachal Pradesh. Trout fisheries in AP are comprised of both brown and rainbow trout and were introduced from

Plate 1

Salmo Trutta Fario Linnaeus

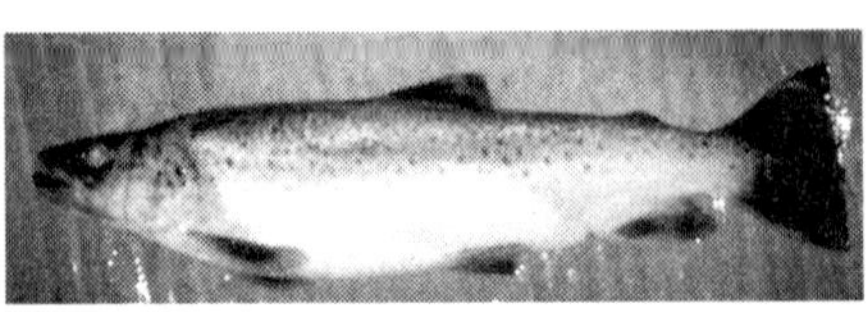

Plate 2

Exostoma Labiatum (McClelland)

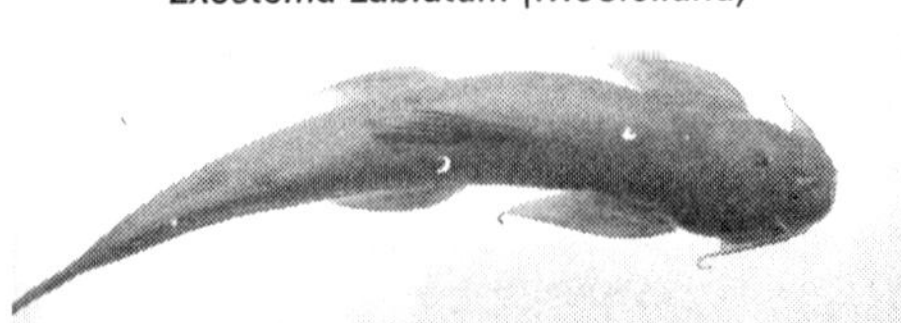

Himachal Pradesh in the government farm at Shergaon, West Kameng district during 1974–75.[5] Besides, there is one naturally occurring fish species which was caught from the opening of an outlet stream. The species was taxonomically identified to be *Exostoma labiatum* (Plate 2). This outlet stream is connected with the river Deopani at the lower altitude of 460 m asl. The high altitudinal difference of the lake and river Deopani; and the steep high gradient fall like stream connecting the lake with the river might have not supported the other locally available fishes of the river to migrate to the high altitude of the lake. Again there is no inlet stream/river into the lake; hence the species *E. labiatum* have been thought to have migrated from the river Deopani. Moreover, this species possess some adaptive morphology like adhesive disc at the ventral of head. The same species is abundantly available at the upper stretches of the river Deopani where the outlet of the lake has joined the river.

The fishes were collected with two special kinds of gill nets prepared by suggesting our own required measurements. The gill nets were very large about 80 metres in length and 10 metres in height. Floats of rubber were tied with the upper rope and dips of iron were tied with the lower rope. The nets were placed into the diaper water with the help of on-spot made small boat of the banana trees. The nets were kept overnight without disturbing the water. The efforts gave successful results. The specimens of *Exostoma labiatum* were collected by diverting and drying portion of the stream water. The details of the survey on fish and fishery of the lake during the period of two years from February 2004 to December 2006 is presented in Table 1. The presence of seeds of Common carp and Chocolate Mahseer suggests that these species have established natural population in the lake.

The surveys reveal that the lake is nearly a kind of isolated water body. The introduced fishes in the lake are thriving well. *E. labiatum* the only available naturally existing fish could not have upwardly migrated from river through the steep cascaded out let stream of the lake. Some geographical barrier might have restricted entry of more fishes into the lake and also probably the escape of trout fishes from the lake. There is a need for thorough survey and collection of fish species available in the river and the outlet of the lake for biological, ecological and particularly ichthyological interest. The migration route of the E. labiatum can also be found out. Also scientific investigation of the lake is required to unfurl much other information on its ecology.

Table 1

Fishery Status of Mehao Lake

	Common Name and Scientific Names of Fishes	*Catch Size Ranges (Weight in Kg) and Numbers of Catches in Parenthesis*
1.	Brown Trout – Salmo trutta fario Linnaeus	= 1.6 (1)
2.	Chocolate mahseer – Neolissochilus hexagonolepis (McClelland)	= 0.0002 to 1.56 (many)
3.	Chinese Common Carp – Cyprinus carpio Linnaeus	= 0.0005 to 1.3 (many)
4.	No common name – Exostoma labiatum (McClelland)	= 0.002 to 0.003 (17)

The data are the outcome of special pilot surveys during the year 2004–06.

Acknowledgement

The paper is a reprint of the original paper title 'Mehao Lake of Arunachal Pradesh: A Biological Treasure', published in the Journal *Sci. & Cult* 76 (1–2): 59–61 (2010).

Notes

1. Raina, H.S. (2005). *Coldwater Fisheries Research and Development in North-east Region of India*, Director, NRC on Coldwater Fisheries (ICAR), Bhimtal, pp. 77–86.
2. Jayaram, K.C. (1999). *The Freshwater Fishes of the Indian Region*, Narendra Publishing House, Delhi, p. 551.
3. Laskar, B.A., A. Pujen, D.N. Das and P. Nath (2006). *Aquacult*, 7(1): 105–10.
4. Laskar, B.A., A. Pujen and P. Nath (2005). *Indian Journal of Environment and Ecoplanning*, 10(2): 525–28.
5. Chaudhary, K.K. (2002). 'Fish Farming and its Prospects in the Hilly Areas of Arunachal Pradesh', in K.K. Vass and H.S. Raina (eds), *Highland Fisheries and Aquatic Resource Management*, India National Research Centre on Coldwater Fisheries (ICAR), Bhimtal, pp. 269–74.

21

Mehao Wetland

A Treasure of Mishmi Hills

FAMES LINGGI

According to Ramsar Convention Bureau, a wetland is defined as areas of marsh, fen, peatland or water, whether natural or artificial, permanent or temporary, with water that is static or flowing, fresh, brackish or salt, including areas of marine water, the depth of which at low tide does not exceed six metres (Barbier et al., 1997: 69). For purposes of this classification, wetlands must have one or more of the following three attributes: (a) at least periodically, the land supports predominantly hydrophytes; (b) the substrate is predominantly undrained hydric soil, and (c) the substrate is non-soil and is saturated with water or covered by shallow water at sometime during the growing season of each year (Cowardin et al., 1979: 03).

Whatever may be the definition and classification of wetlands, they are one of the most threatened ecosystems in the world, whether they are lakes or mangroves. They are disappearing or are getting degraded due to the process of urbanization, industrial and agricultural activities and other formal and informal encroachments from various economic agents. At the formal decision-making also, the contribution of wetland ecosystem is ignored due to their public good/common property nature. Such degradation occurs due to information failure which results in both market and intervention failure. Thus, wetlands have suffered from both quality degradation induced by pollution and from overexploitation because of their open access nature (Turner, 1991: 59). It can be said that information failure denotes the lack of appreciation of the economic value of the conserved wetlands. Market failure is the externality problem, whereby wetlands are damaged by economic activities that are not required to meet the direct consequences of such degradation. It occurs when there is no mechanism to attribute economic values to the public goods provided by the wetlands (Badola and Hussain, 2003: 01).

Generally, wetlands have never been given importance in the development programme and hence poorly valued, and their loss was perceived as a minor cost compared to the expected benefits from wetland development projects. In most cases, any use would seem to have a greater value than the use which wetlands are put. Therefore wetlands have been viewed as wastelands that can be sacrificed for the sake of increasing social welfare. A second reason for wetland loss is the fact that even when individuals are aware of the conservation values of their wetlands, they prefer to drain their lands for intensive cultivation instead of leaving them in their natural state (Seyam et al., 2001). In general, there are four reasons for threat to wetlands (Turner et al., 2003, forwarded from Gilber et al., 2004): (a) market failures due to the public good nature of wetlands; (b) externalities caused by economic activities such as agriculture, industry and water obstruction; (c) lack of understanding of the many values associated with wetlands due to the complexity and invisibility of spatial relationships among groundwater, surface water and wetland species; and (d) frequent failure of poly intervention and land use planning due to inconsistent treatment of wetlands by economic, agriculture, environmental and nature protection policies.

Total Economic Value and Valuation of Wetlands

Broadly, the total economic value of wetlands can be broken into four components namely direct use value, indirect use value, option use value and existence use value. The goods and services which are used for the final consumption or for marketable purposes fulfil the direct use. For example, firewood, timber, fish, etc. constitute the direct use value. Many ecological functions of the wetlands like carbon sequestration, breeding ground for many waterfowl and migratory birds, or all those functions which cannot be measured in market prices are the indirect use value. When the resources are kept for the future use is option use value and getting benefit or satisfaction by merely knowing its existence is its existence use value.

Economic valuation of the wetlands is necessary to understand the importance of wetlands in ecological functions and providing basic needs to us. However, due to absence of property rights and open access nature, its importance has never been realized in the market context. Hence, alternative valuation by using surrogate market prices is needed to evaluate the stream of benefits received by the people. It is an attempt to assign quantitative values to the goods and services provided by such natural resources where market prices are not available (Barbier et al., 1997; Verma, 2001; Badola and Hussain, 2003: 02; Babu et al., 2001: 48). It is concerned with the proper allocation of environmental resources in order to improve human welfare. It thus serves as a very important tool in the hands of the decision/policy makers (Verma, 2001). The main objective is to quantify the benefits (both marketed and non-marketed) that people obtain from wetland ecosystem services. This makes them directly comparable with other sectors of the economy when investments are appraised, activities are planned, policies are formulated, or land and water resource use decisions are made (Millenium Ecosystem Assessment, 2005).

In economic terms, path dependent equilibrium makes it very clear that it is often not possible to revert an old state of affair, once certain things have been destroyed, and destroyed irreversibly (Chattopadhyay, 2001). The need for economic valuation of wetlands arises due to such irreversible character of wetlands and open access nature. Hence, it is imperative to assess the stream of goods and service generated by it before the minimum threshold level is reached. There are innumerable numbers of lakes in Arunachal Pradesh which is yet to be developed for tourist destinations. Beside this, due to scanty population of the State, almost all the lakes are in their natural conditions. Hence, it was never felt by the policymakers to give attention towards it. However, the rapid growth of population of the state suffice that sooner or later these resources might be degraded or converted to some other entities to meet their economic needs. Hence, it is felt that before all the lakes reach the level of degradation, it is necessary to assess the stream of benefits provided by the wetlands and make the people conscious for preservation of that lake. Keeping into consideration of such multidimensional functions and ensuing threat to the wetlands, the present study made an attempt to find out the treasure of resources of Mehao Lake of Lower Dibang Valley District of Arunachal Pradesh. The chapter basically aimed to examine the dependency of the people of nearby villages on Mehao Lake and to estimate the economic value of this lake in terms of user and non-user benefits.

Material and methods of the present study is based on both secondary as well as primary data. Since, only few studies on the topic have been done in India and particularly in North-Eastern region, most of the secondary data have been collected from the internet. Recent Statistical Report and Census of India have been consulted to have an insight on the demographic features of the study area.

The universe of the study is the selected villages on the periphery of the wetland area. The study is basically based on socio-economic survey obtained by a primary survey. The individual households are the ultimate sampling units.

Conceptual Frameworks: Contingent Valuation Method (CVM)

The CVM is a direct method of estimating the non-market value of environmental attributes or amenities such as values of recreational or scenic resources, etc. This method is used when markets do not exist for environmental resources (Mitchell and Carson, 1989). The CVM involves the presentation of hypothetical market scenarios to respondents in a survey format, where the scenario involves some trade-off between the amount of a recreational amenity or environmental good and a monetary attribute. This method uses survey to ask the people about their willingness to pay (WTP) for improved environment or willingness to accept compensation (WTC) for damaged environment.

The CVM has been commonly used as one of the standard and flexible approaches to measure the economic values of non-market goods (Hanemann, 1994). This approach is used for valuation of wilderness as well as of common environmental facilities like forests, common lands, common water bodies, etc. (Kadekodi et al., 2000). The most appealing aspect of the contingent valuation method is that it allows us to estimate both the use value and non-use values of environmental amenity. It gained popularity after the two major non-use values, namely, option value and existence value. The CVM is the only approach to elicit existence benefits of environmental amenity from both users and non-users. There are two approaches to elicit WTP or WTC bids, viz. (a) an open-ended referendum and (b) a close-ended referendum. A closed-ended format tends to anchor the respondent's answer to a range of values presented. Hence, in the present study an open-ended referendum was applied to elicit tourists' and households' willingness to pay for preservation value of the study area.

After obtaining WTP bids from the respondents, a bid curve can be estimated. For open-ended CVM formats a bid curve can be estimated by regressing WTP amounts as the dependent variable against a range of independent variables like age, education, income and total family members, etc. In the functional form, it may be written as

$$WTPi = f(Ai, Ei, Yi, TFMi)$$

The linear form of this function is:

$$WTP = \alpha + \beta 1\ Ai + \beta 2Ei + \beta 3Yi + \beta 4TFMi + \varepsilon_i$$

Where,

WTPi = Maximum willingness to pay (WTP), Ai = Age, Ei = Level of Education, Yi = Annual household income, TFMi = Total Family Members of the household, ε_i = Error Term.

Bid curves are useful to predict the valuation of changes in environmental quality other than those suggested in the survey, and to test the sensitivity of WTP amounts to variations in environmental quality.

Result/Discussion

The Mehao Lake

The 'Mehao' Lake is situated in Lower Dibang Valley district and the geographical position of the lake is 28° 10' to 29° 40' north latitude and 95° 20' to 96° 40' east longitude at an altitude of 1,778 m above mean sea level. The lake comprises of two unequal segments both connected through a link stream of length around 200 m, the bigger one flows into the smaller segment (Sarma et al., 2012; Laskar et al., 2006). The lake covers a water area of 95.27 ha, with periphery of 4,748.33 m. The depth of the lake at a distance of 30 m from shoreline was measured to be 10.4 m. However, the maximum depth as recorded by the District Fishery Department Office of the district is 65 m. The lake water is very much clear, drinkable and safe for life. During daytime, the light transparency of the water was measured upto 7 m, which provided pristine clarity. The upper surface of the lake water is totally open and there hardly exists any floating vegetation in the lake (Sarma et al., 2012).

Sample Villages

In the present study, an attempt was made to survey six villages adjoining the lake in order to understand the dependence on the lake for economic purpose. The villages are Balek, Simare, Abango, Injunno, Koronu and Denlo. These villages are located within 8 to 14 km walking distance from the lake. Between the villages and lake there are forests. All the villages except the Denlo village are located in the foothills.

As per the District Statistical Office, the total population of the surveyed villages is 2,735 persons where male population constitutes 52.21 per cent and female population constitutes 47.79 per cent. The demographic profiles of the surveyed villages are presented in the Table 1.

Table 1

Distribution of Population in the Surveyed Villages as per 2011 Census

Village	*Total Population*	*Male Population*	*Female Population*
Balek	335	275	254
Koronu	740	260	266
Simare	394	115	96
Abango	529	399	341
Injunno	526	176	159
Denlo	211	203	191
Total	2,735	1,428	1,307

Source: District Statistical Report, 2011.

Dependence on the Forest Products among the Surveyed Households around the Surveyed Lake

It was found that the surveyed households were dependent on nearby forests because of firewood. In addition, they used to collect bamboo, building materials and other minor forest products. Around 60 per cent of the surveyed households were dependent on the forest area of the wetland areas to meet their requirements. Among the villages, the highest dependents were from the Balek village which accounted for 35.91 per cent of the households dependent on firewood. On the other hand, there was only one village, i.e. in Denlo village where not a single surveyed household was found to be dependent on firewood of the forests of nearby lake. This may be due to the fact that the Denlo village is located around 14 km walking/distance from the boundary of the wetland areas and as a result the local people preferred to collect the firewood from nearby areas rather than from the wetland areas.

Most of the surveyed households were dependent on the peripheral area of the wetland for hunting purposes. A good number of surveyed households reported that they were depending on this area for their hunting grounds. It is also found from the survey that around 34 per cent of the households from the Korounu village were depending on this forest for hunting. The least dependence was from Simare village which is 5.48 per cent of the households (Table 2).

Table 2

Percentage of Surveyed Households Dependent on Forest Products of Nearby Surveyed Lake (In Percentage)

Forest Products (Values in Rupees)	Village					
	Balek	Korounu	Simare	Abango	Injunno	Denlo
Firewood	35.91	13.26	18.78	16.02	16.02	Nil
Hunting	23.29	34.25	05.48	06.85	08.22	21.92
Timber	20.00	20.00	40.00	Nil	20.00	Nil
Cane	Nil	30.55	02.78	27.78	20.83	18.06
Bamboo	08.20	19.67	01.67	29.50	24.59	16.39
Building materials	53.22	15.51	Nil	09.67	22.58	Nil
Edible items	54.31	08.62	28.44	08.62	Nil	Nil
Others	Nil	40.47	Nil	14.29	45.23	Nil

Source: Field Study, 2012–14.

In timber collection, it was found that only a few households were found to be engaged in timber collection. In fact, timber collection is regarded as illegal and hence, the local people were reluctant to disclose it. Therefore, the information regarding this activity was obtained from a third person and only of those whose main livelihood was from this.

The next important forest product collected by the surveyed households was edible items. For example in Balek village, around 54.31 per cent of surveyed households used the forest for edible items. In many villages, the surveyed households use the nearby forest of Mehao Lake for collection of cane and building materials.

In rural Arunachal Pradesh, people do not have a habit of maintaining any record about their day-to-day activities. However, in the survey, an attempt was made to estimate the approximate number of months in collection of forest products around the surveyed lakes, in order to get an approximate idea regarding the dependence around surveyed lakes. The number of months engaged in such activities was collected on number of days engaged weekly and then converted to number of months as per the duration. The details are given in Table 3.

Table 3

Percentage of Surveyed Households in Collection of Firewood around the Surveyed Lake (In Number of Months)

Forest Products	Number of Months	Surveyed Villages					Total
		Balek	Korounu	Simare	Abango	Injunno	
Firewood collection	Less than 3 months	25	6.25	31.25	25	12.50	8.84
	3-4 months	50.70	18.31	30.99	Nil	Nil	39.23
	5 and above	26.60	10.64	7.45	26.60	28.72	51.93

Source: Field Study, 2012–14.

Table 3 shows that majority of the households (51.93%) used to collect firewood for more than five months in a year, followed by 39.23 per cent engaged in 3–4 months and 8.84 per cent in less than three months. It was interesting to observe in almost all the villages, the surveyed households were engaged in firewood collection for more than five months. Hence, firewood became the important source of fuel for them and they were dependent on nearby forests of the lake for it.

In addition to it, the villagers used to depend on nearby forests of the lakes for bamboo and cane, building materials and edible items, etc. Hence, an attempt was made to examine the number of months spent in a year for collection of those products which are given in Table 4.

Table 4

Percentage among Surveyed Households Collecting Forest Products (In Number of Months)

Forest Products	*Number of Months*	*Surveyed Villages*						*Total*
		Balek	*Korounu*	*Simare*	*Abango*	*Injunno*	*Denlo*	
Hunting	Less than 3 months	29.09	18.18	05.45	07.27	10.91	29.09	77.46
	3-4 months	Nil	100.00	Nil	Nil	Nil	Nil	05.63
	5 months and above	Nil	91.67	Nil	8.33	Nil	Nil	16.90
Cane collection	Less than 3 months	Nil	18.97	3.45	32.76	24.14	20.69	93.55
	3-4 months	Nil	Nil	Nil	Nil	Nil	Nil	Nil
	5 months and above	Nil	25.00	Nil	25.00	25.00	25.00	06.45
Bamboo collection	Less than 3 months	8.47	18.64	1.69	30.51	23.73	16.95	96.72
	3-4 months	Nil	Nil	Nil	Nil	Nil	Nil	Nil
	5 months and above	Nil	50.00	Nil	Nil	50.00	Nil	03.28

Source: Field Study, 2012–14.

From Table 4, it was found that most of the households were engaged in bamboo collection, cane collection and hunting is less than three months in a year. For example, 96.72 percentage households were engaged in bamboo collection and 93.55 per cent households were engaged in cane collection. In case of hunting also, 77.46 per cent of households were reported to be engaged for less than three months.

An attempt was also made to estimate the percentage of surveyed households collecting minor forest products in number of months which is given in Table 5.

Table 5 shows that a larger percentage of surveyed households were engaged in collection of edible items for three to four months. The collections of edible items include bamboo shoot, edible leaves, etc. It was popular in Balek, Korounu and Simare village. Further, it was found that 65.09 per cent surveyed households were engaged for 3–4 months, 32.08 per cent less than three months and only 2.83 per cent for more than five months for collection of edible items. The other products which include minor products like fodder, leaves, etc. were mostly (74.24%) engaged for less than three months.

Table 5

Percentage of Surveyed Households Collecting Minor Forest Products

Forest Products	Number of Months	Total
Edible items	Less than 3 months	32.08
	3-4 months	65.09
	5 months and above	02.83
Building materials	Less than 3 months	98.48
	3-4 months	01.52
	5 months and above	Nil
Others	Less than 3 months	74.24
	3-4 months	03.03
	5 months and above	22.73

Source: Field Study, 2012–14. Notes: Others include fishing, grazing, fodder, etc.

The number of months engaged in collection of forest products may not provide a true picture of dependence of forest of nearby lakes. In order to provide a true picture, value of annual consumption of various forest products is estimated. It was a challenging task since the market did not exist for many of those resources in rural areas. The data on quantities of different items gathered from forests is dependable but the problem is the non-availability of their village level prices. Some of those forest products are, no doubt, locally bartered but the exchange rate of barter does not reveal the absolute price. Under these circumstances we used the prices of their products available in the nearest market. The details are shown in Table 6.

Table 6

Value of Forest Products (In Rupees) by Surveyed Households

Forest Products	Approximate Value (In Rupees)
Firewood	31,54,700 (49.94)
Hunting of Animals	5,81,400 (9.20)
Timber	1,65,000 (2.61)
Cane	3,29,600 (5.22)
Bamboo	1,41,100 (2.23)
Building materials	5,19,900 (8.23)
Edible items	8,59,200 (13.60)
Others	5,66,500 (8.97)

Source: Field Study, 2012–14.

From Table 6, it was found that firewood consumption 49.94 emerged as the most important item in term of value among all the forest products. That means, the surveyed villages of nearby lake were dependent mostly on forests for firewood. This is because of traditional dependence on firewood due to climatic condition as well as non-availability of alternative fuels. The next important item was edible items like leafy vegetables, etc. (13.60%) followed by hunting of animals (9.20%). It was interesting to observe that the timber

(2.61%) consisted of a less percentage of consumption items among the forest products. Hence it appears that the surveyed households were dependent on forests nearby lakes basically for consumption purpose.

Major Activities in Villages around the Surveyed Lakes

The importance of the natural wetlands depends on the dependency level on the various resources collected by the households in surveyed villages. In addition to scenic beauty, the wetland provides many livelihood resources to the people and proper valuation of these resources was not possible through market prices. Hence, the ordinal measurement of the dependency level was used to measure their activities. The surveyed households were asked to specify the major economic activities around the lakes and rank them. The scoring was accorded in the order of their rankings. For first ranking score of five was accorded, four for second ranking, three for third ranking, two for fourth ranking and one for fifth and above ranking.

Table 7 shows that the major economic activity was firewood collection with a total score of 895 which ranked topped among other activities. The other major activities were the collection of minor forest products with 739 score, recreation with 478 score, hunting with 319 score, building materials with 222 score and the least is animal grazing with only eight scores. This supported the evidences that the surveyed households were dependent on lakes, i.e. more specifically on nearby forests around the lakes for firewood collection, collection of minor forest products, recreation and hunting.

Table 7

Major Activities Reported by Surveyed Households in Villages around the Surveyed Lakes

Activities	*Rank (Total Score)*
Firewood collection	1 (895)
Minor forest products (cane, bamboo, edible items, etc.)	2 (739)
Recreation	3 (478)
Hunting	4 (319)
Building materials	5 (222)
Any other (drinking, wet rice cultivation and other)	6 (108)
Fishing	7 (33)
Animal grazing	8 (8)

Source: Compiled from Field Study of 2012–14

Among the villages, the highest number of households of Balek village is dependent on the wetland areas for the firewood resources. Similarly, in the collection of minor forest products which includes bamboo, cane, edible leaves were found to be highest in the Balek village with a score of two hundred twenty-six. On the other hand the recreational activities were also found highest in Balek village where the score was one hundred thirty-nine.

Potential Threats to Mehao Lake

Though the Mehao Lake is in pristine nature and threat to its pristine conditions is not yet detected. The location and the difficult terrain make it free from the anthropogenic disturbances. However, the problems can be perceived in future. Hence, an attempt was made to know the opinion of local people regarding the need for conservation of the lake. Out of 303 households surveyed, 298 households had responded and most of them had perceived threat to these lakes in future. The details are given in Figure 1.

Figure 1
Percentage of Opinion Regarding Need for Conservation of Lakes

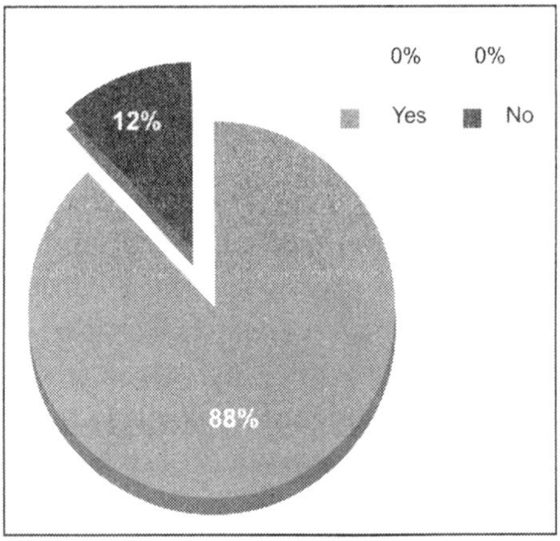

Source: Field Study, 2012–14.

Figure 2
Potential Threats in Percentage

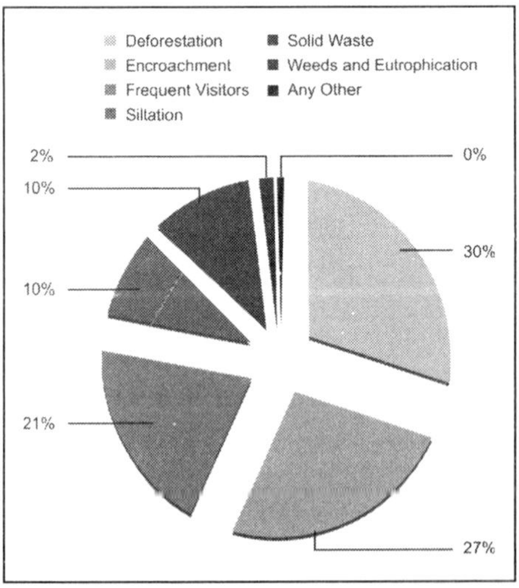

Source: Field Study, 2012–14.

It shows that 88 per cent of surveyed households were of the opinion that there is an urgent need for conservation of lakes. The surveyed households were also requested to identify the future threats.

Around 99.67 per cent of the surveyed households had opinion that the deforestation is one of the threats posing the lake. This deforestation is done for agricultural and the horticultural activities in the vicinity area. Such deforestation has not yet disturbed the ecological balance and the water bodies but it has started affecting the periphery areas and if it is not purposively checked, then certainly it will affect the water bodies in future. The next important threat perceived by the surveyed households is the encroachment of the land for individual purpose. Even then the encroachment of the land for commercial farming was significantly visible. However, both deforestation and the encroachment of the land are intricately related with each other.

Figure 2 shows that the highest potential threats observed by the surveyed households are deforestation which stood at 30 per cent followed by encroachment of land with 27 per cent and frequent visitors with 21 per cent.

Since majority of the surveyed households agreed for the need of conservation of surveyed lakes, an attempt was made to ask them how much they were willing to pay for preservation of lakes.

Figure 3 shows that 92.74 per cent of the surveyed households of villages were willing to pay for preservation of the lake though the economic condition of the surveyed households was found to be relatively poor. The average willingness to pay among the surveyed households was found to be ₹ 229.81.

Figure 3

Opinion on Willingness to Pay by the Surveyed Households

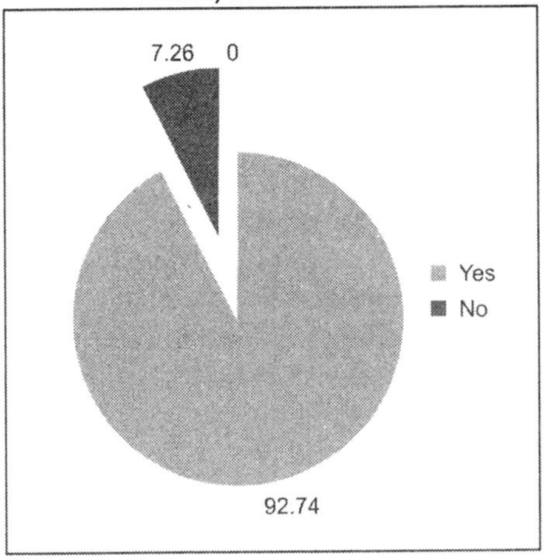

Source: Field Study, 2012–14.

Economic Valuation of Mehao Lake: Contingent Valuation Method

The basic aim of valuation is to determine people's preference – how much they are willing to pay for, and how much better or worse off they would consider themselves to be as a result of changes in the supply of different goods and services. Valuation provides a means of quantifying the benefits that people receive from wetlands, the costs associated with their loss, and the relative profitability of land and resource uses which are compatible with wetlands conservation vis-à-vis those economic activities which contribute to wetland degradation. Valuation helps to predict and understand the economic decisions and economic activities which impact on wetland integrity and status (Emerton, 1998: 1). To understand the economic importance of the Mehao Lake, the contingent valuation method is used to measure its significance to the households. It is a stated preference method for placing monetary values upon environmental assets, which do not have market prices. This is achieved by constructing a hypothetical market and asking individuals what they are willing to pay towards preservation of particular goods (Fanariotu and Skuras, 2004: 146). It is a technique in which respondents were directly questioned to elicit their WTP or WTA for an environmental change (Kumar and Wood, 2010: 106). Willingness to pay refers to valuing the particular dimensions of benefits or projects by determining society's willing to pay for those particular benefits. It requires a listing of the types of benefits and an estimate of the WTP for each one. In our study, the linear regression model is used where the dependent variable is the amount cited as Willingness to Pay and the independent variables are income, total family members, education and age.

$$WTP = \alpha + \beta 1\ Age + \beta 2 Edn + \beta 3 Y + \beta 4 TFM + \varepsilon_t$$

Where

WTP = Willingness to Pay expressed in Rupees, Age = Age of the Respondent's, Edn = Level of Education of the Respondents, Y = Household Annual Income, TFM = Total Family Members, ε_i = Error term.

The result of the regression is as follows:

$$\underset{}{WTP} = \underset{(2.434)}{80.252^{**}} + \underset{(0.332)}{0.173Age} + \underset{(1.862)}{2.318Edn^{***}} + \underset{(14.001)}{0.001Income^{*}} + \underset{(0.436)}{1.118TFM} + E$$

R Square = 0.526, Adjusted R Square = 0.518, F = 65.963, N = 303

Standard error of the estimate = 86.873

Note: 1. The figures in parenthesis are t-values.
2. The asterisk symbols (*, ** and ***) denote significant at 0.01, 0.05 and 0.10 level.

As expected, age, total family members of the household, annual income and educational level, positively influence the willingness to pay. But in the present study, only the education level and income were statistically significant at 0.10 and 0.01 levels. The variable education showed a positive and it was significant at 0.10 level relationships with WTP. This indicates that the relatively more educated people were more concerned about the environment and willing to pay for its preservation. Further, income of the people positively influenced the willingness to pay and it was statistically significant at 0.01 level. This means that the higher the level of income, more the people were willing to pay for the preservation of the lake.

Conclusion

The study highlighted that the natural lakes are the treasure of resources in terms of providing many direct and indirect services to the people. They provide resources in terms of firewood, edible items, source of drinking water, cane, bamboo, fodder, etc. to the nearby villagers. In addition to it, there are indirect services like ecological functions, ecotourism, etc. being performed by the wetlands which are not valuated at market prices. Hence, with growing ecotourism and increasing interest among the stakeholders, there is need for economic valuation of the lakes or wetlands so that various stakeholders can come forward to preserve these lakes or wetlands. The economic estimates which we did, may not be the actual values but it is an information to the people to raise consciousness for preservation of wetlands in general, and lakes in particular, of the state. In fact, the critical need today is to recognize the benefits and interlinkages of the wetlands to manage them in an integrated manner in future. The present study is one of the few studies on valuation aspect of wetlands in the North-Eastern Region. Hence, it is expected that the present study will form the basis of further research work on this topic relating to the entire North-Eastern Region.

References

Babu, C.R. et al. (2001). 'Valuation of Ecological Functions and Benefits: A Case Study of Wetland Ecosystems along the Yamuna River Corridors of Delhi Region', *EERC Working Paper Series, WB-6.*

Badola, Ruchi and S.A. Hussain (2003). 'Valuation of the Bhitarkanika Mangrove Ecosystem for Ecological Security and Sustainable Resource Use', *EERC Working Paper Series, WB-1.*

Barbier, Edward B. (1993). 'Sustainable Use of Wetlands Valuing Tropical Wetland Benefits: Economic Methodologies and Applications', *The Geographical Journal,* 159(1): 22–32.

—— (1994). 'Valuing Environmental Functions: Tropical Wetlands', *Land Economics,* 70(2): 155–73.

Barbier, Edward B. et al. (1997). *Economic Valuation of Wetlands: A Guide for Policy Makers and Planners,* Ramsar Convention Bureau, Department of Environmental Economics and Environmental Management, University of York, Institute of Hydrology, IUCN-The World Conservation Union, www.ramsar.org/sites/default/files/documents/pdf/lib/lib_valuation_e.pdf

Carson, Richard T. and W. Michael Hanemann (2005). 'Chapter 17: Contingent Valuation', in K.G. Maler and J.R. Vincent (eds), *Handbook of Environmental Economics,* Vol. 2, University of California, Berkeley, pp. 821–936, https://asu.pure.elsevier.com/en/publications/chapter-17-contingent-valuation

Chattopadhyay, Kunal (2001). 'Environmental Conservation and Valuation of East Calcutta Wetlands', *EERC Working Paper Series, WB-2.*

Chopra, K. (2004). 'Economic Valuation of Biodiversity: The Case of Keoladeo National Park', in G.K. Kadekodi (ed.), *Environmental Economics in Practice,* Oxford University Press, New Delhi, pp. 86–121.

Cowardin, Lewis M. et al. (1979). *Classification of Wetlands and Deepwater Habitats of the United States,* US Department of the Interior Fish and Wildlife Service, Office of Biological Services, Washington, D.C., http://www.fws.gov/wetlands/documents/classification-of-wetlands-and-deepwater-habitats-of-the-united-states.pdf

Das, T.K. et al. (2000). 'Degradation of Water Bodies and Wetlands in West Bengal: Interaction with Economic Development', *EERC Working Paper Series, WB-3.*

Emerton, L. (1998). *Economic Tools for Valuing Wetlands in Eastern Africa.* IUCN - The World Conservation Union, Eastern Africa Regional Office.

Fanariotu, Ioanna and Dimitris Skuras (2004). The Contribution of Scenic Beauty Indicators in Estimating Environmental Welfare Measures: A Case Study, *Social Indicators Research: An International and Interdisciplinary Journal for Quality-of-Life Measurement,* Springer, Vol. 65(2), pp. 145–65.

Garg, J.K. et al. (1998). *Wetlands in India,* Report No. RSAM/SAC/RESA/PR/01/98, www.moef.nic.in/sites/default/files/wetlands_%20india1998.pdf

Government of Arunachal Pradesh (2008). SFRI Information Bulletin No. 27.

—— (2011). District Statistical Abstract of Lower Dibang Valley District.

Government of India (2007). *Conservation of Wetlands in India: A Profile (Approach and Guidelines),* Ministry of Environment and Forests, New Delhi.

—— (2009a). *Guidelines for Conservation and Management of Wetlands in India,* National Wetland Conservation Programme, Conservation and Survey Division, Ministry of Environment and Forests, New Delhi.

—— (2009b). *National Wetland Atlas: Arunachal Pradesh,* SAC/RESA/AFEGv/NWIA/ATLAS/06/2009, Space Applications Centre (ISRO), Ahmedabad, India, p. 98.

—— (2011a). *High Altitude Himalayan Lakes*, National Wetland Inventory and Assessment, Ministry of Environment and Forests, New Delhi.

—— (2011b). *National Wetland Atlas: North-Eastern States*, SAC/EPSA/ABHG/NWIA/ATLAS/35/2011, Space Applications Centre (ISRO), Ahmedabad, India, p. 318.

Hanemann, W. Michael (1994). Valuing the Environment through Contingent Valuation, *Journal of Economic Perspectives*, Vol. 8, No. 4, pp. 19–43.

Kadekodi, G.K. et al. (eds) (2000). *Water in Kumaon: Ecology, Value and Rights*, Gyanodaya Publications, Nainital.

Kumar, Pushpam and Michael D. Wood (2010). *Valuation of Regulating Services of Ecosystems: Methodology and Applications*, Routledge Publications, New York.

Laskar, B.A. and D.N. Das (2009). 'A Note on Fishery in the High Altitude Lake Mehao in Arunachal Pradesh', in L. Kosugin (ed.), *Wetlands of North East India: Ecology, Aquatic Bioresources and Conservation*, Akansha Publishing House, New Delhi, pp. 334–39.

Millennium Ecosystem Assessment (2005). *Ecosystem and Human Well-Being: Wetlands and Water Synthesis*, Water Resources Institute, Washington, D.C., http://www.millenniumassessment.org/documents/document.358.aspx.pdf

Mitchell, RC and R.T. Carson (1989). *Using Surveys to Value Public Goods the Contingent Valuation Method*, Resources for the Future, Washington, D.C. and The Johns Hopkins University Press, USA.

Sarma, D., Das, D.N., Dutta, R., Baruah, D., Kumar, P., Tyagi, B.C. and P.C. Mahanta (2012). *Coldwater Lakes and Rivers in Arunachal Pradesh, India*, Bulletin No. 19, Directorate of Coldwater Fisheries Research and Indian Council of Agricultural Research, Bhimtal, Nainital, Uttarakhand.

Seyam, I.M. et al. (2001). 'The Value of Freshwater Wetlands in the Zambezi Basin', *Globalization and Water Resources Management: The Changing Value of Water*, 6–8 August, AWRA/IWLRI University of Dundee International Specialty Conference, https://www.utwente.nl/ctw/wem/organisatie/medewerkers/hoekstra/reports/report7.pdf

Turner, Kerry (1991). 'Economics and Wetland Management', *Ambio*, 20(2): 59–63.

Turner, R. Kerry et al. (2003). 'Towards an Integrated Environmental Assessment for Wetland and Catchment Management', *The Geographical Journal*, 169(2): 99–116.

Verma, Madhu (2001). 'Economic Valuation of Bhoj Wetlands for Sustainable Use', ***EERC** Working Paper Series, WB–9.*

22

Managing Tourism Assets

A Case Study of Lower Dibang Valley District of Arunachal Pradesh

RAJEN MIWU

The importance of tourism has been acknowledged by different countries. The proponents of this industry have quoted many benefits of tourism into the economy of the region. This includes economic engagement of the population, which comes in different ways like travel, hospitality, restaurants, etc. The North-East India with its green, white and brown belt of high mountains can provide a very different experience for people from mainland India and people from abroad. With the motive of Act East policy of the government, the importance of Astha Lakshmi to India has been identified with potentials in hydro power and tourism sector.

The state of Arunachal Pradesh is gifted with natural beauty along with varied colourful tribal population residing in different districts of the state. The state has attracted many visitors over the years. Other than Tawang district and Ziro valley in Lower Subansiri district, most of the places in the state are not very popular in terms of tourist visits. This can be attributed to various reasons. This chapter discusses the role of people in taking up tourism-related activities in Lower Dibang Valley district of Arunachal Pradesh. Through a case study approach, this is an attempt to identify the problems and opportunities associated with tourism assets in Lower Dibang Valley district in particular, and Arunachal Pradesh as a whole.

A Brief Theoretical Background

Clancy (2001) has observed that tourism export in Mexico has experienced significant structural changes over the past quarter-century. State policy on tourism has also affected the industry, by way of improvement in infrastructure, growth in transportation and hospitality sector. But the problem was also noticed that development was concentrated in beaches as it was the place which was promoted by the state in a big way. In the context of Arunachal Pradesh, the Government needs to promote different areas of the state as they have different potentials and different nature of tourists to attract. Like, for example, the district of Tawang can be for Buddhist culture and snow, Apatani valley of Ziro can be for the tribe's village life, Dibang Valley for biodiversity, etc. Similar study was carried out by Singh and McDavid (2006) on impact of the hospitality-tourism sector on the Jamaican economy and it was observed that tourism has the capacity to stimulate and induce growth in other sectors of the economy.

Kaplan (2004) has observed that 'Skills development for tourism has attracted only a limited scholarship in the developing world. Skills development has a central role to play in ensuring the effective and sustainable transformation and development of the tourism industry in developing countries and, in the case of South Africa, in ensuring that poorer South Africans begin to benefit from this industry. It is argued that the current lack of an integrated and coordinated approach to tourism skills development seriously limits the potential of skills development to impact positively on tourism transformation and development in South Africa.' This issue of skill development has been an important emphasis for the government at present. The experiences in the tourism sector have shown that people need to be skilled in terms of the need of the industry. This skill should also be in the nature of creating awareness about soft skills like being polite to tourist, welcoming in nature to outsiders, catering to the need and comfort of the visitors. For this, community awareness can be an important factor.

Butts and Briedenhann (2006) observed that, 'Rural tourism development is perceived as both the purveyor of positive benefits and harbinger of negative impacts for host communities. For example, whilst holding substantial potential in attracting tourists, local culture is frequently the victim of exploitation and misrepresentation. Nonetheless, the response of many rural tourist hosts to the sociocultural interaction with their clients is positive. Similarly, a pristine natural environment and the dependence of rural tourism on its conservation as a primary attraction are acknowledged, yet rural tourism is perceived as a degrader and polluter of the very resource on which it is reliant. Economic returns, although avidly expounded by politicians, are generally low and caveats are sounded that rural tourism should not be relied upon as an economic panacea in rural areas. Despite this, it is argued that in adding to the diversity of economic activity in an area, rural tourism may catalyst the provision of additional income, employment and entrepreneurial opportunities for local people, and function as a support for other rural economic activities.' Given the case of North-East India in general, and Arunachal Pradesh in particular, rural tourism can be an attractive proposition due to low investment base. The native people of the regions want to profess and preserve their culture and also engage in livelihood which can be sustainable for them. In this regard, tourism in terms of nature and rural, will help out people in eking out their livelihood without much disturbance.

In a patriarchal society Munshi (2006) identifies that tourism process like other processes and relations in society is gendered. The gender bias is built into the discourse of tourism practices, images and activities which, by and large, privileges the male viewpoint. Indian society is also gendered and Arunachal Pradesh is not different in this regard. Women participation is, therefore, important in this regard because they will be affected by the change in economic activity in their neighbourhood. Therefore, in light of the fact that tourism processes are expanding rapidly in the globalizing world, there is a need to strengthen these voices, both at the local and global levels. For a start, the agenda of women's movements everywhere must include the demand for greater participation of local people in tourism planning and development, especially if rights and interests of people in tourist destinations in the Third World are to be protected. Only then can they share equitably in the benefits that result from tourism (ibid.). Care has to be given by the policy planner in this regard by encouraging gender neutral industry to prosper in the region.

Rogerson (2008) has identified the following challenges faced by small tourism business in Southern Africa. These are to improve market access, enhance marketing, business management and skills development, information communication technologies development and infrastructure, improve understanding of place and culture, support for financing, red tape in tourism, improved understanding for sustainable tourism, expanded institutional support, the need for more research. These similar challenges are faced by tourism business in Arunachal Pradesh where most of the operators are small timers.

According to Levy and Hawkins (2009), tourism can be responsible to strengthening peaceful societies in the destinations around the world. This can be considered important for the North-Eastern part of India, where peace has eluded the region for long to bring in economic prosperity. He noted, 'While limited empirical research has been published in the academic literature on the relationship of peace through tourism; more research on this important area is encouraged.' One can think of tourism being an important factor for encouraging the rural youths in engaging them in some economic activity than towards unlawful activities.

Lower Dibang Valley Experience

The district of Lower Dibang Valley has places of tourist interest like Mayudia, Salley Lake, Mehao Wildlife Sanctuary, Mehao Lake, Bhismaknagar, Iphi River, Ezze River, Forest Park, Nijomghat, Rukmini Nati, Hunli and many more. The district is not very popular in terms of tourist destination when compared to some districts of the state. Even then, the tourist assets that the district has got can attract lots of tourists, either internal or external visitors to these places. Mayudia is a popular place for people from the plains of Assam to witness the snowfall during winter. Even people from Arunachal Pradesh also visit this place during the month of December to February as this place experiences snowfall. Salley Lake, a natural lake three km from the township of Roing is surrounded by thick green forest. This lake can be a potential bird watching area for tourist. Mehao Lake which attracts wild ducks covers an area of four sq km and wildlife sanctuary named after the lake is a living treasure for scientists. There are other places of interest for tourists which can be developed and marketed well to attract visitors from outside the state.

The problem of recognizing and maintaining the tourism assets is very important in developing the potential of the tourism industry. In order to maximize the return from these tourism assets, the government leased out some of the assets on leasehold basis to the public who were interested. In this regard the Salley Lake and its guest house were also leased out to private party. This experiment failed due to various reasons. Some of the factors which can be identified as non-serious business venture on the part of the leaseholder, non-experience in carrying out tourism related activity, non-core business for the leaseholder, etc.

New Development

This lake earlier was a popular place visited by local people and people from outside. It was for some years left unattended due to reasons known only to the leaseholders and the department. Over the years, the guest house and other facilities near the lake got destroyed, almost 80 per cent due to non-attendance of the leaseholder and the department concerned. Friendship Club took over the lake from wildlife department on lease. It was formed by four members, one being a class XII pass out, two members were graduate and one member a law graduate. Using their own savings they invested in clearing the lake side where weeds had grown, some beautification and two boats were procured for boating.

Initial they started boating facility. The place became very popular and they started earning on an average ₹ 2,000 per day from just the rental on boating in the lake. The visitors to the lake were the town people and people from Assam. People who came to the place were very happy about the facility; moreover it also brought in people who could go for dry picnic during weekend days. Therefore, one can notice that people are ready to spend money, provided the tourism asset is presented well and tourist or visitors are made happy. The experience shows that people of the area had forgotten this beautiful lake for some years, because it was left unattended. The place seems haunted for many, but once the place was cleared off and beautified, it automatically attracted people.

The venture of the Friendship Club started in the month of December 2014. During this short experience they faced some problems which can be generalized in the context of Arunachal Pradesh for developing tourism assets and helping out small time tourist operators for engaging them in gainful activity.

Market Access

The major challenge for this club is limited market access because the type of visitors coming to this lake is limited to town people and people from the neighbouring state. For the expansion of the market they need to focus on bird watching which can attract people from abroad and also serious bird watchers from within the country, as the lake is surrounded by lush green forest and hills. Another challenge is the seasonality of the visitors; therefore facilities should come up so that people can come to the place all round the year.

Marketing

Their only source of marketing was by word of mouth and some posts in the Facebook pages in the social network. It received good responses from the net users. But the problem is that it is very limited to people who are connected to these social network groups. Awareness about this beautiful place is very less among outsiders. This is one of the major constraints faced by all the small tourist operators in the state. Other than Tawang district and Ziro Valley, other tourism assets are not marketed well or awareness is very low among potential tourists about other places in the state. The district administration in general have websites for providing general information and tourist interests in the districts but the problem is that they are not marketed well. The need of the hour is that people should be encouraged to market the destination with proper backup through media and financial support should be taken up by the administration.

Business Management and Skills Development

Currently, the club is employing four people. But there can also be other skills required when the club plans to start guesthouse and other facilities. It was also noticed that people in general also should be encouraged to be tourist friendly. This can be taken up by the administration by encouraging and taking up capacity building exercises at the local village level, where proper behaviour is expected and other tourist etiquettes can be taught or encouraged to be adopted by people in general. Involvement of village-level panchayat can also be encouraged.

Information Communication Technologies Development and Infrastructure

Buhalis (1998) has observed that 'Information technologies (ITs) prevail in all functions of strategic and operational management.' The friendship club members have identified the importance of information technology, but the constraints faced by them is that its usage is limited to social networking. Given the tourism assets around the lake, the place can be well marketed using the information technology platform. But for this, higher cost implication is a constraint to small time tourist operators like friendship club. This is where the effort of the government should bring in the needed push for disseminating the information to the outsiders.

Improve Understanding of Place and Culture

For larger role of tourism assets to contribute to the economic conditions of the local people, the development of cultural tourism products is an important element of spreading the economic impact of tourism through the development of new product. Therefore, in the general sense the elements of cultural aspects should be blended to the tourism assets so that larger pool of people take interest in coming and seeing the unique cultures and places. At present, the Friendship Club has concentrated their activity to boating and in future they plan to take up lodging, but in long run, inclusion of culture and art will have to be given attention for sustainable venture. Also, larger people participation is needed for the sustainable growth of the industry and optimum utilization of the tourism assets.

Support for Financing

For the expansion of the operations, the financing support will be necessary. This is one of the major constraints for small-time tourist operators. Tourist cabs were one of the important assets necessary for smooth operation. There are numerous examples where local residents lose access to local natural resources. For example, on Boracay Island in the Philippines, one quarter of the island has been bought by outside corporations, generating a crisis in water supply and only limited infrastructure benefits for residents. Similarly in Bali, Indonesia, prime agricultural land and water supplies have been diverted for large hotels and golf courses while at Pangandaran (Java, Indonesia) village beach land, traditionally used for grazing, repairing boats and nets and festivals, was sold to entrepreneurs for a five-star hotel. Therefore, financial support is necessary for the locals to develop their own assets; else instead of brining in prosperity it will lead to their exploitation.

Improved Understanding for Sustainable Tourism

The current scenario is that the venture is not full time. Therefore, sustainable tourism can happen only if there is steady flow of people. For this, taking care of tourism asset is the foremost important aspect and local people should be encouraged to take care of these assets for the benefit of all. There are other places in the district which can be developed similarly and local youths can take up the task of developing and maintaining the area. Awareness should be created among the population about the importance of tourism and the assets that are around them.

Expanded Institutional Support

Institutional support is very important for handling the tourism assets. Ultimately, it is the well-being of these assets which will generate revenue for the people engaged with the activity. In this case, the need of institutional support was felt by the Friendship Club to develop the tourism assets in the around the area. Local government has an important role in tourism planning and development but has been criticized for not being more proactive. Impediments to local government involvement in tourism planning and policy-making include lack of community interest; lack of resources; lack of appropriate research and information; lack of commitment to implementation; lack of coordination and communication; and lack of technical expertise. Similar situation was also faced in this regard. Therefore care has to be given to take into these factors to improve the situation and increase the productivity of these tourism assets in the area.

Conclusion

From this case study we understand that tourism assets when presented and nurtured can give some value to the people. Nature has gifted lots of tourism assets to the states of North-East India in general and Arunachal Pradesh in particular. These assets are mostly untapped. It needs to be utilized for the benefits of the masses. But in the name of development, care should also be taken on its sustainability. Development need not be concentrated in the few hands or be gendered based. Further, proper government intervention has to be taken care of so that the last poor man is taken care of through trickle-down effect. This in turn will meet the objective of the state as it professes the philosophy of *daridranarayana* as advocated by Swami Vivekananda.

References

Ashley, C., C. Boyd and H. Goodwin (2000). 'Pro-poor Tourism: Putting Poverty at the Heart of the Tourism Agenda', *Natural Resource Perspectives*, 51: 1–6.

Buhalis, D. (1998). 'Strategic Use of Information Technologies in the Tourism Industry', *Tourism Management*, 19(5): 409–21.

Butts, S. and J. Briedenhann (2006). 'Rural Tourism: Projects, Environment and Viability', *Acta Turistica*, 18(2): 109–37.

Clancy, M. (2001). 'Mexican Tourism: Export Growth and Structural Change since 1970', *Latin American Research Review*, 36(1): 128–50.

District Administration, Lower Dibang Valley (2015). http://roing.nic.in/tourism.htm. Retrieved on 17 March 2015 from http://roing.nic.in/default.html.

Dredge, D. (2001). 'Local Government Tourism Planning and Policy-making in New South Wales: Institutional Development and Historical Legacies', *Tourism*, 4(2–4): 355–80.

Kaplan, L. (2004). 'Skills Development in Tourism: South Africa's Tourism-led Development Strategy', *Geo Journal*, 60(3): 217–27.

Levy, S.E. and D.E. Hawkins (2009). 'Peace through Tourism: Commerce Based Principles and Practices', *Journal of Business Ethics*, 89(4): 569–85.

Munshi, I. (2006). 'Tourism Processes and Gender Relations Issues for Exploration and Intervention', *Economic and Political Weekly*, 41(42): 4461–68.

Rogerson, C.M. (2008). 'Developing Small Tourism Businesses in Southern Africa', *Botswana Notes and Records*, 39: 23–34.

Singh, D.R. and A.B. McDavid (2006). 'Impact of the Hospitality-tourism Sector on the Jamaican Economy, 1974–93: An Input-output Approach', *Social and Economic Studies*, 55(3): 183–207.

23

Probable Economic Impact of Hydropower Project

A Case Study on 3,000 MW Dibang Multipurpose Project

RIKO MIHU

Economic development occurs with the expansion of the economic base of a community, region, state or nation through the efficient allocation and use of scarce resources. In general, economic development is any activity that results in additional jobs and income of the people at community level. Economic development suggests an improvement in the quality of life for the community. But in the process of economic development the life of tribal communities is at large risks which need to be advocated before project developer or the State Government to ensure that such development does not harm the downtrodden tribal people. Even having the protective legislation and special constitutional provision of tribal people, the increasing contacts with the mainstream has alienated them from their natural resource base and its impact on tribal communities have been devastating. Resource, tribal and development has been one of the three dynamic concepts which demands active participation from economist, anthropologist, environmentalist, social scientist, bureaucrat and civil society to address the contradictory interest of different stakeholders.

Economic development, though essential for satisfaction of basic needs of the people because of its contribution to material prosperity, per se cannot promote human development with social justice, generally referred to as a social development. It is widely accepted today that human beings are most important without whose proper development, even economic development cannot take place. Mahler (1979: 11) has aptly pointed out that, 'Without human energy, there would be no kind of progress either socially or economically.'

Hydropower project is the basis for much needed economic development and industry, transportation and energy production in the state like Arunachal

Pradesh. It is also fundamental to agriculture, recreation, and the tourism infrastructure which can accelerate the pace of overall development activities. The present study deals with the Dibang Multipurpose Project (DMP) of 3000 MW which is a Hydropower-cum-Flood Moderation Scheme located at Dibang River, about 1.5 km upstream of the confluence of Ashupani River with Dibang River, in the Lower Dibang valley district of Arunachal Pradesh. It also covers the aspects of socio-economic impact, as well as the possible benefits of such huge mega dam project by comparing and contrasting the performance and activities of the project executing agency National Hydroelectric Power Corporation (NHPC) through Corporate Social Responsibilities Schemes.

Precisely, the first basic objective of the present work is to highlight the probable impact of hydropower project on socio-economic development of the region. Secondly, the study has been focussed to understand the contribution of Corporate Social Responsibility (CSR) in mobilizing the social economic status of the indigenous population of the study area.

Research Methodology

Data have been collected through primary and secondary source. For primary data, well designed questionnaire and schedules have been used extensively. To supplement the primary sources, attempts have been made to collect information from secondary sources also, which includes research journals, books, government publication and webpage information also have been referred. The study has been conducted during the period 2011–12.

Discussion

The human development model enacts radical shifts of focus from the basket of commodities and service approach to human beings and their choice sets, their freedom, and especially their action space in shaping their capabilities and well-being.[1] Human development is defined as a process of enlarging people's choice to enable them to lead long and healthy life, to acquire knowledge and be educated and to have access to resources needed for a decent level of life. Human Development Index (HDI) which is used as a summary measure of three dimension of human well-being are – long and healthy life, education and decent standard of living is usually constructed by combining three indices, i.e. the life expectancy index, the education index and human index. The main theme to understand the probable impact on socio-economic life of community is on the following economic variables:

Health and Hygiene

National Hydroelectric Power Corporation (NHPC) has also CSR policies and programmes to improve the socio-economic and environmental aspects in a sustainable manner, while recognizing the interest of its stakeholders. Corporate Social Responsibility extends beyond philanthropic activities and reaches out to the integration of social and business goals. These activities need to be seen as those which would, in the long term, help secure a sustainable development of the communities as a whole. As part of CSR, NHPC pursues good gesture of philanthropic activities towards the development of health scenario of the local people. It is part of their business plan, but local people are getting directly or indirectly support from the NHPC as grants and aids for health and medical purpose for the local communities.

Table 1

Expenditure Under CSR Towards the Health and Hygiene

Particulars	*Yearwise Break-up*			
	2012–13	*2011–12*	*2010–11*	*2009–10*
Financial assistance	–	–	7,300	-
Medical camp	–	–	1,60,249	97,334
Conducting eye camp	–	–	20,000	6,75,890
Purchase of ambulance	–	–	8,17,256	–
Purchase of ambulance	9,29,914	–	–	–
Health awareness	–	–	82,000	–
Total	9,29,914	–	20,76,805	7,73,224
Grand Total (₹)		37,79,943		

Sources: NPHC officials, Roing.

Dibang Multi Purpose (DMP) as a proposed project undertaken by NHPC has already started its expenditures towards the economic development of the society. As per above Table 1, it depicts that NHPC has undertaken many minor steps to upgrade the medical and health facility for the project affected areas. The most important initiative was the donation of two Ambulances to the State Government for Hunli and Arzoo Primary Health Centre (PHC). In addition to that, project developer was contemplating to construct one hospital with all basic facilities in the project affected area. To ameliorate health consciousness among the local community, NHPC had conducted various health camps and also made a documentary film of the region and the community. This shows how the project developer is wining the trust of the local communities through their corporate responsibilities and strategies.

Education

Human development of the community is also largely determined by the level of the literacy rate. Education policy in India has been to achieve equity in education by gender, caste and socio-economic groups and to reduce regional disparity. If we see the social responsibility of NEEPCO, the executing agency of Ranganadi Hydropower Project of Yazali, Lower Subansiri District of AP, it has had tremendous achievements in the development of educational scenario of the community. They had constructed boundary wall, football ground, free toilet room and provided computers (2 nos.) in the Government Higher Secondary School Yazali for Project Affected People (PAF). Apart from these, to encourage the talented student of the community, they facilitate Merit Scholarship by providing financial assistance to students. In the year 2009–10 NEEPCO had earmarked and expended an amount of ₹ 2,11,75,163 under Corporate Social Responsibility. Looking into the facts of such initiatives, power developer will surely foster educational development of the community and enhance the living standard of the project affected people.

In Lower Dibang valley also Merit Scholarship Award has been initiated by the NHPC, for students of Industrial Training Institute (ITI), Roing. The scholarship award which started in September 2009 is sponsored by Dibang Multipurpose Project, NHPC Ltd, under its initiative of adopting the ITI. This initiative is taken under the Government of India's scheme formulated in 2007 for the upgradation of ITIs into Centre of Excellence through Public Private Partnership (PPP). Forty students from the Institute undergoing training in different trades, received the scholarship, which includes a certificate and cash prize of ₹ 3,000. The important landmark in the development of education is that NHPC is considering introducing NHPC College of Science, Technology, Arts, and Commerce, at Tawang district of Arunachal Pradesh. All these are the positive move from the project developer which ultimately helps the indigenous population to excel in education scenario.

Following are some prominent areas where NHPC has already undertaken initiatives under CSR to arrest and improve the education system in the two districts, i.e. Dibang valley and Lower Dibang valley districts of Arunachal Pradesh.

Total amount of ₹ 34,50,315 under CSR have been expended towards the education sector of the proposed project areas. Apart from the ITI students, scholarships are provided to the meritorious students of Government higher secondary school, Roing which was started on 2009 and so far, implemented amounting to ₹ 12,86,425 including donation to ITI, Roing. NHPC is also helping NGOs and other education institution in purchasing school items like books, computers and other essentials infrastructural items in and around project affected areas (see Table 2).

Table 2

Expenditure Under CSR Towards Education

Particulars	*Yearwise Break-up*			
	2012–13	*2011–12*	*2010–11*	*2009–10*
Scholarships	–	10,67,550	1,33,000	85,875
Sports	–	10,000	65,000	20,000
School upgradation	–	5,32,945	86,377	–
School items and accessories	–	85,000	5,54,368	–
Upgradation of ITI, Roing	–	84,200	7,26,000	–
Total	–	17,79,695	15,64,745	1,05,875
Grand total (₹)	34,50,315			

Source: NHPC officials, Roing.

To provide basic education to the project affected areas, NHPC has proposed to construct a school up to class XII standard with boarding facilities. Presently, NHPC engages in the supplying study materials and others items like school bags, books, library development, stationary, etc. and extends financial assistance to meritorious students by providing scholarships. Several such activities under CSR policies are expected to come up through consultation and participation of all the stakeholders.

Income Generation

Levels of income generation in the community determines the healthy human development. Given the binary role of income – both as an end and a means – a steady growth of income is essential for overall development. It is worthwhile to mention here that undivided Dibang valley had the highest income index and human development index and ranked second in the whole of Arunachal Pradesh as per HDR Arunachal Pradesh 2005. As per the proposed project it is to be installed in the lower Dibang valley and Dibang valley where income of the people are directly connected with the natural resources. Once the project is installed, agricultural land will be exploited. The main income sources and livelihood will be hampered. Now it is to note that how proposed project will give better status on the human development status of local people.

Project proponent claims that there will be massive employment generation. This will substantially increase the income level of the local community. Local people can also become entrepreneurs and start sound new business venture. They can lend their house and land on lease which can be good sources of income generation. As there will be influx of the population, local community's resources can be used in various merchandized purpose and to establish marketing hubs. It will inculcate a regular income generation by exploring traditional food items, vegetables, etc. that are just hypothetical assumptions which may not be sure to happen but at least the local people have choice to make decisions.

NHPC being a socially responsible corporate citizen, they are responsible and committed to health, education, peripheral development and others through the comprehensive CSR policy for the sustainable development of the local populace. Apart from the R and R amount and its commitment of 12 per cent free power to the state and one per cent free power from the project would be provided and earmarked for local area development fund by the developers. The state Government shall also provide a matching one per cent from its share of minimum 12 per cent free from power as recommended in the Government of India's hydro power policy–2008, if considered necessary by the state Government keeping in view the development requirement of the area.[2] The project proponent states that State Government can get a revenue of ₹ 300 annually from Dibang Multipurpose project but hydropower policy however, doesn't promise that this amount of money will be used for the benefit of the project affected areas. That is the area where project developer and state Government need to ponder upon. The local community may not be directly benefited by the proposed project but power developer and state Government need to focus on regular Income generation scheme by conducting socio-economic survey and provide inclusive development vision for the downtrodden populace.

Irrigation

Land is the major income earning asset in the area and people are highly depended on the land for the agriculture. The proposed project is located in an area with low population density. DMP being a multipurpose project can be used for irrigation purpose. The water will be stored in the reservoir, thus the flow regime of the river can be tamed and channelized. According to the top NHPC officials DMP will be beneficial for the downstream even in the Assam plains for agriculture purpose if water is properly tamed in collaboration with concerned department in the state. Immediate beneficiary of the canal will be only the downstream people who are very beneficial for community in the long run. For that Substantial investment in irrigation infrastructure, institution and capacity building should be made before the water is stored in the reservoir.

Tourism Potential

The economic developments of the community also depended on the tourism prospect in the locality. Large dam may be designed to attract the tourist in the project area since it has beautiful natural scenic beauty which attract tourists from outside the state and the globe. This could be a good source of earning for the local people by exploring its cultural heritage, natural scenic beauty, water sports, and navigation in the reservoir. One of the attractions in the Dam site will be its natural beauty which may augment the film industries too.

As per proposed project, with the collaboration of state Government and agencies of tourisms, navigation, water sports can be taken up after the completion of the projects (NHPC officials, Roing). Development of the tourist sector can boost the state economy as Dibang Valley is known for its natural beauty, having large diversity in flora and fauna. The potentialities of cultural tourism can be enhanced by properly integrating institutional development in the proposed areas. Eco-tourism and natural tourism around the proposed multipurpose project can be good option for state Government to regain the trust level of communities, since people are more comfortable to accept tourism industry than to the proposed project. At this juncture it will be wrong to portray that installation of proposed project will enhance tourism industry since project is yet to come up. Education can encourage such industry and collective responsibility will induce behavioural changes that will support sustainable development.

Employment Generation

Dibang multipurpose project is one of the largest mega dam to be installed in the lower Dibang valley, Roing of Arunachal Pradesh. The project will give ample opportunities for employment. The generation of employment will boost the living standard of the people, especially to the project affected families. To ensure economic well-being of the community, many power developers provide employment avenues for the local community. The project developer in Jammu & Kashmir, Chutak HE, provides vocational training for development of entrepreneurship to take up self-employment project like fruit growing, poultry farm, weaving of pashmina carpets, animal husbandry, etc. in Sikkim Teesta power station. The power developer provides regular job to one person in NHPC from each displaced family. Apart from all these avenues from the power developer, local people can start good business units. Such recruitment policies and programmes will enhance living standard of the local communities and deviating young generation from the unproductive activities which will ensure human development in the regions.

The power developer of hydropower projects shall reserve the specific jobs for the projects affected people. The hydropower policy 2008 of Arunachal Pradesh specify following categories of posts to be filled by the local tribals, subject to the incumbents fulfilling the job requirement as stipulated below:

1.	Managerial/Professional post	25%
2.	Ministerial/Clerical post	50%
3.	Skilled jobs	25%
4.	Unskilled jobs	75%

It is surprising to find the lacunae in the hydropower policy and Memorandum of Agreement between Government of Arunachal Pradesh and NHPC Ltd. For execution of Dibang Multipurpose Projects (3,000 MW) on Dibang river in Arunachal Pradesh they are not in conformity with above cited provisions on hydropower policy. Employment for the local in other posts are not clearly mentioned in MoU which was signed on 24 June, 2007. ... that after deployment of the requisite skilled/semi-skilled manpower from the existing project(s) of the corporation, all new recruitment against the newly sanctioned posts for the project(s) in the categories of class III and IV, i.e. C and D staff shall be made 100 per cent from the State of Arunachal Pradesh, as per requirement from time to time. In the events of non-availability of suitable candidates meeting the prescribed qualification with the local employment exchange, the posts shall be filled-up from other candidates. However, for recruitment of executives category post through press advertisement, an examination centre will be introduced at Itanagar for convenience and to provide easy opportunity to candidates from Arunachal Pradesh.[3]

Viewing hydropower policy 2008 of Arunachal Pradesh, employment generation will be there but the question that arises is how local people are made skilled and qualified to be employed in the post apart from the C and D categories? Since, employment avenues are there but qualified people are few it can be construed that availability of employment to all local people will be a wrong notion. What if Projects affected family are not qualified then how will state Government and Power developers ensure job opportunities? It is therefore, implied that project will not necessarily increase job avenues to local or indigenous people of Arunachal Pradesh, rather it depends upon the qualification and skill they are possessing.

Infrastructure Development

Infrastructure is the basic physical and organizational structure (that provides the framework supporting the entire structural development) indispensable for the operation in the modern complex society. It is the lifeline on which development process of the state relies upon, without which other development activities would not take place. Infrastructure development of the community is possible when there is development in communication, transportation, water supply, electrical grids, and telecommunication. Infrastructure developments are very much needed in the society to enhance social living conditions and to ensure regional balance in development.

NHPC, the largest Central Government hydropower utility in India, presently implementing 13 projects with installed capacity of 5,655 MW in the country is constructing 2,000 MW Subansiri Lower HE Project, the largest hydro-project of the country in Arunachal Pradesh. The project sanctioned by Government of India in September 2003 at an estimated cost of ₹ 6,285 crore is under the active stage of implementation. In addition to Subansiri, NHPC has signed a Memorandum of Agreement (MoA) with Government of Arunachal Pradesh on 24 June 2007 for execution of Dibang Multipurpose Project (3,000 MW) costing about ₹ 14,530 crore and Tawang I and II HE Project (1,500 MW) costing about ₹ 6,600 crore. These projects involve an investment of about ₹ 27,000 crore in coming years in Arunachal Pradesh, which is the largest investment ever made by NHPC in any state. On completion, Subansiri HE Project, Dibang Multipurpose Project and Tawang I and II will be generating annually 7,421 MU, 10,668 MU and 6,636 MU respectively. On completion of all the above four projects the revenue earned by the beneficiary state/s will amount to about to ₹ 600 crore in the form of 12 per cent free power. Subansiri Lower HE Project will be commissioned in the 11th Plan itself, while Dibang and Tawang projects will be commissioned in the 12th Plan and beyond. With execution of these projects by NHPC, whole of North-Eastern region will have benefits that are both tangible and intangible in nature. The local project area will have the benefits like development of public health centre, school and community centre. Resettlement and rehabilitation package of these projects will include providing financial assistance for construction of cattle shed o. poultry farm, agriculture land depending on availability, subsidy for seeds/fertilizers/land management, vocational training to the locals, preference in allotment of shops in NHPC's shopping complex, special measures for tribal and renovation/relocation of religious structures. With the implementation of these basic amenities like road, communication network, electricity, medical facilities will improve in North-Eastern states. Prior to NHPC, Brahmaputra Board was implementing the projects in Arunachal Pradesh. Ministry of Water Resources in the year, 2000 had handed over Lower Subansiri projects (7,300

MW) comprising Subansiri Lower, Subansiri Middle and Upper projects as well as Lower Dihang (Siang) projects (13,400 MW) comprising Lower Siang, Middle Siang and Upper Siang projects to NHPC. NHPC has been engaged since then in the state of Arunachal Pradesh, conducting S&I and preparing DPRs of projects in Subansiri, Siang, Dibang and Tawang basins. NHPC has so far prepared Pre-feasibility Reports of 25 schemes with an installed capacity of 17,403 in Arunachal Pradesh under the '50,000 MW Hydroelectric Initiatives' of Government of India.

State Government can improve its worse infrastructural development through proper utilization of the 'Upfront Premium'. The power developers of viable projects have to deposit non-refundable amount including Processing Fees as stipulated hereunder:

Project Capacity	*Minimum Upfront Premium*
25 MW–100 MW	₹ 1.00 Lakh per MW
101 MM–500 MW	₹ 2.50 Lakh per MW
501 MW–1,000 MW	₹ 3.50 Lakh per MW
1,001 MW–2,000MW	₹ 5.00 Lakh per MW
2,000 MW and above	₹ 6.00 Lakh per MW[4]

As per Dibang Multipurpose Project, the concerned state Government had already received a giant amount of ₹ 15,000 Lakh from the NHPC, as a free power. This free power is an optional purchase from the power developer over and above the 12 per cent free power share, the state Government will guarantee payment for such purchases. If this money received is properly channelized, Arunachal Pradesh will be the richest state of the country considering the hydropower potentials in the state.

Table 3

Expenditure Under CSR Towards Infrastructure Development

Particulars	*Yearwise Break-up*				
	2012–13	*2011–12*	*2009–10*	*2008–09*	*2007–08*
Eze mini hydel project	55,900	–	50,000	22,500	–
Rain shed	–	–	9,80,674	–	–
Improvement of helipad	–	–	–	–	38,00,000
Mule track	–	–	5,18,388	–	–
Total	55,900	–	15,49,062	22,500	38,00,000
Gross Total			54,27,462		

Source: NPHC officials, Roing.

Dibang Multipurpose Project will be one of the biggest hydropower projects in the entire country if proposed projects are installed. Infrastructural development and hydropower project are very interdependent and for this reason, future prospect of state development is largely dependent upon the project development in the region. In Lower Dibang valley, Roing NHPC pioneered DMP project cost at ₹ 15,886 crore. This unit of Lower Dibang valley has started its CSR schemes in the vicinity areas of the proposed project for local area development. Table 3 shows the expended amount under CSR for local area development made by NHPC so far.

The above discussion affirms how NHPC as a corporate body initiated numerous initiatives under CSR (Corporate Social Responsibility) in the study area. All these initiatives are a part of corporate strategy so as to create confidence in the minds of people of the region. Beyond any doubt, dams will bring many socio-economic benefits to the region but harbinger of large dams remains a core issue before the community at large. Socio-economic transformation of the region is possible when such projects are encouraged with best practices being adopted. Project affected people (PAP) shall be entitled to get fair compensation along with other business avenues like commercialization of indigenous resources, handicrafts and handlooms, more market exposure and most importantly, creating opportunities for market hub in the region which has cumulative impact in the society as a whole.

At the same time, large dams engulfed many oddities in the society and outbreaks of many social unrest during the past three years in the study areas. By and large, community of the proposed dams expressed their discontent through agitations, bandhs and other democratic means and started slogans like 'temporary benefits permanent loss'. One of the important elements of apprehension and contention regarding the DMP is marginalization and loss of ethnic identity. Idu Mishmi population which is not more than 12,000 in the proposed areas shall have direct effect to local residence in terms of socio-economic and political rights. The influx of workers from outside will increase the vulnerability of new threatening diseases which will effect in the demographic profile of the community as a whole. Other elements of contention include destruction of natural resources, unhealthy ecosystem and improper R and R policy of the corporate continues to be centre of communities concern. If all these issues are addressed with cohesive dialogue between, corporate, State Government and PAP, it shall reap desired outcome with least interruption. Following Table 4 shows total number of dams proposed to be constructed in the state in different river belts of Arunachal Pradesh.

Table 4

Proposed Hydo Power Projects

	Name of Rivers/Basins	*No. of Projects*	*Probable Hydro Potentials (MW)*
1.	Tawang	15	2,815.90
2.	Kameng	56	5,346.50
3.	Subansiri	28	11,557.00
4.	Dikrong	10	577.00
5.	Siang	45	18,426.00
6.	Dibang	17	9,775.00
7.	Lohit	11	7,910.90
8.	Tirap	5	203.00
9.	Total	185	56,611.30

Source: Hydropower Policy, 2008.

In May 2003, the Prime Minister of India launched 50,000 MW hydropower initiatives to increase the hydropower development. Under this scheme, detailed project reports are being prepared for 73 schemes. Of these schemes (total about 32,000 MW), 70 are located in the Brahmaputra basins especially in the Arunachal Pradesh. At present 42 HEPs are under Prime Minister's 50,000 MW hydropower initiatives in Arunachal Pradesh. Initially, Dibang Multi-purpose Project of 3,000 MW was not included in these schemes. Later, recognizing the significance and feasibility of the project it was also included in these schemes by 2008 for early installation of the project. On Dibang river basins, 10 projects along with DMP, were allocated with installation capacity of 9,775 MW. Many projects are to be executed by private parties such as Reliance, Anthena, Jindal, M/s Soma Enterprises, etc. Private sectors participation has been low in the hydropower sector, although the sector was opened up in 1991, since investors looked at it as a higher risk proposition compared to thermal projects. Also, concerned civil society opposed many projects in the single river basin that too being executed by Private parties which have no prior experience in constructing such hydropower projects. People are questioned about the level of integrity and commitments towards the development of all stakeholders. The level of trust towards the private parties is a matter of concern for project proponents. Issues and concerns of mega dams is the least concern for political leaders of the state which lead to many MoUs and MoAs with least known private corporates who do not have any experience in hydropower dam construction. It has become a source of the State Government to earn and receive money as an upfront money from the corporate which has immense effect in the future state's exchequer. NHPC has already paid an amount of ₹ 225 Cr. as advance to the state Government of Arunachal Pradesh for execution of project on ownership basis, such as Tawang HE Project Stage-I (750MW), Tawang HE Project Stage-II (750MW) and Dibang Multipurpose Project (3,000 MW). That amount as an advance to the state Government in respect of said project shall be recovered/adjusted together with nine per cent per annum to be compounded annually from the value of free power (12%), for which the state Government is entitled. All these monetary benefit have already been used by State Government without any successful execution of even one of the hydropower project in the state. Therefore, developing power project with an idea of creating electricity with mega dams is a distant dream for a state like Arunachal Pradesh.

Mega projects are in most cases considered as the necessary evil of development. Before their benefits can be reaped, a lot of sacrifice and tough choices have to be made. The fear and uncertainties surrounding such projects range from the impact on the local people and environment which leads to mass critics and agitation from the local people, civil society, scientist and environmentalist. Today, it is more of a requirement than a belief that all the stakeholders' involvement and their participation in all decision-making process concerning a project is the surest way of minimizing conflicts and ensuring social justice. Tribal development and project execution should be made with outmost care considering the primitive state of the local communities, to avert future conflicts and successful execution of the project in a time.

Conclusions

What about the issues of corruption in HEP in Arunachal Pradesh? The analysis should have been more critical by looking into how benefits could be ascertained within the vicious circle of politics and corruption in the state politics. Government can make the local economy to boom or even destroy it depending upon the strong and implicit programmes and policies to upgrade the local economy. Local economy can be upgraded through supplementing of fishing, recreation, navigation, tourism in the water channel reservoir lake, etc. – development of proposed project in the study area can avail such opportunities.

The economic development of the state is not an isolated phenomenon but it is an integral part of the economic development process of the country as whole. It is not denying the fact that development of the state is fully dependent upon the abundance of natural resources. But at the same time, development process requires an inclusive approach towards sustainable development. Only having natural resources is not enough for nation's development but programme and policies of development process should be based on long-term structural development considering interest of all stakeholders. In the process of development process, communities' interest needs to be emphasized, specially in the hydropower development prospects. In Arunachal Pradesh, many hydropower projects are proposed but couldn't be fast tracked for necessary clearance due to mass agitation by NGOs, civil societies, economists, anthropologists, social scientists and the student community. Under these circumstances power developer and state Government need to address the problems and grievances of local community, considering the fact that development must not create islands alone, it must be internalized by the people. Development must be with equity. Development must be, by and for human race (Bhattacharjee, 1958: 253).

Project development in the state is not a new buzzword for the tribal people of Arunachal Pradesh. Many projects are being executed in the state but fail to meet the state exchequer requirement due to ill political will, unorganized market mechanism and lack of goodwill, Example is, Namchik-Namphuk coal block in Changlang District which is the epitome of state failure in project development. The project was initially under the control of State Government itself but later on in 2007 the Arunachal Pradesh Mineral Development and Trading Corporation Limited (APPMDTCL), a state Government undertaking, auctioned it to private firm to extract coal from the block which adversely affected state exchequer. It has been argued that state is losing ₹ 500 crore annually from Namchik-Namphuk coal block due to irregularities in revenue returns, tax evading and illegal mining. Therefore, it is required that every project be installed to increase regional balanced development by ensuring a broad based programmes and policies which integrates state interest with communities' interest.

Hence, it is imperative to note that economic development through hydropower development is not a sure shot method and not to be taken as guaranteed. But it can be hypothetically accepted as base of economic development until cohesive, inclusive and long-term visionary are prepared and actualized. The impact of such proposed dams on the tribal communities; their lifestyle and identity need to be understood so as to ensure democratic process of economic development. Large dams promised to solve poverty, infrastructure, hunger and starvation by providing irrigation, controlling floods and providing much needed electricity for domestic and industrial development. It was a grand promise that prompted Pandit J. Nehru, the first Prime Minister of India to call dams, 'Secular Temple of Modern India.' Environment and social cost of such large dams is thought to be an inevitable price that one has to pay for such development. It invokes utilitarian logic of 'few people have to sacrifice for the greater national good.' Howsoever, there must be a justified and well accepted socioecological study and assessment of the proposed projects through democratic and unbiased agencies to realize the true sense of development by bridging the expectations of all the stakeholders.

Notes

1. Human Development Report, Arunachal Pradesh, 2005.
2. Arunachal Pradesh Extraordinary Gazette, 20 November 2008.
3. Memorandum of Agreement between Government of Arunachal Pradesh and NHPC Ltd. for execution of DMP (3000MW) on Dibang River in Arunachal Pradesh, Itanagar signed on 24 June 2007.
4. Hydropower policy, 2008.

References

Barua, Indira, Sarthak Sengupta and Deepanjana Dutta Das (2002). *Ethnic Groups, Cultural Continuities and Social Changes in Northeast India*, Mittal Publications, New Delhi.

Baviskar, Amita (2007). *Waterscape*, Permanent Black, Uttaranchal.

Bhattacharjee, R.P. (1958). *Economic Development of Arunachal Pradesh*, Himalayan Publications, New Delhi.

D'Souza, Dilip (2002). *The Narmada Dammed*, Penguin Books India Pvt. Ltd., New Delhi.

Dreze, Jean, Meena Samson and Satyajit Singh (2002). *The Dam and the Nation*, Oxford University Press, New Delhi.

Iyer, R. Ramaswamy (2003). *Water: Perspective, Issues, Concerns*, Sage Publications, New Delhi.

Krishna, Sumi (1996). *Environment Politics: People's Lives and Development Choices*, Sage Publications, New Delhi.

Siebert, Horst (2008). *Economics of the Environment*, Springer-Verlag, Berlin.

Singh, Surendra Singh (2008). *Social Development, Human Rights and Social Justice*, New Royal Book Company, Lucknow.

Thukral, Enakshi Ganguly (1992). *Big Dam Displaced People*, Sage Publications, New Delhi.

Web References

http://nvda.nic.in/triaward.htm
http://www.boloji.com/wfs/wfs022.htm
http://www.cea.nic.in
http://www.jstor.org/stable/4411528
www.ohchr.org/en/about

Contributors

Ambika Aiyadurai, Assistant Professor, Humanities and Social Sciences, Indian Institute of Technology (IIT), Gandhinagar, Gujarat.

Athuko Tayu, Assistant Professor, Department of Geography, Rangfra Government College, Changlang, Arunachal Pradesh.

Boni Amin Laskar, Scientist D, Zoological Survey of India, MoEF & CC, Freshwater Biology Regional Centre, Hyderabad.

D.N. Das, Senior Professor, Department of Zoology, Rajiv Gandhi University, Itanagar.

Eva Umpo, Research Scholar, Department of Anthropology, Rajiv Gandhi University, Itanagar.

Fames Linggi, Assistant Professor, Department of Economics, Indira Gandhi Government College, Tezu, Arunachal Pradesh.

Justina Umbrey, Research Scholar, Arunachal Institute of Tribal Studies, Rajiv Gandhi University, Itanagar.

Kenjum Bagra, Research Officer, Arunachal Pradesh Biodiversity Board, Itanagar, Arunachal Pradesh.

Maya Pulu, Project Assistant, Centre for Women Studies, Rajiv Gandhi University, Itanagar.

Mite Lingi, Member, Idu Mishmi Language Development Committee, Lower Dibang Valley, Roing and Dental Surgeon, District Hospital, Roing, Lower Dibang Valley, District, Arunachal Pradesh.

Rajen Miwu, Assistant Professor, Department of Commerce, Indira Gandhi Government College, Tezu, Arunachal Pradesh.

Rajiv Miso, Assistant Professor, Department of History, Jomin Tayeng Government Model Degree College, Roing, Arunachal Pradesh.

Razzeko Delley, Assistant Professor, Department of English, Jomin Tayeng Government Model Degree College, Roing, Arunachal Pradesh.

Riko Mihu, Assistant Professor, Department of Commerce, Government College, Tezu, Arunachal Pradesh.

Roger Blench, McDonald Institute for Archaeological Research, Cambridge, United Kingdom and Kay Williamson Educational Foundation, Nigeria.

Rumo Meto, Assistant Professor, Department of English, Tadar Taniang Govt. Degree College, Nyapin, Arunachal Pradesh.

Samiran Roy, Assistant Professor, Department of Environmental Science, Nabin Chandra College Badarpur, Dist: Karimganj, Assam.

Sarit K. Chaudhuri, Director, Indira Gandhi Rashtriya Manav Sangrahalaya (IGRMS), Bhopal and Former Head, Department of Anthropology, Rajiv Gandhi University (RGU), Itanagar.

S. Simon John, Director, Arunachal Institute of Tribal Studies, Rajiv Gandhi University, Itanagar.

Tarun Mene, Assistant Professor, Arunachal Institute of Tribal Studies, Rajiv Gandhi University (RGU), Itanagar.

Tilu Linggi, Research Scholar, Centre for International Legal Studies, Jawaharlal Nehru University (JNU), New Delhi.

Index